Reformation

Petra Bosse-Huber, Serge Fornerod,
Thies Gundlach, Gottfried Locher
Editors

REFORMATION

Legacy and Future

World Council
of Churches
Publications

REFORMATION
Legacy and Future

WCC Publications is the book publishing programme of the World Council of Churches. Founded in 1948, the WCC promotes Christian unity in faith, witness and service for a just and peaceful world. A global fellowship, the WCC brings together 345 Protestant, Orthodox, Anglican and other churches representing more than 550 million Christians in 110 countries and works cooperatively with the Roman Catholic Church.

Opinions expressed in WCC Publications are those of the authors.

Scripture quotations are from the New Revised Standard Version Bible.

Cover Design: Adele Robey
Typesetting: Ann Katrin Hergert and Michelle Cook/4 Seasons Book Design
ISBN: 978-2-8254-1660-0

World Council of Churches
150 route de Ferney, P.O. Box 2100
1211 Geneva 2, Switzerland
www.oikoumene.org

Contents

Preface

When did the Reformation take place? And what is it about, exactly? Protestant churches traditionally celebrate Reformation Sunday around 31 October. In fact, the tradition goes that, on this day in 1517, Martin Luther, a young German friar and theology professor, posted 95 theses on the door of the Castle Church in Wittenberg. The theses criticized the practice of indulgences, which enabled believers to buy a piece of their salvation with some coins. This invitation to a debate among theologians marked the beginning of a conflict among different theological perspectives that were plainly irreconcilable. Over a very short period of time, thanks to political support and the extensive use of the printing press, a large segment of the Roman Catholic Church changed its practice and some of its thinking at that time. This movement proliferated throughout Europe at such a high speed that Luther's arguments against indulgences could not possibly be the sole cause.

In 2017, the Protestant churches born of this movement commemorate the fifth centennial of the Reformation. But what exactly will happen in 2017? Why celebrate this event, which seems so distinct from the situations that churches face today and from the spiritual concerns of our contemporaries, even if we admit that it thoroughly changed the history of Europe and is of worldwide historical importance? Did the Reformation not also cause significant disorder, some of it violent? What, concretely, do we want to commemorate and celebrate? What does this Reformation consist of? To what extent can it affect today's church and world?

The Evangelical Church in Germany (EKD), stemming from the Lutheran Reformation, and the Federation of Swiss Protestant Churches (FSPC), originating from the Reformation initiated by Huldrych Zwingli and John Calvin, decided in 2012 to set an example of the unity of Protestantism by organizing a joint preparation congress for the Reformation Jubilee 2017. In taking this step, FSPC and EKD underscored that through the theological consensus reached in 1973 among Protestant families on the hill of Leuenberg in Switzerland, known by the name of the "Leuenberg Agreement," the forthcoming celebrations of the Reformation Jubilee have reached a new, pan-Protestant meaning, without which the Protestant churches are no longer comprehensible. By dint of this congress, which was held in Zurich in October 2013, EKD and FSPC sought to take stock of the aforementioned questions right at a time when most churches have started planning their own activities. Above all, we wanted to discuss "what we celebrate" and "why we do so" with signatory churches of the Leuenberg Agreement, that is, members of the Community of Protestant Churches in Europe (CPCE), and partner churches from all over the world. The Reformation is no longer defined in terms of Luther in Germany or those of Calvin or Zwingli in Switzerland alone, whatever decisive importance may be attached to these personalities. The Reformation has to be understood in plural terms and as a European movement whose roots date back to earlier centuries. First and foremost, however, a new light should be cast on it to reflect the current context of global Christianity: We see on the one side secularization and erosion, on the other growth and fundamentalist tendencies—an increasingly multicultural and pluralistic religious landscape. We also take note of the achievements, the reality, and future of ecumenical dialogues and of global concerns about the future of the earth. Thus, for Protestant churches, 2017 will not be or, rather, not *only* be a matter of remembering what happened and following its traces in history. Rather, it is about reclaiming the message of freedom that Luther and other Reformers rediscovered as we read the Bible anew. We want to reinterpret the discoveries of that era for Christians today. If 2017 is to be a jubilee and celebration, it can only be a celebration of the gospel and of Jesus Christ.

The texts compiled in this volume, therefore, only reflect a part of what constituted the whole wealth of this congress. They are intended to invite and provoke discussion and exchanges among the churches as to what the message of the gospel means for today's society and how to celebrate it in the best and broadest way in 2017 and beyond. These are the main reason for and the added value of the congress documented in this volume. It thus provides authentic points of reference of international appeal for all those who are preparing for the celebration of the fifth centennial of the Reformation, with neither triumphalism nor misplaced modesty, with neither denominational polemics nor underestimation of the ecumenical challenges.

The congress was attended by nearly 250 participants coming from 35 countries—professors, church leaders, interested pastors, evangelists, and ecumenical specialists. The global dimension of the Protestant churches thus became apparent and palpable. The texts presented here stem from very different authors and contexts. Some have a more academic form, others are rather narrative or descriptive. For many authors, the congress was not held in their native languages. All of this is noticeable in the style of the different contributions. We did not want to unify all these elements, however, which readers may find disruptive and irritating at first. We see the strength and the quality of these contributions precisely in these elements. Rather, they are an indication that a goal of this congress was reached: to gather Protestant voices from all over the world around our common identity today without prejudice, preassigned rules, or standards.

The book follows the intrinsic logic of the congress:

- The first four parts deal with questions about the theological foundation and legacy of the Reformation. The analyses revolve around the significance of the discovery of the Reformation for today, on the one hand, which obviously requires an ecumenical and international approach. On the other hand, they update specific themes around which the Reformation historically crystallized. There indeed has been remarkable progress in historical and theological research in recent years, clarifying anew the question of what the Reformation actually generated and how much it was also the fruit of that epoch.
- The fifth part of this volume deals with the opportunities and limitations for today with respect to different contexts or dialogue partners of the jubilee: What is the commonality between the German and Chinese situations? How can our message be understood from a Roman Catholic or an African perspective?
- Finally, this volume contains assessments and retrospectives of the congress, especially from the standpoints of Free Churches and the radical wing of the Reformation.

We hope that the variety and richness of these perspectives of 2017 will encourage the readers to undertake their own projects and preparations.

Acknowledgments

This congress and publication were only successful due to the concrete and active support during the preparations, implementation, and follow-up work of numerous people and institutions. We extend our heartfelt gratitude especially to:

The following in Bern and Hannover: Dine Fecht, Thomas Flügge, Nicole Freimüller, Simone Gawarecki, Ann Katrin Hergert, Martin Hirzel, Henning Kiene, Kerstin Kipp, Michèle Laubscher, Reinhard Mawick, Christiane Rohr, Michael Schneider, Daniele Waldburger.

The following in Zurich: Martin Breitenfeldt, Philippe Dätwyler, Roland Diethelm, Rita Famos, the parish council, the pastors and the team of Walter Jucker from the congregation Neumünster, the Freie Gymnasium Zürich, the community centre Riesbach, Nicolas Mori, Brigitta Rotach.

The stewards: Joel Baumann, Bettina Birkner, Fritz Boller, Friedel Goetz, Tamara Jenny, Lia Knobel, Anna Luedke, Johannes Seyfarth, Alexander Stölzle, Jonas Stutz, Annina Villiger.

The musicians and artists: Elisabeth Berner and the quartet "Berner in Fusion," the yodeling club of Ebnat–Kapple with Hansueli Hersche, Hans Hürlemann, the Bismärkli–Schuppel and the Helvetic Fidlers, Walter Neff, Christian Scheifele, Andreas Thiel, Hans Thomann.

The translators and editors: Suzanne Bollinger, David Dichelle, Daniel Dubach, Elisabeth Gerber, Peter Glatthart, Christoph Renfer, Pia Schell, Hartmut Lucke, Roland Revet, Hera Moon, Monique Lopinat, Christine Sutter.

The Swiss Reformation Foundation, DM—échange et mission, the World Communion of Reformed Churches, the Reformed Church of the canton of Aargau, the Reformed Churches of Bern–Jura–Solothurn, the Evangelical-Reformed Church of the canton of St Gallen, the Evangelical Reformed Church of the canton of Thurgau, the Evangelical-Reformed Church of the canton of Vaud, the Reformed Church of the canton of Zug, the Evangelical-Reformed Church of the canton of Zurich, the Office of Culture of Appenzell Outer-Rhodes, the canton and city of Zurich, as well as Zurich Tourism.

Contributors

Michael Bünker: ThD; general secretary of the Community of Protestant Churches in Europe (CPCE); bishop of the Evangelical Church A.B. in Austria, Vienna.

Anne Burghardt: MDiv; Secretary for Ecumenical Relations, Department for Theology and Public Witness, Lutheran World Federation, Geneva.

Marianne Carbonnier-Burkard: PhD in history of philosophy; honorary lecturer at the Protestant Institute of the Faculty of Theology in Paris; vice president of the Society for the History of French Protestantism, Paris.

Christophe Chalamet: ThD, professor of systematic theology at the Theological Faculty of the University of Geneva; 2003–2011 professor of history of Protestant theology, Fordham University, New York.

Christine Christ-von Wedel: PhD; historian specializing in humanism and the Reformation; president of the Board of Mission 21, Basel.

Erik Alexander De Boer: ThD; professor of Reformation history at the Free University Amsterdam and of church history at the University of Theology in Kampen; associate professor of patristics at the Free State University in Bloemfontein.

François Dermange: ThD; professor of ethics at the Theological Faculty of the University of Geneva.

Frédéric Elsig: Litt.D.; professor of medieval art history at the Unite of Art History of the University of Geneva.

Fulvio Ferrario: ThD; professor of systematic theology at the Theological Faculty of the Waldensian Church, Rome.

Walter Fleischmann-Bisten: ThD; historian and theologian; general secretary of the Protestant League in Germany since 1984; director of the Institute for Confessional Studies Bensheim.

Frank Fornaçon: pastor of the Evangelical Free Church Kassel-West "Kirche im Hof"; member of the Presidium of the Union of Evangelical Free Churches (Baptists) in Germany (BEFG); representative of the Association of Evangelical Free Churches in Germany (VEF) for the Reformation Jubilee, Ahnatal.

Thies Gundlach: ThD; vice-president of the Church Office of the Evangelical Church in Germany (EKD); head of the department "Priority Areas of Church Works," Hannover.

Anne-Marie Heitz-Muller: ThD in Protestant theology, specializing in history of women and Reformation; parish assistant, Strasbourg.

Martin Ernst Hirzel: MDiv, ThD; executive secretary for Ecumenism and Religious Communities of the Federation of Swiss Protestant Churches (FSPC), Bern; till 2006 professor of church history at the Theological Faculty of the Waldensian Church, Rome.

Hanspeter Jecker: PhD.; lecturer at the Theological Seminary Bienenberg; research associate in various research projects regarding Anabaptism; member of the Swiss Mennonite Conference (Anabaptists), Basel.

Margot Kässmann: PhD, Dr h.c.; ambassador of the Council of the Evangelical Church in Germany (EKD) for the Reformation Jubilee 2017, Berlin.

Cardinal Kurt Koch: president of the Pontifical Council for Promoting Christian Unity, Rome.

Ulrich H. J. Körtner: ThD; professor of systematic theology at the Evangelical-Theological Faculty of the University of Vienna.

Volker Leppin: ThD; professor of church history in Tübingen; professor of church history in Jena, 2000–2010.

Athina Lexutt: ThD; professor of church history and history of theology at the Institute for Protestant Theology of the Justus Liebig University Giessen.

Gottfried Wilhelm Locher: PhD; president of the Council of the Federation of Swiss Protestant Churches (FSPC), Bern; member of the Presidium of the Community of Protestant Churches in Europe (CPCE), Vienna.

Viorel Mehendinţu: ThD; archpriest of the Romanian Orthodox Church, Stuttgart.

Michel Müller: MDiv; president of the Church Council of the Evangelical-Reformed Regional Church of the Canton of Zurich.

Peter Opitz: ThD; professor of church and dogmatic history from the Reformation to the Present at the Theological Faculty of the University of Zurich and the director of the Institute for Swiss Reformation Studies, Zurich.

Jong Wha Park: ThD, Dr. h.c.; senior pastor at the Kyungdong Presbyterian Church in Seoul; chairperson of the board of directors of the Kukmin *Daily Newspaper*, Seoul; managing chairperson of the Korean Host Committee of the 10th Assembly of the World Council of Churches (WCC), Busan, South Korea until November 2013.

Johanna Rahner: PhD; professor of systematic theology at the Institute of Catholic Theology of the University of Kassel.

Martin Sallmann: ThD; professor of modern church history and modern history of theology as well as confessional studies at the Theological Faculty of the University of Bern.

Martin Schindehütte: MDiv; since December 2013 retired, before bishop for Ecumenism and Ministries Abroad of the Evangelical Church in Germany (EKD), Hannover.

Nikolaus Schneider: Dr h.c.; chairperson of the Council of the Evangelical Church in Germany (EKD), Berlin.

Klára Tarr Czelovszky: ThD; director of the Department for Ecumenical and External Relations of the Evangelical Lutheran Church in Hungary, Budapest; member of the Presidium of the Community of Protestant Churches in Europe (CPCE), Vienna.

Wolfgang Thoenissen: ThD; professor of ecumenical theology at the Theological Faculty Paderborn and presiding director of the Johann Adam Möhler Ecumenical Institute, Paderborn.

Karen Georgia A. Thompson: MDiv; minister for Ecumenical and Interfaith Relations, United Church of Christ, Cleveland, Ohio, USA.

Olaf Fykse Tveit: MDiv, ThD; general secretary of the World Council of Churches, Geneva.

Douwe Visser: ThD; executive secretary for Theology and Communion, World Communion of Reformed Churches, Hannover.

Martin Wallraff: ThD; professor of church history and history of theology at the University of Basel.

Aiming Wang: MDiv., ThD, Dr. h.c.; full professor (systematic theology, historical theology, hermeneutical theology), vice-president of Nanjing Union Theological Seminary, Nanjing, China.

Lord Rowan Douglas Williams: ThD; The Rt Revd & Rt Hon Baron Williams of Oystermouth, dean of Magdalene College, Cambridge, UK; former archbishop of Canterbury.

Ibrahim Yusuf Wushishi: ThD; reverend of Nigerian Baptist Convention; member of the National Executive Committee of Christian Association of Nigeria (CAN); executive committee member of Christian Health Association of Nigeria (CHAN); general secretary of the Christian Council of Nigeria (CCN), L

Part One

Introducing the Reformation Jubilee

CHAPTER 1

Michel Müller

"Who Am I to Stand in God's Way?"

Opening Sermon

Dear brothers and sisters,
Many of you will be spending three, possibly four days and nights here in Zurich for the convention that opens today with this worship service. I can imagine that most of you will have to report back about all the meaningful things you accomplished during your stay. Historically speaking, you find yourself in one of the most important cities of Christendom. For that reason, you have come to this place. Others come to Zurich for the Street Parade or perhaps the Zurich Film Festival, which just ended yesterday. Here you may even buy an exorbitantly overpriced designer handbag or a luxuriously expensive watch. Will your loved ones at home ask reproachful questions about your shopping spree? Will *your* purchase turn viral in the international media? Probably not. In any case, there is another, much more decisive question being posed to all of us: Can God's Spirit confront us in such a place, here and now, and in such a way that a great storm will be incited? Are we even expecting something like this? What else are these conventions good for, anyway?

As we reflect on the Reformation, must we stand accountable for what we accomplish? Or even for whatever we choose *not* to do? Does it even depend on us and what we do? Together with Peter, we ask the equivocal question: Who am I to stand in God's way? (Acts 11:17).

Initially, the apostle posed his question rather cautiously—just as Moses and Jeremiah once did. *God's Spirit* is building God's church! Who, then, were these individuals, even if one of them was destined to become the first pope, to encounter the Spirit? According to Luke, the Spirit is free to create regulations and facts, which the church can and *must* follow in all her subsequent doings. In the book of Acts, the receiving of the Spirit is always followed by a baptism. At times, however, Luke reverses the order so that the Spirit is received following a baptism. The Spirit is free, for it is the Spirit of God. That does not mean that the Spirit is idle. Its ministry may be expected, actually anticipated, surprisingly and even in contradiction to our own well-groomed theological convictions. Correspondingly, the history of the church has always been, according to the third article of the Apostles' Creed, a history of the Holy Spirit. Christian churches have developed ingenious systems to test the ministry of the Spirit, sometimes even to tame and domesticate it. Yes, we have to test the Spirit! The detours and dead ends in different chapters of the church's history, even of our own, oblige us to do so. Consequently, we must ask ourselves: How are we to understand the last 500 years as ministry of the Spirit? How would Luke have continued with his story of the ministry of the Holy Spirit? Would Protestants have been included as one of the signs of the Spirit's ministries?

Several representatives from other churches would undoubtedly still question this—even after 500 years. We in the church of Zurich, however, believe just that. Our church polity confesses that the church "is built up through God's Spirit."[1] And not only we ourselves, but a multitude of churches, which emerged in the last few centuries and spread from Zurich, Wittenberg, and other places of Reformation, perceive themselves in faith as part of the ministry of God's Spirit. However, how can this be and how do we reconcile the one Spirit and the many churches?

The ecumenical theologian Oscar Cullmann (1902–1999) understood all too well the diversity of the Christian churches as defining the ministry workings of the Spirit. He wrote in his famous work *Unity through Diversity*: "Those persons, who do not respect the rich fullness in the workings of the Spirit, and therefore seek only uniformity, are actually committing a sin against the Holy Spirit."[2] Therefore, can we not conversely view the continuing existence

1 Art. 86, Ordinance of the Reformed Church of the Canton of Zurich.

2 Oscar Cullmann, *Unity through Diversity: Its Foundation, and a Contribution to the Discussion Concerning the Possibilities of Its Actualization*, trans. M. Eugene Boring (Philadelphia: Fortress Press,

of the Roman Catholic Church alongside the numerous Protestant churches, as being the working of the Spirit as well? So the following quote may apply: "In all our ecumenical relations, it is of the utmost importance, that we not only know, but also recognize more thoroughly those things, which the Spirit has sown in others, as a gift to us."[3] Those are not Cullmann's words, who thought through the idea of charismatic gifts in all churches. No, that was a quote of the current bishop of Rome! In the very same interview with the Jesuit periodical *Civiltà Cattolica*, which was published just a few weeks ago, Pope Francis went on to say: "Being united in our differences, we must make progress. There is no other way to become one. That is precisely the way of Jesus." "United in our differences" is perhaps not quite the same as the term "reconciled diversity," as we Protestants understand it, but the term also does not totally stray from the basic concept behind our own Leuenberg community.[4] Is this the current challenge facing us all today, especially in regards to the younger churches such as the Pentecostals, whose very name bears witness to the Spirit? Here, we are talking about the second largest group in universal Christendom today. How will we actually celebrate the Reformation with them? How will we discuss, pray, and experience the topics of church renewal together? And how will we encounter the ancient churches? After celebrating 500 years of Reformation, will we in all seriousness have to commemorate a millennium of schism between East and West?

Indeed, we have to examine all of this, all the Spirits. This examination actually can and should be the task of a convention of theologians and church leaders. Together, we must examine history as well as its consequences. Through this process, we will learn and draw our inspiration. For what other reason have we come together in this place? Is not our present situation in a way quite similar to that of that first-century believer in Jerusalem in the book of Acts, who had to examine the Spirit and decide?

So who are we? Who am I? Precisely this question was asked by the very same Peter, who once said that one should obey God more than humans. It is an attitude Martin Luther held during his stay in Worms when he maintained that he must obey his conscience more than the church or the emperor: "Here I stand, I can do no other!" Regardless of its historicity, the appeal of such statements lies in their ability to summarize the occurrences of the time in a nutshell. So, there is one individual standing in front of the

1988). The quote in the text has been translated by this essay's translator, Reverend Ralph W. Miller, from the German edition, *Einheit in Vielfalt: Grundlegung Und Beitrag Zur Diskussion Uber Die Moglichkeiten Ihrer Verwirklichung* (Gottingen: Mohr Siebeck, 1986), 28.

3 From part 2 of an interview with Pope Francis by Antonio Spadaro, SJ, in *Stimmen der Zeit,* 19 September 2013.

4 The Community of Protestant Churches in Europe, CPCE (http://www.leuenberg.eu).

rulers of the world and in front of God, having been moved by the Spirit to remain true to his conscience and the word of God rather than to the rest of the world. Suddenly, such a decisive moment depended on a single person, who bravely gave an account and did a courageous deed in the name of God. This phrase—"to do a courageous deed"—stands here in Zürich as exemplary for Zwingli's work. Although Zwingli wrote this phrase under different circumstances than Luther, it nonetheless applied as well then as it does today: if God's Spirit moves us in any direction by means of scripture, we must follow. Writing in late medieval German, Zwingli penned the phrase: "*Tuont um Gottswillen etwas Dapfers*" ("For God's sake, do a courageous deed"). You may read these exact words in the sacristy of this church. So, who are we to stand in his way? Do you feel the tension here? We have to withstand this suspense, this discrepancy even: church history is not about individual heroic characters, but about Christ's church, which is built by God's Spirit. However, nothing will come into being unless someone follows the Spirit—and that would be us. Even though the church is not about us, it will not work without us. So who are we today?

And who am I? Once more, I would like to borrow a few words, recently uttered by Bishop Francis of Rome: "I am a sinner, whom God has looked upon." A sinner, so that not even so-called infallible decisions can stand in God's place? A sinner who may dare to act precisely because the Lord has looked upon him? In the Protestant tradition, we would rather articulate this with these words: he is simultaneously sinner and justified.

However, what should we as Protestant churches be doing here and now, as well as in the near future? Here in Zurich, we are currently celebrating 50 years of the ordination of women. Naturally, this celebration attracts a certain amount of attention, but surely no applause. In a modern society, this topic seems and should be self-evident. And celibacy? For us Protestants, this is no longer an issue ever since the time of Katharina von Bora, who wed Luther, and Anna Reinhart, who married Zwingli. In numerous Protestant churches, we have ceased to set up systems of norms pertaining to lifestyle issues and to discriminate against those persons who are different from us. We have taken this road not simply out of spite against other churches, but because we are Protestant Christians. So, what still remains for us to do in that future time and place to which the Spirit is leading us?

Here is a noteworthy example: the United Protestant Church of France has taken a great step forward this year in their relations with one another. "*Ecoute—Dieu nous parle*" is their slogan in French, literally translated: "Listen, God is speaking to us." And when God speaks, who can stand in God's way? God is calling us to be witnesses in modern society. Within the German-speaking churches, which are still relatively rich, I see the following question arise: How much longer do we want to support and maintain structures as well as infrastructures that no longer reflect the actual demands and sizes of our churches today? Structures that reduce and withdraw funds from our mission to preach the gospel to all peoples in word and deed?

Who am I to say such things? None other than a person who, within his place, within his own church tradition, and with his individual gifts and talents, should do and wants to do what is necessary. A person who, within the limitations of his own possibilities, tries not to stand in the Spirit's way. For, as Luke summarizes, it is through the Spirit that even Gentiles are granted repentance that leads to life (Acts 11:18).

Allow me to be quite frank with you: the time has come for us to go *outside* of these old walls. Let us go into the world. I am not talking about a world as we would like it to be, but the world as it really is. Let us go out to the people, who simply are the way they are. We must leave our sense of security behind us, which we find in forms of reciprocal affirmation and within the bounds of tightly closed church systems. We must leave ourselves behind and encounter fellow humans and their actual needs, especially their spiritual ones.

To go beyond one's boundaries: this may also be done in a convention. Let us go out of our comfort zones. Let's go outside, have a seat on a bench, watch the people pass by, and perhaps even exchange a kind word with a stranger. They are just people, even here in Zürich. Ecumenism starts with a personal encounter with another human being, my neighbour—someone to listen to, someone to pray for, someone to serve. Who will do such things if I don't?

Only then will the universal church, ecumenism, be a spiritual and diaconal ecumenism; a church that prays and serves, that has been born out of the word of God and is nurtured at the Lord's table. All are invited to come to this table—all, whom the Lord himself invites. Indeed, it is the same Lord who once explained to Peter: "Do not call anything impure that God has made clean" (Acts 11:9).

Indeed, who am I to stand in God's way?

Amen.

CHAPTER 2

Gottfried Locher

The Reformation: Remembering for Our Future

Reformation: The Gospel at Its Centre

The Reformation is going to be 500 years young: in 2017, the churches of the Reformation will be commemorating how Martin Luther famously nailed his 95 Theses to the door of Wittenberg's Castle Church. And in 2019, the beginning of Huldrych Zwingli's ministry of the word from the pulpit of the Grossmünster will be commemorated. It has already become apparent that the Reformation Jubilee has the potential to gather considerable momentum around the world. It is an occasion to lend expression, in a variety of ways, to our joy over the rediscovery of the liberating message of the gospel, whose centre is the message of our justification before God solely through faith in Jesus Christ. Or, put differently: human beings can exist in time and eternity because God loves them. The gospel shall be at the centre stage and be celebrated. This is the message of the Reformation—a liberating and exhilarating message. The Protestant churches, therefore, are not celebrating themselves. The Reformation was about the renewal of the *one* church. The Reformation Jubilee has thus had an ecumenical dimension right from the very beginning.

The Preparation Period

Preparations have already begun for the Reformation Jubilee here in Switzerland and especially in Germany as well. However, there is still much to be decided. Both the Federation of Swiss Protestant Churches and the Evangelical Church in Germany have grasped this opportunity and invited you all here to Zurich to an international preparatory congress. The goal is to come together to reflect upon how we would like to celebrate the Reformation Jubilee and what significance the message of the Reformation can have for church and society in the future.

We are glad that you have all come to Zurich from near and far, from over 35 countries and five continents. You symbolize that the message of the Reformation has expanded throughout the world into a wide variety of contexts and has continued to move people to this day. The range of experiences and perspectives that you have to offer will enrich our congress and, hopefully, build bridges between people with church and university backgrounds. We seek to enter into a critical-constructive dialogue with one another on the Reformation era as a means of opening up new perspectives for our churches and society today.

Protestant Churches Celebrating Together throughout Europe and the World

The decision to join together as we move towards the 2017 Reformation Jubilee and to celebrate the 500th anniversary of the Reformation lies behind this congress, beginning today. This is the *first* time that Protestant churches in Europe have sought to celebrate a Reformation anniversary together. While in 1917, only a few individuals were campaigning for unity among Protestants in Switzerland, advocating for a celebratory worship service to take place in Zurich's Grossmünster on 31 October, today the Protestant churches of Europe wish to celebrate together. This was all made possible by the Leuenberg Agreement, the 40th anniversary of which we are celebrating this year. In 1973, Europe's Lutheran, Reformed, and United churches met at Leuenberg near Basel to come to an understanding about the common basis of faith, recognizing that the remaining doctrinal differences among the churches of the Reformation were no longer of a church-dividing nature. Ever since, the Protestant churches of Europe have formed a church community, including fellowship of table and pulpit and a common proclamation of the gospel in word and deed. The Community of Protestant Churches in Europe (CPCE)–Leuenberg Church Fellowship has served as an example for churches in North and South America as well as in the Middle East, and will hopefully also bring Protestants closer together at the global level. What, then, could be more fitting than the Protestant churches in Europe and throughout the world celebrating the Reformation Jubilee together? Therefore, at its autumn 2012 General Assembly in Florence, the CPCE called upon its member churches to celebrate a Reformation festival at the European level that "illuminates the European-wide dimension of the Reformation." While 2017 will play a central role in this regard, 500th-anniversary celebrations will begin before that and continue well past 2017, especially here in Switzerland.

Discovering Each Other's Riches

"We are past the times in which we played the Reformation traditions against each other. We would much rather discover the riches found within them." This quote by Wolfgang Huber on the occasion of the Calvin commemorations in 2009 is also leading the way forward for us here today and as we move toward 2017. We wish to recognize the riches of our respective traditions and learn from one another. The ecumenical community is a learning community.

Zurich: One of the Places of Origin of the Reformation

The Evangelical Reformed Church of the Canton of Zurich is hosting this congress here in Zurich, which is one of the places of origin of the Reformation. It is well known how the Reformation took its own turn in Zurich and in other places in Switzerland, including Bern, St Gallen, Basel, and then Geneva. The irreconcilable judgments of Luther on Zwingli and the regrettable failure of the 1529 Marburg Colloquy have not yet been completely forgotten. Following the Leuenberg Agreement, however, and in light of previous positive experiences that also existed throughout church history, we know that, aside from confessional differences between Luther and Reformed Christians, the Reformation was an era of Protestant commonalities, even if not everybody involved recognized it due to political and, at times, personal reasons. Our joy is therefore all the greater over the fact that Lutherans, Reformed, United, and members of other denominations are meeting for the first time in this way here in this city, a place that, alongside Wittenberg and later Geneva, holds great importance for Protestants around the world. Without figures such as Zwingli, Bullinger, and Calvin, the Reformation would likely have remained a German-speaking and northern

European phenomenon. A Protestant catholicity will thus become apparent in this congress, one among which there is diversity. We have already experienced some of this just now during the worship service.

Remembering for the Future

"Remembering for the Future" shall be our motto for the next few days. Reformation commemoration should primarily involve asking about the value of the Reformation message for the Protestant churches and society today. Are the churches able to provide a sufficiently strong witness to God's word of reconciliation and change? Is their proclamation clear and understandable? The interpretation of the Reformation message of liberation today and connected theological questions are to be at the centre of this congress and of the jubilee.

The Lasting Effects of the Reformation

As part of a culture of remembrance, the Reformation Jubilee also involves the task of recalling the past. The Reformation had an impact on the world. It had a diverse effect on early modern society. Some of these imprints, as reflected, for example, in the church–state relationship, are to be traced here over the next few days. What is the relationship of culture, economics, and politics today to the Reformation? Such questions will be addressed in this Zurich congress as well. As already said, however, discussions will centre on the Reformation as a task for us now. Aspects of Protestant faith and responsibility for the world continue to influence our societies today. What potential does the Reformation message hold for the church and society of tomorrow?

The Reformation Anniversary as an Ecumenical Task

The commemoration of the Reformation should thus not serve as a means for the self-promotion of churches, denominations, and cultural areas, but instead incite a productive and cooperative form of how to be church today. This requires us to rethink the theological questions that were posed back then, while also continuing to pursue questioning ourselves critically. I am very happy that we will be challenged with another view on the Reformation right from the beginning with the opening address of Rowan Williams, the former archbishop of Canterbury (while this is not, in fact, an external viewpoint if we take into account that the early church of England was closely connected to Zurich's reformers).

If the commemoration of the Reformation is to support our work on how to be church today, this will involve an ecumenical dimension, as mentioned in the beginning. At this congress, we wish to seek consciously the dialogue with ecumenical partners. With respect to relations with the Roman Catholic Church, it would constitute a major step if we were to succeed in attaining a common view of the history of the Reformation era, as suggested in "From Conflict to Communion," a recent document by the Pontifical Council for Promoting Christian Unity and the Lutheran World Federation (LWF). We know that the Reformation not only coined the "Protestant" churches but the Roman Catholic Church as well. This offers the promising opportunity for a common ecumenical discourse today. This could be the great defining characteristic of the Reformation Jubilee in the early 21st century. With a view to the relationships with the Free Churches that invoke the radical and once-persecuted Reformation movement, the ecumenical dimension of the Reformation Jubilee entails for us a critical engagement with our own past.

The Congress: An Invitation to Cooperate

In addition to focusing on reflection, this congress will also provide a practical platform for the exchange of ideas. Plans and perspectives will be provided by different churches with regard to the Reformation Jubilee. It would be nice if cooperative opportunities could be envisioned and mutual projects initiated at the local, regional, national, and international levels. Foremost, however, this congress shall seek to foster in all of you the motivation to participate actively in the Reformation Jubilee, and to kindle your interest for the Reformation and its significance for the present day. Thereby, the Reformation shall be highlighted in its diversity and Protestantism made visible as a global and as a plural movement.

Finally, I find the words that Zwingli wrote at the end of his 1525 "Commentary on True and False Religion"—the very first exposition of Protestant doctrine—to be of particular relevance to this congress, and to the Reformation Jubilee in general: "Everything I said here, I did for God's glory, for the benefit of Christian society, and with the best conscience. Thanks be to God."

CHAPTER 3

Nikolaus Schneider

Why Are We Gathered Together?

The Reformation Jubilee 2017 is a global event!

In Germany, the opening kick-off for the big topic of "Reformation Jubilee" was launched as early as 2003 from the milieu of the Roman Catholic Church, namely by Cardinal Kasper, at the General Assembly of the Lutheran World Federation held in Winnipeg. Cardinal Kasper highlighted this landmark year 2017 and raised the question of the ecumenical dimensions of this event. Soon thereafter, Wolfgang Böhmer, then minister-president of Saxony-Anhalt, picked up the ball and invited state and church to embark upon the Reformation Jubilee 2017 together.

We are grateful that not only the German federal government but also many federal states and concerned municipalities are currently participating in the preparation for the Jubilee. And this event no doubt marks one of the rarest events in the history of the German Bundestag: in October 2011, all parties including the left adopted in a united voice the resolution to promote and support the Reformation Jubilee 2017 at the federal-government level as a "world-class event."

So, we will have a year of great celebration in Germany with the church congress and a world exhibition of the Reformation in Wittenberg. People will be enticed to come to the "heartland of the Reformation" to visit national exhibitions and other tourist attractions in the form of top-notch educational museum events in magnificently restored historical buildings in Wittenberg, Eisenach, Eisleben, and Torgau. Insiders will be attracted to big, specialized congress events in Wittenberg, Halle, and Berlin.

The Academic Advisory Board, which provides the government and the church partners with materials and information, published a paper entitled "Perspectives for the Reformation Jubilee 2017" in 2009. It reads therein:

> On the way toward the Reformation Jubilee 2017, it is important to identify the relevance that the Reformation has, going far beyond theology and the church, for a variety of areas of our contemporary culture and to raise questions about its potential for interpretation in our times characterized by individualization, pluralization, and globalization. Given the distinct Protestant hallmark in the Western modern culture, such present-day interpretation . . . constitutes a contribution to the conservation as well as evolution of the identity of this culture.[1]

Now the question arises, Is it good and right for the church and state authorities to take over the preparations for the Reformation Jubilee? Does not a revised comeback edition of the old alliance between throne and altar, state and church—well, Prussia and Protestant church—shimmer through this, an alliance that nobody seriously wishes for? On the other hand, the cultural "Protestant hallmark" engraved on our society, which also coins the living environment of Europe, remains only a "hallmark." It is only one of the bricks to be integrated into the edifice of the Reformation Jubilee to be built upon a sound informative and theological basis. We are convinced that our genuine theological contributions can forestall the danger of the "revised comeback edition" of the old throne–altar alliance.

Please allow me to elucidate this point in two content-centred emphases:

The Reformation Jubilee Celebrates God's Redemptive Work in Jesus Christ!

The date 31 October 1517 is a symbolic date for the rediscovery of the liberating power of the gospel. The ever-fascinating story of Martin Luther's nailing of the 95 Theses calling for repentance on the door of the Castle Church in Wittenberg has been engraved in the cultural memory of our country. We do not celebrate the birthday of our Protestant church by celebrating

1 "500 Jahre Reformation—Luther 2017," *Perspektiven für das Reformationsjubiläum 2017* (Wittenberg), 10.

this date; we see this taking place more aptly in the redemptive work of Jesus Christ and the community-founding discourses and works of the apostles. With this event, we are going to celebrate the fact that the gospel found a new way to approach people. And we shall celebrate the liberating theological leitmotivs that are expressed in the four solae/soli of the Reformation:

Solus Christus, the underlying Christ centrality;
Sola scriptura, the newly discovered biblical piety;
Sola gratia, the awe-inspiring theology of grace;
Sola fide, the focus on liberating faith.

These are the determinant substantive orientation points for the celebration and presentation of the Reformation Jubilee. In a world that readily forgets its own religious roots, it is increasingly important to be guided by theologically significant symbolic dates and leitmotivs.

People in present-day society are searching for a merciful God in a quite different way than people did in Luther's time. Those who are trimmed, right from the cradle, to become competitive packages attractive in the labour market need a different kind of voice to reflect God's saving action in their lives. While the spiral of performance and efficiency and even-higher performance and even-greater efficiency is continually swirling, people need to be awakened by the appeal of the gospel: it is not performance and proficiency, nor my efforts and my own success, that have power over me and decide my value.

People need to be reminded of the fundamental insights of the reformers: that faith in Christ makes it possible to live a life without fear, without the inner constraint for self-justification and self-aggrandizement; that faith makes us free before God and for God; and that this freedom calls us to the responsible ministry to the people and the world. The gospel is dealing with key issues of all people. The gospel is about the questions of inalienable human dignity, awareness of freedom for the benefit of the whole community, and sustainable social responsibility of all people for all people and for the world.

It is our common task to formulate these core insights of the Reformation for our time in such a way that they are understood within and outside our churches. We seek and need such a hub for information, discourse, and existential support that can make it clearly understandable to outsiders and neophytes why the Reformation Jubilee is a commemorative event recalling God's redemptive work in Jesus Christ and at the same time has a central implication for living in the modern society now and in the future.

Reformation Jubilee 2017 Belongs to Our Ecumenical Church Community!

The Evangelical Church in Germany will celebrate 2017 cheerfully, with self-confidence and self-criticism and openness to our ecumenical brothers and sisters.

In Germany, beginning back in 2008, we agreed on a Reformation decade with yearly topics spread over these ten years, progressively moving from one topic to another. Throughout these ten thematic years, we are trying to fathom the "length and breadth and height and depth" (cf. Eph 3:18) of the implications of the Reformation revolving around the gospel—including the shadows and boundaries of this movement. The topic for 2013 was "Reformation and Tolerance," in which we were invited to reflect also on the cruelty and destruction that Luther and the Reformation disseminated with their intolerance. In this context, we are to rectify the picture of the "German hero Martin Luther," often painted with a national pathos. Recent Luther research unambiguously demonstrates that Luther had an ambivalent personality with admirable traits and long-lasting theological inspirations, but also one marked by fierce polemic and shameful anti-Judaism.

In view of this "dark side" of the Reformation, an interdenominational committee between the Evangelical Church in Germany (EKD) and the Roman Catholic Church in Germany came into being, under the motto of "healing of memories," to attempt to clarify the images and typifications of the Reformation that constitute a substantial burden for us even today. Before God and each other, we wish to bring forward the wounds that are engrained in our memory to this day. Should this attempt succeed, the joint celebration of a reconciliation service in 2017 would be a clear signal for the liberating and healing power of the gospel and a landmark event of great ecumenical significance.

We have invited our Roman Catholic, Orthodox, and Free Church partners to participate in the Reformation Jubilee, even though some might rather think of the Reformation in terms of the schisms and separations of the Western church, or have no explicit awareness of direct involvement in the Reformation themes, or, like the Free Churches, have a memory of painful history with the established churches. The EKD has reached some agreements with the German Bishops' Conference to strengthen our community: thus, not only are the 95 Theses being commented on ecumenically, but a Protestant–Catholic joint document is being drafted under the working title of "What everyone should know about Christianity."

The ecumenical dimension and the international orientation of the Reformation Jubilee 2017 is a central concern of the EKD. That is what distinguishes us from the earlier jubilees that have been celebrated since the first centenary in 1617.

From a historical perspective, not only is it doubtful whether the event of the famous 95 Theses being nailed on the door of the Castle Church in Wittenberg actually took place in 1517; it can also be questioned whether these 95 Theses can be considered a new Reformation theology or, rather, constituted a good Roman Catholic theology in the context of that time. Regardless of such doubts, it remains incontestable that the upheaval wrought by Martin Luther and his generation of reformers influenced all of our churches, albeit at different times and in different ways. Therefore, the Dutch tell a different Reformation history than brothers and sisters in Africa. The Italian Protestant churches are living with their own Reformation stories quite different from those of the big Scandinavian churches.

But this is precisely why we have come together here in Zurich: we want to listen to one another's histories of Reformation, to detect the roots on which our Reformation churches stand, and to consider what forms their present and what hopes guide them. We shall learn from one another which theological insights are of particular importance to us and which differences constitute common wealth. Amidst the diversity we represent and our polyphonic voices, we shall seek to find common formulations for the core of the Reformation events that were disseminated 500 years ago out of Zurich, Wittenberg, and many other places, so that the story of Christ will gain in importance as a story of liberation for the people and world today.

Let's talk about it and work together here in Zurich!

Part Two

Biblical Studies

CHAPTER 4

Karen Georgia Thompson

Romans 3:21-31

The passage we heard this morning is one that is quite familiar to us. This passage is one that was central to the Reformation and in particular to the arguments of Martin Luther. In his day, Luther was faced with a church that was corrupt, a people who were taught that they had to buy their way to eternity, and clergy who were caught in carrying out the will of a defined clerical hierarchy that in turn was supported by the will of the emperor. Church and state were unified in supporting the selling of indulgences as a means of escaping God's retributive justice. Giving money to the church through the purchase of indulgences rendered penance for sin into a financial transaction rather than the act of repentance and contrition that it is.

With his extensive work on the book of Romans, Luther dared to challenge the church at a time when few options existed for other Christian religious views and thought that countered the dominant Christian doctrine of the day. Luther concluded from his reading of the book of Romans that it was the free gift of God's grace that provided justification, which was received through faith and could not be bought. Luther challenged the authority of the pope and the Roman Catholic Church when he taught that the Bible is the only source and authority for the church.

Luther, after all, was not a Lutheran but a Roman Catholic priest who was critical of the exploitation of the poor and the misuse of the papacy. As a result, he voiced his strong critique of the very institution to which he was called to serve. Luther paid the price for his daring when he was later excommunicated by the pope and condemned as an outlaw by the emperor. For Luther, we are saved *sola Scriptura, sola gratis, sola fides*—"by scripture alone, by grace alone, and by faith alone."

As we contemplate the fast-approaching quincentennial anniversary of the Reformation, this is certainly an occasion to revisit the past and the work of those who have gone before. The occasion also invites us to look at the present and think of the future of the church.

Romans 3:21-31 is as familiar as it is challenging. Paul's first-century Christian audience in the Roman churches had never met him and did not know him. The text picks up where Paul concludes in Romans 1:17 and follows on the conclusion of Romans 3:20, where Paul writes: "For 'no human being will be justified in his sight' by deeds prescribed by law, for through the law comes the knowledge of sin." This sets the stage for what Paul has to say.

In their book *The First Paul*, Marcus Borg and John Dominic Crossan devote an entire chapter to their discussion of "justification by grace through faith." They offer that when Paul

> spoke of justification by grace through faith, he was not thinking about how we get to heaven, but about transformation of ourselves and of the world in this life here below. Moreover, when he contrasted faith and works, he was not thinking of *faith-without-works*—which cannot exist because faith always includes works—but about *works-without-faith*, which unfortunately exists all too often—sometimes from habit or guilt, sometimes from thoughtless repetition or calculated hypocrisy.[1]

The grace of God given to us in Christ Jesus is what provides the place and the space for works, not as prescriptive, but as an outgrowth of God's transformative power at work. Because we are recipients of God's grace, we are motivated to be a part of God's justice at work in the world.

Faith is the action of the individual, not works. Faith is our response to God. However, the activity of faith is not independent of God's present work. If faith were solely the action of the individual, then one would have the right to boast of one's faith, much the same as one could boast about works.

---

1 Marcus J. Borg and John Dominic Crossan, *The First Paul: Reclaiming the Radical Visionary Behind the Church's Conservative Icon* (New York: HarperOne, 2009), 155.

Walter Brueggemann and others note that a reading of the text which implies faith is the sole ownership of the individual "makes the text into a statement centered on the consequences of God's righteousness for human beings . . . the focus of the text is not on the human quest for a gracious and loving God, but is on the radical act of God in reclaiming all humankind."[2] Even when the individual has faith, it is God's righteousness that is evident.

Right relationship with God is not for some, but for "all." Paul repeatedly emphasizes the universal nature of sin: "all have sinned and fall short of the glory of God," just as the "righteousness of God through faith in Christ Jesus" is for all who believe. For Paul, God shows no partiality in the offer of justification. There are no conditions or stipulations placed on acquiring the grace of God.

Paul holds this idea of "all having access" up against the law, which was accessible to a singular people. There are no prescriptions to be upheld to attain what God has to offer. Salvation is available to all who have faith in God.

God is the agent at work bringing humankind back to right relationship. God desires to be in right relationship and, as a result, we experience the righteousness of God at work on our behalf. Paul writes: "irrespective of law, the righteousness of God has been disclosed, and is attested by the law and the prophets, the righteousness of God through faith in Christ Jesus" (v. 22).

As Brueggemann and his colleagues write, "God's righteousness is not simply a quality comparable to God's goodness or God's immutability. Although God's righteousness is never severed from God, God's righteousness is a gift graciously bestowed on human beings. . . . God's righteousness is a way of talking about God's actions of reclaiming the world for God."[3]

Luther engaged this text almost 500 years ago in a world that was not in right relationship with God. Luther looked out into the world around him and saw change that was needed and necessary. The corruption in the church was not new. The sale of indulgences did not target the rich exclusively, but also targeted the poor. The church was getting richer while the people were getting poorer. Luther's motivation was not solely about changing the church; it was also about action on behalf of the poor and the marginalized. The Reformation changed lives. The Reformation changed the church. The Reformation changed the world.

Five hundred years later, we can see the differences the actions of the reformers made in the church and outside the church. The Reformation was not a perfect experience; there were those who were excluded because they

---

2 "Proper 4," in Walter Brueggemann, Charles B. Cousar, Beverly R. Gaventa, and James D. Newsome, *Texts for Preaching: A Lectionary Commentary Based on the NRSV—Year A* (Louisville: Westminster John Knox, 1995), 352.

3 Ibid., 351.

were thought to be wrong in their interpretation of scripture and understanding of God. The Reformation anniversary will take place in the context of an ecumenical community that is still looking to a day when the church will be united, as Jesus prayed with his disciples: "that they may all be one" (John 17:21). Some point to the Reformation as a place where the church was fractured. The bifurcations are further present in our Protestant ranks where churches have split again and again because of differences. We have Christians by many names: Methodists, Anglicans, Orthodox, Lutherans, Baptists, Pentecostals, Holiness, Evangelicals, and within each of those groups there are subgroups. Why are we so divided over how we understand God, Jesus, the Holy Spirit, or the sacraments when God has made a way for all to be redeemed to God through Christ?

Regardless of how we choose to reclaim the content of Romans 3:21-31 during these days and months leading to the Reformation celebration, we are confronted with the life and work of Luther and the reformers as well as their contribution to shaping—or perhaps reshaping—Christianity to be the religion we practice today.

CHAPTER 5

Margot Kässmann

John 3:1-15

What a text for an early morning! It is a really tough nut to crack, and hard to get into in only 30 minutes. It is a well-thought-out, profound, and thoroughly composed passage. Only in the gospel of John do we come across this intriguing Nicodemus dialogue. What does it all mean? If you are thinking after reading it for the first time that it is much too complicated and hard to understand, I can put you at ease: even Rudolf Bultmann, the great exegete of John's gospel, felt the same way. He found that the entire conversation breathed "the atmosphere of the mysterious," developing "the secret of rebirth, of the Son of Man, and of testimony."[1]

Let us now look into the situation more closely. A man named Nicodemus, who was apparently well known, and even regarded by Jesus as a "teacher of Israel" (3:10), came to Jesus after dark. This has been interpreted in many sermons and literature as a sign of fear: a man high up in the Sanhedrin was afraid to speak with Jesus in public. But what was he afraid of? Losing

1 Rudolf Bultmann, *Das Evangelium des Johannes* (Göttingen: Vandenhoeck & Ruprecht, 1978), 93.

his reputation? John the Evangelist himself seemed to view Nicodemus as an opportunist. In any event, he says of the "authorities" that they were afraid to confess their belief in Jesus publically: "Nevertheless many, even of the authorities, believed in him. But because of the Pharisees they did not confess it, for fear that they would be put out of the synagogue; for they loved human glory more than the glory that comes from God" (12:42-43).

New Testament scholar Klaus Wengst thus puts forward the thesis that, for John, Nicodemus was mostly uninteresting as an individual, but stood more for a group of "secret upper-class sympathizers, who did not confess publically for fear of being excluded from the synagogue. Because they did not wish to risk their social status."[2] Strong words, indeed—but John does clearly reproach Nicodemus, and many who acted the same way, for speaking of Jesus as a "teacher who has come from God" (3:2), while not, however, confessing their faith in him. We can probably detect a latent form of anti-Judaism here in John. Additionally, we can observe how this continues to flare up in the exegetic views on our text, such as that of Emmanuel Hirsch, who writes: "The Jew is bound to a service that closes his eyes to a state of being God's child, which is a miraculous gift of God, descending into earthly life."[3]

Nicodemus appears several times in John's gospel. He advocates for a fair trial for Jesus (7:50f.) and is the one who, together with Joseph of Arimathea, provides for a burial in dignity (19:39ff.). Is it not in fact possible that Nicodemus was just interested in Jesus' teachings, gave them considerable thought, and openly sought a dialogue with him? It would not be unusual for such a conversation to take place in the evening. The Talmud describes how rabbis often delved into the Torah at night: "Come, bless the Lord, all you servants of the Lord, who stand by night in the house of the Lord! (Ps. 134:1) What is the meaning of 'by night'? Rabbi Yochanan responded: This refers to the scribes who engage with the Torah at night. Scripture accredits them as though they were engaged in sacrificial service" (Mas. Menachoth 110a).

The situation could be quite straightforward: two men come together in the evening and have an intensive conversation about the basic questions of life and faith. This, of course, still occurs today—perhaps even here at our congress in Zurich! And even with and among women! Beyond all our busy, everyday lives, evening can provide space for dialogue to feel things out and ask questions without any pressure to achieve results. That is how I understand this conversation, as a struggle for answers of faith, which are never easy to find. And it is good when such a dialogue occurs. Much too rarely do we ask ourselves questions of faith such as: Do you believe in resurrection?

---

2 Klaus Wengst, *Das Johannesevangelium*, vol. 1, chs. 1-10 (Stuttgart: Kohlhammer, 2000), 119.

3 Emmanuel Hirsch, *Das vierte Evangelium in seiner ursprünglichen Gestalt verdeutscht und erklärt* (Tübingen: J. C. B. Mohr, 1936), 135.

Can I say for myself that Jesus Christ is the way, the truth, and the life? What do we mean when we refer to the son of God? What does baptism mean to me? And are we open enough to people like Nicodemus, who are interested but do not wish to convert or confess right away? I think that we need more Nicodemus dialogues today!

But let us look more closely at this dialogue, which Bultmann incidentally understands as being a traditional "pronouncement story"[4] in John: to begin with, Nicodemus does not even ask a question but recognizes Jesus as a teacher in faith. We are indeed at the very beginning of the gospel. John the Baptist recognized that the Spirit of God was with Jesus and the miracle at the wedding of Cana as well as the cleansing of the temple were, first, symbolic acts. Nicodemus understood that nobody could do those signs if God was not with him. Jesus responded with the central idea that "no one can see the kingdom of God without being born anew" (3:3).

In John, the kingdom of God is only mentioned within this context in verses 3 and 5. In the synoptic gospels, it is often presented with the idea that we need to be like children to gain entry. As we read in Mark 10:14: "Let the little children come to me; do not stop them; for it is to such as these that the kingdom of God belongs"; and in Matthew 18:3: "Truly I tell you, unless you change and become like children, you will never enter the kingdom of heaven." John is actually even more radical, speaking not only of becoming like a child but being born anew. What can this mean?

Precisely this is what Nicodemus was asking: "How can anyone be born after having grown old? Can one enter a second time into the mother's womb and be born?" (John 3:4). This I find to be a quite pleasantly realistic question! Can in fact an old man start over? Is it really possible for an old woman to leave everything behind and start all over again? I have been viewing theses like these with a growing feeling of concern. I was, for example, on a panel on the future of aging in Germany at the Hamburg *Kirchentag* ("church gathering") this past May. One researcher described how we are all getting older and need to learn new things all the time, start new careers, take on new perspectives. . . . I just felt great exhaustion. We are all expected to make ourselves younger in our society, be it with Botox or hair implants. We are supposed to go on new journeys, remaining flexible and mobile. But maybe I do not want to keep starting afresh. Maybe I just want my peace and to leave everything the way it is. So, the demand to be born again could in fact lead to stress! Or does this mean something entirely different than today's obsession with youth? Birth is a radical and unique event. John actually speaks of an experience of becoming new that reorients your life. I do not live a life anchored in myself but in grace, and I find my meaning of life based in God's

4 Bultmann, *Das Evangelium des Johannes*. 93.

commitment to life and not my own achievements. I find strength in faith, whether in life or in death—*sola gratia* and *sola fide*, as the reformers expressed it so concisely.

What can it mean, however, to be born of the Spirit? John speaks first of the Spirit and then of water: "No one can enter the kingdom of God without being born of water and Spirit" (3:5).

And we are now in fact coming to a tricky ecumenical minefield! There are those, Baptists in particular, who say: first comes the Spirit and then the water—of the baptism! For Reformed Christians, this question of the work of the Spirit is of particular importance. Question 53 of the Heidelberg Catechism, the 450th anniversary of which we are celebrating this year, asks: "What do you believe concerning the Holy Spirit?" The responses to this go as follows:

First,
he is, together with the Father and the Son,
true and eternal God.
Second,
he is also given to me,
to make me by true faith
share in Christ and all his benefits,
to comfort me,
and to remain with me forever.

For those who are baptized, therefore, the Holy Spirit is, in this tradition, God's everlasting succour. But I am a Lutheran myself and wonder, of course, why the ecumenical congress chose to present me in particular with a text like this.

For Martin Luther, it became increasingly clear that baptism was the central event and sacrament. Through baptism, God promises people grace, love, care, and meaning of life. All our failure and all of life's wrong turns cannot revoke this. In baptism, we do not require penance or a sacrament of penance: we are redeemed and we have long been children of God. *Baptizatus sum*—"I am baptized." During the most difficult times of his life, Luther told himself that and found solace in it.

Additionally, everyone who has emerged from baptism is a priest, a bishop, a pope. It was from this understanding that Luther developed his respect for women. They are baptized and are thus all of equal status. To say that we are baptized and therefore equal before God was a theological breakthrough as well as a social revolution. From this understanding of baptism, the conviction developed over the centuries that women are indeed able to take on any kind of church ministry. I find it important to highlight the theological background, particularly in regard to the ordination of women as pastors and as bishops and how different churches question that practice. This is not a question of *zeitgeist*, but one of theology.

This holds true with regard to racism as well. In South Africa, one missionary told of the many white farmers, during the apartheid era, who tried to prevent their black workers from being baptized. "Then they are just like us"—a deep theological insight, indeed, since that is precisely how it is. Baptism is a sign in opposition to all racism, sexism, and other forms of exclusion within the church community.

Before the Reformation, the celibate life was considered to be the direct path to heaven, so to speak, held in high regard by God. For many reformers, to embrace marriage was a sign that family life, with sexuality and children, was also a life blessed by God. The public weddings of previously celibate priests, monks, and nuns were a theological sign. Theologian Ute Gause explains that it was a symbolic act that would "illustrate something that was fundamental to the Reformation: how the new faith turned toward the world and was demonstrative in its sensuality."[5] Some may claim in this country today that Protestants are actually less sensually inclined than Roman Catholics or the Orthodox. The reformers, however, sought to demonstrate that life in the world is of no lesser value than the priestly or monastic life. The goal is to live a life of faith in our everyday world—and there Protestants may also be sensual.

And I find this to be confirmed in this morning's Bible text. We read in John 3:6: "What is born of the flesh is flesh, and what is born of the Spirit is spirit." This does not, however, need to be a form of dualism, even if it is so frequently viewed that way in exegesis: *σαρχ* and *πνευμα*! As human beings, we are tied, of course, into the contexts of our lives. It would indeed be irresponsible for us to shake off everything having to do with the here and now for the sake of a supposedly Spirit-driven future! It is precisely in this connection that Luther admonishes us to take on responsibility in this world, with his view that the occupation which we pursue is our vocation, wherever God has placed us in our lives. And still, the question of spiritual birth serves as a kind of corrective: Is there not also an entirely different sort of divine reality? One in which property, honour, wives, and children, or indeed everything that we own, everything our hearts cling to, is fully relegated to the background? Or as Bultmann wrote, a person can know that "he actually belongs to the being beyond even as he in fact tumbled into being in the here and now."[6] I do not think that this is suggesting a renunciation of the world. The question being asked here involves, rather, the perspective in which we understand our lives.

5 Ute Gause, inaugural address, Bochum 2011, unpub. ms., 2.

6 Bultmann, *Das Evangelium des Johannes*, 100.

Are we entirely caught up in *σαρχ*, flesh, the worldly? Or are we aware of the divine reality, *πνευμα*, which many in fact do not wish to recognize, especially in today's secularized age? Do we see it instead as the "opiate of the people," as self-deception, or as a way to run away from the realities of life? These are questions regarding the light in which we view our lives.

As we know, this morning's Bible passage presents us with certain difficulties as churches in ecumenical community. Is the baptism of children effective if people do not also embrace their baptism with their minds and with a conscious "yes"? Would there not also have to be a second baptism for adults or only one adult baptism?

This was already a point of contention during the Reformation era, and those who were labeled Anabaptists by their opponents were harshly persecuted by the "mainline" Reformation. A baptism of faith or an adult baptism was of importance to them, as baptism was to be preceded by a personal confession to Jesus Christ. They saw the baptism of infants as unbiblical and therefore invalid, with adult baptism to be the first baptism.

We have now overcome certain differences. On 22 July 2010, at its general assembly in Stuttgart, the Lutheran World Federation (LWF) issued a statement of contrition toward the Mennonites as the spiritual heirs to the Anabaptist movement so brutally persecuted during the Reformation era. The declaration states:

> Trusting in God who in Jesus Christ was reconciling the world to himself, we ask for forgiveness—from God and from our Mennonite sisters and brothers—for the harm that our forebears in the sixteenth century committed to Anabaptists, for forgetting or ignoring this persecution in the intervening centuries, and for all inappropriate, misleading and hurtful portraits of Anabaptists and Mennonites made by Lutheran authors, in both popular and scholarly forms, to the present day.[7]

That was important—and healing. In 2007, nearly all of Germany's churches formally recognized each other's baptism, thus providing an important sign of community. The Roman Catholic bishop Gerhard Feige said at that time that the mutual recognition showed that baptism is something that "fundamentally connects divided churches and Christians." This refocus on baptism does not yet, unfortunately, include everybody everywhere. The recognition of baptism can, however, still constitute an important ecumenical step. I remember well how there were discussions about what visible signs of community could be made at the 2003 First Ecumenical *Kirchentag* in Berlin. In the end, this turned out to be a remembrance of baptism during the closing worship service. Protestants, Catholics, and Christians of other

---

7 http://www.lwf-assembly.org/uploads/media/Mennonite_Statement-EN_03.pdf.

denominations drew the sign of the cross with baptismal water on each other's foreheads. I was very touched.

But what is spiritual birth? Our Bible passage this morning is a clear challenge for us. All of the exegetes whose works I consulted underscore how meticulously this conversation was composed in John's gospel. John already seeks to show Jesus, here at the beginning of his ministry, to be the one he proves to be after his resurrection: Son of Man, Messiah, Son of God. According to this gospel, John the Baptist saw how the Spirit of God descended upon Jesus during his baptism in the form of a dove. In the speech and work of Jesus, God becomes detectable for human beings. You find out what God is like: like a loving father, like a searching widow, like a caring vineyard owner, and like Jesus, inviting one and all to convene at a single table.

But what is the relationship between Spirit and baptism? Does baptism bring about the Spirit's presence? As Klaus Wengst writes: "God's Spirit is sovereign. People cannot determine how the Spirit works—not through baptism either."[8] This is certainly true. Baptism does not tame the workings of the Spirit. Sometimes, we actually are more afraid of too much activity of the Spirit. This was already the case among the reformers: Luther, for one, raced back from Wartburg Castle to Wittenberg when he began to feel the effects of too much free spirit. Both Huldrych Zwingli and John Calvin also valued clear-cut order instead of an overabundance of free spirit.

Even today, we seek balance between necessary order and the equally necessary freedom of spirit. A church as an institution can indeed be irritated at times by such an abundance of spirit. I recall the conciliar process for justice, peace, and the integrity of creation, which was viewed by some in West Germany as a factor of annoyance. In East Germany, it led to overcrowded churches, which provided a stage for political debates—so that some feared that it would damage the church. In the end, however, it led to a peaceful revolution instead. I am also remembering Switzerland, where Basel hosted the First European Ecumenical Assembly in 1989, and one could sense how things were brewing in the churches of Eastern Europe, where a spirit of freedom was urging for room. Our partner churches in the countries of the South are also familiar with this, when questions are asked about issues such as how much patriarchy the church can endure, whether one can adapt too much to a dictatorship, or whether one can even begin to talk about homosexuality.

But how do we distinguish among the spirits? Is something purely libertinism or the Spirit of God? Is God's *ruach* at work here or the spirit of chaos? I believe there are two criteria. First: Jesus Christ. As we read in the text: "So must the Son of Man be lifted up, that whoever believes in him may

8 Wengst, *Das Johannesevangelium*, 1:126.

have eternal life" (3:15). This is about believing in Jesus, who stands for God's word in the world and in whom, precisely for this reason, death does not have the final word. The Spirit may so joyously roar, but those who refer to the Spirit need to face the question of whether it is all about them and their own chosen goals, or about Jesus Christ, who stands for this Spirit.

The second criterion involves the formation of the congregation. This also stands in connection with baptism. One last time we turn here to Wengst, who writes:

> Since baptism is at the same time the rite of admission into the congregation, it also becomes clear that the Spirit does not bring forth individuals in isolation from one another, but that the birth from the Spirit moves one into the community of the congregation. Baptism by water is thus, in relation to the primary action of the Spirit, to be seen as a human act of obedience, which publically and bindingly recognizes this action as one that calls one into the congregation.[9]

Baptism draws us into a community. And wherever the Spirit acts, it seeks to build up this community. All too often, the freedom of the Spirit is referred to in the name of individuality. Individuality does indeed not have negative connotations for Protestants. However, whenever this turns into an egomania, where community no longer matters but only one's basic personal convictions, other spirits are in play. We know distinctions among spirits from other institutions as well. We need think only of the Olympic games, where the spirit of sport and understanding among nations is supposed to prevail, and which lose their credibility when it turns out to only be a spirit of money and doping.

Our churches will have to always be judged by whether their spirit is guided by the *solus Christus* of the reformers—and whether they serve the community. For Protestants, this also means, particularly with view of the 500th anniversary, reflecting on what it means that they have so often been moved by the spirit of division. This is a justified question. When I was in the United States in June 2013, I was again troubled by the fact that there are 22 Lutheran churches there, not all of which are sharing in table fellowship. What kind of sign is this?

Thank God that the Reformation has also had a 500-year-long history of learning. With the Leuenberg Agreement, we have now had a form of church community in Europe for 40 years that respects differences while nonetheless making it possible for churches to recognize each other and embrace a common communion.

"No one can enter the kingdom of God without being born of water and Spirit" (John 3:5b). Maybe John mainly wants to say, "You need to open

9 Ibid., 1:123f.

yourself up to the Spirit." Nicodemus actually vanishes from this scene in a peculiar silence as the dialogue segues into Jesus' words of revelation. Does this allude to Nicodemus not being able to open up, not being able to follow Jesus? Bultmann views the word as an "admonition—indeed not a moralistic one, but an admonition to question oneself."[10] It is not about an "improvement of the person,"[11] but about finding one's origin in God and understanding that one does not have life under control. I find this to be an extraordinarily helpful thought. Salvation cannot be manufactured or purchased but is grace—a gift of God. I need to open up and place all of my trust in God when it comes to my own security in questions of life and faith, and not in those things that may otherwise seem so right and important: money, conformity, and orthodoxy.

Baptism is a sign of belonging. Allowing God's Spirit into our lives is a sign of trust in God. This applies to our personal lives, but also to churches as institutions, which need, again and again, a roaring of the Spirit when they make themselves too comfortable in the world. I am thinking of our structures but also of the challenges, of finding the courage for brave words and deeds when facing all the issues involving justices, refugees, war, and weapons sales, as well as threats to the future of our planet. In the end, as those who are baptized, we can, in all our struggles, only place our trust in God and in the action of God's Spirit, which we are able to sense again and again.

10 Bultmann, *Das Evangelium des Johannes*, 95.

11 Ibid., 97.

CHAPTER 6

Klára Tarr Cselovszky

Matthew 5:13-16

A major flood occurred in Budapest in 1838, similar to 2013's spring flooding in Ulm, on the Danube, in Germany's Elbe region. Back in 1811, a church was built there on Deák Square, the church that my husband currently serves as its pastor, and to which we live next door. The church is a tall and solid building, located on the Pest, a low-lying side of town, which was built up higher due to the sandy ground. When the city was flooded in 1838, only the church remained dry. Hundreds of people found their safety there, including the members of the nearby Jewish congregation. Once the water had receded, the Jewish congregation gave our Lutheran forebears a communion chalice, ever since known as the "Flood Chalice." The church was a place of refuge, a mighty fortress, a city on the hill. We can read about this and other imagery in Matthew 5:13-16:

> 13 *You are the salt of the earth, but if salt has lost its taste, how shall its saltiness be restored? It is no longer good for anything except to be thrown out and trampled under people's feet.*
>
> 14 *You are the light of the world. A city set on a hill cannot be hidden.*

[15] Nor do people light a lamp and put it under a basket, but on a stand, and it gives light to all in the house.
[16] In the same way, let your light shine before others, so that they may see your good works and give glory to your Father who is in heaven.

The essence of these verses can be summed up in one German word, *Ausstrahlung*, which is akin to "radiance." This word can be found in numerous contexts today. In meteorology, it is used to describe how heat is radiated from the earth's surface and atmosphere. People are considered to be radiant as well, with regard to their personal magnetism or charisma. The word *radiance* is connected to the ideas of "mission" and "transmission" (sending something, beaming). It stands in opposition to the words *reception* and *inquiry*. The word *Strahl* itself can mean "ray" or "line." It is used in mathematics and physics to refer to "an infinite line in one direction, beginning at a fixed point," or "electromagnetic waves emitted from a single source of energy."

The key words in our text—the light, the city on the hill, the salt—are small items that have great effect, great radiance. One cannot cover them up, deny them, and change their effect once they have begun to do that which constitutes their being: the light radiates brilliance to fully destroy the darkness; the city on the hill serves as a beacon, guide, and protector, to be seen from a vast distance; and salt lends taste to bland foods.

It is remarkable how precisely language reflects the biblical sense of the word *Ausstrahlung/radiance*: mission and transmission. In physics, the term means that rays come from *a single source of energy*. This source is often not even perceived, and we only sense its effects: brightness, taste, and the sense of security. Jesus' followers are only instruments as well. They transmit the gospel through their acts, their lives, and their words. They work like a painkiller: they are small but have a large impact. I myself come from Hungary, the land of peppers. A German acquaintance of mine once bought pimentos, those little cherry-shaped peppers. He wanted to eat them in a sandwich. But when he bit into it, he could not eat the pimento because it was too hot. And he felt the effects of it on his tongue for a long time. This is the way I experience the church. Being in diaspora in no way means that the church is near its end. I have been part of a diaspora church ever since I was born. That was always something completely natural for me, as the impact of a church does not only depend on its size. We also need solid cities that are big and strong, but not everyone can live near such a mighty fortress. The Austrians are probably the only exception to this, with a city that has two of our images in its name, Salzburg, referring to both salt and a city on a hill.

Light: Well into the modern era, it remained unclear what light actually was. Some people believed that "rays" were emitted *from* the eyes as a means of being able to see the environment. However, the eyes are in fact not the source of light, but it is actually with the assistance of light that the human brain and eyes are able to perceive the environment. Without light, we cannot see or perceive what is around us at all.

Light features in numerous biblical passages, first and foremost in the book of Genesis. The third sentence of the creation narrative reports that God created light already on the first day—immediately after creating the heavens and the earth! Light is the detachment of brightness from darkness. As György Jakubinyi, a Catholic theologian from Transylvania, wrote in 1991: "Light is redemption through Jesus Christ from the darkness of the separation from God." Wilhelm Stählin analogously wrote in 1958, "It is the light that allows things to be distinguished from one another: good from evil; light from dark." The image of light, the flame itself, has great significance, as fire is not an object but a process. Something very important occurs in the process of change: out of an object, of wood, and of a spark emerges light. This is the disciples' mandate: becoming the light in the world.

Salt: Adding salt improves food. Salt cannot be taken back from food: once the flavour is in it, it cannot be removed. The spoken word cannot be taken back either, or its meaning reversed. Jesus' word is like salt in food: it changes one's being, just as flavour change s food.

He does this through us. He does not speak to us in conditional terms, but in actual terms: *You are* the salt of the earth, the light of the world. Jesus does not say we should try to be salt and light, but "you are" already!

His words have the power of creation. Just as God says in Genesis, "Let there be light," so does Jesus say, *you are* the light and the salt. He creates disciples of simple people, through whom he radiates his power out into the world. This message of Christ is an unimaginably great honour, receiving the mandate to be a disciple. Amen.

Part Three

Theological Legacy of the Reformation

CHAPTER 7

Rowan Williams

The Reformation's Legacy

What exactly is it to celebrate today the heritage of the 16th-century Reformation? Many commentators in recent decades have expressed their sense that we have lost or are losing any clear idea of what it is to be a European Protestant in the "classical" mode; in Britain, several observers have noted that if there is any residue of popular religion now, it is of what most would see as a distinctively "Catholic" stripe, preoccupied with rituals and holy places and the numinous quality of the beloved dead (the reaction to Princess Diana's death being the most dramatic illustration). A popular British Christian identity grounded in the Bible, family-based devotion, and anti-papalism (together with a certain sense of the providential role of the nation) has conclusively disappeared. And something comparable is reported elsewhere in Europe. While secular commentators will refer to "Catholic social teaching" as a coherent and identifiable presence in general debates about social well-being and political justice, there is relatively little recognition, in the wider culture, of a distinctive Protestant voice in social ethics, despite the extensive and sophisticated contributions made by so many in church and academy. It is not surprising if there are signs of uncertainty about the Protestant—and specifically the Reformed—identity in Europe and beyond. "Protestant" identity is often conflated with a distinctively American brand of biblical literalism and social conservatism, itself understood as opposed to an equally distinctive "liberal Protestantism," which is unconcerned with doctrine and committed to broadly progressive causes. Such a framework is no help at all in making sense of most of the Reformation itself, let alone of what Reformed theology has meant in the last 100 years or so. Students are often bewildered as to where they should locate Karl Barth on a theological map defined by the simple oppositions of left and right, conservative and liberal.

In these brief observations, I want to attempt a very broad analysis of what the contributions of a recognizably "Protestant" theology have been to Christian culture overall; to suggest what some of the lastingly constructive elements have been, as well as noting those things that have had more ambivalent effects. I write as an Anglican—that is, as someone whose ecclesiastical identity is shaped by a reluctance to see the Protestant/Catholic divide as a simple binary opposition, but who is bound to be conscious of the essential role of Reformed theology in the self-definition of the Church of England. My personal formation was in the "catholic" wing of the Anglican family, but marked also by a childhood in the Welsh Presbyterian Church and a continuing interest in and enthusiasm for various strands in the Reformed tradition represented by writers like Richard Baxter, Thomas Torrance, and, of course, Barth himself. It is against that personal background that I venture to identify three themes in Reformed theology and practice which I believe to be of lasting and crucial significance for the theological health of the Christian community; and also to reflect on another three themes that have been less obviously fruitful and which indeed bear some responsibility for aspects of our current cultural desolation and confusion. My tentative conclusion is that these latter themes can only be countered by a better theological understanding of the former ones—so that we may after all be able to identify a positive, distinctive, and creative role for the legacy of the Reformation today.

Very briefly, the three themes that seem to be positive are these. First, the Reformation affirmed the absolute difference of created and infinite action; its consistent emphasis on the sovereignty of God is a way of underlining the truth that God's action and ours can never be in *either* competition *or* collaboration. Second, the Reformation established the principle that scripture was not only a source for true teaching and for illustrative clarification of that teaching but also a *critical* presence in the church, in some sense "intervening" in the church's life, never simply the church's instrument. Third, the Reformation, in questioning any suggestion that the means of grace could be "managed" by human intermediaries, affirmed that the church was first and foremost the assembly of a people, not of rulers and subjects.

The ambivalent legacy of the Reformation might be summarized in these ways. First, the emphasis on the sovereign dignity of God's word allied itself with a developing rationalism to produce a one-dimensional picture of human knowing, in which the nonverbal was regarded as inferior. Second, the suspicion of hierarchy encouraged a half-hearted theology of the church and a privileging of individual piety and individual exploration at the expense of understanding corporate identity in Christ and the Spirit, and of intelligent appropriation of the Christian past. Third, the stress on divine sovereignty came to suggest (in a way directly contrary to its proper theological meaning) an opposition between human and divine to be resolved by simple submission on the part of the created will—so that human emancipation was thought to require the abandonment of theological discourse.

Taking the first three in order: the focus of the Reformation protest against the popular theology and practice of the late Middle Ages was a pattern of language and habit which seemed to presuppose that the reconciled or grace-filled life was something that could be "negotiated" with God. This world of piety was seen (not always fairly) as a way in which human beings could use specific created means whose effects were guaranteed by God in order to obtain rewards promised by God; and, although the prior agency of God is acknowledged in such a framework, the *immediate* impression is of a sort of spiritual technology in which God is bound to honour the conditions God has laid down. The created agent knows what God is "bound" to do. And this is where the difficulty arises. God's action is seen as removed from the present situation; it becomes an abstract frame within which human action plans and seeks to control human destiny (not least, of course, by the very particular kinds of control associated with the ordained ministry, which controls the administration of the means of grace). The result is either a complacent reduction of the life of discipleship to compliance with a new "law"—or, as Luther discovered, a corrosive despair of encountering the grace of God as a direct and living reality, a state in which there is a dissonance between what is authoritatively declared to be the case by the authorities of the church and the personal sense of guilt or abandonment.

Luther reinstates divine sovereignty by appealing to a God who is systematically hidden; a God who cannot be negotiated with, whose presence is always to be found in the heart of God's own apparent absence, not in the places where God can be *predicted* to be present according to some systematic map of God's workings. And such a theology makes full sense only when there is a serious recovery of what had always been a fundamental principle of Catholic theology but had been regularly overlaid—the principle that God's action and finite action are not two instances of the same thing: they cannot compete, they cannot be thought of as fighting over a single contested territory. It is this principle that in fact pervades Aquinas's theological world (it can be seen at work in very interesting ways in his Christology especially). But the Reformation protest insists that this has to be worked through at every level of theology and practice. Any theological idiom or devotional habit that seems to imagine God as responding to human initiative is to be excluded from genuinely theological discourse, because God's action is not in any sense conditioned by human action. The contested, even shocking theology of predestination advanced by Calvin is essentially about this fundamental noncommensurabilty of created and uncreated act: temporal succession, logical consequence, moral appropriateness—all these are fatally mistaken frameworks for thinking about the relation of God to creation. And the rather paradoxical implication—not as alien to Calvinistic thought as some would think—is that the dignity of the human can never be threatened by the majesty of God any more than that majesty can be threatened by the affirmation of concrete human liberties, because there is no competition between the finite and the infinite. The Reformation principle of God's unconditional sovereignty *ought* to deliver us from both anxiety and resentment in regard to God, and to allow a robust theology of human calling and freedom in the social/political sphere.

This is not unconnected with the second positive point. If scripture is "the word of God written," it is a vehicle for that same unconditional divine action. It is not a passive instrument for human discovery, expressing truths that can be distilled into a neat conceptual schema (which is why fundamentalism is, in an important sense, antithetical to a fully Reformed theology); it is alive and active, a field of records and songs and maxims in which human discourse may at any moment become tangibly the vehicle of an authoritative communication and summons to discipleship. And this means that scripture is always a critical presence in the church. Although there were and are some Reformed theologians who interpret this as meaning that scripture provides a detailed constitution for the church, so that anything not prescribed there is implicitly forbidden (a view expressed by some English Calvinists in the 16th and 17th centuries), this is not quite how most mainstream Reformed thinkers have developed the point. The principle that everything in the life of the church needs to be tested by how well it serves the proclamation of the gospel of God's free election and grace is not the same as saying that scripture is a comprehensive law book for the church. But it does mean that scripture can never be regarded simply as a tool for the church's purposes or a source of material to illustrate the church's teaching. It is something that has to be heard as a question from outside the church's life, even though scripture is itself bound in with the church's life and does not exist in a vacuum. It is always a book read by the church; but it is read by the church *so that* the church is able to hear what it would not otherwise hear.

Thus the church's life—including and especially the church's worshiping life—is one in which we are brought into question. We are to be led into attentive silence as well as praise and affirmation; and the reading and hearing of scripture is a primary embodiment of this dimension. It is not that, as we listen, we automatically hear the precise expression of God's will; as we have already seen, we cannot treat the agency of God as automatically predictable in any way. But we listen in the expectation of being changed into a more Christlike way of being. Sometimes, this is in ways we can see and grasp; most often, it will be in ways we do not immediately perceive. But the discipline of listening expectantly means that we are bound always to ask what we should be discovering about our discipleship that we did not previously know. This is not a matter of working out new interpretations of familiar texts or producing radically new doctrines: there is a given framework of teaching and practice, the shared identity of those baptized into Christ, which gives meaning to all our actions in worship; without it we could make no sense of what we were doing. But within this we constantly ask to be instructed and enlarged in our reading, and so in our service and witness. The characteristic shape of worship can be seen as this attitude of expectant listening combined with the unceasing expression of gratitude for what has been heard and given.

The much-misunderstood Reformation principle of the open Bible, the accessibility of scripture to all, was in its context a protest against authority that was not accountable to either the community as a whole or to the prior reality of God's communication in scripture. It was not meant to be a charter for unlimited individual interpretation, but a way of opening up the life of the church to a shared process of reading and discerning, in which all baptized people had a voice. The grace of Christ was not passed on to the body of the faithful by a priestly caste; ordained ministry in the church was a solemn and lifelong charge, and the assurance of its continuity was a serious matter, but it was not an induction into a governing elite. The classical Calvinist distinction between ruling and teaching elders was an attempt to reflect the concerns at work here. Although it did not take long for the teaching ministry to become, in many contexts, as much of an authoritarian system as what it had replaced, the ideal of a "conversational" process of studying the text to which all were equally accountable was a deeply theologically motivated effort to embody the principle of the dignity of all the baptized. An "open" Bible is what gives to the community a common language in which all have the right to speak, and it is no longer acceptable to limit access to this shared world so as to reinforce the power of a governing class. There is a solid element of classical republicanism in this (a feature that ironically echoes some aspects of Aquinas's political thought). It is no surprise to see it worked out in various national histories. But this does not mean either an anarchy of love or a democracy, as we understand the word. It could involve aspirations to real theocracy as much as ideals of participatory, perhaps syndicalist, debate and decision. The significant point is that making universally available a shared authoritative cultural resource in the form of scripture meant the creation in principle of a theological conversation in which all could be held to account, and there was no exclusion in advance of any voices. The challenge that the Reformation did not always succeed in handling had to do with discovering the kinds of consensus that would have and hold authority.

In the light of this discussion, the positive legacy of the Reformation is very much bound up with the idea of a society (secular and ecclesiastical) capable of self-questioning, confident in the prior affirmation of God's action in a way that undercuts anxiety and rivalry, united by a common conversation around the narrative of scripture and wakefully alert to the possibility of new insight or new challenge in this context. It is not simply identical with what we have come to think of as "modern" society, let alone "enlightened" society, though these latter would not exist without it. The main differences are to do with the particular way modernity privileges autonomy, so that God's sovereignty is seen (despite the all-important Reformation clarifications) as a menace to human dignity, and the individual's liberty is likewise seen as threatened by the language of accountability. The Reformed picture of human flourishing involves obedience—and thus understands the deepest liberties to have something to do with submission to being questioned by a reality, a truth, beyond our individual agendas.

Modernity, in fact, appears in this light as a systematic misreading of the Reformed picture. What I earlier called the ambivalent features of the Reformed legacy are all, in their ways, inversions of the basic theological principles of the 16th-century Reformation, reinstating much of what the movement sought to overthrow. The way in which a certain model of rationality came to be seen as all-important and normative reflected a deep suspicion of claims to knowledge that could not be defended by the kind of argument proper to reasoning and adult persons. Against mystification and manipulation, Reformed thinkers insisted that God communicated in ways that were accessible to all. When symbols were used, they had to be understood as essentially illustrations of things that could be put more clearly—even if less vividly—in other ways. Despite Luther's sophisticated theology of the dialectic between hiddenness and manifestation in the actions of God with us, Protestant thought moved increasingly toward the assumption that truthful knowledge was necessarily a matter of clear verbal communication.

It was hard to include in this an understanding of what more recent thinkers have called "tacit" knowledge, or of the material dimensions of knowing (the capacity to recognize a face, to play an instrument, ride a horse, interpret the sky so as to foresee the weather)—let alone the codes in gesture, sign, and, indeed, visual image that convey what cannot effectively or satisfactorily be codified in speech. Words *ought* to be enough for everything, which is why—as Torrance and others note—the Reformation so stressed hearing over seeing as the paradigm for knowledge.

The result was, eventually, to polarize different accounts of human knowing. Either we know because we hear/read in scripture the simple propositions of divine truth or we read off from the natural world around us all we need to know and ignore all claims to knowledge that do not conform to particular processes of gathering evidence. We are on the road to the futile and unintelligent standoff between "science" and "religion" that still dominates the thoughts of so many in our culture. And to recover a more integral view of knowing, we need—as I have already suggested—to turn the best insights of the Reformation against its distortions.

Luther's revolution in theological thinking implied that no state of affairs in the world carried an obvious meaning that could be grasped and deployed as an instrument of human power. To understand the hiddenness of God in the crucified Christ required us to be silenced, brought to nothing, faced with a potential abyss of meaninglessness, so that we were at last free to receive God's gift without the presumptions of our own agenda, our individual needs and ambitions. The clarity of words alone will not alter this need for being dispossessed; and the more we let go of a view of language that assumes we can produce a comprehensive picture of the world that fits into a single system of consistent explanation, the more we see that our learning as human beings is bound up with our capacity to respond to a variety of signs and signals, consciously or not. Our reasoning must follow the appropriate method for its subject; it has to be molded by that subject and to come to "share" something of that subject's life. And in this, without trying to reinstate a late-medieval obsession with symbolic readings of texts and world, we do recover a sensitivity to communications that are not simply verbal—or, if verbal, then working with irony and indirection (a point very clear in the Protestant poetics of Fulke Greville or George Herbert in the 16th and 17th centuries).

The weakness in thinking about the church, which I have suggested as another ambivalent legacy, rises from a complex distortion of the notion of the "invisible" church. Once again, a point originally developed as a way of underlining the hiddenness of God's act and thus its absolute freedom and transcendence became a fixed position of skepticism in popular Protestantism toward any doctrine of the necessity of the Christian community as shaping Christian identity. The obscurity of the church's limits, the truth expressed by the early Calvin as perceiving " churches half-buried," the resistance to making institutional adherence a vehicle of almost automatic grace—all these things encouraged in many a vague sense that Christian identity need have nothing visibly corporate about it. Again, it is the Reformation's own principles that will help us escape such a distortion, above all the emphasis on the open Bible as the field of *common* language. The individual taking refuge in private piety (in ways that would have shocked Calvin as much as Luther) has not yet grasped that an inner realm beyond any shared discerning and testing of God's will is precisely the kind of inward-curving of the human spirit that consolidates the reign of sin. And while the stress on how the fullness of grace in the eucharist depends on the communicant's faith is an understandable reaction to what was thought to be a mechanical and thus graceless approach in which God's presence was automatically assured, popular piety readily took this to mean that the outward form was a purely practical way of reinforcing a mental lesson—rather than a corporate and objective act of pleading with God to bear witness to Godself and God's work in Christ through the effective operation of the Spirit. Believing in the absolute sovereignty of grace does not mean that we are bound to see grace at work in the private experience of individuals rather than anywhere else; quite the opposite. Such a belief relativizes private experience no less authoritatively than it relativizes shared experience. And our common worship directs us to the abiding realities of scripture and sacrament as objective testimonies to God's act, independent of our subjective state or aspirations.

And just as a properly understood Reformed theology dissolves the polarity between corporate and individual by insisting that God's act is free in regard to both of them, so it dissolves the haunting and persistent sense of rivalry between God and creation, that rivalry which, as I noted earlier, makes so many assume that for humanity to be free, God must be dethroned. God's sovereignty is not a vastly inflated variety of human power. And once we have grasped this, we can begin to see the radical implications of God's creation of human beings in the divine image and God's purpose of endowing them through Jesus with a share in the divine life. As Calvin well understood, this is disturbing for a Reformed theology only if God is capable of being threatened by human dignity or flourishing—which is, *ex hypothesi*, unthinkable. An uncompromising stress on the absolute difference of God's power ought to result in an enhanced theological affirmation of human dignity: there is no reverence given to actual finite humanity that in itself takes anything away from what is due to God. Idolatry is ascribing to what is created what belongs only to God—that is, treating creatures as more than creatures. The true

Christian challenge is to love and revere humanity for what it is—mortal and vulnerable, yet immeasurably glorious because made by God as the site of divine manifestation and agency. And—to connect this with themes touched on earlier—our capacity for radical self-questioning as individuals and as a society is made possible by this basic conviction that our mortal and fallible human state is affirmed in its fragility by God, who undertakes to absolve and transform it, never to abolish it. Or, in other terms, we can question everything about our humanity, its precise capacities, its habitual behaviour, we can live with an almost corrosive pessimism about what fallen nature is actually like, yet we cannot question the dignity unconditionally bestowed by the God who has no jealousy of our state, since the divine life does not share the same space as ours.

It is the ability of Reformed theology to affirm this that gives it a role in our current cultural struggles. To proclaim Christian hope is in no sense to advance an optimistic view of human capacity or character; a theological perspective allows us to assume the worst (in just the way associated with Augustinian and Calvinist thought in the popular mind), but it does not allow us to think less of our humanity than its maker does. And by proposing to us the language and world of scripture as the house we inhabit together and the dialect we speak, it tells us that we may find direction and, indeed, transformation as we make our own the story of God's dealings with a people with whom God makes covenant. To speak of Christian hope is to speak of divine fidelity; our social vision is grounded in the belief in a God who freely promises to be the God of those who have not "earned" or been obliged to compel God's love. The radical otherness of divine love and commitment, and the consequent irreducible mysterious extent of God's election, entails a systematic reverence for human persons, whatever their status or achievement or ethical performance. All are potentially part of a story of unpredictable divine faithfulness, part of the scriptural story in which we may find common ground.

This is a legacy that challenges a number of negative forces. Its emphasis on growing into a maturity that can handle self-questioning is a challenge to a public/media culture preoccupied with the management of personal images. It suggests that genuine and honest exchange in personal and public debate is essential and that for this to work there must be a basic willingness to silence one's dreams of invulnerable rightness. In the face of a vague spirituality that can easily turn into consoling and sentimental "inwardness," it stresses the need in spiritual practice, public and personal, for listening with care and attention, ready for what will not be welcome to the lazy ego—listening in "the fear of God," to use the old-fashioned vocabulary. In contrast to a general unwillingness to think in terms of shared narratives that are more than local or communal, it proposes a universal narrative of divine grace and election, crystallized uniquely in scripture, focused on the events in which the true image of humanity is restored in the crucified and risen Christ. It is worth underlining that Calvin himself repudiates the idea that our salvation is only a formal or external and mechanical relation with a Christ who has declared us righteous but makes no "real" change in us: "He imparts to us his life and all the blessings which he has received from the Father" (Comm. Jn 17.21).

Against anxious and fundamentalist religion, this Reformed tradition affirms a God who cannot and *need* not be persuaded by our efforts or our success: the language of our faith, especially our prayer, is characteristically shaped by gratitude for unearned and uncaused love and forgiveness, gratitude for God being God. Against a rebellious or resentful atheism, suspicious of alien and coercive power, it presents a God who can have no interest in diminishing God's creatures and whose absolute sovereign freedom is such that God need not bully or coerce those creatures; God's free will is a will for forgiveness and healing and for the extension of the divine love and bliss to creation.

Out of all this emerges the outline of a theology that imposes a demanding spiritual discipline, a sober and thoughtful style of worship, a freedom constantly and without panic to have one's own integrity under scrutiny and to do the same for the community as a whole and its institutions, a Christ-centred understanding of human history and a radical political vision, challenging inequalities and arbitrary domination of all kinds. In brief, the governing themes of authentic Reformed theology do not only represent a recovery of many of the most radical ideas of patristic thought, but offer as robust and profound a resource for addressing contemporary social crises as the tradition of Catholic social teaching—not that these are rivals, but complementary understandings, with the Reformed tradition contributing above all its emphasis on the incomparable sovereignty of God which liberates us from moralistic assessments of merit and invites us to reflect in our own actions and relations the same "causeless" fidelity to the promise of love that belongs to God.

The greatest theologians of the Reformation were not zealots seeking to expunge history and symbol from the Christian mind, or individualists committed to the autonomy of private conscience, or theocrats determined to impose on all human society an unreconstructed version of the Mosaic law, or rationalists obsessed with words at the expense of both silence and sign, or biblical literalists with a mechanical model of inspiration. The accidents of history have associated Reformed Christianity with all of these in various contexts, and there are, of course, elements in Luther, Calvin, Melanchthon, or Zwingli that might foster and encourage such ideas. The popular picture of Protestant Christianity in the West is still largely dominated by one or all of these stereotypes. But if we are now seeking to articulate for our own day what is distinctive and valuable about the legacy of the Reformation, it becomes necessary to disentangle them from the fundamental insights and questions of the reformers. In this very modest contribution to such a task, I have tried to indicate where I believe the emphasis should fall. I have been helped and encouraged by that strand in recent writing about Calvin which sees him as a humanist scholar retrieving insights from the early Christian centuries, offering a fresh way of focusing on the eucharistic transformation of the believer and the community—not a logician determined to establish the omnipotent liberty of God at the expense of both reason and human dignity. There is in him, undoubtedly, a "tragic" element that is most visible in his stress on the comprehensive corruption of fallen humanity and the (consequent) arbitrariness of predestination; Calvin—and much of the tradition that stems from him—is no more successful in handling this than Augustine. But this is an outgrowth from the main stem of his thought, and needs to be kept in perspective. What is most significant is the way in which Calvin explores so comprehensively the leading themes of a renewed theology that gives such space to human maturity—political and psychological—while at the same time keeping human capacity within a relentlessly realistic framework. A Christian faith that does not require any kind of infantilization on the part of the faithful—that is, perhaps, the greatest aspiration of the 16th-century reform, and an aspiration that today is more than ever an imperative if Christian belief is to persuade and attract and convert.

CHAPTER 8

Ulrich H. J. Körtner

An Exclusive Faith

The Fourfold "Alone" of Reformation Theology

If we want to think about what it means today to be Protestant, we must first distinguish between "Protestant" and being faithful to the gospel.[1] The upcoming Reformation Jubilee 2017 is a good occasion for reflecting on the core message of the Reformation, which restored the intrinsic value of "Protestant" in the sense of being committed to the gospel. The gospel of Jesus Christ is a critical measure for the proclamation of all churches and denominations, which takes a firm stand against certain developments and some current trends in Protestantism. The question of what is Protestant today should also be posed from the broad angle of the ecumenical arena, not merely as an expression of denominational self-assurance. My understanding of the Reformation Jubilee is an invitation to all churches and denominations to think about the ecumenical implications of the insights of the Reformation as we reflect today on what the gospel means and on being committed to the gospel.

1 Abbreviated version of the speech held on 8 October 2013.

What is expounded in the following presupposes that the doctrine of unconditional acceptance and justification of the ungodly and the Reformation critique of the church based thereupon is, while not being the sole content of the Reformation theology, at its theological core. It is the foundation for the Protestant understanding of Christian freedom as well as Protestant ecclesiology and its core concept of the priesthood of all believers.

Reformation Theology

The guiding principle of the Reformed understanding of justification is the unconditional granting of salvation, and thus the clear distinction between the recipient and the acting entity of faith. This distinction is expressed by the four exclusive formulae whose meanings I will explore for today's society: by faith alone—*sola fide*—a human being is justified before God, through faith in Jesus Christ because Christ alone—*solus Christus*—can bring salvation and redemption to sinful humanity. This occurs solely out of grace—*sola gratia*—and is validly testified to only through the scripture alone—*sola scriptura*—as the source and the criterion of justifying faith, of the life springing from faith, and of all the preaching and theology.

The gist of the Reformation message becomes manifest only if one keeps in mind and takes into consideration how these four so-called exclusive particles are interpreting each other interactively. None of them may be considered independently. Even the medieval Catholic Church could testify that human salvation depends solely on God's grace. And in its decree on the doctrine of justification, the Council of Trent also attested to the sole efficacy of divine grace—however, in a way that this was not duly equated with the sole efficacy of faith. The Reformation view of faith, however, becomes obscured if it is understood as a general intrinsic trust, transcendental consciousness, or awareness of dependence per se that basically all humans share inherently. Faith in the sense of the Reformation is faith in Jesus Christ as the sole foundation of divine acceptance and absolution. Its significance, however, must be explored from the perspective of trinitarian theology, as I will expound in what follows. The justification of sinners for the sake of Christ is a trinitarian event. A question arises thereupon: How do the believers know this? On what do they ground their trust and confidence? The answer of the Reformation tradition is that it is the Bible, the Old and New Testament, that testifies to this assuredly because Christ himself might be heard through its words.

Thus, according to the Reformation understanding, a justifying faith is an exclusive faith—exclusive in the sense that salvation is granted only by its virtue. This exclusive faith becomes manifest, however, only within the scope of these four interactively interpretive exclusive particles of the

Reformation. Therein, *solus Christus* deserves the position of primacy among the quadruplet, since faith is, in the sense of the Reformation, although a human deed, not a human work. In faith, the believer plays a passive role typical of humans because the ability to believe is neither a human faculty nor any aptitude provided by nature, but it is and remains a gift beyond human reach. However, the act of faith consists of believing in the message of Christ—the gospel—and trusting it in life and death.

Such an exclusive understanding—namely, with a pointed christological emphasis—of faith turns out to be offensive not only in the past, but still today. *Sola gratia*, taken alone, may be more or less acceptable. Apart from that, as far as the whole issue of exclusive particles of the Reformation theology is concerned, do they not have to be adapted in the face of today's pluralistic cultures and interreligious dialogues? Is the *solus Christus* not hugely intolerant in regards to non-Christian religions? Does *sola fide* not undermine ethics and commitments undertaken to improve the world? And as for the so-called Reformation principle of scripture, *sola scriptura*, is it still defendable given the findings of historical-critical research?

Now, even an additional, fifth exclusive particle is occasionally mentioned when attempts are made to bundle up the message of the Reformation theology: *solo verbo*—by word alone. It is true that faith abides by the Protestant understanding of the word that testifies to and assures humans of divine grace. The word provoking and witnessing to faith is understood as God's word in human words that ultimately witnesses to that which is understood and believed as God's life-creating and liberating Word in the person of Jesus Christ. Even though the formula *solo verbo* is occasionally mentioned in Luther's works, its classification as one of the exclusive particles of the Reformation has a more recent origin, namely as an influence of the theology of the word of God in the 20th century. Compared to the Reformation era, however, substantial conceptual shifts and new emphases are found in the theology of the word of God. The *solo verbo*, as suggested by Eberhard Jüngel,[2] can replace *sola scriptura*, thus proving to be a response to the much-discussed crisis of the Reformation principle of the scripture. In my following discourse, I will stick to the four classical exclusive particles of the Reformation theology and try to fathom their hermeneutic potentials. I will not juxtapose *solo verbo* with *sola scriptura*, less replace it with it. I understand it as an interpretation applicable to all four exclusive particles because it raises the issue of the fundamental interrelation between word and faith in all four cases. Nevertheless, this interpretation is to be guarded against some restrictions imposed on the theology of the word of God by critics who criticize

2 Cf. Eberhard Jüngel, *Das Evangelium von der Rechtfertigung des Gottlosen als Zentrum des christlichen Glaubens* (Tübingen, 1999), 169ff.

the overdominance of the word and have sparse experience of Protestant worship.[3] Nor should it be hastily declared as a distinctive feature of controversial theology to mark the difference between Protestant and Catholic traditions, as has occasionally been the case with the debates about the Joint Declaration on the Doctrine of Justification (JDDJ).[4]

Nonetheless, the question remains whether the gist of the Reformation doctrine of justification—with all due respect for the efforts undertaken to reach ecumenical consensus—remains sufficiently safeguarded in the JDDJ. However, our primary concern here is not to check the state of ecumenical dialogue on the doctrine of justification but, rather, to address the question as to what extent the exclusive particles of the Reformation can contribute to exploring the doctrine of justification and making it understandable for the present.

Justification Today

A superficial view of the Reformation doctrine of justification gives the impression that it is obsolete in modern society in which the notion of the last judgment, the quest for the merciful God, and the fear of punishment have faded and the existence of God has become questionable all together.[5]

The modern skepticism of the doctrine of justification is closely associated with the problem of theodicy. Theodicy mutates into anthropodicy. If God does not exist, only humans are left as the sole actors in the world. The welfare and salvation of the world depend solely upon human beings. Because God is missing, the justification of humans is replaced with the barbarism of self-justification, as the German writer Martin Walser states.[6] Thus the putative obsolescence of the Reformation doctrine of justification is at peculiar odds with the now-ubiquitous compulsion of public justification today and the "tribunalization" of the modern reality of life.[7]

3 An example of such critiques: Ulrich Kühn, "Solo verbo?—Die sakramentale Bedeutung des christlichen Gottesdienstes," in *Jahrbuch für Liturgik und Hymnologie* 41 (Göttingen, 2002), 18–30.

4 For example, see Ingolf U. Dalferth, "Ökumene am Scheideweg," *Frankfurter Allgemeine* Zeitung (FAZ) 26 (September 1997): 10f., and the "Stellungnahme des Vorstands der Arnoldshainer Konferenz zur Gemeinsamen Erklärung" of 4 June 1997, in epd-Dokumentation 49 (1997): 57f., 59f. Criticisms: Kühn, "Solo verbo?," 20; André Birmelé, *Kirchengemeinschaft. Ökumenische Fortschritte und methodologische Konsequenzen*, Studien zur Systematischen Theologie und Ethik 38 (Münster, 2003), 136.

5 The succeeding paragraphs in this section have been taken from Ulrich H. J. Körtner, "Rechtfertigung—Botschaft für das 21. Jahrhundert. Eine Thesenreihe zum bevorstehenden Reformationsjubiläum 2017," *Materialdienst des Konfessionskundlichen Instituts* (MdKI) 63, no. 6 (2012): 113–15.

6 Cf. Martin Walser, *Über Rechtfertigung, eine Versuchung* (Reinbek, 2012).

7 Cf. Odo Marquard, *Abschied vom Prinzipiellen*, Philosophische Studien (Stuttgart, 1981), 39ff.

The message of justification is for humans who, in modern terms, struggle for recognition. Existential and social conflicts cannot be explained by the mere struggle for self-preservation; they are, rather, a struggle for recognition.[8] Social conflicts can therefore not be reduced to economic issues, but they are always also moral and—as we have seen them resurge in recent years—religious ones. In the struggle for recognition, appreciation, and attention, staged as well by mass media, people are driven by the fear of being stigmatized with insignificance.[9]

The question of guilt and its parallel question of forgiveness and acceptance also have not really disappeared. The conscience frightened by moral guilt mutates, rather, as Klaus Winkler writes, into narcissistically mortified conscience,[10] which is—to put it in psychoanalytic parlance—oppressed less by the failure vis-à-vis the superego than the ego ideal. Even so, an experience that incurs guilt in a moral sense is also a lasting reality.

So, the question of guilt and the question of forgiveness and acceptance have not really disappeared. Thus, the meaning of the message of justification opens up only when we look not only into different forms of guilt, but of sin as well. Sin means a misguided relationship to God, which manifests itself in a misguided self-relationship and a misguided relationship to fellow human beings and the whole creation. It constitutes the deep structure of the struggle for recognition. Already in the biblical tradition, the struggle for recognition is pinned down at every turn. The phenomenon of sin and quest for recognition belong together already in the Old Testament understanding. Paul radically defines a sinful man as God's enemy. The Pauline doctrine of justification says, however, that God overcomes human enmity, and thus recognizes and accepts humans unconditionally for Christ's sake in spite of their sins.

Justification of the sinner also means that the justified sinner acquires a new self-image as God's creature. The goal of justification is a new understanding of human creatureliness. By restoring the relationship to God that has been disturbed, humans also gain a new relationship to nature, which now burgeons as God's creation.

8 Cf. Axel Honneth, *Kampf um Anerkennung. Zur moralischen Grammatik sozialer Konflikte* (Frankfurt am Main, 1992). Honneth refers to Hegel's early philosophy.

9 Cf. Erich Fromm, *Die Furcht vor der Freiheit* [1941] (Munich, 2000). Fromm interprets the fear of insignificance at the end of the late Middle Ages as an important driving force of the Reformation preaching of Luther and Calvin (pp. 76ff.), though with a criticism that the faith championed by Luther did not really overcome this fear, but merely compensated for it.

10 Cf. Klaus Winkler, *Seelsorge* (Berlin/New York, 1997), 282.

By Christ Alone

In Luke's Acts of the Apostles, there is an abrupt sentence that sounds extremely repugnant to the ears of modern people living in a time of religious tolerance and pluralism, and also of religious indifference. The apostles Peter and John are brought before the Sanhedrin. In his defense speech, Peter talks about Christ: "Salvation is found in no one else, for there is no other name under heaven given to mankind by which we must be saved" (Acts 4:12).[11] This bold statement reads like an echo of the Christ hymn of the apostle Paul in Philippians 2:9-11 and Roman 10:9.

Martin Luther and the Reformation put these statements in a nutshell with the succinct formula "*Solus Christus*—Christ alone." However, this formula had not yet acquired it famous church-critical meaning in Luther's early works; it obtained this only after his Reformation discovery.[12] That salvation can be found in Christ alone is in itself a good Catholic formula on a par with "*Sola gratia*—by grace alone." "*Solus Christus*" is given its intensified reforming significance and concurrent delineation from the late medieval Catholic doctrine of grace after the Reformation discovery due to its close association with "*Sola fide*—by faith alone," in association with *sola gratia* and *sola scriptura.*

In a way, the aforementioned four exclusive particles can be embraced in the formula "God alone."[13] Such a radical view of the sole redemptive work of Jesus Christ appears to be hardly admissible in light of today's demands for tolerance, especially in interreligious dialogues. Can this biblical statement still claim theological validity today? Or is it necessary to mitigate its pungency within a framework of a theology of religions? I would like to stress that this question is being raised as a common ecumenical challenge, not merely as a problem of a Protestant theology of religions.[14]

In a critical delineation from today's conceptions of a theology that declares religion as its leitmotiv and would like to start out from the lived religion in its diversity, let it be posited here that the main concern of Christian faith is not religion or spirituality, but God. The gospel does not promise "small transcendences" that we can experience on vacation or in a football stadium, but it answers the question as to what my only comfort in life and in death is, as expressed by the Reformed Heidelberg Catechism (1563). The

11 Unless otherwise indicated, Bible passages are cited according to the New International Version.

12 Cf. Bernhard Lohse, *Luthers Theologie in ihrer historischen Entwicklung und in ihrem systematischen Zusammenhang* (Göttingen, 1995), 67.

13 Cf. Gerhard Ebeling, *Luther. Einführung in sein Denken*, Uni-Taschenbücher (UTB) 1090 (Tübingen, 1981), 296.

14 Cf. Dorothea Sattler and Volker Leppin, eds., *Heil für alle? Ökumenische Reflexionen*, Dialog der Kirchen 15 (Freiburg/Göttingen, 2012).

pressing problem of today's churches is not the lack of a certain type of spirituality, but the linguistic deficiency of faith that manifests itself in an occasionally appalling trivialization concerning Christian faith, which is justifiably criticized as self-secularization of the church.[15] The respiritualization that some recommend in response to the crisis faced by the church is actually no alternative, but may foment such self-secularization even more.

While it is true that religious concepts cannot be waived in theological matters, distinction should be made first and foremost between religion and belief in God. Additionally, distinction should be made between the question of God and the question of meaning. Not everyone who seeks the meaning of life is seeking God for that. Whoever wants to talk about God in the biblical sense today cannot take it for granted that God is always an object of the quest. The point of departure of a prior question of God is by no means self-evident and inevitable. Therefore, the chance of talking about God does not depend on the question of God, but the memory track of the biblically testified revelation of God.

Posing the question of God today is only possible because people in the past spoke of God and witnessed to God's work. The New Testament texts, however, do so in such a way that they speak of Jesus Christ at the same time.

However, we cannot speak properly of Jesus in view of his person and life without speaking of God at the same time, so that the meaning of Christ's life is revealed within the horizon of God—just as, conversely, the word *God* is given its ultimate meaning only in connection with the life of Jesus. The fate of Jesus makes it evident that the essence of God is love.[16] What this love consists of, which is God, can only be determined by referring to the life of Jesus. Thus, the word *God* is given its Christian meaning when God and Jesus are spoken together. Moreover, we can only speak of God and Jesus of Nazareth together by speaking of the God of Israel, as testified to by the Old Testament, as the Father, and Jesus as the Son, and the Holy Spirit; in other words, by speaking of God in trinitarian terms.[17]

In this sense, I see the churches challenged to refine the profile of what is Christian. Christian faith is differentiated from all other forms of religion first and foremost by the confession to Jesus Christ as saviour. It is precisely for this reason that his believers have been called Christians. However, this confession of faith includes the faith in the God proclaimed by Jesus, who, in turn, is the God of Israel. Yet, not a vague openness for God, but the

---

15 Cf. Wolfgang Huber, *Kirche in der Zeitenwende. Gesellschaftlicher Wandel und Erneuerung der Kirche* (Gütersloh, 1998), 10.

16 Cf. 1 John 4:16.

17 Cf. Eberhard Jüngel, Gott als Geheimnis der Welt (Tübingen, 1986). For detailed trinitarian discourse about the Holy Ghost, see Ulrich H. J. Körtner, *Die Gemeinschaft des Heiligen Geistes. Zur Lehre vom Heiligen Geist und der Kirche* (Neukirchen-Vluyn, 1999), esp. 47–62.

confession in Christ is the determinant "marker" that distinguishes the label "Christianity" in the market of religious possibilities and impossibilities. The identity of faith and church is to be determined from there.

By Grace Alone

By grace alone—and that for Christ's sake—the sinful humankind is justified before God and accepted by God. By grace alone—also for Christ's sake—the justified sinner lives as a renewed creation of God. "If anyone is in Christ," Paul writes in 2 Corinthians 5:17, "the person is a new creation." Thus, justification involves not only the forgiveness of sin and reconciliation with God, but also the renewal of creation. Therefore, the doctrine of justification and *sola gratia* are, in the Protestant understanding, the criterion for *all* of the church's proclamation[18] and the understanding of the gospel of Jesus Christ, as well as of the world as creation and human beings as God's creatures.

This can be elucidated very aptly by Luther's interpretation of the first article of the Apostles' Creed. What is meant by the statement: "I believe in God, the Father Almighty, Maker of heaven and earth"? Luther replied:

> I believe that God has made me and all creatures; that He has given me my body and soul, eyes, ears and all my members, my reason and all my senses, and still takes care of them. He also gives me clothing and shoes, food and drink, house and home, wife and children, land, animals, and all I have. He richly and daily provides me with all that I need to support this body and life. He defends me against all danger and guards and protects me from all evil. All this He does only out of fatherly, divine goodness and mercy, without any merit or worthiness in me. For all this it is my duty to thank and praise, serve and obey Him. This is most certainly true.[19]

Thus, Luther gave the belief in creation a frame of the message of justification. *Sola gratia*: in terms of the theology of creation, this means to receive life as a good gift from God's hand—"All this He does only out of fatherly, divine goodness and mercy, without any merit or worthiness in me." In Luther's understanding, faith is equivalent to the certainty of salvation *sola gratia*. This is underpinned by the concluding phrase of his interpretation of the first article of faith: "This is most certainly true."

Additionally, *sola gratia* also stands in contrast to the mercilessness of the overtribunalized, present-day living environment that provokes the pressing

18 Cf. also Leuenberg Agreement, Art. 12, according to which "the unique mediation of Jesus Christ in salvation is the heart of scripture and that the message of justification as the message of God's free grace is the measure of all the church's preaching."

19 Martin Luther, *The Small Catechism* (St. Louis: Concordia, 1986).

question of a culture of compassion and forgiveness. According to Christian understanding, Jesus Christ, as the incarnate Word of God, is the source and criterion of such a culture of forgiveness.

The gospel is the promise of unconditional love. Given that the earthly Jesus already claimed for himself the authority to forgive sins in the name of God, the New Testament sees a final act of divine forgiveness in his death and resurrection. Agreeing with Paul, we are to understand the death of Jesus as the epitome of divine love of enemies (Rom. 5:10), so that the basis for the commandment of love of neighbours culminates in the commandment of love of enemies (Matt. 5:38-48). In the end, however, divine forgiveness aims at an ultimate and universal reconciliation.

It is, most of all, its religious dimension that makes Christianity a standard resource of a culture of forgiveness. This has also been highlighted by Hannah Arendt.[20] Particular attention deserves to be paid to her elaboration of the deeds unforgivable for humans because there is no earthly punishment through which they can be atoned for. This idea is helpful for understanding afresh the meaning of the biblical discourse of the last judgment. A right understanding of the notion of judgment represents the Christian certainty that nothing is impossible for God when it comes to forgiveness, exactly because God is the judging, justice-rendering God. Without the idea of the judging God, the idea of the merciful God loses its plausibility.

Then again, under the sign of justification and reconciliation, the idea of the last judgment undergoes a shift from a symbol of fear to a symbol of hope, as already demonstrated in question 52 of the Heidelberg Catechism.[21] The biblical idea of the last judgment and the doctrine of justification of the sinner both express a hope that applies not only to the victims of history, but also to the culprits in such a way that killers do not triumph over their victims.[22]

---

20 Cf. Hannah Arendt, *Vita activa oder Vom tätigen Leben* (Munich, 2001), 304.

21 Question 52 reads as follows: Q. "What comfort is it to you that Christ will come to judge the living and the dead?"—A. "In all my sorrow and persecution I lift up my head and eagerly await as judge from heaven the very same person who before has submitted Himself to the judgment of God for my sake, and has removed all the curse from me. He will cast all His and my enemies into everlasting condemnation, but He will take me and all His chosen ones to Himself into heavenly joy and glory." (A version authorized by the Canadian and American Reformed churches, chosen by the translator.) Whereas the aspect of hope in the idea of tribunal may be underscored in the Heidelberg Catechism, the adoption of double-standard judgment and eternal condemnation of God's enemies ("His and my [!] enemies'), though supported by biblical passages, should undergo a theological revision. Such an apodictically asserted certainty of faith, as is the case with the Heidelberg Catechism, is not to be tolerated at any rate.

22 Cf. Max Horkheimer, *Die Sehnsucht nach dem ganz Anderen. Ein Interview mit Kommentar von H. Gumnior* (Hamburg, 1970), 62.

For the Christian faith, the idea of the last judgment is addressed from the redemptive significance of Jesus' death. The link between *sola gratia* and *solus Christus* becomes apparent. To paraphrase the Apostles' Creed, Christians hope for the second coming of Christ in the last judgment. That the judge of all humans is none other than Jesus Christ tells us that God wants a salvific restoration of the world and that God's righteousness is imbued with the spirit of love.

The goal of justification is reconciliation. All human efforts at reconciliation are ultimately anchored in the reconciliation between God and humans endowed by God in Christ. Living out of the power of reconciliation is living in the hope of God's reign. This hope includes the memory of the dead and their sufferings. It forms the unreachable horizon of all worldly efforts at reconciliation.

By Scripture Alone

According to the classical Reformation doctrine, scripture alone is the source and criterion of Christian faith, doctrine, and life. Luther's formula "*sola scriptura*," of course, does not stand alone, but belongs to the quadruplet of the interexplanatory exclusive particles: *sola scriptura—solus Christus—sola gratia—sola fide.*[23] Scripture alone is the source and criterion of faith, because it bears witness to Christ, who alone is the source of salvation, namely, to the gospel that acquits sinners. Justification of sinners is by grace alone for Christ's sake, and that by faith in the gospel alone, as testified by the scripture.

According to the Lutheran Formula of Concord of 1577, "the scriptures alone remain the sole judge, rule and norm; they are the touchstone according to which all teachings must be recognized and judged, whether they are good or wicked, right or wrong."[24] A similar formulation is found in the Reformed confessions.[25] Apart from the fact that the Formula of Concord reduces the Reformation principle of the scripture to a mere criteriological function in comparison to Luther, it has both in Lutheranism and in Reformed churches an anti-Catholic—or more precisely, an anti-Rome—thrust. Neither the church tradition nor the teaching ministry, but only the scripture, is the authoritative standard for theology and preaching.

23 Cf. for the following, Ulrich H. J. Körtner, "Rezeption und Inspiration. Über die Schriftwerdung des Wortes und die Wortwerdung der Schrift im Akt des Lesens, " *Neue Zeitschrift für Systematische Theologie und Religionsphilosophie (NZSTh)* 51 (2009): 27–49.

24 *Bekenntnisschriften der evangelisch-lutherischen Kirche* (hereafter BSLK) 769: 22–27.

25 Relevant passages in *Bekenntnisschriften der evangelisch-reformierten Kirche* (BSRK*)* 154f. (Zurich Confession of Faith, 1545); 234:15-22 (*Confessio belgica*, 1561); 500:35–37 (Waldensian Confession of Faith, 1655); 506f. (Anglican Articles, 1552/62); 526f. (Irish Articles of Religion, 1615); 542–47 (Westminster Confession of Faith, 1647); 871f. (Confession of Faith of the Calvinistic Methodists, 1823); 905:12–14 (Confession of the Free Church of Geneva, 1848).

"The" Bible, "the" scripture, on which the Reformation *sola scriptura* insists, is indeed a canon of anti-Catholic thrust that has to be described as a hybrid in the light of the canonical history. The reformers refer to the purported original texts of the Old and New Testaments under the humanistic slogan "*ad fontes*" ("[back] to the sources")! Therefore, they gave the *Biblia Hebraica* preferential treatment over the Septuagint, on which the Old Testament of Latin Vulgate was based. The reformers evoked thereby the prior provision, externality, and incontestable authority of God's word. In truth, however, they did not use a preexisting canon, but *created* "a hybrid canon that had never existed before and has existed only in national translations ever since."[26]

The scripture invoked by the Reformation churches is, strictly speaking, not the starting point, but a product of the Reformation, namely a canon presented as a mixture of Hebrew scope and Greek structure with the involvement of a third language, be it German,[27] English, or any other modern language. Thus, similar to the case of the Septuagint, the translation is actually the original.

The aforementioned interrelatedness of canon, translation, and denominational identity must be taken seriously from the Protestant perspective as a question regarding the Reformation principle of scripture.[28] Irrespective of the fact that the Protestant hybrid canon is only available in translations, there are a wide variety of German, English, or other foreign-language translations, whereby a clear distinction should be made between private translations, editions, and scientific translations as well as those approved by the church, that is, approved for liturgical use. Before the act of reading, one can choose a Bible version from among different translations, which shows the truth that not only the meaning of individual texts, but also the Bible itself, is created anew each time as a macro-text in the act of reception.

Does this mean that the Reformation principle of scripture, whose crisis has been at issue since the beginning of the historical-critical exegesis,

---

26 James A. Loader, "Die Problematik des Begriffes hebraica veritas," *Harvard Theological Studies* (HTS) 64 (2008): 227–51; here 247.

27 The first complete Bible translation in German during the Reformation period was not Martin Luther's translation, as is well known, but the "Zurich Bible" of 1531 (the "Froschau Bible," whose separate parts were published between 1524 and 1529). Its translation of the NT was indeed based on Luther's translation, which in its full version was not published until 1534. Cf. Albrecht Beutel, art. "Bibelübersetzungen II.1," *Religion in Geschichte und Gegenwart* (RGG)4 I (Tübingen, 1998), cols. 1498–1505, here col. 1500.

28 The following passage has taken from Ulrich H. J. Körtner, "Im Anfang war die Übersetzung. Kanon, Bibelübersetzungen und konfessionelle Identitäten im Christentum," Marianne Grohmann and Ursula Ragacs, eds., *Religion übersetzen. Übersetzungen und Textrezeption als Transformationsphänomene von Religion,* Religion and Transformation in Contemporary European Society 2 (Göttingen, 2012), 179–201, here 194–98.

is ultimately dismissed?[29] Is it to remain in its *de*construction,[30] or is there any possibility for a *re*construction of a more acceptable aesthetics of reception that is convincing not only under literary criteria, but also theologically? Accordingly, is it possible to explore afresh the doctrine of the inspiration through scripture in its Reformation understanding, without succumbing to the self-deception of the old Protestantism?

The unity of the scripture can be determined neither formally in the sense of a canon list—of which there are still many—nor through a dogmatized inventory of significance. Rather, this unity presents itself anew at each continued reading, although distinction should be made between the outer and the inner unity of the canon.

Nonetheless, the Reformation tradition professes that the canon is not a product of the church, that is, the church plays no active part in the formation of the canon. It is only on this premise that the Reformation principle of scripture, "*sola scriptura*," according to which scripture alone is the source of faith and the basis for the rejection of the church privilege of interpretation, makes sense. However, to what extent is this assertion plausible under the conditions of modern historical consciousness and the historical-critical research?

The various forms of the Jewish Bible or the Old Testament as well as the Christian Bible with its dual canon can be understood in terms of the modern concept of intertextuality.[31] As Gerhard Ebeling explains, the biblical canon is, analogous to the Reformation principle of scripture, "no text demarcation principle, but a hermeneutical principle in a decisive way."[32] Taking this idea seriously entails "the respect for mutual *demarcation* and therefore enriching *complement* which bring about various text traditions and organizations," not only in dialogue between Christianity and Judaism, but also among Christian churches.[33] If each canon is understood as a particular implementation of the idea of holy scripture, which is dependent on the exchange with

29 On the crisis of the scriptural principle, refer to Ulrich H. J. Körtner, *Theologie des Wortes Gottes. Positionen—Probleme—Perspektiven* (Göttingen, 2001), 302ff.; Jörg Lauster, "Prinzip und Methode," *Die Transformation des protestantischen Schriftprinzips durch die historische Kritik von Schleiermacher bis zur Gegenwart*, Hermeneutische Untersuchungen zur Theologie (HUTh) 46 (Tübingen,2004).

30 Hector Avalos, *The End of Biblical Studies* (Amherst, NY, 2007), 37ff., 65ff.

31 Cf. Thomas Hieke and Tobias Niklas, "Die Worte der Prophetie dieses Buches," in *Offenbarung 22,6-21 als Schlussstein der christlichen Bibel Alten und Neuen Testaments gelesen, Biblisch-theologische Studien* (BThS) 62 (Neukirchen-Vluyn, 2003); Stefan Alkier and Richard B. Hays, *Kanon und Intertextualität*, Kl. Schriften des FB Ev. Theol. der Goethe-Universität Frankfurt/Main, Bd. 1 (Frankfurt am Main, 2010).

32 Gerhard Ebeling, *Dogmatik des christlichen Glaubens*, vol. 1 (Tübingen, 1982), 34.

33 Loader, "Die Problematik des Begriffes *hebraica veritas*," 249.

other forms of its implementation, a hybrid such as the Protestant canon is also theologically legitimate.

Interpretation of scripture does not only happen inevitably in a pluralistic way, but it is always subject to presuppositions; still, it takes place within the church or respective denominations as interpretive communities.[34] In this respect, the postulate of "church hermeneutics," which is discussed today as a "hermeneutics of consent,"[35] stands to reason. Consent with the biblical text can be, at most, a result of a process of understanding, rather than the premise itself. Consequently, according to the Protestant understanding, there can be no interpretive privilege under ecclesiastical or doctrinal-magisterial authority that is to control and domesticate the plurality of the—in principle, interminable—interpretation process.

According to the Reformation tradition, the church, specifically the worshiping community, is indeed not the subject, but the object of interpretation. The church is a creation of the word: "*creatura Euangelii*" (Luther),[36] that is, a creature of the gospel or "*creatura verbi divini*," creation of God's word.[37] As Luther writes, the church is "*nata ex verbo*,"[38] whereby the birth of the church from God's word is not a one-time past event, but a continuous one. Similarly, as a new Christian daily comes forth from baptism, according to Luther, [39] so the church as a community of believers is always born anew from the word. It is precisely in this sense that the church is *creatura verbi* and not its *creator*.

By Faith Alone

How, then, is faith to be understood in Reformation theology, which alone can justify human beings? Gerhard Ebeling puts Luther's understanding of faith in a nutshell, using a simple formula: "Faith is a good conscience."[40] A good conscience does not come from the works and services that we perform ourselves, but solely from the work of God in Jesus Christ. It is a liber-

34 For the concept of the interpretive community, see Stanley Fish, *Is There a Text in This Class? The Authority of Interpretive Communities* (Cambridge, MA, 1980).

35 Peter Stuhlmacher, *Vom Verstehen des Neuen Testaments. Eine Hermeneutik*, Das Neue Testament Deutsch (NTD) Erg. 6 (Göttingen, 1979), esp. 205ff.

36 WA 2:430, 6–8.

37 The expression "*creatura verbi*" to describe the church is not traceable to Luther. However, there are at least quotes similar to this description, e.g., WA 6:560,36–561,1; WA.B 5:591,49–57. Cf. M. Trowitzsch, "Die nachkonstantinische Kirche, die Kirche der Postmoderne—und Martin Luthers antizipierende Kritik," *Berliner Theologische Zeitschrift* (BThZ) 13 (1996): 3–35, here 4 n.6.

38 WA 42:334,12.

39 Luther, *Small Catechism* (BSLK 516:30–38).

40 Ebeling, *Dogmatik des christlichen Glaubens*, 1:191.

ating conscience, as the faith consists of the experience of a newly attained freedom from sin and for God and other humans.

The doctrine of unconditional acceptance and justification of the ungodly is, finally, none other than a doctrine of freedom. The Reformation understandings of saving event and salvation history are actually a story of freedom or, more precisely, a story of liberation. Faith is the awareness of a newly attained freedom to which the believer is freed by Christ (cf. Gal. 5:1).[41]

Freed to believe, a human being can "fear, love, and trust God above all things," as Luther reaffirms in his interpretation of the First Commandment.[42] It is within faith as well that the nature of sin comes to light: sin is essentially unbelief, which is tantamount to the lack of fear of God, love of God, and trust in God.[43]

Faith, however, is neither a human work nor asset nor a virtue, in the sense of a philosophical theory of virtue, but exclusively God's work and gift. This is ascertained as the believer participates in the act of faith as a subject. Luther describes faith in his interpretation of the third article of the Apostles' Creed as the work of the Holy Spirit: "I believe that I cannot by my own reason or strength believe in Jesus Christ, my Lord, or come to Him; but the Holy Ghost has called me by the Gospel, enlightened me with his gifts, and sanctified and kept me in the true faith."[44] As the justification, faith is also to be understood as a trinitarian event that is effectuated by the Father, the Son, and the Holy Spirit.

By the same token, the Heidelberg Catechism, the most important confession of the Reformed churches, states in the response to Question 21 what true faith is: true faith "is not only a certain knowledge, whereby I hold for truth all that God has revealed to us in his word, but also an assured confidence, which the Holy Ghost works by the gospel, in my heart; that not only to others, but to me also, remission of sin, everlasting righteousness and salvation, are freely given by God, merely of grace, only for the sake of Christ's merits."[45]

The gospel is, in the sense used by Luther and the Heidelberg Catechism, χήρυγμα Ἰησοῦ Χριστοῦ ("the kerygma of Jesus Christ"), as the apostle Paul said in Romans 16:25. In this formula, both objective genitive and subjective genitive are used on an equal footing. Thus, the kerygma of Jesus Christ is not only the proclamation *of* Jesus Christ as object, but also the

41 In his work "*De captivitate Babylonica*" (1520), Luther mentions "*scientia libertatis Christianae*" (WA 6:538,30).

42 Luther, *Small Catechism* (BSLK 507:43-44).

43 Cf. Rom. 14:23: "[E]verything that does not come from faith is sin."

44 Luther, *Small Catechism* (BSLK 511:46–512:5).

45 The Heidelberg Catechism (trans. note: the version as taught in the Reformed churches and schools in Holland and America; source: http://www.prca.org).

proclamation originating *from* Christ as subject. It is precisely for this reason that word and faith directly belong to each other according to the Reformation understanding.

Wherever the message of Jesus Christ is received, it is Christ himself who is at work. Quoting Rudolf Bultmann, it can be said that Christianity begins when the proclaimer becomes the proclaimed. Through the fact that he is being proclaimed, Christ himself speaks within the present.

In the New Testament, Jesus of Nazareth is called the Word of God. Though not physically present, he is indirectly present by the Christian proclamation; in Pauline dictum, by kerygma. Kerygma is the word of faith, also in the dual genitive meaning: it bears witness to the faith in Jesus Christ and is simultaneously the medium that evokes faith. In the *message* (not report!) of faith, in which faith in Jesus as the Christ of God is *professed*, *God* comes up. Thus, God is the entity that brings forward the message of Christian faith as a self-mediated, faith-provoking message, manifested as such. In this way, God appears as the basis of faith and thus as the basis of all reality.

A more detailed explanation is necessary to clarify why the "word of faith" is to be understood as a confession of faith on the one hand, and as a provocation to faith on the other. A lexical meaning of "provocation" is "to call forth." Insofar as the word of faith is the way in which God's *creative* word becomes perceivable, "to call forth" means "to call into being," not only "*to challenge*," as we usually translate "to provoke." The provocation of the word of faith is not to be understood as a mere demand, that is, an appeal to faith. Rather, the word of faith speaks "of faith in the way that it promises and gives instead of just demanding and claiming it."[46] Faith in the sense of the New Testament is therefore "an integral part of the event to which it testifies."[47]

If the way in which we encounter God's word in human words is none other than the word of faith, faith itself—as we can still learn from Bultmann—is to be interpreted as a way of *understanding*. However, faith as a peculiar way of *self-understanding* sees itself in a passive way as *being recognized and understood* by God. The Pauline eschatological hope is also directed toward being subjected to a final revelation of the self, as expressed in 1 Corinthians 13:12: "Now I know in part; then I shall know fully, *even as I am fully known*." Faith is thus not a way of active self-determination, but a passive state of *being* determined.[48] Although the believer understands *him- or herself* anew in the faith, respectively the believing self grounds *itself* in God, faith is merely

46 Gerhard Ebeling, *Dogmatik des christlichen Glaubens*, vol. 3 (Tübingen, 1979), 251.

47 Paul Tillich, *Systematische Theologie*, vol. 2 (Stuttgart, 1977), 128.

48 Cf. Bultmann, *Theologische Enzyklopädie*, ed. Eberhard Jüngel and Klaus W. Müller (Tübingen, 1984), 129 n.67, where the believer is described as the object of divine action.

something *passively experienced* that cannot be understood as a self-driven act in whatever activities the subject may be engaged, but only as a gift. As such, mentioning human self-determination in view of the faith can be at best in a way that a previously determined state is recognized and reenacted in faith by God.

Nevertheless, faith does not rest self-sufficiently by itself, but it is paired with the love of God and of fellow human beings as well as with hope. In the Johannine writings of the New Testament, God's nature is described as love, and faith as being in the love. According to Luther, however, faith and love relate to each other as a person and his/her work,[49] and actor and action.[50] Faith becomes manifest in the gratitude[51] that is practiced in a lived ethos. However, it cannot be reduced to a mere means of motivating action.

The message of justification presupposes that a conceptual distinction be made between the action of God and that of humankind. When Luther speaks of the deeds of love as the fruit of faith, human action is certainly not juxtaposed unconnectedly next to God's action, but it actually relates to none other than that which is God's work alone, namely faith. The doctrine of justification talks about God's exclusive act of grace upon human beings and the world. The discourse about the justifying act of God opens up a specifically theological understanding of freedom, which is the basic condition of all action. Accordingly, all common concepts of action as well as a general understanding of ethics are subjected to the critique. An ethics founded on the theology of justification is, if understood correctly, not so much an ethics of doing as an ethics of letting be. Using the reversed order of the sentence of James 1:22, its boldly formulated motto reads: "Be hearers of the word and not doers alone, thus deceiving yourselves!"

Hearing the word of God directs us to an ethics of letting be—letting God be God and others be others instead of using God and the world arbitrarily.[52] By no means, to quote Marx, is it not a matter of changing or improving the world or our fellow humans in accordance with our ideas of salvation, but of sparing them. To leave others and the creation as they are includes, of course, deeds of kindness, which, however, can always carry the risk of showing a paternalistic attitude of patronizing others. An ethics anchored in justification is therefore always an ethics of self-limitation of the acting subject as well.

It is necessary to protect the gospel, that is, the good news of the justification of the ungodly by faith alone, against its reduction to a particular

49 Cf. WA 17/2:97, 7-11.

50 Cf. WA 17/2:96, 25.

51 Cf. Part III of the Heidelberg Catechism.

52 The two closing paragraphs have been taken from Körtner, "Rechtfertigung," 114.

morality. The fourfold *solus* of the Reformation theology may be invoked also in this respect. The message of justification should also be guarded from the misunderstanding that human doings or nondoings do not matter at all. On the contrary, faith encourages and empowers us to take responsibility before God and fellow humans. The task of a Protestant ethics is to elucidate the interrelation of freedom, love, and responsibility, and to bring it to bear fruits for the benefit of current conduct in society and politics.

CHAPTER 9

Peter Opitz

The Swiss Contribution to the Reformation Movement

The Historical Contribution of the Swiss Reformation to the Reformation Movement

The Swiss Reformation as the historical root of worldwide Reformed Protestantism

In early January 1523, the mayor and members of the city council of Zürich invited all preachers, pastors, vicars, and priests in Zürich and the adjoining region to the town hall to take part in a "disputation" to be held at the end of the month, which aimed to arbitrate a conflict: a dispute between those who claimed to preach the word of God from the pulpit for the common people, thereby relying on the gospel, and their opponents who reproached them for being "false teachers, debauchers, and heretics." The bishop of Constance was also invited. The council members had taken this initiative only after the bishop's failure to comply with the request to establish peace and order in his diocese, declaring that the disputing parties should be granted the opportunity to justify their standpoints in compliance "with the true divine scripture in the German language." Ulrich Zwingli had conceived his doctrine in 67 articles, which were to be presented for debate.

The outcome of the disputation was conclusive, and the decision of the council indicatory: as nobody could refute Zwingli's standpoints on this ground, he was allowed to continue his preaching as previously. What is more, not only Zwingli himself, but also all other pastors and priests in town and country were instructed to preach henceforth only what they can "prove true by virtue of the holy Gospel and other true divine scriptures."

It was not until a considerable time later that the Reformation finally prevailed and was established in Zürich, but its course was set by this event. The Zürich council had taken the reins of church and religion into their own hands and stood behind the controversial preacher Zwingli, thus recognizing the gospel as found solely in the holy scriptures (*sola scriptura*) as the criterion by which the Christianity of the Roman Episcopal Church should be measured to justify its claim to power as true spiritual authority in the Christian Europe.

While it is true that the Swiss Reformation would hardly have been imaginable had it not been for Luther's emergence and the far-reaching echo that it triggered, the Zürich council's decision was the first event of its kind and was groundbreaking for the entire European Reformation movement. A sovereign political authority of that time had decided as a fundamental rule that the proclamation of the gospel should occur in accordance with the "divine word" as its sole measurement. This inevitably resulted in "reforming" some of its own Christianity-based political community, regardless of all ecclesiastical and religious traditions and political threats coming from the empire. Zwingli masterminded this event with his unique theological profile on which the later "reformed" theologians could draw directly or indirectly, not least John Calvin, in whose works hardly any theological thoughts can be found that had not already been expressed and discussed in the Swiss Reformation years before. Likewise, the Zürich decision triggered the impetus for building a "Reformed" church "according to the Word of God" that entered into the Reformation movement. Just consider the recourse of a public disputation to introduce the Reformation, which was then emulated across the empire. Even admitting its distance from the modern ideal of a common search for the truth without sovereign intervention, it is definitely closer to this ideal than to papal edicts or princely decrees of religion. Also to be considered are the founding of theological "superior schools" and academies for the education of pastors under the influence of humanistic biblical philosophy, or the introduction of synods, pastors' conferences, and consistories as church-governing bodies and as countermodels of the episcopal-hierarchical governing structure.

An important historical contribution of the Swiss Reformation to the Reformation movement was its emergence as a mainly municipal or communal Reformation, which became the root of worldwide Reformed Protestantism. This imagery of "root" at the same time shall hint at its rapid growth and development, spreading its branches in various domains in Europe, occasionally merging with the impetuses and traditions of the Wittenberg Reformation, and taking on various theological colours and ecclesiastical shapes. Unlike Lutheran Protestantism, which has kept its identity anchored on its founding father until today, albeit de facto with very different interpretations, it is part of the nature and self-identity of the movement originating from these Zürich roots to defy being characterized or defined by one single reformer. Later, however, this was often done, as exemplified by the adoption of the term *Calvinism*, which was initially used as a derogatory name, as self-designation. This may be explained historically, and gave Calvinism from the 17th century onwards a certain "confessional" identity, but not without problematic facets and consequences. This identity, in fact, restricted the historical wealth and theological claims of this movement that emerged from the Swiss Reformation.

The Swiss Reformation as European Reformation

Contemporary understandings define the (Reformed) Swiss geographically as areas directly influenced by Zwingli, marked by the cities Zürich, Schaffhausen, Basel, and Bern. However, a closer look at the reformers who were the spiritual leaders of the movement in these areas readily transforms the Swiss Reformation into a European Reformation. Already, Zwingli himself was not a genuine Confederate, as he came from Toggenburg, an area affiliated to the Old Swiss Confederacy, but endowed with limited political rights. The secretary of the Second Zürich Disputation and a later Anabaptist martyr was Balthasar Hubmaier, who hailed from Friedberg near Augsburg. Zwingli's successor Heinrich Bullinger grew up in "condominium" Aargau. Leo Jud, Zwingli's closest colleague and ally, pastor of the Zürich Municipal Church of St Peter, came from upper Alsace. William Reublin, the first Zürich pastor who married publicly, also came from Alsace, precisely from Selestat. Konrad Pellikan, the famous Hebraist and teacher of the Old Testament at the Superior School of Theology in Zürich, was another Alsatian, coming from Rouffach. His colleague at the Superior School of Theology of no less reputation, Theodor Bibliander, came from Bischofzell. And Peter

Martyr Vermigli, the widely acclaimed scholar, was an Italian. The situation in Basel, Bern, and Schaffhausen was not different in regard to the origins of their respective formative reformers. This was especially true for Lausanne, Neuchâtel, and Geneva, where almost exclusively French reformers left their traces. This phenomenon can be explained by the close association of the Swiss Reformation with European humanism. It is not coincidental that the Roman Catholic Erasmus settled down in Basel and that his funeral oration was delivered by the reformer Oswald Myconius, Zwingli's former ally, who originally came from the Roman Catholic Lucerne.

Theological Contributions of the Swiss Reformation to the Reformation Movement

What can be described as the specific *theological* contributions of the Swiss Reformation to the Reformation movement, not only in recognition of its historical significance, but also in terms of its potential implications for the future? Our question here is not concerned with theological history, but with building on the aforementioned distinct features of the Swiss Reformation and making it fruitful for the Reformation movement of today and tomorrow. Therefore, these contributions have to be looked into more closely one by one.

The gospel of reconciliation

The content of the gospel as defined by Zwingli at the First Disputation of Zürich of 1523 is none other than Christ himself; God's will and act of reconciliation was revealed in Christ for us: "The essence of the Gospel is that our Lord Jesus Christ, the true Son of God, revealed to us the will of his heavenly Father and, with his innocence, freed us from death and reconciled us with God."

This does not give rise to a "new teaching." It is ultimately and solely a call to listen to "Christ alone" (*solus Christus*) and to entrust oneself to him as the place of reconciliation with God. Calling the reformers "new believers" and juxtaposing them with the Roman Catholic "old believers" was a polemical propaganda or misinterpretation. What was intended by the Swiss Reformation was nothing else than a return to the (unclouded) source and concentration on the essential and the fundamental of the common Christian faith. The Swiss reformers identified themselves as representatives of the "old faith," as expressly emphasized by Heinrich Bullinger. Regarding this fundamental concern of the Reformation, they felt profoundly allied with the Wittenberg reformers. A closer look, however, reveals a prominently distinctive Swiss profile—which nevertheless would not have been the cause for an inner-Protestant division, at least from the Swiss perspective. Unfortunately, Luther saw the matter differently. My task is now to elaborate on this Swiss profile a bit further.

Luther's piety and thought remained deeply influenced by his experience as a monk. Even though his liberating "reformative discovery" completely changed the way of the penitent piety of the late Middle Ages, the centre of gravity of his understanding of the gospel continued to be a question of individual appropriation or affection of the divine grace, as proven by his attitude in the eucharistic controversy, by his catechisms, as well as by his extremely reserved attitude in presenting measures of reform in ecclesiastical life and worship practices.

It is not by chance that Zwingli's description of the gospel does not revolve around the justification, but around reconciliation and God's will—both to be found in Christ. Reconciliation means, however, restoration of community. For Zwingli, the community of humans with God is inseparably linked with a "reconciled" community of humans shaped by the divine will as manifested in Christ, that is, a Christian congregation. Zwingli's concern as a "people's priest" (pastor of the people) was as much his personal salvation as the salvation, that is, the nearness to God, of the congregation entrusted to him. Thus, it is no coincidence that Zwingli chose Matthew 11:28 as the slogan of his proclamation on the title page of his writings entitled "Christ who calls people to himself, in his community": "Come to me, all you who are weary and are carrying heavy burdens, and I will give you rest" (Matt. 11:28).

An important theological consequence is that the leitmotivs derived from the Swiss Reformation are not law and gospel, but election and covenant. Later on, as is well known, the lawyer Calvin took over the baton from Martin Bucer, who was influenced by Zwingli, and further developed the notion of "election" as God's claim on the congregations worshiping God. In contrast, Heinrich Bullinger was more preoccupied with the concern of not overshadowing divine love as the base for the divine will for community. The notion of God's will to save all people (1 Tim. 2:4) was important for him, so that he was ready to forfeit logical speculations for it. He focused on God's "covenant" with God's people, thus becoming the founding father of the Reformed covenant theory.

Accordingly, it may be said that the place where Zwingli's message was conveyed was not the confessional, but the public assembly. The gospel aims at community and is mainly experienced in the community. It thus necessarily constitutes Christian congregations, giving them a special, "evangelic" form. Three further aspects shall here be mentioned.

The church as a community of learning

A well-known institution of the Zürich Reformation was the so-called Prophecy founded in 1525. A Bible passage from the Old Testament was interpreted daily, except for Fridays and Sundays, in the choir of the Grossmünster. First, the exegetes would spring into action and interpret the passage of the day on the basis of the Hebrew original and the Greek Septuagint version. Then, the results of the exegetical study were presented in German to the congregation. This institution had symbolic value: the Bible was now being interpreted in a place where the Latin Bible text, which no one understood, had previously been sung in the form of hymns. This was done in a way that aimed to approach the original text as closely as possible, on the one hand, and searched for the contemporary interpretation of the word of God, on the other. This institution evolved into the "Superior School" of Zürich. Learned scholars worked there to train theologians, especially in the biblical languages and in Bible exegesis. In fact, however, the intention was not just to train theologians, but also to educate a community of common people in biblical truth. Everybody should get to know and understand the word of God.

The Zürich Bible translations also emerged from the *Prophecy*. In 1529—five years before the completion of the Lutheran Bible—six volumes of the complete Zürich Bible were published. In the year of Zwingli's death (1531), they were amalgamated in one volume and published as the "Froschau Bible." In the ensuing years, a large number of different versions of the Bible and Bible commentaries were printed, both for scholars and for the general public. The Bible was at the very centre of the Swiss Reformation, in particular of the Zürich Reformation; it was more important than confessional writings, catechisms, or writings by the reformers.

In an effort to interpret the Bible with the best methods available, they gratefully resorted to humanistic education. The common steps of Bible interpretation included not only the consideration of different genres of biblical texts, their philological and rhetorical analyses, and their contextualization in the respective events and discourses, but also the consideration of Armenian paraphrases of the Bible as well as exegetic literature dating back to the Talmudic era, the time of the church fathers, and the Middle Ages. Heinrich Bullinger wrote a study guide for theology students, in which he introduced studies of classical antiquity and its philosophical, historical, and poetic works as a mandatory course to be completed before beginning biblical exegesis.

Bible study and exegesis were always a joint undertaking. There is no Zwingli Bible, but only a Zürich Bible. For the Swiss reformers and scholars, teamwork was a matter of course. This included discussions over difficult passages and acceptance of varied interpretations. The decisive criterion was better argumentation in terms of philology and context. This principle was also applied to the understanding of communion, which, according to their understanding, was to be interpreted in line with the Hebrew biblical tradition and in conjunction with other words by Jesus. On this point, two different cultures collided in Marburg.

Many of the writings by Zwingli and Bullinger end with this sentence: "Whoever can prove me wrong or improve my knowledge by referring to the Bible is hereby requested to do so." The biblical exegesis, the search for the divine word for the contemporary society, was a joint effort and study. And everybody was in need of learning. No single person possessed the truth. The fact that there were no bishops in the churches of the Swiss Reformation is consistent with this Reformation understanding of the priesthood of all believers. Bullinger called church officials *remigatores*, "rowers."

The church as a community of reconciliation and justice

Zwingli's communion liturgy provided that the bread be passed around in the community and that everyone break off a piece thereof. This was a revolution in view of the sacramental piety of that time, which was deeply rooted in the church's liturgical life as well as in the perception of the general public. Zwingli justified this rite with the following argument: if everyone passes the bread on to the next person, it may bring about reconciliation between two antagonized neighbours during the communion. Therefore, communion would have induced something important as a meal of reconciliation. By the same token, Zwingli argued against the exclusion from communion: the Lord's supper as a celebration of reconciliation could also be a place where impenitent sinners may return and repent. Therefore, nobody should be excluded from partaking in communion. The church as a place where the reconciliation with God in Christ is being celebrated can only be centred on reconciliation among individuals. Although ecclesiastical authorities, such as the marriage courts in Zürich in Bern and the consistory in Geneva, from a modern perspective had some strange features, they also attached more importance to the reconciliation between antagonized individuals within a Christian community than to "moral orders."

Reconciliation is not possible, however, without naming the injustice and reestablishing justice. It belongs to the particularities of the Swiss Reformation that the gospel was largely associated with political, judicial, and economic systems right from the start. The scope of the Reformation mandates endowed to the Christian authorities was not confined to the religious realm. They were also intended to rectify injustice, protect the weak, prevent usury and unlawful enrichment, make sure that nobody had to beg, and saw to it that the sick were attended to. Already, in one of his Disputation Articles, written in 1523, Zwingli used the rediscovered gospel to formulate the demand to the authorities: "Therefore all their laws ought to conform to the divine will so that they protect the oppressed person, though he may not actually lay a charge" (Article 39).

In his book *On the Divine and Human Justice,* Zwingli distinguished very clearly between the kingdom of God and the realities of the world. Religious utopias were not his concern. Yet, he was of the opinion that it is the duty of Christian communities to participate in modeling the worldly conditions whereby they might orient themselves to divine justice. This can only be done in a fragmented way, inchoately and incompletely, in consideration of realities, but that is just the way it should be done.

The so-called *Fürtrag* (petition) was established in Zürich under Heinrich Bullinger: pastors were given the right to appear before the political council and to admonish it, as the Old Testament prophets admonished their kings. This prophetic ministry was an important element of the Swiss Reformation. And it by no means only dealt with religious matters: poor relief as a duty of the entire polity, regulation on interest rates, the establishment of schools, mercenary and refugee policies, even public spending were on the agenda of daily political issues on which Bullinger pointed out to the council God's will for justice.

The church as a community of grateful confession

In his *Commentarius* of 1525, Zwingli formulated his doctrine of communion first and foremost as a "token of confession" and "gratitude." That is how he understood the biblical passages regarding the Lord's supper, and saw his understanding confirmed in the etymology of the Latin word *sacramentum* as meaning "oath of allegiance," as well as in the early-church designation of communion as "eucharist," a celebration of thanks.

As is well known, Zwingli attracted much criticism for this theological reading. Later, he attempted to take this criticism into account. Although his writings on communion from the last two years of his life have hardly been acknowledged until this day, the Swiss reformers after him took over and further developed his approach. Bucer and Calvin tried to find a middle ground between Zwingli's position of his later years and that of Luther. Heinrich Bullinger developed a doctrine of communion in which he tried to avoid overemphasizing a single aspect or a single Bible verse at the cost of others, but to let all aspects of the "Lord's supper" mentioned in the Bible come into play. The Lord's supper was thus understood as a celebration in which the whole life of the church is emblematically condensed. It is "eucharist," a celebration of the congregation that in gratitude remembers Christ's work of reconciliation ("Do this in remembrance of me"; 1 Cor. 11:24); as a celebration of the community, it is a form of proclamation of Christ, and it is at the same time an expression of the anticipation of the second coming of Christ, the one who was raised to be seated at the right hand of God ("For as often as you eat this bread and drink the cup, you proclaim the Lord's death until he comes"; 1 Cor. 11:26). What is celebrated is Christ's presence in his congregation (Matt. 18:20), which is invited to his table. Additionally, as a meal of fellowship, there is also an ethical dimension to the supper, for fellowship is impossible without mutual care and respect (cf. 1 Cor. 11:17-34). Bullinger's doctrine of communion has fallen far into oblivion, but only as far as the name of its author is concerned, for anyone who compares the doctrine of communion in the Lima document with Bullinger's doctrine will find many parallels. This is not as coincidental as it may appear at a first glance. The thoughts of "eucharist," of gratitude, and of confession are indeed always present, for public confession and thanks are essential parts of the life of the church. This theme of confession became a particularly pressing topic in the Protestant churches living in diaspora and in the persecuted churches. Here, a new culture of confession came into being to which especially Calvin made substantial contributions.

In the tradition of the Swiss Reformation, confession takes place not only vis-à-vis people but, first of all, vis-à-vis Christ himself, to whom the confession is made in responsibility before him. The "Reformed" do not refer to their own faith when they "confess." They invoke Christ. As part of their foundation, Swiss reformers share the conviction that no Christian simply has the true faith or true knowledge of faith—and can thus just simply "pass it on." No church has the right to present itself as the extended arm of divine grace, and no sacramental celebration is simply a distribution of the body of Christ. Every religious discourse and action is first and foremost a responsibility before God and can only occur in a prayer for the Holy Spirit. The Christian church is nothing other than a part of the world. However, the church is a praying world: *Veni creator spiritus!* Therefore, it is a thankful world, always confessing anew. This is the critical and, at the same time, beneficial significance of putting emphasis on the divine Spirit in the Swiss Reformation. It is only in this way that a Christian church or group can strive not for itself but for the advent of the reign of God, and thus implement its mandate.

What is the special contribution of the Swiss Reformation to the Reformation movement today?

Many of the aspects expounded above are by no means particular to the Swiss Reformation. As has already been pointed out, founding a religious sect was the last thing intended by the Swiss Reformation. Instead, it was committed to carrying out the simple and, at the same time, the most demanding task of taking seriously that which is basically Christian, namely, Christ himself as the Word of God and a place of divine reconciliation. The revival of confessionalism or the reverence of the founding fathers is opposed to the spirit of the Swiss Reformation. Yet, it is worth paying attention to the particular manner in which the Swiss reformers formulated their insights and tried to apply them to shape the church. A brief look into their writings soon reveals, however, that they were also not different from other reformers, in that they were all children of their time and thus shared its measurements and blind spots. We have only to recall such things as the brutal punishment system blatantly running counter to the Christian faith that none of those reformers challenged, the class society that they called into question only rudimentarily, the matter-of-course attitude with which they justified with Bible texts the necessity of a single official religion, thus carrying on or even aggravating the religious "intolerance" that humanity had known since ancient times, and the like. Is not precisely the upcoming jubilee a good opportunity for us also to distance ourselves from the reformers—in respectful criticism supported by Christian theological arguments—with respect to their *failures* to say and do right things in fulfillment of the missions with which they were entrusted? Zwingli and Bullinger, who expressly invited their readers to criticize or at least correct their standpoints on the basis of the gospel, should be especially open to—even thankful for—gospel-based criticisms.

From our brief historical excursion, the following conclusion may be drawn: the special contribution of the Swiss Reformation to the global Reformation movement of today and tomorrow consists mainly in one task, namely, the task of recalling and ensuring that all "Christian" churches built on Christ remain true places of a community of learning, of reconciliation and justice, and become increasingly more so—including the acknowledgment of our own guilt and failures—as well as being places to express gratitude and confession in a more visible and tangible form of political and social radiance. Whether the upcoming Reformation Jubilee will be an occasion to promote this task is yet to be seen.

CHAPTER 10

Jong Wha Park

Protestantism and Postconfessionalism in Korea

I am very happy to be here to talk about the Reformation and confessionalism, and to let you know how the Reformation is realized, accepted, and practiced in Korea, a country so distant from Europe. Korea does not belong to the so-called places of origin of the Reformation.[1] But this is merely a geographical distance. Korea is indeed coming closer to Germany and its Reformation. Therefore, we would like you to accept us as an authentic member of the Reformation. The doctrines of the Reformation are practiced by the Christian churches and confessions across the world and Korea shares them as such.

I am a Presbyterian and Reformed pastor. In the second half of the 1970s and up to the early '80s, I had an opportunity to work in the field of world mission and ecumenism while serving in a church in Württemberg. So

1 Editor's note: Dr Park's speech was delivered partly in English and partly in German. The languages were unified for the purpose of this publication and the text adjusted accordingly.

I thought, aha! This is ecumenical: Reformed and Lutheran together. I also learned that Wittenberg was the cradle of the churches stemming from the Reformation in this country. Through collaboration with the Protestant Mission Society of Southwest Germany, I came into contact with the churches here in Switzerland. This means that I worked with the authentically original Reformation churches in Europe. I came to form the idea that Reformation is a main topic in Europe, especially in Germany and Switzerland: they were living in the Reformation, with the Reformation, and for the Reformation.

After six years in pastoral service, I decided to continue my studies to enhance my chance to find a good job back home. So, I obtained my doctorate under the famous Reformed theologian, Jürgen Moltmann. Back in Korea, I became a university professor. This experience led me to the following insight: Reformation is not only a matter limited to church; rather, it is an epoch-making global event that we would like to celebrate together. This insight is viable from an academic standpoint on theology. This is also what I had experienced firsthand in Europe, in Germany and Switzerland. By that time, I thought and acted beyond the confines of confessionalism.

After ten years of service as a professor, I was given the post of the general secretary in a church-governing body. Shortly afterward, I suddenly realized: aha! I actually am a confessionalist. As a church official, in my capacity as general secretary, I of course had to represent and foster my confessional church. Without the office I was holding, I would probably have remained a nonconfessional theologian, but by virtue of this post, I became a Protestant pastor knowledgeable of and loyal to the confession I represent.

After another ten years of service, I again took a new office, this time as a parish pastor. Church members have little interest in confessionalism. Congregational changes and exchanges are quite common even beyond confessional borders, for instance, moving from a Methodist to a Presbyterian church or from a Pentecostal to a Presbyterian church.

So, as it were, church members have little interest in confessions or confessionalism. Church officials and church-governing boards are more or less interested in confessionality and confessionalism, and, indeed, in a way that, in my opinion, should not *necessarily* be continued. Only theologians are genuinely interested in it.

My conclusive note of this introduction before continuing is therefore the following: in Europe, I learned that the Reformation is concerned with confession. I remember a French theologian who said, "So listen, Jesus preached the kingdom of God. Through history emerged the church." What I actually mean by that is that the reformers put great efforts to reform the church, but confessional churches emerged as a result. Much reflection should still be made about the kingdom of God and the church, *basileia* and *ecclesia*, as well as about the Reformation and confession and their interaction and relationship, if we really want to celebrate this Jubilee together.

Further, we must say that the Reformation is always handed down through fixed rails of confessions, over which the train of church always rolls. We non-Europeans have to learn this as well. However, I must add that the confessions have to reform themselves as well, in order to hand down the spirit of the Reformation in a better and more authentic way, as shown in the example of Korean churches. I shall now elaborate on this further.

Korean Christianity in a Multireligious Context

Talking about religions in Korea, we can deal only with those religions in South Korea. It is generally agreed that religions enjoy a peaceful coexistence: Buddhism, Confucianism, Roman Catholicism, and Protestantism, and other traditional folk religions. Folk religions and newly arising religious societies like Islam together represent less than 0.5 percent of the total population in South Korea. Confucianism, which had replaced Buddhism as the state ideology during the five-century rule of the Yi Dynasty (1392–1910), has up to now been regarded as the standard for public ethics, social norms, or personal and filial loyal rules (e.g., ancestor worship, etc.). The primary living faiths and religions in Korea nowadays are mostly Buddhism and the two Christian religions. Nevertheless, there still exist interreligious dialogue and cooperative institutions and organizations at work, including various small religious societies.

To get a picture of the present state of mainline religions, let me offer some statistical observations from the Korean Ministry of Culture and Tourism's 2008 Population Census. In the years 1985, 1995, and 2005, the statistics respectively show the following percentages of believers relative to the total population:

- Religious believers: from 42.6 percent (1985), up to 50.7 percent (1995), and up to 53.1 percent (2005).
- Buddhists: from 19.9 percent (1985), up to 23.2 percent (1995), and down to 22.8 percent (2005).
- Protestants: from 16.1 percent (1985), up to 19.7 percent (1995), and down to 18.3 percent (2005).
- Roman Catholics: from 4.6 percent (1985), up to 6.6 percent (1995), and up to 10.9 percent (2005).

The 2008 Population Census shows the number of the believers as follows:

- Buddhists: 10,726,463 members in 21,935 temples with 49,408 monks.
- Protestants: 8,616,438 members in 58,404 churches with 94,615 pastors.
- Roman Catholics: 5,146,147 members in 1,511 churches with 14,597 priests.

Buddhism remains still the oldest and largest religion in Korea. It had been the state religion for more than 1000 years, until 1392, when Confucianism replaced it and drove it into the mountainside spiritual retreats. Almost at the end of the Confucian Yi Dynasty, first Roman Catholicism came into Korea from the European West, and then Protestantism arrived a century later from the American West.

Roman Catholicism began officially with the founding of the first house church in Seoul (1784) by the first baptized Korean, Lee Seung Hoon. He had gotten in touch with Jesuits in China and brought with him and his elite colleagues new techniques and scientific developments like the compass and telescope—so-called *so-hak* ("science from the West")—back to Korea. In the midst of decades of long political struggles during the Yi Dynasty, the power elites of the reform-minded, but eventually defeated, "Namnin Faction" took sides with the *so-hak*. Thereby, they received the then still-exotic Roman Catholicism as their faith community. The power struggle was then aggravated by the tabooed actions of the *so-hak* party. They refused the ancestor worship rite, which was the core symbol of Confucian political and filial ethics, as "idolatrous." Massive persecutions of "blasphemous" Catholics followed. In the light of these massacres, Napoleon's French Navy threatened several times with invading maneuvers. The conservative ruling dynasty and its elites reacted to this threat by further strengthening the persecutions, which led to increasing numbers of victims among priests and believers. The initial mission situation for Roman Catholicism in Korea was therefore filled with political and social turmoil as well as severe persecution.

Present-day Roman Catholicism enjoys the reverse side of its historical experiences. Its membership grows constantly, as is shown above. Its social credibility is among the highest of the religious communities in Korean society. Its interreligious dialogues and cooperation are going smoothly and well. Today, more people are converting from the Protestant to the Roman Catholic faith than vice versa. This challenges Protestants to think about and reshape their way of living and sharing their faith.

Two Tracks of Protestant Mission and Church

The sons and daughters of the Reformation, the Protestants in Korea, had perfect conditions to start as missionaries and establish a church life. At the beginning, the first track of mission was through traditional common Christian missionaries' work. Church historians agree that the arrival of two missionaries from U.S. Methodist and Presbyterian churches, Rev. Appenzeller and Rev. Underwood, in the harbour city of Inchon on Easter Sunday, 5 April 1885, marks the beginning of the Protestant mission and church in Korea. This occurred a century after the Roman Catholic's arrival in Korea. Unlike the persecution against the Catholic Christians, the royal house of the declining Yi Dynasty officially welcomed Protestantism from the USA as a "credible friend and supporter" for the self-reliance and freedom of Korea. On the international level, Korea then suffered increasingly from foreign threats and invasions, as Japan, China, and Russia all used the Korean peninsula as a battlefield for their hegemony in the region. Protestantism was seen as a religion of the USA, as the spiritual bastion of the actual power of the USA. Missionaries reported that the last king of Korea had almost declared Protestantism as Korea's "state religion." However, these efforts were in vain.

For Koreans, it is evident that "mission" and colonialism" do not belong together. Mission came from the American West, whereas colonialism was compelled by the non-Christian neighbouring country, Japan. In the Korean context, the Protestant mission in its beginning meant a protesting Christian mission against Japanese colonialism. For the mission-receiving people of Korea, mission was a protest for liberation. It was, therefore, a protest both for and against: a protest against suppression and for liberation. Mission was an act of protesting in both ways. It included a protesting "reaction against oppressive bondage" and "pro-action for liberating commitment." In this respect, such a practical Protestantism may, for instance, be referred to Martin Luther's dual concept of the freedom of a Christian: "A Christian is a perfectly free lord of all, subject to none" and "A Christian is a perfectly dutiful servant of all, subject to all."[2]

In a broader sense, the Protestant mission in the Korean context was initially understood and received as a carrier of the "political" or "social" gospel. An example thereof is the initiation of the March 1 Independence Movement in 1919 by Protestant leadership and congregations, which were actually still a minority at that time. This movement was joined and actively participated in by Buddhists and traditional religions' leaders (unfortunately,

---

2 According to Martin Luther, "The Freedom of a Christian," trans. W. A. Lambert, in Harold J. Grimm and Helmut T. Lehman, eds., *Luther's Works*, vol. 31: *Career of the Reformer I* (Philadelphia: Fortress Press, 1957).

there is no record of Roman Catholic participation). This was the beginning of Korean Christians' interreligious and interfaith dialogue and cooperation.

In another sense, the Protestant mission and church was also understood and received as a platform for "personal" comfort and salvation. Congregations and church gatherings were well attended from the start and abundant in personal and intercessory prayers. Important to mention in this context is the traditional "early morning prayer" of the Korean Protestant churches. Prior to going to work, people are invited to kneel down and to worship, praise, and pray. This explains the early morning prayer that takes place every morning in every church. According to the Japanese colonial police report, participants in the early morning prayer should be "in keen alert, because they not only pray for the salvation of souls, but are prayerfully crying and yearning for their national independence and freedom." Prayer in words and deeds belong together in the Protestant practice of faith.

The second track of Protestant mission and church had been paved by means of the Bible being translated into the common Korean language. In Korea, Chinese characters are perceived similarly to Latin in the Western world, meaning that they are not really accessible by the common people. *Hangul*—which is the common language for Korean people, like Koine for the people in Jesus' time—was the instrument through which the Bible, in the Protestant mission's initial period, was part by part translated and transmitted even into the hands of women and lower-class people who did not have access to literary education and training. The Bible worked miracles. Translations gave the language a systematic grammar. The translated Bible communicated with people, leading to rapid and meaningful evangelism and mission. What exactly happened with Luther's translation of the Bible in the time of the Reformation?

It is a historical fact that the Bible had been translated into Korean even before the arrival of first Protestant missionaries. Some reform-minded people of literacy and nobility had already been in contact with European (Scottish) scholars of the Bible Society of Scotland. They were working as missionaries in Manchuria, China, early in 1882, and then in Japan in 1887. They translated the Bible into Korean from Chinese and, respectively, from Japanese. Interestingly, Appenzeller and Underwood already carried some parts of the Bible translated into Korean when they first arrived in Inchon in 1885.

This initiative of Bible translation within Korea and the arrival of missionaries from outside intertwined to become the backbone of Protestant mission and church in Korea. The translation of the Bible suited the cultural context of Korean society, with its high and absolute educational fervour, which also largely represents aspects of Korean-Confucianism. The introduction and opening of modern schools—that is, modernized mission schools—by the missionaries and mission boards contributed greatly to the Protestant mission works. By "modern," I mean especially the equality of educational opportunities beyond differences in gender, social status, class, and economic standing. Just think of the thousand-year-long, male-dominated social structure and the hereditary class discrepancy between nobles and servants, rich and poor.

It is true contextually that Roman Catholicism had a difficult position in Korea, since, during its emergence, it struggled with the still-powerful feudalism of Korean society, whereas this same Korean feudalistic society later received Protestantism as a favoured salvific force due to its own dismantling and collapse. However, not only the living context varies, but also the mission and church life.

Confessionalism or/and Postconfessionalism

Missionaries stood for their own confession. The arrival of foreign missionaries began with the Northern Presbyterians (with Underwood) and the Northern Methodists (with Appenzeller) from the USA in 1885. Simply said, they were followed by the Anglicans in 1890, the Australian Presbyterians in 1891, the Southern Presbyterians/USA in 1892, the Southern Methodists/USA in 1896, the Canadian Presbyterians in 1898, and the Salvation Army in 1908.

In terms of mission and unity, I would say the Korean experience is twofold: mission in unity was impracticable, unity in mission was impossible. In the early church history of Korea, first Korean Protestants were eager to do mission and build churches by establishing a "firm" and healthy faith. However, the first Protestant missionaries were also eager to do mission and build churches by holding up a more solid and loyal "order." That was the picture of "faith and order" ecumenism in the early Protestantism in Korea.

In the time of colonialism (1910–1945), of the Korean War (1950–1953), and the national division thereafter, Korean Protestant churches and missions had lived through ups and downs. In 1905, there was a serious unity discussion and agreement among Korean church leaders and mission societies to build a Church of Christ in Korea. However, this enterprise later failed.

The Japanese colonial government actually rejected a united church of Koreans and missionaries, as it was perceived as a potentially strong antagonist to their rule. Confessional loyalty and missionaries' meritocratic way of thinking eventually lead to the dictum: "March separately for more souls." Not only missionaries but also home-mission boards had few commonalities in understanding mission and church ecumenically yet. Their main concern was mostly with creating a confessional order to be effective and supportive for their own mission works.

Confessionalism and confessional allegiance were just given without any consideration or discernment. It was not a choice at all. In view of the imminent de jure colonial rule of 1910, there was a big conflict between Korean leaders opting for a uniting church and confessionally—or, rather, denominationally—oriented missionaries. The 1907 mass revival gatherings, resulting in a successful evangelization, targeted a strengthening of faith for life, on the one hand, and a reconciliation between two conflicting partners, on the other. In the later period of colonialism, Japanese rulers compelled all the confessions and denominations of Korean Christianity to join the one United Church of Christ in Japan. This coerced unity, naturally, was cast off with the liberation of Korea from Japanese colonial rule in 1945. National liberation brought Korean churches' confessional division forth more strongly.

Today, confessional missionary societies are all integrated into their local partner churches of the same confession. It was not even the question of confessional identity and confessional unity, but denominational divisions and separations within one and the same confession. An example of this is the harsh denominational divisions among Presbyterians. Theological disputes, regional and factional conflicts, ecumenical and antiecumenical conflicts, political-ideological disparities—all these are basically nontheological factors. At present, more than 200 Presbyterian denominations are registered, though they together confess the same Presbyterian credo and share, for example, the Westminster Confession. Once a denomination is orderly established, it acquires a fixed political and organizational structure. Interconfessional ecumenism is a challenge. This can be seen in the work of the National Council of Churches, which does not include the majority of confessional churches. Even more difficult is an interdenominational ecumenism within a confession like in Presbyterianism, because one and the same credo does not prove to be a binding force of unity in the face of power relations and political struggles among churches. A unity in faith, as expressed in creedal statements, is not always visible. And even such an invisible unity in faith is not always to be experienced. So, what now?

Korean Protestant churches are used to saying, "Marching forward in separation!" Confessional and denominational divisions and competition eventually helped churches to grow faster. Growth comes first and has been the top priority in mission work. In the wake of this growth movement, small churches have been established. Theirs is not a separate form of ecclesial institution, but they serve just as a temporary shelter for becoming bigger and larger. About 80 percent of all Protestant churches comprise such shelters, which depend on subsidies from self-reliant large churches or megachurches.

The problem is that their growth has stopped in recent years. Megachurches and large churches swallow members even from among these small churches. The "rich and poor" discrepancy among congregations and churches grows constantly. These are the consequences of an unlimited competition for quantitative growth of church and mission without ecumenical cooperation and dialogue in faith and practice.

People in Korea say that in the past the churches had been concerned about the world, but that now it is the other way around: the world is concerned deeply about the churches, their struggle for self-existence, and the church's shaky public mandate, which has lost its resonance within the world. "Churches" here mean Protestant churches, which seem to be losing their dynamic power of "Protestant-ism."

Now: A Second Reformation?

1. Structural renewal of the Protestant churches

We need to stop new church-planting actions in this unlimited denominational/confessional competition and build interconfessional cooperation at a local level to establish a common parish church.

Mission and diaconal services need to be restructured and coordinated in an interconfessional way to avoid duplication of resources and to foster commitments.

We need to facilitate pulpit exchanges and enhance congregational encounters among different confessions for closer mutual understanding and acceptance.

2. Building ecumenical cohesiveness

We need to nourish tolerance toward neighbouring religions in a multireligious living context by:

- Respecting other confessions in a multiconfessional church context;
- Identifying together things to be protested (critical solidarity);
- Building consensus about things to work for (seeking alternatives).

We need to work for a paradigm change in attitude of Protestants toward Roman Catholics: from a church of *reformata* (alone) to a church of *semper reformanda* (together).

CHAPTER 11

Olav Fykse Tveit

The Legacy of the Reformation and Its Significance for the Ecumenical Movement Today

This reflection on the legacy of the Reformation and its significance for the ecumenical movement comes from the perspective of the World Council of Churches (WCC). Our global fellowship of churches includes the Evangelical Church in Germany (EKD), the Federation of Swiss Protestant Churches (SEK-FEPS), and the many churches you represent, and indeed, most of the people in this gathering. As this is a real but partial gathering of our global fellowship of churches. I find it natural to make my primary common reference point in this presentation the convergence text on ecclesiology from the Commission on Faith and Order, *The Church: Towards a Common Vision* (2012). My foreword to *The Church* identifies this text as a reflection of "the constitutional aims and self-identity of the WCC as a fellowship of churches who call each other to the goal of visible unity."[1]

1 *The Church: Towards a Common Vision* (Geneva: WCC, 2013), vi. I thank my colleague, Rev. Dr John Gibaut, Director of Faith and Order, for his valuable contributions to this presentation in the light of this Fairh and Order document.

The constitution of the WCC states

> The primary purpose of the fellowship of churches in the World Council of Churches is to call one another to visible unity in one faith and in one eucharistic fellowship, expressed in worship and common life in Christ, through witness and service to the world, and to advance towards that unity in order that the world may believe.[2]

From the perspective of the WCC and its commitment to Christian unity, an inescapable starting point for any ecumenical reflection, including on the ecumenical impact of 16th-century Reformation can only be an ecumenical hermeneutic of mutual accountability being humble, honest, and hopeful.[3] This corresponds to the essence of Lutheran theology, namely the renewal of the gospel as the basis for anything and for everything we are and do as church.

It is sobering to remember that the decision to identify 31 October 1517 as the beginning of the Reformation was made in 1617, making it the first centenary celebration in the modern era.[4] The choice was no accident. It was made in Saxony, where the memory of Martin Luther nailing his theses to the door of the Castle Church in Wittenberg was strong. It was clear in 1617 that Europe was heading toward conflict, a war of religion. The Protestant communities in Germany and throughout continental Europe needed a central authority or a common point of reference to galvanize a sense of identity. That is what 1517 provided: a common narrative, a point of reference. So, the first commemoration of 1517 was a prelude to a series of devastating religious wars, the Thirty Years Wars, transforming the memory of Luther's bold act in 1517 into a weapon.

As a Norwegian I will also remind you that for Norway the Reformation was a sovereign act by the Danish King in 1536, and not something that grew out of a change of faith in the people of the church.

Intra-European and colonial wars have continued into our own 20th century, and while the root causes have not necessarily been religious, the divided disciples of Jesus continued to find themselves on different sides of lethal conflicts. At the beginning of the ecumenical movement in the wake of the First World War, the churches knew that they could not authentically be makers of justice and peace as long as they were divided from and against one another. And so, a significant element of the modern ecumenical movement

---

2 See Article 3, Constitution and rules (as amended by the 9th WCC Assembly, Porto Alegre, Brazil, February 2006).

3 See Olav Fykse Tveit, "Unity: A Call to be Strong or Humble? " *Ecumenical Review* 65.2 (July 2013), 171-80.

4 See "Reformation Centenary Broadsheet," in Neil MacGregor, *A History of the World in 100 Objects* (London: Allen Lane/Penguin Book, 2010), 552-58.

was the reaction of the churches to all wars. In this context, the 1925 Conference on Life and Work in Stockholm said to the churches:

> … The sins and sorrows, the struggles and losses of the Great War and since, have compelled the Christian Churches to recognise, humbly and with shame, that "the world is too strong for a divided Church." The Conference itself is a conspicuous fact. But it is only a beginning.
>
> We confess before God and the world the sins and failures of which the Churches have been guilty, through lack of love and sympathetic understanding. The call of the present hour to the Church should be repentance, and with repentance a new courage springing from the inexhaustible resources which are in Christ.[5]

Or, as the message of the First World Conference on Faith and Order said in its message to the churches in 1927:

> God wills our unity. Our presence in this Conference bears testimony to our desire to bend our will to His. However we may justify the beginnings of our disunion, we lament its continuance and henceforth must labour, in penitence and faith, to build up our broken walls.[6]

This lament corresponds deeply to the core message of the theses on the doors in Wittenberg in 1517. Only through real penitence, regret, and remorse can there be real experiences of the life-giving grace of God, or in other words, God's grace cannot be a commodity or token, only received by being humble, honest, and hopeful: in other words, in faith.

The shadow of war hung over the First Assembly of the WCC in 1948. The message of the assembly states bleakly: "Over all mankind hangs the peril of total war. We have to accept God's judgement upon us for our share in the world's guilt."[7] The stark starting point of the WCC in 1948 from "Man's disorder and God's design" did not stem from the divisions of the 16th century alone but from much earlier, as well as much later. The continuing ecclesial divisions from the Council of Chalcedon in the mid-5th century belong to the memory of division of the Oriental Orthodox churches, rather than 1517. For the Eastern Orthodox and the Western Catholic churches, the mid-11th century marks the significant experience of ecclesial division, rather than 1517.

---

5 §§2-3 from the "Message" from the Universal Christian Conference on Life and Work, Stockholm, 1925. In *The Ecumenical Movement: An Anthology of Key Texts and Voices,* ed. Michael Kinnamon and Brian E. Cope (Geneva: WCC, 1997), 265.

6 "The Call to Unity," First World Conference on Faith and Order, unanimously adopted by the full Conference, 20 August 1927.

7 "The Message of the Assembly," in *The First Assembly of the World Council of Churches,* ed. W. A. Visser 'T Hooft (London: SCM Press, 1949), 9.

Even within the churches of the West shaped by the Reformation, 1517 is not a common commemoration. Anglicans, Anabaptists, Evangelicals, Methodists, and many others have different histories of reform and division.

These observations are not to minimize or relativize the significance of the year 1517, or its 500th anniversary in 2017. I hope that they will serve as a reminder that from the ecumenical perspective of the fellowship of the WCC, the Reformation and its beginnings need to be seen, assessed, and commemorated from wider historical and ecumenical perspectives.

These same observations also highlight the ecumenical significance of both Reformed and Lutheran communities being able to celebrate 2017 together. The difference between the situation when Martin Luther and Ulrich Zwingli left Marburg in 1529 and that of today when EKD and FEPS hold this consultation together in Zurich, which is also 40 years after the Leuenberg Agreement, is remarkable.

The effect of the 16th-century Reformation on global Christianity, and indeed, on world history, is undeniable. Let me identify some of the legacies of the Reformation to the ecumenical movement, legacies that are both affirmations of the theological focus of the Reformation and accompanying challenges for today.

Bible and Hermeneutics

The recovery of the Bible as a primary source of authority is one of the great legacies of the Reformation to be affirmed ecumenically. As the Faith and Order text *The Church: Towards a Common Vision* succinctly states: "All Christians share the conviction that the Scripture is normative."[8] The translation and proclamation of the scriptures into vernacular, printed Bibles, biblical preaching, biblical hymnody, and biblical scholarship all contributed to making the Bible a living authority in the churches—one of the great legacies of the 16th century to global Christianity. Its legacy continues through the ecumenical movement in things such as common translations of the Bible and the recovery of a common lectionary for the proclamation of scripture at the eucharist and in services on the word on Sundays, largely derived from the Roman Catholic lectionary produced after the Second Vatican Council. The flourishing of biblical scholarship, the study of the Bible in universities, colleges, and seminaries, and congregational Bible studies have been ecumenical achievements. While the goal of visible unity in one eucharistic fellowship has yet to be achieved, the churches already find their visible unity in the biblical word of God.

An ongoing challenge of the Reformation for the churches and the ecumenical movement is biblical hermeneutics: How is the Bible to be read and

8 *The Church*, §11.

interpreted, and by whom? What is the relationship between the Bible and Tradition? How are the scriptures authoritative in the life of the church today? What are the relationships between individual and community readings of the Bible? These issues have long been on the agenda of the ecumenical movement, such as the Faith and Order study. A convergence on these questions was proposed at the Third Conference on Faith and Order in Montreal, 1963, offering also the Lutheran hermeneutical key to the common reading of the scriptures, namely the liberating word of the gospel:

> … we can say that we exist as Christians by the Tradition of the Gospel (the paradosis of the kerygma) testified in Scripture, transmitted in and by the Church through the power of the Holy Spirit. Tradition taken in this sense is actualised in the preaching of the Word, in the administration of the Sacraments and worship, in Christian teaching and theology, and in mission and witness to Christ by the lives of the members of the Church.[9]

Faith and Order reflection on "Scripture, Tradition and traditions" continues into the present in study texts such as "Treasure in Earth Vessels: An Instrument for an Ecumenical Reflection on Hermeneutics," and more recently in the reflection on "Sources of Authority." Yet despite the vast ecumenical study on biblical hermeneutics, unresolved issues from the Reformation regarding biblical interpretation surface in recent instances of Christian division between the churches and within them, especially around questions of moral discernment. The ecclesiological issues are the role of the church as an interpreting community, the relationship of the Christian believer and the community, and the diminished capacity for divided Christians to discern together. As the message of the Amsterdam assembly succinctly stated:

> As we have talked with each other here, we have begun to understand how our separation has prevented us from receiving correction from one another in Christ. And because we have lacked this correction, the world has often heard from us not the Word of God but words of men.[10]

The 9th Assembly at Porto Alegre posed the same challenge in a different way:

> The relationship among churches is dynamically interactive. Each church is called to mutual giving and receiving gifts and to mutual accountability. Each church must become aware of all that is provisional in its life and have the courage to acknowledge this to other churches.[11]

9 "Scripture, Tradition and Traditions," I.45, in *The Fourth Conference on Faith and Order: The Report from Montreal 1963*, ed. P. C. Rodger and L. Vischer (London: SCM Press, 1964), 51-52.

10 Amsterdam 1948, "The Message of the Assembly," 9.

11 "Called to be the One Church," in *God, in your grace… Official Report of the Ninth Assembly of the World Council of Churches*, ed. Luis N. Rivera-Pagan (Geneva: WCC, 2007), 257, §7.

Culture and Catholicity

The Reformation gave a renewed accent on both culture and context. An obvious example is language and the vernacular in biblical translations and liturgy. In the German states, Luther's vernacular translation of the Bible gave rise to a common form of German and a growing sense of cultural cohesion. The same can be said about the legacies of the 16th-century Book of Common Prayer and the 17th-century authorised version of the Bible in England and their impact on the development of the English language. That today English has become the international language, not least amongst ecumenical and other church-based institutions such as the WCC, is something of a legacy from the English reformation in the 16th and 17th centuries.

The Reformation emphasis on culture, context, and diversity is a legacy to the ecumenical movement that is affirmed in *The Church*:

> Legitimate diversity in the life of communion is a gift from the Lord . . . The disciples are called to be fully united, while respectful of and enriched by their diversities. The Gospel needs to be proclaimed in languages, symbols and images that are relevant to particular times and contexts so as to be lived authentically in each time and place.[12]

And yet the same legacy is also an ecumenical challenge. Culture-based churches claimed autonomy in the 16th century, largely in opposition to Roman primacy, but apart from one another as well. Many of the churches that asserted their local cultures at the Reformation, in their later colonial and missionary enterprises imposed much of those same cultures on other peoples. *The Church* continues on this point:

> Legitimate diversity is compromised whenever Christians consider their own cultural expressions of the Gospel as the only authentic ones, to be imposed upon Christians of other cultures.[13]

As an accentuation of culture may threaten catholicity, Faith and Order cautions:

> The essential catholicity of the Church is undermined when cultural and other differences are allowed to develop into division. Christians are called to remove all obstacles to the embodiment of this fullness of truth and life bestowed upon the Church by the power of the Holy Spirit.[14]

Threats to catholicity ultimately threaten the unity and mission of the church:

> At the same time, unity must not be surrendered. Through shared faith in Christ, expressed in the proclamation of the Word, the celebration of

12 *The Church*, §28.

13 Ibid.

14 Ibid., §22.

the sacraments and lives of service and witness, each local church is in communion with the local churches of all places and all times.[15]

Liturgy, Sacraments, and Ecclesiology

Questions around culture identity and diversity in the 16th century were expressed concretely in the lives of ordinary Christians in weekly liturgy and sacramental theology. The colloquy of Marburg failed because of significant disagreement on eucharistic theology, leaving the eucharist as one of the theological and pastoral battlefields of the Reformation.

And yet there was a common zeal for eucharistic renewal that was common to most of the major reformers from Jan Huss in the early 15th century to Martin Luther, Martin Bucer, John Calvin, and Thomas Cranmer in the 16th century and into the 18th century with John Wesley. The renewed vision of the eucharist (Lord's Supper or Holy Communion) was one in which there was a balance of word and sacrament, celebrated in the vernacular, every Sunday, where the laity and clergy together would receive holy communion in both the bread and the cup—the sacramental body and blood of Christ. It was a compelling vision of the church as a eucharistic community. The common vision of weekly communion for laity and clergy was a direct challenge to the theology, piety, and canon law of the late medieval church, where only the clergy would regularly receive, and the laity once a year. The insistence that laity receive both bread and wine was a radical recovery; in the medieval church, and in the Roman Catholic Church until the liturgical reforms of the Second Vatican Council, communion in both kinds for lay people was forbidden. In Western Christianity, the utraquism (*sub utaque specie*) of the early 15th-century teaching of Jan Hus was a grassroots mark of the Reformation from the 16th century to the 20th century, and expressed a different ecclesiological vision of the equality and dignity of the baptised lay person who would receive holy communion in both kind and on every Sunday. The implicit ecclesiological consequence was not to distinguish "church" and "people," but rather to express that Christian people are the church. Sadly, this liturgical vision of the church was never fully achieved in the 16th century, but it was received in the liturgical renewal of the 20th century through the ecumenical movement.[16] With some irony, the Reformation legacy around eucharistic praxis would find expression in the liturgical reforms initiated by the Second Vatican Council.

15 Ibid., §29.

16 Cf. "The liturgical renewal among some churches may be seen in part as a reception of the convergence registered in ecumenical dialogue about the sacraments." Ibid., §43.

The challenge of the Reformation to the ecumenical movement on the eucharist is in terms of theology as well as praxis. The failure of Marburg and the protracted disunity between Lutheran and Reformed Christians until the Leuenberg Agreement of 1973 was due to the central question of Reformation sacramental theology: Is the risen and ascended Lord present in the eucharistic bread and wine? While both Luther and later Calvin disagreed with Zwingli, subsequent Swiss and German reformers continued to disagree with one another. Where they were united was in their common opposition to classical Western Catholic teaching on eucharistic theology. One of the deeply disturbing features of the 16th century was that Christians were prepared to kill—and to be killed—because of their beliefs about the eucharist, the sacrament of unity.

Questions around eucharistic theology have been on the agenda of the ecumenical movement, both in the bilateral dialogues between the churches and at the multilateral level of the Commission on Faith and Order. The convergence reached on the eucharist in Baptism, Eucharist and Ministry (1982) was one of the most well received parts of the text. Through the use of the biblical term *anamnesis*, Faith and Order resolved the two great 16th-century eucharistic controversies: eucharistic sacrifice and the presence of Christ. By first identifying the eucharist as the "living and effective sign" of Christ's sacrifice, BEM states that "Christ himself with all that he has accomplished for us and for all creation is present in this anamnesis granting us communion with himself. The eucharist is also a foretaste of his parousia."[17]

The simple yet profound resolution in Baptism, Eucharist and Ministry of some of the deeply divisive issues from the 16th century shaped bilateral dialogue on the eucharist and contributed to the renewal of eucharistic liturgies of the churches, as well as in their eucharistic theology and praxis. Western liturgical renewal has been one of the most exemplary instances of receptive ecumenism.

In *The Church*, the vision of the eucharist as the operative paradigm for understanding Christian unity as *koinonia* only makes sense in light of ecumenical convergence achieved in Baptism, Eucharist and Ministry on the sacramental theology and praxis:

> There is a growing consensus that koinonia, as communion with the Holy Trinity, is manifested in three interrelated ways: unity in faith, unity in sacramental life, and unity in service. The liturgy, especially the celebration of the eucharist, serves as a dynamic paradigm for what such koinonia looks like in the present age. In the liturgy, the people of God experience

17 *Baptism, Eucharist and Ministry* (Geneva: WCC, 1982), §§ 5, 6.

> communion with God and fellowship with Christians of all times and places. They gather with their presider, proclaim the Good News, confess their faith, pray, teach and learn, offer praise and thanksgiving, receive the Body and Blood of the Lord, and are sent out in mission. . . . Strengthened and nourished by the liturgy, the Church must continue the life-giving mission of Christ in prophetic and compassionate ministry to the world and in struggle against every form of injustice and oppression, mistrust and conflict created by human beings.[18]

We have significant manifestations of this *koinonia* in the agreements of Leuenberg, Meissen, and Porvoo and many others in other continents, particularly in North America.

And yet, despite the affirmations in *The Church*, a challenge from the 16th, 11th, and 5th century divisions is that some of us are still unable to receive one another in one eucharistic fellowship. Despite the degree of agreement in eucharistic theology achieved in the bilateral dialogues, and especially in the convergences reflected in the responses to Baptism, Eucharist and Ministry, the underlying issues continue unresolved. They are what Faith and Order identifies as "the most difficult issues facing the churches in overcoming any remaining obstacles to their living out the Lord's gift of communion: our understanding of the nature of the Church itself."[19] This is one important reason why a proper perspective on 2017 should be how we focus on the witness to the values of the kingdom of God, the gifts of justice and peace of the church, and look at the church from that perspective. This is also what we will do in the forthcoming assembly in Busan.

Martyrdom and Memory

Protestant critique of medieval Christianity includes the perceived lack of lively faith and understanding in their pre-Reformation forebears. More recent study points to different conclusions, and suggests both the vitality and limitations that are true of any era. A sign of the vitality of late medieval Christianity was its capacity for reform and renewal. Luther, Zwingli, Calvin, Bucer, Cranmer, and the other reformers are legacies of the late medieval Catholic Church. I marvel at the capacity of every part of Western Christianity to change and grow in the 16th century, including the Roman Catholic Church before, during, and after the Council of Trent. That capacity for conversion in the sense of metanoia is a legacy of the time of Reformation.

The challenge to the ecumenical movement is the legacy that not all in the 16th century discerned the word of God in the same way. The diversity in biblical interpretation, doctrine, and practice led to irreconcilable differences,

18 *The Church*, §67.

19 Ibid., 1.

over which Christians were prepared not only to separate from one another but to go to war with one another. The memories and martyrs of separation are legacies from the 16th century that continue to be an ecumenical challenge.

There is an interesting project from Faith and Order called The Cloud of Witnesses that explores the commemoration of saints—the holy women and men of faith. It raises the question of a mutual receiving from one another our martyrs of the Reformation era. Is it possible to receive as "saints" in one church the martyrs whom their forbears killed of another church? Such a reception of each other's martyrs belongs to the ongoing process of the healing of memories.

There have been recent acts of healing of memories. At this gathering in Zurich let us remember when in 2007 the Swiss Reformed churches asked the descendants of the Swiss Anabaptist movement for forgiveness for the martyrdoms that took place here in the 1520s, as well as the apology given in 2010 by the Lutheran World Federation at its assembly in Stuttgart to representatives of the Mennonite World Conference for the persecution of Anabaptists from the 16th century and beyond.

The WCC journeys to Busan with the prayer "God of life, lead us to justice and peace." Within an ecumenical hermeneutic of mutual accountability about our histories, this prayer evokes repentance for the violence perpetrated by Christians against each other and in conflict with peoples of other faiths and toward people of other religions. We are recalling the lament of Amsterdam 1948: "We have to accept God's judgement upon us for our share in the world's guilt." There is a healing of memories that needs to continue. There is a need to continue with the insights and challenges of the 2011 International Ecumenical Peace Convocation. There is the challenge of the Pilgrimage of Justice and Peace after the assembly this year. The ecumenical movement needs to engage new partners in the Pilgrimage of Justice and Peace from civil society, other faith communities, and especially within the Christian family. Why is it, for instance, that so few of the historic peace churches belong to the WCC? Why are there only two Mennonite churches from Europe who are part of our fellowship? Is this also a challenge to the ecumenical movement from the 16th century?

Ecclesia Semper Reformanda or Renovanda?

The 16th century was not the beginning or end of reform, but a trenchant moment in a process that is as old as the church itself. It is unique in the scope of its reforms, but also in its consequences, namely a dramatic experience of Christian disunity. As the churches today continue to respond to the different demands of proclaiming the gospel in rapidly changing contexts, we are again in a time of fresh expressions of reform and renewal. As Faith and Order notes in *The Church*:

> Today the proclamation of the kingdom of God continues throughout the world within rapidly changing circumstances. Some developments are particularly challenging to the Church's mission and self-understanding. . . . The "emerging churches," which propose a new way of being the Church, challenge other churches to find ways of responding to today's needs and interests in ways which are faithful to what has been received from the beginning. In some places, the Church faces the challenge of a radical decline in membership and is perceived by many as no longer relevant to their lives, leading those who still believe to speak of the need for a re-evangelization.[20]

The WCC is often asked how it can assist the churches, especially from the global North, to be renewed. What from the 16th century can the ecumenical movement harvest in order to discern how the Holy Spirit is renewing the churches today? What are experiences that the Spirit invites us not to repeat?

The topic of reform and renewal has also been raised in a very different context. In 2006 the Conference of Secretaries of the Christian World Communions asked Faith and Order to convene a World Conference in 2017 on "Reform and Renewal." In light of the anticipated celebrations in Germany and in Europe that year, in the Lutheran World Federation and its member churches, and throughout the Protestant world more generally, the Conference of Secretaries wanted an ecumenical contribution that includes Orthodox and Roman Catholics as equal members.

The title "Reform and Renewal" was problematic for Faith and Order, particularly for the Orthodox members who do not speak about the ecclesial body of Christ as being reformable or changeable, although they affirm that it stands in constant need of renewal. So, the theme in 2017 is simply "Renewal." The work begins in a few weeks in Busan in the Ecumenical Conversation "Transformed by Renewal." I have strongly supported this idea several times. The issue of renewal is at the heart of the proposed Unity Statement of the assembly:

> Only as Christians are reconciled and renewed by God's Spirit will the Church bear authentic witness to the possibility of reconciled life for all people, for all creation. It is often in its weakness and poverty, suffering as Christ suffers, that the Church is truly sign and mystery of God's grace.

Renewal is an ecumenical challenge, for while all churches recognize the biblical call to renewal, different expressions of renewal continue to be

20 Ibid., §7.

church-dividing. Thus, theological clarity on the authentic signs and fruits of renewal is vital. The aims of the WCC conversation on renewal are to articulate ecumenically what renewal means from a theological perspective; to identify authentic signs of renewal pastorally; and to receive the fruits of each other's experiences of renewal ecumenically. As Faith and Order proposed in its 1990 study document *Church and World: The Unity of the Church and the Renewal of the Human Community*,

> The church too stands under the judgement of the word of God, and in its human and historical reality is called to repentance and renewal. It is called "to become what it is," to embody in its historical and institutional life its true nature as a holy, reconciled and reconciling community.[21]

It will ask why some renewal movements divide churches. *Church and World* insists that the search for unity and the search for renewal are inseparable and flow from God's will, revealed in Jesus that the churches are called "both to visible unity among themselves and to common witness and service for the renewal of human community."[22] This belongs to an understanding of purpose of the church as the "sign and servant" of "God's design to gather humanity and all creation into communion under the Lordship of Christ" as articulated in *The Church: Towards a Common Vision.*[23] The same spirit of renewal is reflected in *Together Towards Life*, the new WCC mission statement:

> God's love does not proclaim a human salvation separate from the renewal of the whole creation. We are called to participate in God's mission beyond our human-centred goals. God's mission is to all life and we have to both acknowledge it and serve it in new ways of mission. We pray for repentance and forgiveness, but we also call for action now.[24]

From the ecumenical perspective of mutual accountability, we have to ask: What are the theological distinctions between reformation, transformation, and renewal? The ecumenical commemoration of 2017 should be humble, honest, and hopeful—asking how and praying that the gospel can both renew and unite us as churches.

---

21 *Church and World: The Unity of the Church and the Renewal of the Human Community* (WCC: Geneva, 1990), 2-3.

22 Ibid., 4.

23 *The Church,* §25.

24 *Together Towards Life: Mission and Evangelism in Changing Landscapes* (WCC: Geneva, 2013), 38, §105.

Part Four

Themes and Impact of the Reformation

A. Church History

CHAPTER 12

Fulvio Ferrario

Earlier Reformations and the Reformation

Pierre Valdo, Jan Hus, John Wycliffe, Girolamo Savonarola

Four figures are depicted on the rather impressive pulpit (so impressive, in fact, that it is not normally used) of the Waldensian Church located at Rome's Piazza Cavour. Two are well known (Martin Luther and John Calvin), the others not so much: Arnaldo of Brescia and Girolamo Savonarola. Arnaldo (1099–1155) preached poverty, the renunciation of the worldly power of the church, the value of lay preaching, the invalidity of sacraments administered by unworthy priests, and the right of laypeople over against those of priests. He was excommunicated, hanged, and, subsequently, his corpse burnt. Savonarola (1452–1498), a Dominican, preached for an ethical renewal of the church and society in the heyday of the Florentine Renaissance. While he seemingly had the aura of the prophetic, a good number of his contemporaries and historians viewed him as not entirely free of fanatical tendencies. The ruling Medici family and Pope Alexander VI conspired to have him convicted of being a heretic and agitator. He, too, was hanged and burnt. In 1997, the Archdiocese of Florence began the canonical process for his beatification.

Why should the people who built the Waldensian Church at Piazza Cavour, over a hundred years ago, have wanted to draw attention to these two figures alongside Luther and Calvin? The answer is simple enough. First, this Protestant church in the midst of the papal city wanted to provide a reminder in images, pseudo-mosaics, and windows painted with early church themes that Protestant Christianity is rooted in the apostolic tradition (!). The figures of Arnaldo and Savonarola, moreover, aim to call attention to the fact that there was a pre-Luther and pre-Calvin Reformation history, especially also in Italy. The church of *sola scriptura* thus does not only *have* a *tradition*, but *is tradition*, even in Italy, and it is no *less* so than the Roman Catholicism, but, indeed, *differently so.*

This, however, allows us to recognize the difficulty of the entire topic: Is it enough to be "against Rome" in one way or another in order to count as "pre-Reformation"? Are "our Protestants"—as the Waldensian historian Emilio Comba, at the end of the 19th century, described men such as Petrus Valdus, but indeed also Arnaldo and Savonarola—really to be viewed as the predecessors of Luther and Calvin? Or does this only inappropriately overextend the term *Reformation*, theologically and historically? A reasonable answer should, of course, be one of nuance, particularly so if viewed within the European context. So, it is impossible to speak of Valdus and Savonarola, Arnaldo and Wycliffe, all at the same time. We can with certainty, and not even unjustifiably, list a number of topics that could be described as characterizing a particular continuity: for example, the theological significance of scripture, a more or less radical questioning of the medieval classification of word and sacrament, critique of clericalism, and an emphasis on the role of the laity. This would, however, lead directly to the major discussion on the continuity and discontinuity between the "first" and "second" Reformation, a discourse that would be impossible to summarize here, and much less to improve upon with new ideas. I will therefore limit myself to two dimensions, whereby "dimension" means more than just a "topic" here. Rather, it represents dynamics that form that which makes the church the church, and which, in my opinion, are decisive for today's spiritual, social, and ecumenical state of European Protestantism.

The first dimension can be introduced with a well-known Luther quote:

> I have taught and held all the teachings of John Hus, but thus far did not know it. John Staupitz has taught it in the same unintentional way. In short we all are Hussites and did not know it. Even Paul and Augustine are in reality Hussites. See the monstrous things into which we fall, I ask

> you, without the Bohemian leader and teacher. I am so shocked that I do not know what to think when I see such terrible judgments of God over mankind, namely, that the most evident evangelical truth was burned in public and was already considered condemned more than one hundred years ago. Yet one is not allowed to avow this. Woe to this earth. Farewell. (Luther's letter to Spalatin, February 1520)

Augustine and Luther were unconscious Hussites because Paul was one: because they, like Jan Hus, taught what Paul had taught. This is in regard to the apostolicity of the church, or more precisely, in regard to a particular understanding of apostolicity: "apostolic" refers to that which the apostles taught (which Luther is known for having brought to a head as *Was Christum treibet*—"whatever advances the cause of Christ"). The apostolicity of the church is characterized by the apostolic content of the church's proclamation: the *tradictio* depends decisively and, in the end, exclusively on the apostolic *dictum*. This implies a specific ecclesiology which, in particular, Hus expressed in a theologically reflected way: the church can and must bear witness to, and serve the truth of, the gospel. The church can, however, never possess and administer a guarantee of this truth. The gospel guarantees itself. This was precisely what the medieval Waldensians meant to say when they emphasized their apostolicity, even as later generations would undergird this conviction with the odd legend that placed their origins in Paul himself having visited the Waldensian valleys. This also applies to the other representatives of the "first" Reformation: they fought for a particular content-based (and not doctrinal) interpretation of the apostolicity of the church, that is, the apostolic succession as a continuity in the truth.

If I understand matters correctly, however, Luther was the first to offer a complete theological presentation of this viewpoint, in his category of *promissio*: the truth of the gospel is grasped in faith as *certitudo*, in the power of the promise (and not as *securitas*—in contrast even to the Waldensian legend!), and thus not as a possession but as the free grace and fidelity of God that "each morning brings us fresh outpoured." In Luther's expanded interpretation, the apostolicity of the church cannot, strictly speaking, be taken as a "claim," but only be received in the gratitude of faith. The category of *promissio* is, in my view, the Protestant alternative to the Roman Catholic implementation of the concept of the ecclesial (or, more practically speaking, the episcopal) "guarantee" of apostolicity.

Luther, in any event, picks up a question from Hus and the "first" Reformation that remains decisive today, not only in ecumenical dialogue, but also with regard to the character of the witness and very being of the church. This question is the very question of what is apostolic and, hence, what is and who is the apostolic church. I would like to take the liberty to assert that ecumenical topics debated so often and so intensively even today (including the often-discussed "ethical questions") are, ultimately, not theologically genuine if they, as dialectical and indirect they may be, are not traced back to this question of the apostolicity of the ecclesial message.

The second heritage of the "pre-Reformation" tradition that I would like to discuss here confronts "classical" central European Protestantism with a critical question. This involves criticism of the "Constantinian" view of the relationship between church and state and, in general, the entire constellation of financial, political, and social power. "Constantinism" and similar categories are, of course, concepts that cannot be easily specified historically, let alone theologically. The political entanglement of the medieval church, which the Waldensians rejected, just to name one example, can hardly be compared with the entanglement of the empire in Luther's day. Nonetheless, one simple fact remains: various "pre-Reformation" movements supported an idea of the discipleship of Jesus, which saw the Christian congregation as an "alternative" or "countercultural" community. The central European Reformation of the 16th century, by contrast, framed its radical discipleship in a way that the church seeks to be *within* society and developed a suitable theology (which was, in fact, also adopted by persecuted minority churches of the Reformation such as the Huguenots and the Waldensians). While this did not indeed entail an uncritical and automatic acceptance of prevailing social conditions, it did create a particular constellation that we could call *Volkskirchentum* (a concept of national people's churches). This constellation made it possible for millions of men and women, in the course of the centuries, to hear the gospel and to lead Christian lives. Those whose background lies in another aspect of history (practically speaking, from a free-church background, as is the socioreligious case in various minority churches) must realize that this *Volkskirchentum*, in its various versions, represented an ecclesiological and pastoral possibility and often still does. But it is indeed just *one* such possibility. Will this possibility continue to exist in future Europe? Once again, a simple yes-or-no answer would be pointless; however, the statistics concerning both parish membership and financial resources speak quite clearly. It can no longer be taken for granted that the cooperation between church and state, as is the case today in countries such as Germany, will remain unchanged in the long run. Indeed, such cases are currently already more of an exception than the rule within Europe and throughout today's world. Can the heritage of the non-Constantinian "first" Reformation bear fruit in a post-Constantinian era?

In order to be able to pose this question responsibly, we first need to reject decisively any sort of idealization. A smaller, poorer, and socially less-established Protestant Christianity will not necessarily become a more convinced and convincing messenger of the gospel, as the state of a good number of diaspora churches shows much too clearly. It is also apparent that the Protestant church, as it has been formed through the Reformation and the diverse history of Protestantism, is constantly to be found in the tension between being a community of profession and one of "inclusion." This dialectic takes on a variety of contours in the large churches of the people—as well as in minority churches—but it exists for both, and not only for socioreligious but also, and especially, for theological reasons. The balance between these two dimensions needs, however, to be reconsidered in the new situation. Smaller and poorer churches, if they wish not only to survive but also to thrive, need to assert their distinctive identities as professing churches more decisively, especially with regard to their daily practice.

There is a great deal of space between the people's churches' understanding of the Protestant (but also the Roman Catholic, to say nothing of the Orthodox) past and the one of the sect (following Troeltsch's definition); a space in which European Protestantism can seek its path forward. The "pre-Reformation" heritage can provide much enrichment in the course of this difficult, but fascinating and spiritually deeply challenging search. The church, indeed, does not live from its heritages, but from the coming future of God. However, we have seen that this future comes to us through a word, that through a *dictum* that became and becomes *tradictum*, in the dimension of the diachronic communion of saints. In this light, this *tradictio* of the pre-Reformation church is not just a historical "example" but a living witness and theological contribution toward formation of our path forward into the future.

CHAPTER 13

Volker Leppin

Breaking Away or Emerging from the Middle Ages?

The Middle Ages do not hold a good reputation among Protestants—whether they are Lutheran, Reformed, or members of United churches. The same is true for those who celebrate the achievements of the European universities, whose roots actually reach back to the 13th century, and those who worship in churches that were built long before the Reformation, such as the Zurich Grossmünster and Wittenberg's Town Church. One could view this simply as an instance of neglecting history—such attitudes are, however, often connected to views of theology and history that are linked in defining their identities through separation and dissociation.

This has indeed a long tradition within Protestantism. When Karl Holl recalled the significance of the doctrine of justification for Martin Luther in 1917, the year of the last Reformation centenary, he did so following a conceptual model that had Luther breaking from the Middle Ages in both his biography and his theology in one single moment. Things were only to be seen as new if they emerged from a break with the old. This model had an impact on the entire interpretation of the Reformation, including the Reformation in Switzerland. In a way, this lent theoretical expression to a pre-theoretical self-conception.

This was met, shortly before and after World War II, with a view that continues to be predominant in Roman Catholic research today, developed in particular by Joseph Lortz and Erwin Iserloh: they afforded the Reformation, from a Roman Catholic point of view, certain legitimacy as a reaction to medieval times, which, in fact, had no longer been particularly medieval. They explained that in the late Middle Ages, and within the Scholasticism of the *via moderna* in particular,[1] the unity of philosophy and theology was broken, piety was externalized, and the link to Christian truth was lost. In the run-up to the Second Vatican Council, this approach was overtly an ecumenical offer, with the catch, however, that there was behind-the-scenes agreement that the problems that the Reformation had addressed eventually had been acknowledged, corrected, and eliminated within the papal church at the Council of Trent. Even as the protest that Luther and Zwingli launched appears justified within this model, it did not afford any permanent status to the Reformed and Lutheran churches.

Protestants, therefore, needed to react to this accordingly. This was done in particular by researchers from both major Protestant denominations who were able to gain an overview of the Reformation as a whole. Despite a certain Luther-centrism, this holds true for Bernd Moeller as well, who cleverly replied to Joseph Lortz and Edwin Iserloh's *decadence model* with a *culmination model*, holding that the Middle Ages did not reach a low point, as these other researchers would have it. On the contrary, there was no time more pious than the 15th century—only, this piety was misguided and therefore had to be corrected by the Reformation. Thereby, Bernd Moeller discovered more possible continuity with the late Middle Ages in terms of the social structure of the southern German and Swiss towns than in theological terms, which he generally analyzed in line with Luther's paradigm and a very traditional view of its opposition to the Middle Ages. The Reformation theologian Heiko Oberman countered this competently by placing the multifaceted roots of both Zwingli and Luther in the theology of the late Middle Ages—going as far as to explain the Marburg Colloquy of 1529 in terms of the late medieval conflict between the *via moderna* and *via antiqua*.

This important impulse for a more nuanced understanding of the relation between the late Middle Ages and the Reformation has now been

1 In general terms, *via moderna* represents a variety of language-critical theology following in the footsteps of William of Ockham. The *via antiqua*, on the other hand, is a philosophy and theology that claims to be able to construct reality from concepts. Thomas Aquinas served as its foremost authority.

developed further in the work of Berndt Hamm and myself into a *polarity model.* The Middle Ages should thus no longer be viewed as leading up to the Reformation in a linear manner. Instead, I find it more appropriate to acknowledge especially the late Middle Ages in all of its diversity. There were various, at times nearly mutually exclusive, but in any case polarly opposed, movements within the single church. The tension between the *via moderna* and *via antiqua* is one such case, to which more can be added: there was not just one area of contention within academic theology—to be carried out occasionally in open dispute—but a strong alternative to the universities' exclusive claim upon the transmission of truth was also developed. The humanistic circles of scholars—in its most extreme form, the Florentine Academy as well as the *sodalitates* of the northern Alps and of southern Germany and Switzerland in particular—but also the rich correspondence of humanistic scholars such as Joachim Vadian serve to show that one could attain and transmit scholarship in other ways, at times in particularly strict distinction from Scholasticism. This is attested by the polemic and at times rather arrogant *Epistolae Obscurorum Virorum.*

As humanism emerged, so did the call for an inner understanding of theology in contrast to Scholasticism, which was experienced as externalized and rigid and following its logical rules instead of a clear understanding anchored in one's own perception of scripture and the church fathers. The slogan *ad fontes* also encapsulated the drive to look into these church sources anew to ascertain and adopt their inner character. The psalm interpretations of Faber Stapulensis demonstrate this, as do Zwingli's first sermons in Zurich, where he no longer wished to follow the disjointed order of the lectionary but, instead, the order of the books of the Bible themselves. The contrast between inner adoption and mere externalization was, however, not only a cognitive contrast but, indeed, found great resonance in its affective terms: the late Middle Ages saw the emergence of an abundance of mystical literature and derivatives. Particularly the *devotio moderna* movement reflected intensive efforts to adopt faith not only externally but with one's heart and soul. Not for nothing did Thomas à Kempis's *Imitation of Christ* become one of the most widely read Christian books of all time—representing as it did a type of piety that stood diametrically opposed to the various externalizing forms of the late Middle Ages. Not only were people able to count their years of purgatory, but they could also purchase the necessary indulgences, swapping coins for years of suffering. In Wittenberg, thanks to a guide by Lucas Cranach, one could find out exactly how many years of indulgence each of the relics there stood for. Quantity became a decisive criterion of religiosity.

Laypeople participated in both externalization and internalization, and in both they—in yet another polarity—entered into increasing opposition to the dominant clerical class, who were often socially and legally separate from them. One of the great nuisances of the late Middle Ages was the fact that the clergy insisted on having their own court proceedings in Rome, thus extracting themselves from the local jurisdiction. Additionally, they also led lives that had little to do with the notion of an apostolicity. A common reaction to this was "anticlericalism," with Boccaccio's *Decameron* being the most amusing expression of this, but also a thoroughly representative one at that.

The further development that was of particular importance, however, had to do with an institutional tension between central and decentralized church governance. This polarity has two facets, both with significance for the century of the Reformation. The 15th century, for one, was characterized by the opposition between the pope and the councils, resulting in conciliarism, beginning at the Council of Constance and reaching its peak at the Council of Basel. It emerged in reaction to the papal schism of the late 14th century, which had revealed that the church could not expect intermundane rescue from its own highest echelons, but only from a General Council as the representative of the universal church. In the shadow of the Council of Basel, however, this polarity took on yet another form: the king of France succeeded, in the 1438 Pragmatic Sanction of Bourges, in attaining far-reaching rights over the church in his country and thus to lay the foundations for the phenomenon of "Gallicanism," in which the French church attained autonomy with respect to the pope. This success in France was reflected in the German-speaking world in the local efforts of numerous territories and towns to take church administration into their own hands. Whether this entailed control of the ministry of proclamation in a town church or the establishment of dioceses in Meissen and Naumburg, the variety of phenomena all had the same driving force of decentralizing the church and thus tying it more closely to local authorities as well as to local congregations.

Following a model that operates with these tensions or polarities does indeed make it possible to describe the transition from the Middle Ages to the Reformation with greater nuance than do the decadence and culmination models. This also holds for the turning of the two great reformers, Zwingli and Luther, against the predominant Scholastic theology. There, Zwingli's humanistic background in particular remains beyond question. However, Luther's scholarship is also clearly attested, as evidenced in his theses on the Heidelberg Disputation. Protesting against "the" Scholastic movement from such standpoints was, as discussed above, nothing new.

Even when theological protest turned into protest at the church level and hence intensified sharply, one can still categorize this as late medieval alternatives. It is therefore quite evident that Luther's and Zwingli's protests against the prevailing situation in the church were initially aimed at externalization.

As far as Zwingli is concerned, this becomes evident in the reports on his first sermons, in which, as Canon Hoffmann complained, Zwingli criticized, among other things, purgatory and the cult of the Virgin Mary and the saints. The basis for this was the volatile mixture of the heritage of late medieval Scotism and the influences of humanism on Zwingli's theology, which led to his strong emphasis on setting in opposition all that represents the external-material and the spiritual-intellectual realms of faith. While still remaining quite parallel within the polarity model, Luther's protest evolved in a slightly different way. Derived in particular from his reading of mystical authors—Johannes Tauler and Theologia Germanica—Luther developed his protest against the externalized form of the sacrament of penance as manifested in indulgences. This can be seen in the first of his 95 Theses against indulgences: "When our Lord and Master Jesus Christ said, 'Repent,' he willed the entire life of believers to be one of repentance." In this way, mystical spirituality entered into Protestant memory.

Just as both reformers clearly came out on the side of internal piety within that polarity, they also took a clear stand within the polarity between clergy and laity. Like Luther in his "Appeal to the German Nobility," Zwingli also called in his 1522 sermon "On Clarity and Certainty of the Word of God," one of his first Reformation works, for the universal priesthood of all believers, as founded in baptism. In both cases, this basic theological principle developed into a crucial catalyst for political action, with Zurich moving faster than Wittenberg and Saxony in the matter. The variously interpreted First Zurich Disputation of 29 January 1523 served to show, in particular, that laypeople were ready and able to take on responsibility for God's word in their own area of influence. And when the sovereigns of Hessen and Saxony set out to introduce the Reformation to their lands, they also followed the principle of laypeople being able to be called to reform the church, just as Luther had put it in his "Appeal to the German Nobility."

It would stand to reason that this can also be linked to the distinction, already known to the late Middle Ages, between centralization and decentralization. The reformers and their ideas supported the decentralized, and—from the viewpoint of the medieval church—disintegrative forces. In return, they were faced, Luther in particular, with the church leadership's unconditional demand for obedience: Silvester Prierias, who was commissioned with an evaluation of Luther's case, represented the papal central church leadership with a severity that was by no means a matter of course in the late Middle Ages. In the same way, Johannes Eck, otherwise not entirely disinclined to conciliar ideas, brought the Leipzig Disputation to a head in the papal question.

These few sketches demonstrate that the beginning of the Reformation can be understood as an intensification and radicalization of the polarities of the late Middle Ages. The Reformation is easier to understand once it becomes clear that there was no single (decadent or climactic) instance of the Middle Ages but, instead, a plurality of religious forms. Explaining the Reformation with the help of late medieval polarities does not entail a claim that these polarities were later simply allocated to the emerging denominational churches. To provide just one example: even the Roman Catholic Church of the modern era maintained the internal element, and it became significant to the development of the Protestant churches that externalized elements in structure and ministry would be reclaimed as well.

This type of polarity model permits us to see what developments helped the reformers to come to their views. Even the decisive difference may be understood this way: in the polarity of the question of centralization and decentralization, in which an agreement could no longer be found. Until this day, it is not for nothing that it is ecclesiological issues that still divide Protestant from Roman Catholic doctrine. The developments that led to this, however, cannot be separated from the late medieval roots of both parties.

CHAPTER 14

Christine Christ-von Wedel

Humanism, Reformation, Enlightenment

Connections and Divisions

Johann Salomo Semler (1725–1791), a representative of the rationalist neology movement within the Protestant Enlightenment, postulated a clear thesis on the concepts of humanism and the Reformation. As a young professor of theology, he had already become aware that especially Erasmus, but also Valla, Cusanus, Vives, Pico dela Mirandola, Wessel Gansfort, Faber Stapulensis, as well as the mystics, had "already seen and honestly spoken out on all truths that faced the common unhealthy religion of the church" and that "Erasmus had achieved the most without having left the Roman Catholic Church" so that "neither Zwingli nor Luther had discovered or found a single entirely new sentence or concept."[1] Moreover, in historical-critical exegesis, the particular area in which Semler himself stood out, he added that hardly anyone had followed the "proper path of investigation as impartially, as purely historically" as Erasmus, the great 16th-century humanist, did.[2]

1 Johann Salomo Semler, *Lebensbeschreibung*, vol. 2 (Halle, 1782), 178f. (hereafter *Lebensbeschreibung*).

2 Ibid., 124.

As an enlightened theologian, Semler thus seems to have followed in the footsteps not of the reformers, but of Erasmus. However, he indeed praised Luther highly at different times so that Gottfried Hornig believed that Semler, as a theologian, built his work on Luther's thought in particular and was inspired by him alone, not least when it came to his biblical criticism.[3]

The relations between the great movements of intellectual history thus do not seem absolutely clear. To shed some light on this—and do allow me this most enlightened metaphor—I invite you to look into four aspects of Enlightenment thought:

The question: What do reason and revelation each contribute

1. to knowledge?
2. to the belief in progress?
3. to the historical approach?
4. to the call for tolerance?

Since humanism, the Reformation, and the Enlightenment are highly complex movements with completely different schools of thought within them set against each other, only certain and, for the Reformation churches, particularly influential representatives of the movements will be presented here.

Written in 1784, Kant's well-known phrase in support of that which he himself already termed the "Enlightenment" was: "*Sapere aude*: Have the courage to use your own understanding!"[4] It was important to the proponents of the Enlightenment that one use one's own understanding critically, which is to say, to maintain a critical view of authorities and of tradition. With regard to theology, they critically examined the traditional dogmatic and their creeds as well as traditional forms of worship. However, they also evaluated the biblical record in accordance with their own rational-seeming criteria. The relationship between revelation and reason became the problem at hand: Do they complement each other, or can reason reinterpret revelatory truths as rational truths, or does one need to give up on the idea of revelation entirely? One such enlightened theologian, Johann Joachim Spalding (1714–1804), maintained the concept of revelation, but postulated that biblical revelation "essentially and in its main purpose" corresponded with the "truths of nature and reason."[5] Johann Friedrich Wilhelm Jerusalem (1709–1789) went a step further, wishing to give up the doctrine of the Trinity "because reason cannot

3 Gottfried Hornig, *Die Anfänge der historisch-kritischen Theologie: Johann Salomo Semlers Schriftverständnis und seine Stellung zu Luther* (Göttingen, 1961), esp. 37.

4 Immanuel Kant, "Beantwortung der Frage: Was ist Aufklärung?," in *Immanuel Kants populäre Schriften*, ed. E. von Aster (Leipzig, n.d.), 1.

5 Cited from Emmanuel Hirsch, *Die Umformung des christlichen Denkens in der Neuzeit. Ein Lesebuch mit Quellentexten* (Tübingen, 1938), 29.

grasp it at all," letting the term remain in the baptismal formula only due to traditional reasons.[6] The appointed Lutheran court preacher and consistorial councilor in Dresden, Christoph Friedrich Ammon (1766–1850), even dared using reason-based considerations to attack the doctrine of justification, stating that "the people can only be pleasing to God . . . through the awareness of their virtue and righteousness (Rom. 2:14f.), which derives from the observation of the purer moral commandments of the Gospel (Rom. 1:16)."[7] In so doing, Ammon thus provides a reinterpretation of Pauline thought. The sentence "one is justified by one's faith" becomes "one is pleasing to God through the awareness of one's righteousness." This reinterpretation fits in well with the moral Christianity of many theologians of the Enlightenment era. From there, it is only a small step to reject fully a religion of revelation, a step in fact already taken by Hermann Samuel Reimarus (1694–1768), whose ideas were published by Gotthold Ephraim Lessing in his *Fragments by an Anonymous Writer.* This included a fragment, published in 1777, with the title "The impossibility of a revelation that can be believed by all on a founded basis." This led to the famous "fragments controversy" (*Fragmentenstreit*), which kept the entire late 18th century in suspense.[8]

The relation between revelation and reason was a problem for Christianity from the very beginning.[9] Sixteenth-century thinkers vacillated between having the greatest trust in the supposedly God-given human powers of reason and great skepticism. In 1510, Agrippa von Nettesheim (1486–1535) grandly pronounced that people can investigate and evaluate everything as they comprehended and contained God.[10] In 1526, however, the same author wrote on the uncertainty and vanity of all knowledge and art, not trusting humanity on any ability to have knowledge of one's own accord. Instead, people depended entirely on God's revelation, which they could only understand if they were "illuminated by God."[11]

Erasmus vacillated more moderately in this regard. In his early 1503 work, he explained that biblical revelation was rational and corresponded with human reason through the "equal consistency of nature (*quae consentaneae sunt*

6 Ibid., 34.

7 Ibid., 39.

8 Ibid., 47.

9 Cf. for the following: Christine Christ-von Wedel, *Erasmus von Rotterdam. Anwalt eines neuzeitlichen Christentums* (Münster, 2003), 125–30 (hereafter Christ-von Wedel 2003).

10 Agrippa von Nettesheim, *De occulta philosophia*, ed. Perrone Compagni (Leiden, 1992), 508, 20.

11 Agrippa von Nettesheim, *De incertitudine declamatio* (Köln, 1539), cap. XCVII, cf. cap. XCVIII—C.

aequitati naturae)."[12] Twenty years later, however, he warned that "to search out knowledge of the nature of God by human reasoning is recklessness; to speak of the things that cannot be set out in words is madness; to define them is sacrilege. . . . And in order to achieve eternal salvation it is enough for now to believe about God those things that he himself has openly made known about himself in Holy Scripture."[13] Human beings were therefore entirely dependent on God's revelation for their ability to recognize God. "God had sprinkled in human hearts some tiny spark of percipient intelligence, but bodily passions and the darkness of sins had blinded it."[14]

Luther was not entirely clear on this matter either: in connection with Romans 1:19-20, he stated in 1515/16: "God's invisible qualities . . . could and can be seen from the creation of the world and evermore."[15] In his 1524 dispute with Erasmus on the freedom of the will, he emphasized the clarity of scripture, the understanding of which human reason cannot be in any doubt as "Christ's words need be certain and clear, otherwise one does not indeed have them at all; we do however have a certain text and our reason, and the simple word as it stands, and we are not at odds over it."[16] In a 1537 sermon, however, Luther found no bridge between faith and reason; instead, one had to believe the Holy Spirit in that what "he speaks is God's truth, and believe his words, which blind the eyes of reason or even put them out."[17]

With regard to the relation between reason and revelation, the Enlightenment was able to build on the questions of the 16th century. A clear dependence on humanism or the Reformation cannot, however, be derived from this. The proponents of the Enlightenment were even less able to appeal clearly to humanism or the Reformation to support their belief in progress. Erasmus had, for example, hoped until 1516 that a new golden era was arising. In the following years, however, his great hopes were soon dashed.[18] Zwingli could keep his optimism for the future somewhat longer but eventually only

---

12 H. S. Desiderius Erasmus Roterodamus, *Ausgewählte Werke*, ed. Hajo Holborn (München, 1933), 57, 16f. (hereafter H).

13 *Desiderii Erasmi Roterodami opera omnia*, ed. Johannes Clericus (Leiden, 1703–1706), Bd. VII, c. 497 C/D (hereafter LB). Translation here by Jane E. Philipps, in "Paraphrase on John," *Collected Works of Erasmus* (Toronto, 1991).

14 Ibid., VII, c. 500 E.

15 Martin Luther, *Kritische Gesamtausgabe*, 73 vols. (Weimar 1883–2009), 56:176, 15-21 (hereafter WA).

16 Ibid., 16:263.

17 Ibid., 46:545, 15-22.

18 Cf. Christine Christ-von Wedel, *Erasmus of Rotterdam: Advocate of a New Christianity* (Toronto, 2013), 93–95 and 251f.

until 1522,[19] and in Luther's work, there was very little to find of use to this end.

Enlightenment thinkers could find, however, a rich bounty in Erasmus's historical approach and his tolerance. Enlightened theologians responded to the recent discoveries of naturalists such as Nicolaus Copernicus, Giordano Bruno, Johannes Kepler, Galileo Galilei, and Isaac Newton. They no longer explained the world teleologically, but mechanically and causally using mathematical laws, while investigating the world empirically. Their results were no longer reconcilable with the ideas about nature provided in the Bible. In the beginning of the 18th century, Isaac Newton (1642–1727) already attempted to pursue historical-critical considerations to liberate the biblical message from outdated ancient points of view, as a means of preserving its witness to faith.[20]

Johann Salomo Semler, in particular, then laid the foundations for the historical-critical method, which continues to dominate our theology today. This method allows us to distinguish between the manner of the text that is in line with the changing historical context and the specific conditions of the time in which the biblical authors expressed matters of faith, and those matters themselves. Once these historically dependent conditions were filtered out, these matters of faith could be paraphrased in new words to be proclaimed convincingly for one's own time. Semler made precisely this methodically possible in his great life's work. He explained that the "healthful effects" that emanated from the words of the apostles and "always, as all reality, come from God" did not depend "on the words that were spoken or written" but on the "content and the ideas of these matters."[21] God revealed Godself through "mediators." The "formulation . . . of written revelation . . . was always their own . . . in accordance with their own circumstances."[22] The prophets and apostles expressed the revelation in their view of the world and ideas about nature. This explains why already the early Christians spoke of God's actions in different ways. As Semler put it: "Paul did not write for Christians in Palestine; Matthew did not write for the followers of Paul and

19 Cf. Christine Christ-von Wedel, "Erasmus und die Zürcher Reformatoren: Huldrich Zwingli, Leo Jud, Konrad Pellikan, Heinrich Bullinger und Theodor Bibliander," in *Erasmus in Zürich. Eine verschwiegene Autorität*, ed. Christine Christ-von Wedel and Urs B. Leu (Zürich, 2007), 95.

20 Cf. Albrecht Beutel, *Kirchengeschichte im Zeitalter der Aufklärung* (Göttingen, 2009), 48 (hereafter Beutel 2009).

21 Johann Salomo Semler, *Abhandlung von freier Untersuchung des Canon; nebst Antwort auf die tübingische Vertheidigung der Apocalypsis*, vol. 1 (Halle, 1771) fol. a[8]r-v (hereafter Canon).

22 Johann Salomo Semler, *Historische Einleitung zu Baumgartens Glaubenslehre*, in: Siegmund Jacob Baumgarten, *Evangelische Glaubenslehre*. vol. 1 (Halle, 1759), 40 (hereafter *Einleitung zur Glaubenslehre*).

John."[23] "Biblical truths" were thus expressed in very different ways depending on "place and time."[24] This was not a failure, according to Semler, but "this variance was probably even God's order."[25] It was indeed a false and tyrannical principle in opposition to the teachings of Christ to say that all Christians had to have "the same unchanged Christian perception throughout all times" and a "uniform Christian language";[26] a principle that was thus a "human insolence . . . against God, who alone judges people, each according to his conscience."[27] This led to a fundamental skepticism with regard to dogmatic teachings (even one's own) and an unlimited tolerance for confessional variances. Semler also explicitly included Jews in his call for tolerance and firmly established that fighting over dogmatic questions and especially damning others was "useless."[28] He did, however, allow that the public churches had to uphold doctrine and forms of worship that united their membership. Their creeds could only be changed by a majority. The personal Christianity of individuals, however, was what mattered before God. Christians should and must express their divergent personal opinions freely. Individuals should only hold back when speaking publically in the name of their church. Semler thus distinguished distinctively between personal and public Christian lives.[29]

Semler's historical approach allowed him to question the biblical canon critically in a monumental four-volume work.[30] In it, he put forward the view that Old Testament books such as Esther, Ruth, Nehemiah, Judges, but also Revelation were specific to their times and thus of little use for Christians,[31] while in general reducing the status of the Old Testament in comparison with the New Testament.[32] He favoured certain books of the New Testament over others as well, writing paraphrases of those books he found most useful, the gospel of John and selected epistles. He rewrote and explained biblical texts anew to present them in a manner appropriate and comprehensible for the people of his own time. As Semler explained, a teacher "must thus present biblical truths in such expressions, idioms, and a succession of sentences

23 Johann Salomo Semler, *Ueber historische, geselschaftliche und moralische Religion der Christen* (1786), ed. Dirk Fleischer (Nordhausen, 2009), 20, §7 (hereafter *Religion der Christen*).

24 *Einleitung zur Glaubenslehre*, 71–73, 77.

25 *Lebensbeschreibung*, 149.

26 *Religion der Christen*, 27, §13.

27 Ibid., 30, §15.

28 *Lebensbeschreibung*, 352, cf. 268, 271, 293, 298, 330, 366.

29 Ibid., 171f.; cf. Fleischer in his *Einleitung zu Religion der Christen*, IX–XII.

30 Johann Salomo Semler, *Abhandlung von freier Untersuchung des Canon*, 4 vols. (Halle, 1771–1775).

31 Cf. *Lebensbeschriebung*, 139.

32 Ibid., 135.

that an understanding, which is possible in his time and place, requires and permits."[33]

Semler's method appalled his orthodox colleagues, who, as representatives of a doctrine of verbal inspiration of God's revelation, equated God's revelation and the traditional writings. They continued to control the pulpits and theological faculties, and Semler, along with his students and colleagues, were strongly defamed as a result. He and his pupils were threatened that they would meet "a terrible end."[34] Semler was, therefore, happy to rebuke his opponents with the fact that even the reformers had pursued biblical criticism and that Luther has critiqued the canon in particular.

Luther saw God's word, scripture, and the Spirit as a unit, understanding them as the living Word. Our task is thus to find the living Christ in scripture, as "the Gospel teaches nothing else but Christ, and thus scripture also has nothing else but Christ."[35] Luther thus criticized the canon from within the core of his theology and, for instance, called the epistle of James an "epistle of straw" because, while it refers to Christ, it did not "teach of him" and goes "directly against St. Paul and the rest of scripture by ascribing justification to works."[36] He was not particularly interested, however, in the critical-historical line of inquiry and, beginning in 1523, tended increasingly toward a doctrine of inspiration, which would pave the way for the highly orthodox doctrine of verbal inspiration. Luther denied any contradictions within the Bible and warned that every iota of it was more significant than heaven and earth.[37] A similar development appeared in Zurich following Zwingli's death.[38] The reformers learned the biblical languages and established effective philological methods of exegesis, but subordinated historical considerations, inasmuch as they pursued any, to their dogmatic conclusions.[39]

Erasmus, however, was different. Semler could see adumbrations of his own most important principles in his work, something that Semler

33 *Einleitung zur Gaubenslehre*, 71f.

34 *Canon*, vol. 1, *Vorrede*, fol. a5v.

35 WA 10,1/1: 625–28, esp. 628, 2.

36 D. Martin Luther, *Biblia, das ist die gantze Heilige Schrift, Deutsch auffs new zugericht* (Wittenberg, 1545), ed. Hans Volz (München, 1974), vol. 3, 2454f.

37 WA 40, 2/1: 419b and WA 40, 2/2: 57b, 17-22.

38 Cf. here and for the entire paper: Christine Christ-von Wedel, "Zur Genese der historisch-kritischen Methode in Humanismus, Reformation und Aufklärung," in *Fiat voluntas tua. Theologe und Historiker—Priester und Professor. Festschrift zum 65. Geburtstag von Harm Klueting,* ed. Von Reimund Hass (Münster, 2014).

39 Cf. the last part of the essay to appear in the series *Spätmittelalter, Humanismus, Reformation*, ed. Volker Leppin, et al., to be published by the Siebeck Verlag: Christine Christ-von Wedel, "Leo Jud als Beispiel für die Erasmusrezeption zwischen 1516 und 1536," in *Basel als Zentrum des geistigen Austausches in der frühen Reformationszeit*, ed. Christine Christ-von Wedel, Sven Grosse, and Bernd Hamm (Tübingen, 2014).

appreciated and acknowledged. Seldom had an interpreter of scripture "pursued the proper path of investigation as impartially, as purely historically" as Erasmus, Semler explained. Indeed, later German theologians did not even understand what Erasmus was talking about.[40]

Erasmus's criticism of the canon derived primarily from historical-critical considerations.[41] As for Semler, many parts of the Old Testament were also, in his opinion, of questionable significance for Christians.[42] He explained, in particular, that the biblical authors wrote for their times and that there was much that was no longer of importance to his contemporaries: "There are passages which are meant to apply solely to the disciples and their time, others apply to all; certain allowances are made for the feelings of those times and some are to be laughed at with irony."[43] The aim was now to reformulate the biblical text in a manner appropriate to one's own time.

Erasmus also wrote paraphrases of the books of the New Testament; however, he did so for all the books apart from Revelation. Additionally, derived from his historical approach, Erasmus also had a fundamental skepticism of dogmatic doctrines and systems that made absolute claims.[44] He fought for a tolerant stance toward heretics[45] and declared the dogmatic differences between denominations to be inconsiderable.[46]

Following on this overview, I will attempt to provide answers, in all modesty and as best I can, to the following three questions that were presented to me from the organizers of this conference:

1. *What is the relationship between humanism, the Reformation, and the Enlightenment?* We do not need to go as far as Semler, who posited that the Reformation had nothing new to offer theologically and that everything had already been conceived before in humanism.[47] It does, however, often hold for those teachings that survived the Enlightenment and which are generally accepted today.[48] The proponents of the Enlightenment drew on the humanists themselves and on Erasmus in particular. For them, the reformers' main contribu-

40 *Lebensbeschreibung*, 124–26.

41 LB, IX, c. 863D; LB VI, c. 1124-1126, fn. 3; c. 1023f, fn.18; c. 1038 fn. 30; c. 1088; c. 1026 B; 1038 D and esp. c. 1124-1126, fn. 3.

42 H, 70f.

43 H, 157f.; translation cited in Christ-von Wedel, *Erasmus of Rotterdam*, 84.

44 Christ-von Wedel 2003, 182f.

45 Cf. z. B. LB, VII, 79-81; IX, 580-83 and 1054-60; *Opera omnia Desiderii Erasmi Roterodami* (Amsterdam, 1969ff.), vol. IX/1, 304, 623-26.

46 Cf. Christine Christ-von Wedel, "Erasmus von Rotterdam zwischen den Glaubensparteien," in *Zwingliana* 37 (2010): 21–39.

47 *Lebensbeschreibung*, 178f.

48 Cf. Christine Christ-von Wedel and Urs B. Leu, *Erasmus in Zürich. Eine verschwiegene Autorität* (Zürich, 2007); and Christ-von Wedel, "Leo Jud als Beispiel."

tion was the liberating act in setting an example of daring to do something new. Many humanistic elements were given up again in the Reformation orthodoxy, but the recollection of the reformers' readiness to take risks surely paved the way for the breakthrough of the Enlightenment in the Protestant churches. In any event, enlightened Christian ideas gained particularly rapid acceptance in the Protestant milieu.[49]

I cannot answer the other two questions in my position as a historian attempting to be as objective as possible, but can only make a few suggestions from my own subjective point of view:

2. *What critical questions would Protestant theology be right to ask of the Enlightenment?* The Enlightenment, in my opinion, was not able to place reason and revelation in a convincing relationship. Time and again, 18th-century thinkers ran the danger of subordinating revelation to their supposed rational-moral ideas, instead of allowing themselves to be challenged scholarly by the biblical witness. We need to think further about the relationship between reason and revelation.

3. *What are the churches of the Reformation still able to learn from the Enlightenment?* Historical-critical thinking, as it emerged from humanistic philology, has gained acceptance as an exegetical method in the Christian—and not only Protestant—churches. In my opinion, however, there still is a lack of historical awareness in spite of it all. Our Protestant churches now join the Enlightenment thinkers in seeking a broad ecumenism, but do they also ask themselves whether the various formations of faith throughout history and in the different cultures could be the will of God? One seeks to pursue a contextual theology, but do Christians also consider that God's revealing Godself in history means that history, in all of its contradictions and atrocities, is intertwined with God's acts, and do we ask what that means for our faith?

It could, furthermore, be useful to connect Enlightenment thinkers in considering the relationship between personal and public Christianity—in other words, to reflect on the relationship between desirable variety in individual professions of faith and forms of worship, on one hand, and the necessary unity for an communal faith and generally recognized and practiced forms of worship in our churches, on the other. It is, thankfully, uncontroversial today to "let every man seek heaven in his own fashion" (Frederick the Great), but can every minister publically act in his or her church and for his or her church in his or her own fashion? At what point does a publically pronounced individual confession of faith turn into arbitrariness and when is it instead necessary for a community of faith to thrive?

CHAPTER 15

Martin Wallraff

New Media and New Networks

The Reformation and the Printed Book

"The Reformation and the printing press" is a frequently examined and discussed topic. The interest in the subject is quite valid, of course, as the Reformation would not have taken the course it did without the printing of books. (And, indeed, vice versa: the nascent art of printing benefited greatly, both in terms of economics and substance, from the public discourse of the Reformation.) It was not for nothing that Martin Luther spoke of printing as the *summum et postremum donum*, the "greatest and ultimate gift"—and he himself actually made use of this gift massively and masterfully. Wittenberg's local book production took on a quasi-industrial character, the existence of which almost completely derived from Luther or, at least, from the reformers in general. It would, however, be wrong to say that the art of printing was simply a chance find and a stroke of luck as an instrument that carried the Reformation throughout Europe, a kind of megaphone for a message that had originally been independent of books. The relationship between the Reformation and the printing press is, in fact, frequently reduced to this "megaphone" function, that is, the amplification and dissemination of a message. Naturally, it undoubtedly served in this function. This is illustrated well by the small leaflets that generated a vast audience for Luther's first significant Reformation writings practically overnight; writings such as the title page of his 1520 "Address to the Christian Nobility of the German Nation Respecting the Reformation of the Christian Estate." We can also name some of the impressive numbers involved: whereas 180 copies of the renowned 1454 Gutenberg Bible were produced and sold, 100,000 copies of Martin Luther's New Testament were disseminated in the first 15 years of its publication alone. These numbers demonstrate impressively that, although printing had been invented around two generations before the Reformation, it was not until the Reformation era and partly under its influence that it became a true mass medium.

While the megaphone function did thus exist—and it is important for our understanding of the Reformation and printing—there is more to the topic than just this function. This becomes immediately apparent when, instead of looking at the world from the point of view of Wittenberg, we choose a city such as Basel as our point of reference. I choose Basel, in particular, for two reasons. The first is quite substantial, in that Basel is the Reformation town in which the book-publishing tradition had already been established the longest and at the highest level. It is the location where the interplay between humanism, printing, and the Reformation is most visible in all its complexity. The second reason admittedly involves the institutional dimension, as I am a representative of Basel and, in particular, its theological faculty. The Reformation and the printing press remains a topic in Basel until this day, and it is of particular importance to us that this be apparent in the context of the Reformation celebrations as well.

I would like to highlight three aspects of this topic, and put forth three theses in the process, developing and illustrating them by using three particular books that were printed in Basel.

I will work through these books chronologically, beginning with one of particular renown (with the second example being less well known). I speak here of the first publication of the Greek New Testament, which Erasmus had published in Basel in 1516. This is, more specifically, only the first publication and not the first printing of the text, as its direct competition, the *Complutensian Polyglot*, had already been printed previously in Spain but could not be distributed until later for legal reasons. The parallel development of both projects makes it clear that certain ideas are simply "in the air" at particular times. If one party does not carry them out, another one will—or both do so independently of one another in two different places at the same time. In this particular case, we have to say that the quality of scholarship was undoubtedly higher in the Spanish project. The manuscripts it was based on, the philological standards, and the breadth of the materials collected were all superior. Erasmus's advantage, however, did not lie solely in his edge in the race against time, but also in the theoretical reflection put into his project—something that is of particular interest to us here.

Erasmus's New Testament was not simply a new kind of "copy" of the Bible with a significantly greater scope of resonance (i.e., not just a "megaphone"), but a completely new project. The editor gives account to this in his preface, in which he explains that his goal was to make it possible to develop a new "true" picture of Christ, one based on a reliable biblical witness. This witness is being liberated from the falsifications of the Vulgate and given an entirely new basis. Erasmus did indeed see his main achievement in replacing Hieronymus's old Latin text with his own, entirely new translation from the Greek original. The fact that the Greek text was also provided—as a sort of countercheck—was actually of secondary relevance. It was, however, significant that the new printing medium, the printing press, allowed for a new depth of historical scope in the shaping of the text. While the medieval text of the Bible had always been in flux—like a stream of lava, which pushed its way through the centuries, sluggishly but not without a certain dynamic—a fixed snapshot in time now became possible. This stream of lava came to a halt in hundreds of identically printed texts. This fixed text was able to provide a precise impression of the "original"—at first, more in terms of an intention, but later also in its implementation all the way through to Nestle/Aland. This is indeed as Erasmus intended it: a true picture of Christ in the text. It is about "genuineness," "truth," and "fidelity to the original," which had not previously been possible or pursued.

Additionally, I begin with this book because the 500th anniversary of its appearance is right around the corner. In 2016, we hope to make people aware again of this important book through a variety of initiatives. This will include a major exhibition at three locations—including, among others, the well-known painting *Body of the Dead Christ in the Tomb* by Hans Holbein. It was not our idea to place this famous image as a sort of illustration alongside the New Testament, as common witnesses of the same cultural contexts. The connection is, instead, a deeper one: in both cases, entirely new technical and artistic means were used to draw a picture of the "historical Christ" that had not previously existed. "The Archeology of Christ" is one suggested working title.

While the 1516 book was released before the beginning of the Reformation, it goes without saying that they are very closely substantially connected. This is not only because the Greek New Testament served as the immediate basic text for both Luther and Zwingli's translations, but especially because—and this is my first thesis—the new medium constituted a new relationship to both text and scripture. Establishing a fixed text through printing formed the basis for new historical and religious appreciation—pointing the way toward the subsequent Protestant principle of scripture.

As previously mentioned, my second book is not as well known. While it was also printed in Basel, this does not become apparent at first glance, as the title page provides no information on the place, year, or publisher. There are, in fact, reasons for this, as it was quite a "hot item" at the time. As one can surmise from the title page, this was the conciliar paper of Enea Silvio Piccolomini, which is to say, the commentary on the Council of Basel written by the council secretary, who would later become Pope Pius II. Why is this then a "hot item"? The council had actually taken place nearly a century before the Reformation even began, and Pope Pius II had died decades earlier. We only need to recall a few facts about church history, however, to understand the controversy. The call for a free council endured throughout the early part of the Reformation, and late medieval conciliarism, that is, the conviction that the council was the Archimedean point from which one could dislodge the papacy, provided the continual theological background. The fact that a later pope had once supported this theory earlier in life and that this paper had remained mostly unknown until then was enough to render its publication an attractive yet also dangerous undertaking.

Moreover, the title only represents the content to a very partial degree. The book did offer the prominently billed Piccolomini piece, but a great deal more as well. Upon closer inspection we may see the volume as a wealth of sources with a strong antipapal tendency. The publisher collected every medieval text of this category that he could find. The title was apparently taken from the piece that promised to attract the most attention and thus sell the best—the conciliarist writing of a future pope.

The further details on the content are of lesser interest to our purposes than the background of its development. When, where, and by whom was the book in fact printed? As mentioned above, it was printed in Basel. However, it is only from modern research that we know of this and of any other answers to these questions. The book itself is completely anonymous and provides no hints as to how it came about. We do now know, however, that it was printed in 1523 by Cratander in Basel, and edited by a Cologne-based humanist by the name of Sobius. Two aspects of this are of particular interest: first, the fact that it was not a homegrown Basel product, but that a scholar far afield apparently shared the opinion that Basel provided the right "stage" for his controversial project. Second, all of this occurred several years before the Reformation was officially introduced in Basel. For several reasons, unfortunately, it is not easy to reconstruct any further specific details regarding this cooperation.

We can, however, establish that printing does not only provide a medium for the dissemination of a message, but that interregional networks of scholars and printers had already formed before the Reformation, to open the doors to an exchange of manuscripts, information, and religious convictions. This is my second thesis, which, if nothing else, serves to highlight the atmosphere in Basel of the 1520s.

The same thesis can also be illustrated by my third book, and in some ways even to a greater extent, as we know more about it. I will return to this further at the end. The third book is a relatively well-known work. More precisely, it consists of several volumes, an entire series of weighty tomes that were printed in the 1560s in Basel. They are the so-called *Magdeburg Centuries*, which are given that name because their actual title is too long to cite on a regular basis. It begins with the words *Ecclesiastica Historia*, and it is known for being the first monumental treatment of church history from a Protestant point of view and, indeed, the first independent work of this genre in around a thousand years. In its full length, the title is also interesting as a sort of theological program for historical scholarship: the history is ordered by centuries (hence the title) while the content is also categorized by *loci*, that is, diachronic cross-sections within individual topics.

The formal working process at play here, however, is of greater interest to us. This was a major cooperative project (today it could be called a "third-party funded project") with its main centre in Magdeburg. This is in itself surprising, as the printing site was in far-off Basel. The *spiritus rector* of the undertaking, Lutheran theologian Matthias Flacius Illyricus, had had excellent relations there from earlier times, and his *Catalogus testium veritatis*, a sort of manifesto for the actual presentation of history, was published with Johannes Oporinus in Basel, in 1556, despite the long distances involved. The publisher Oporinus played a key role in this major project as well, in a much more expansive and important manner than we would expect from a publisher today. Materials not only found their way from Magdeburg to Basel (in terms of the completed manuscripts to be printed), but were also sent in the other direction. Oporinus went to lengths to provide the Magdeburg scholars with resources for their work in the form of important, newly printed source editions, of which a large portion was released in Basel. The network was in fact even larger, and effectively spanned all over Europe. In addition to Flacius himself, who travelled far in search of rare manuscripts, the diplomat Caspar von Nidbruck, who was an imperial councilor in Vienna and a secret Protestant, also played a key role in this process. He purchased manuscripts for the Vienna Court Library throughout Europe, both as part of his own personal passion but also in the service of the emperor. Before they were deposited there, however, he lent them to the Magdeburg authors for them to extract.

Martin Hartmann has recently investigated this exchange: "The manuscripts and prints were packed into barrels, marked with consecutive letters, and shipped up the Danube to Regensburg, where they were copied by scribes in the house of Superintendent Nikolaus Gallus. They were then sent back to Vienna the same way." Nidbruck also exchanged letters with Oporinus to coordinate these activities.

This would lead to a network that permitted an expansive system of processing information that was hitherto unparalleled. This is my third and final thesis. It remains impressive today to see how comprehensively the *Centuries* scholars were able to refurbish all the material: the portrayal was based on actually *everything* one could know at the time (and a large portion of what we know today), thus representing a new standard of research. Here again, printing is by far not only a means of efficiently disseminating information ("megaphone"), but the new medium brought about an entirely new culture of information processing.

It is hardly necessary to explain by means of a conclusion that the Reformation did not merely make use of the new medium but was also strongly shaped by it. The Reformation would not have occurred as it did without the printing press. It would not only have grown somewhat more slowly and quietly. The medium and the message, rather, condition each other: from the understanding of scripture and personal relationships through to scholarly ideals, the media conditions of communication left their mark on what we now call the European Reformation.

CHAPTER 16

Athina Lexutt

The Princes' Reformation and the People's Reformation

A Farewell to "the" Reformation

It is no longer a secret: there has never been "the" Reformation. Despite all of the long-lasting trends of heroization, especially in the 19th century, all media distortion, and even in spite of all that is entailed in having an extensive program planned for the 2017 Reformation anniversary, the supposed nailing of the 95 Theses on a church door in a small town in Electoral Saxony on 31 October 1517 did not set "the" Reformation in motion out of the blue. The Reformation did not take place solely within the territory of that state, and it was not led by Martin Luther alone as a defiant and heroic Herculean figure. Some reformational movements can be observed well before 1517, if we include the reforms of Jan Hus and John Wycliffe as well as those of the European humanist circles. They can be observed far away from Wittenberg, whether in Zurich, Geneva, England, Scotland, France, Scandinavia, Poland, or Hungary; they did not only bear the signature of Luther, but also of Huldrych Zwingli, John Calvin, Martin Bucer, John Laski, Konrad Cordatus, and others; and they encompassed a broad period of time after 1517 as the Reformation gradually became enshrined in church orders and church life with great geographical variety. The confessionalization debate set a number of balls in motion and has brought into focus what a multifaceted and ambivalent phenomenon "the" Reformation has been.[1]

The fact that books on the topic are still given such titles is due to two things (and is justified as such). First, the departure from talk of "the" Reformation does not necessarily entail the end of the epochal term as such; it is evident that "secular" and church historical perspectives diverge in this regard, something that prompts further discussion. This is closely connected to the fact that one also needs to distinguish clearly between "the Reformation" and "the reformational." Even if the Reformation, as a historical movement, can and must be referred to in its diversity, the task still remains, in view to the question of the Protestant identity and its unique character, to search for its common impetus and centre, and, indeed, for the "reformational" that all have in common. The diversity of the Reformation does not set aside a potential specificity of all that is reformational.

The task at hand lies in investigating more closely one of these aspects, namely, the diversity of the Reformation. The main idea, as reflected in the title, is that—in broad terms—there are two forms of the "Reformation": one that was guided by the state authorities "from above," and another that emerged from the people, from the congregations and *Landstände,* "from below." The true, multifaceted nature of this phenomenon, however, is demonstrated in the six volumes[2] on the confessionalization of the territories of the *Reich.*[3] Among all of these labels, there were other variants and forms with

1 For a research report on this with a comprehensive bibliography, see Athina Lexutt, "Konfessionalisierung—neuer Schlauch für alten Wein?," in *Verkündigung und Forschung* 45 (2000): 3–24. Thomas Kaufmann, in his well-received *Geschichte der Reformation* (Frankfurt a.M./ Leipzig, 2009), speaks self-evidently of plural "Reformations." It remains to be seen whether that is an elegant solution. The confessionalization paradigm is, however, by no means the only attempt at meeting the requirements of the plural phenomena of the time. An overview of several different recent research approaches can be found in Stefan Ehrenpreis and Ute Lotz-Heumann, *Reformation und konfessionelles Zeitalter*, Kontroversen um die Geschichte, (Darmstadt, 2002); concerning our context, cf. in particular 29–47.

2 To avoid any confusion, vol. 7 includes a summary of the results of the contributions of the first six volumes. See n. 3 for a full description of the series.

3 Anton Schindling and Walter Ziegler, eds., *Die Territorien des Reichs im Zeitalter der Reformation und Konfessionalisierung. Land und Konfession 1500–1650*, vol. 1: *Der Südosten*, Katholisches Leben und Kirchenreform im Zeitalter der Glaubensspaltung (hereafter KLK) 49 (Münster, 1989); vol. 2: *Der Nordosten*, KLK 50 (Münster, 1990); vol. 3: *Der Nordwesten*, KLK 51 (Münster, 1991); vol. 4: *Mittleres Deutschland*, KLK 52 (Münster, 1992); vol. 5: *Der Südwesten*, KLK 53 (Münster, 1993); vol. 6: *Nachträge*, KLK 56 (Münster, 1996); vol. 7: *Bilanz—Forschungsperspektiven—Register*,

their own qualities, and there could well be mixtures or successions of various forms in one and the same region.[4] These six volumes also make it clear that the presentation in the following can only be a rather schematic sketch of examples of the Reformation movement types that existed in different parts of Europe.[5] This will draw upon the results of the confessionalization debate as well as the latest documentation on Reformation history as far as it is relevant to this context.

The Reformational Movements: An Encounter

As we view the Reformation century and the decades that led up to it, we first and foremost see shifts at various political, social, and cultural levels. The questioning of imperial power, which we will now be looking into more closely, corresponded with the discussion on authority within the church, which was settled in favour of papal power after the reform councils of the 15th century, but which also open up the "council" alternative in the long run. In economic terms, the introduction of the monetary economy, among other things, led to banks, through the lending of money, being able to become unofficial political forces by financing the purchase of offices, warfare, and prestige objects. On the other hand, this would coincide with the impoverishment of the peasantry, rural nobility, and the knighthood, which led to uprisings and riots.[6] The flourishing cities represented further competition, with their rise in power and

KLK 57 (Münster, 1997). This is joined by the three large conference volumes on Reformed, Lutheran, and Catholic confessionalization: Heinz Schilling, ed., *Die reformierte Konfessionalisierung in Deutschland—Das Problem der "Zweiten Reformation." Wissenschaftliches Symposion des Vereins für Reformationsgeschichte 1985*, Schriften des Vereins für Reformationsgeschichte (hereafter SVRG) 195 (Heidelberg, 1986); Hans-Christoph Rublack, ed., *Die lutherische Konfessionalisierung in Deutschland. Wissenschaftliches Symposion des Vereins für Reformationsgeschichte 1988*, SVRG 197 (Heidelberg, 1992); and Wolfgang Reinhard and Heinz Schilling, eds., *Die katholische Konfessionalisierung. Wissenschaftliches Symposion der Gesellschaft zur Herausgabe des Corpus Catholicorum und des Vereins für Reformationsgeschichte 1993*, SVRG 198 (Heidelberg, 1995), as well as numerous individual studies outside of these volumes.

4 Kaufmann remarks that the "relationship between the sovereigns' Reformations and the parish and rural town Reformations is complex. In some territories such as Electoral Saxony, Brunswick-Lüneburg, and Ansbach-Bayreuth, one will have to presume that the process of unification and normalization, which took the form of a church order in the legislation of the sovereign, in many places did not simply create Reformation innovations but also regulated and fenced in a previously extant reformational diversity." Kaufmann, *Geschichte der Reformation*, 4.

5 The individual depictions are not provided in accordance with a particular formula or even a consistently set period of time. It is not meant as a comprehensive history of the Reformation but, instead, as a selection of information relevant to the context being discussed.

6 Whether and in what way a parish Reformation can be derived from this has been discussed in depth following Blickle's theses; cf. again Ehrenpreis and Lotz-Heumann, *Reformation und konfessionelles Zeitalter*, in particular 41–47.

political influence. In terms of culture, the Renaissance constituted the beginning of a return to anthropological questions that were not necessarily discussed in a theological context and/or within the basic structures. They sought expression first in art and philosophy, and then in theology, thereby gradually displacing the dominance of the methods of Scholasticism. Humanism brought these threads together and blazed the path for free scholarship; for a constructive coexistence of individuality and hierarchical interests; for personal autonomy in decision making supported through educational programs; for an irenic and tolerant attitude; and, not least, for a cosmopolitan point of view that went beyond territorial boundaries. Adopting certain mystical elements as well, humanism was also reflected in the new *devotio moderna* form of piety, which then also entailed a serious challenge to the theological system and not just to the method of Scholasticism.

In sum, it is no exaggeration to speak of a time of crisis or at least a time of change in Europe, in which much was in flux and it was not yet quite clear where these new paths would ultimately lead. We can, in any event, observe a struggle between old and new forces at all levels, which led to greater uncertainty and instability. Recent research has been right to look into the degree to which the turn of the century, which also constituted a turn of the half-millennium, contributed to this insecurity. End-of-the-world scenarios were hardly more virulent than they had been in similar landmarks in prior times. Of greater relevance was the lack of a central power that could hold everything together—or, indeed, the wish and will to impede such a power. This provides us with a picture of a divided Europe led by many different interests, a Europe that is not yet a single one. Instead, we can observe countless mini-states, which are mostly in turn composed of numerous territories with their own traditions and interests, with their own political and social structures and their own religious backgrounds.

A look at the political map of Europe upon the eve of the Reformation underscores these impressions, showing various forces with different competing interests. The House of Habsburg, which was at the centre of most of these conflicts, controlled large areas of Europe through its adept marriage and inheritance politics along with successful campaigns of conquest. Their claims were countered, however, by three main opponents: France to the west, which had developed into a sovereign nation-state and made its own claims to the imperial throne; the Ottoman Empire to the east, which was pushing continuously westward; and the princes of the empire, who generally remained loyal to the emperor in their aspirations toward sovereignty, but who also made expensive demands in return for this loyalty. The Golden Bull of 1356, which installed the emperor as an electoral position, was already a move in such a direction, extending unprecedented power to the elector princes; the imperial reform under Maximilian I, however, further granted the individual imperial estates, with the three colleges of the Imperial Diet, new responsibility and powers that did not simply assist the emperor, but actually did quite the opposite. Even the hereditary lands of the Netherlands showed an interest in attaining their independence from the House of Habsburg. England, Scotland, and the Scandinavian countries had little part in the continental disputes, as they were strong monarchies themselves and waited to see what would happen in order to make use of it for their own purposes. Politically independent since the 1499 Peace of Basel, the Swiss Confederation developed strongly autonomous political systems in its towns and cantons, although with great social, economic, and political differences between the rural areas with their community-oriented type of constitutions in central Switzerland and the towns, which were run by guilds and town patricians.[7]

Given this, it becomes clear how much the Habsburgs' power was under threat from all sides, and how the Reformation could be used as a political instrument by all those who sought sovereignty and freedom from the clutches of the Habsburgs. The Reformation thus appears to have been carried consistently by a mixture of political and theological-religious motivations. Typically, the Reformation was at least given support "from above," and was mostly initiated by the regional sovereigns or—in the free imperial cities and cities of the Swiss Confederation—by the city councils.[8] In the Netherlands, at most, there were several movements that emerged from the people so that one can speak of a Reformation "from below." The clear political interests of the princely and urban Reformations make it more difficult to determine the degree of theological and spiritual motivation in each case. One can, for

7 Cf. Hans Berner, Ulrich Gäbler, and Hans Rudolf Guggisberg, "Schweiz," in *Die Territorien des Reichs*, 5:278–323.

8 Cf. Manfred Rudersdorf, "Die Generation der lutherischen Landesväter im Reich. Bausteine zu einer Typologie des deutschen Reformationsfürsten," in *Die Territorien des Reichs*, 7:137–70. From the beginning he establishes: "The estate-based sovereign state thus became a dominating political power under the banner of the Reformation and confessional dualism, and a trailblazer and successful shaper of the early modern state in Germany. [. . .] It became clear early on that the sovereign's authority, commitment, and initiative were essential for the breakthrough of the Reformation. [. . .] Without the decisive will and instinct for reform of the sovereigns who were inclined toward the Reformation, the proclamation of the new doctrine, and the expansion of the new territorial churches in terms of organization and personnel would never have attained such wide appeal, and a long-term and extensive confessional rootedness in terms of both quantity and quality in the minds of the people would not have been possible, which ultimately was only attainable and maintainable in a territorial state with the potential of sovereign pervasion and unification" (ibid., 137f.). Rudersdorf contrasts this concept of a sovereigns' Reformation with Bernd Moeller's idea of an urban Reformation, and Blickle's concept of a parish Reformation, which are indeed valid for certain areas of the empire. On urban Reformation and its conditions, cf. Kaufmann, *Geschichte der Reformation*, 411–28.

example, certainly say of the Saxon Elector Frederick that, by founding his own university in Wittenberg, in a humanistic framework, he met his advisors' call for reform while also indeed fulfilling his own will to reform. Having his own university, however, also meant paying his own professors, and attracting students who would carry forth the renown of Saxony back to their own territories, which would entail a wide and sustainable influence that was not to be underestimated. Additionally, Landgrave Philipp the Magnanimous, who brought Hesse[9] into the Reformation with the 1526 Homberg Synod and founded the first Reformation-oriented university in Marburg in 1527, could also be seen to have been motivated in two different ways, as was underscored in his later tactical stance poised between the Schmalkaldic League and the emperor in view of his bigamous marriage. His efforts toward finding a compromise in the dispute over the eucharist were also motivated both by theological interests and by political concerns, in terms of avoiding a fragmentation of the Reformation. We can indeed observe such political interests in all of the territories that joined the Reformation in the 1520s and 1530s. The banished Duke Ulrich of Württemberg could actually only reclaim his territory by asking the Swiss as well as Philipp of Hesse for their support, so that "his" Reformation would have to accommodate both theological strains.[10]

---

9 Cf. Manfred Rudersorf, "Hessen," in Die Territorien des Reichs, 4:254–88; on the figure of Philipp, cf. Gury Schneider-Ludorff, *Der fürstliche Reformator. Theologische Aspekte im Wirken Philipps von Hessen von der Homberger Synode bis zum Interim* (Leipzig, 2006). Landgrave Philipp at first personally espoused Protestant doctrine, which he attained especially through his conversations with Melanchthon. In addition to Wittenberg, he also turned toward Zurich and Strasbourg and found an influential advisor in the southern German Martin Bucer. An officialdom with a strong internal network involving relatives and acquaintances provided the Reformation movement with a basis that allowed it to establish and use selected strong, long-lasting structures, and to maintain them even in turbulent times.

10 Cf. Hermann Ehmer, "Württemberg," in *Die Territorien des Reichs*, 5:168–92. This had the apparently curious consequence that the South of the country was reformed by Ambrosius Blarer in line with Zwingli, while Erhard Schnepf, a follower of Luther, reformed the North. The Lutheran movement did not prevail until the Wittenberg Concord of 1536. As a consequence, the University of Tübingen was to be given a clear Protestant identity; only the change of the statute in 1537, however, would allow for the duke's appointment policies to prevail, after the university rector had long fought against the duke's involvement. A number of free imperial cities (Weil, Schwäbisch Gmünd, and Rottweil) were within the territory of Württemberg, as well as domains of imperial knights and the clergy, and remained Catholic or had been re-Catholicized. This situation made it difficult to introduce the Reformation everywhere. Under the rule of Ulrich's son Christoph, the Reformation was solidified further organizationally and structurally, while some of the structures would become exemplary for the political administration, providing a basis for the old Württemberg territorial state. Württemberg developed under Christoph into a model Lutheran country (the Lutheran Spain), while its influences derived, all throughout, from the duke himself and from Tübingen-based theologians such as Jakob Heerbrand and his students (including Ägidius Hunnius and Polykarp Leyser),

In addition to progressive sovereigns of this type, there were those who were seen as friendly to the Reformation but who did not yet take the decisive steps, in particular because they were interested in pursuing a reform within existing structures—if, indeed, at all. At different times and under certain conditions, they took a position that was not entirely clear. This had, however, a variety of reasons. In the Electoral Palatinate, which had lost its prominent position of power within the empire with its defeat in the 1503 War of the Succession of Landshut, religion completely served politics. Luttenberger was thus surely right when he said that this involved "an understanding of order that lacked a truly religious dimension."[11] The very existence of any reformational movements there must be understood as serving just such political calculations. While the Duchy of Jülich-Kleve was inclined toward the Reformation due to its humanistic influence, directly informed by the ideals of Erasmus of Rotterdam, and the Electoral Brandenburg due to its interest in the ideals of early church reforms, religious and theological motivations were greatly lacking in the Palatinate, at least with regard to the electoral prince himself. While not hiding from ongoing developments, support was not truly forthcoming. This indecisive attitude, however, permitted Reformation forces to develop with relative ease, or, at least, without being constantly scrutinized by the sovereign, as was really most appropriate to the cause, that is, academically and theologically (one need only think of the stance of the representatives of Brandenburg and Jülich-Kleve, especially at the Religious Colloquy of 1540/41, where they presented wholly Lutheran arguments with regard to the doctrine of justification) as well as in terms of actual worship practice and in the eucharist *sub utraque* in particular.

The Reformational Movements: Selected Examples

Saxony

When we refer to "Saxony," we need to remember both states of that name: the Ernestine Electoral Saxony, which held electoral rights through 1547 and which is seen as the origin of the Reformation; and the Albertine Duchy, which artfully pried the electoral rights from Electoral Saxony.[12]

---

and later especially Jakob Andreae, whose work on the Concord would also serve to shore up the political peace.

11 Cited from Anton Schindling and Walter Ziegler, "Kurpfalz: Rheinische Pfalz und Oberpfalz," in *Die Territorien des Reichs*, 5:17.

12 Cf. Thomas Klein, "Ernestinisches Sachsen, kleinere thüringische Gebiete," in *Die Territorien des Reichs*, 4:8–39; and Herbert Smolinsky, "Albertinisches Sachsen," in *Die Territorien des Reichs*, 2:8–32.

If we first take Electoral Saxony into consideration, the territory that Luther called home and where he was protected by the electoral prince, we are able to observe strong humanistic movements that emerged from Erfurt in particular, which belonged to the Archbishopric of Mainz. Especially the humanistically inclined council members, and then the court chaplain and secretary George Spalatin, who was closely connected to Luther, worked toward the ideas of the movement being firmly planted at the court. These efforts culminated in the founding of the town's university in 1502, which can certainly be seen as the cradle of the Reformation. With Luther's appointment as a professor in *lectura in biblia* and Melanchthon's as a professor of Greek, Wittenberg would serve as a home base for both leaders of the new movement. Elector Frederick III (1486–1525) supported and nurtured the movement tactically in terms of diplomacy and politics, making particular use of his influence at the election of the emperor. However, only his brother and successor John (1525–1532) as well as John Frederick I (1532–1554) would publically espouse Luther and play a prominent role in the Reformation throughout Germany as leaders of the Schmalkaldic League. The interests of the Reformation were also supported to a great extent by the cities of the territory, which began quickly to implement the movement in practical terms. It was not, in fact, necessary for the sovereigns to take direct action to this end, as students, city council members, and congregations supported the reforms at all levels: schools were either founded or reformed in line with humanistic ideas, and institutional poor relief, the "common chest," was introduced. Subsequent to the visitations that occurred, especially in the late 1520s, which put an end to uncontrolled religious outgrowths and confusion, and brought order to church, society, and schools, the movement also reached, to a broader extent, rural parishes and the nobility, with the reforms often being introduced upon the communities' own initiative, while sometimes being decreed from above as well. The well-ordered training of new pastors and the orientation toward a binding creed brought about the needed inner stability in a sustainable manner, particularly in contrast to the Duchy of Saxony, which had developed into Electoral Saxony's opponent.

Under Duke George (1500–1539), the duchy had maintained a pro-Habsburg stance until 1539. While George did, in fact, support humanistic reforms in the implementation of a form of territorial church regiment—even before the Reformation movement there was administrative reform (in which the nobility was increasingly replaced by commoner officials), a new educational program, and printing presses in Leipzig that supported new ideas in their own way—these reforms would, however, only occur within the old order. With the Leipzig Disputation taking place within his territory in 1519, George understood that Luther's influence was leading in a direction that he himself no longer supported. The continued competition with Electoral Saxony also played a role in the process, and the duke thus took the side of the old faith, and ensured the strict implementation of the Edict of Worms—in opposition to the prevailing trends, especially in Leipzig, where large portions of the citizenry identified with the Reformation, including craftspeople, the university, and, not least, the printers. Facing such irrepressible sympathies with Lutheranism prompted George to increase the pressure against Luther and his followers, while also pushing for reforms within the Catholic Church. This stance, along with several advisors who joined his efforts, led to religious discussions with Mainz, Hesse, and Electoral Saxony, discussions that failed but paved the way to the Religious Colloquies of 1540/41 in terms of ideology and content. The tables turned, however, when George's brother Henry came to power in 1539. He was strongly influenced by his wife and his advisors; he had already introduced the Reformation to his own territory and immediately extended it to the entire duchy. He was succeeded by his son Maurice, who was politically adept at moving tactically between the emperor and the Schmalkaldic League, his father-in-law Philipp of Hesse in particular. When the time seemed ripe, in the mid-1540s, to wage war and resolve the religious question in favour of the emperor, he supported the Habsburgs in return for a few not insignificant promises, such as the right to be an elector should the Schmalkaldic League and Electoral Saxony lose the war. Maurice's "treason" was only rewarded partly, however. As he never really had sought to re-Catholicize Saxony, it was not difficult for him to change sides again to join a strong group of princes that had risen to oppose Charles. The bridges had, however, already been burnt between Ernestine and Albertine Saxony, as would be expressed at a variety of levels. The effects of this on the academic level would be consequential indeed in the long run. As a means of presenting themselves as the true successors to the Reformation, the Ernestine branch founded its own university in Jena, which would become the centre of Gnesio-Lutheranism, especially after the appointment of Matthias Flacius.

In any event, the new elector Maurice continued to support the Reformation in its incipient stages within his territory. August, his brother and successor, lacked the necessary temperament to take risks, and his reign was instead marked by two factors: a clear loyalty to the emperor (and thus a continuation of Albertine policies) and a resistance to the pressing ahead of the Electoral Palatinate and its opening to European Calvinism, as well as to the attempt to come to an agreement with the Ernestine branch, beginning politically with the Naumburg Treaty of 1554. From that point on, efforts were made to anchor the Reformation agenda at the academic and institutional levels and to resolve disputes among Protestants so as not to endanger the religious peace, as it had been represented in the territory by the Universities of Wittenberg and Leipzig and continued to be pursued in the opposition to the University of Jena. The Reformation, as it were, was brought back to focus on the reformational and into the university. As August's son Christian (1586–1591) began his reign, his opening to Philippism entailed, at the same time, also a small opening to Calvinism. There was, however, strong resistance to this "Calvinization" on the part of the cities and nobility, and so such tendencies came to a swift end following Christian's death.

Palatinate

The Palatinate[13] is perhaps the most impressive example for the degree to which church politics depended on individual territorial sovereigns, as it went through a particularly changeable path of confessionalization under its different electors.

The Electoral Palatinate had lost its particular position of power in the empire at the beginning of the 16th century, and thus took on a vacillating stance with regard to religion for tactical considerations. Elector Louis V (1508–1544) was obvious in his maneuvering between loyalty to the emperor, which was to help the Palatinate to return to its old honour and glory—certainly influenced by the strong humanistic circles in the territory and at the University of Heidelberg (which was, however, not particularly significant at first)—and trends more favourable to the Reformation, which were certainly also due to the friendly relations with Electoral Saxony. Louis employed both Protestant and Catholic officials and preachers. His brother and successor Frederick II (1544–1556) did not have trouble in restrengthening elements related to the old church, as the Schmalkaldic War made it impossible to remain neutral any longer. The influence of neighbouring territories and cities was significant both for the Reformation and the maintenance of the traditions of the old Catholic faith. Strasbourg, Esslingen, and Landau are particularly responsible for southern German influences gaining an early and strong foothold in opposition to Lutheranism. Wittenberg and Nuremberg, by contrast, pushed in the Upper Palatinate for a "gradual growth into a life of general church reform"[14] with Lutheran convictions, in which the members of the city council and the sovereign's officials would become supporters of the movement.

It was not until Otto Henry (1556–1559) that the Reformation was introduced as an act of the sovereign, with strong southern German accents due to the influence of Johann Marbach of Strasbourg, but without these tendencies, however, taking over entirely. On the contrary, Otto Henry was

13 Cf. Schindling and Ziegler, "Kurpfalz," 5:8–49.

14 Ibid., 5:21.

able to tolerate all variety of Reformation movements and to unite them at his court, convinced that they could only address the emperor and other Roman Catholics effectively if the various strains of Protestantism were to be united. His successor, Frederick III (1559–1576), turned toward Calvinism, as he put more trust in his southern German and Swiss-oriented advisors, and opened himself up to Philippism. The Heidelberg Catechism was programmatic in this regard. Frederick's very comprehensive implementation of the Reformation in Calvinistic terms (including iconoclasm and the removal of all altars) endangered, on the one hand, his position in the empire, as the security of the Religious Peace of Augsburg was no longer guaranteed (which they attempted to circumvent with the CA *Variata*); on the other hand, this implementation was a significant opening toward western Protestantism for this reason and due to relevant political measures (and especially the support of emigrants and the struggle for freedom in the Netherlands). When Louis's son Louis VI (1576–1583) came to power, the Palatinate returned to Lutheranism—albeit for a short time—linking to Otto Henry's reforms. Within Palatinate-Lautern, the realm of Louis's brother John Casimir, however, Calvinism remained undiminished so that it could return to predominance when Casimir took the reins of the electoral regency following Louis's early death in 1583. Casimir picked up where his father left off in terms of politics and the church. This political stance would reach its apex in 1608, under Frederick IV, when anti-Habsburg resistance was organized in a coalition of the estates under the directorate of the Electoral Palatinate. Apart from internal conflicts of interest and the challenge of a Catholic counterleague, it was the intentional absence of Electoral Saxony that led to a weakening of the alliance. Its chairman of the war council, Christian of Anhalt, who was a passionate opponent of the Habsburgs and did all he could to turn confession into an object of interest for the political powers, proved successful in his efforts to have Frederick V, the not particularly outstanding successor to Frederick IV, crowned as king of Bohemia. These events, which led to the Thirty Years' War and turned Frederick into a mocked "Winter King," show that Christian's ideas did not come into fruition at all, but in fact meant catastrophe for the Palatinate. The opposition to the emperor came at the expense of the Palatinate's electoral status, which was instead given to Bavaria. Additionally, its territory was divided up and occupied on the left side of the Rhine by Spain and on the right side of the river by Bavaria. Re-Catholicization came as an unavoidable consequence, although the segments of the population with Lutheran leanings (a majority in the Upper Palatinate) also worked toward the repression of Calvinism. For the Palatinate and its confessionally diverse parts, the war meant the beginning of a true struggle of confessions, which came again to the fore during the peace negotiations. In the end, the attempt of Charles Louis (1649–1680), the elector of the Rhenish Palatinate, which had been restored as the eighth electoral territory, to rebuild the area with its confessionally mixed immigrants, led, in particular, to the multidenominational character of this area.

Zurich

Thomas Kaufmann speaks of Zurich as the "first Reformation of an autonomous city."[15] Zurich is indeed a classical, exemplary model of a movement steered by influential city authorities, resulting in the expansion of their own area of power, while reducing that of the bishop of Constance. This was another case in which political motivations were at least partly decisive. The most important theologian of this network, Huldrych Zwingli, did not stand apart from the municipal leaders, but was in fact quite useful for them, as he fit in well with their interests in terms of his humanistic, namely Erasmus-oriented biblicism, his anti-French and anti-Habsburg positions (as articulated in particular in his attacks on the Swiss mercenary system), and his wish to embrace the gospel in its power also to form society. That the city council was the decisive force in this play for power became evident at the visible beginning of the Reformation, the Breaking of the Fast in 1522, which was justified by Zwingli: it was no longer the new practice that needed to be legitimized but the traditional practice, instead. Following a disputation, the council announced the "winner," which further underscored his prominent position in questions of church doctrine. As the struggle became more heated between Zwingli and the Zurich council versus the bishop of Constance and the Swiss Diet (*Tagsatzung*), it was again the council that acted clearly in support of Zwingli's views, and demonstrated at the First Zurich Disputation of 1523 how the public order was to be maintained and whose responsibility this was—even if they stressed that the leadership was only an interim solution in accordance with emergency law. Thomas Kaufmann states this well:

> The great career that city disputations had as a type of event throughout the broad history of the Reformation, attests to the fact that this public-civic model of presentation, demonstration, and negotiation provided particularly advantageous opportunities to adjudge Reformation doctrine, to align the clergy of a municipality or city territory with a particular theological position, to oblige them to bear loyalty to the city authorities, and to orchestrate the self-driven autonomy with regard to the church hierarchy.[16]

15 Kaufmann, *Geschichte der Reformation*, 392.
16 Ibid., 402.

The Second Zurich Disputation of the same year revealed, however, that not everyone agreed with virtually placing doctrinal authority in the hands of a lay body. Zwingli was met with opponents from among his own supporters, who consequently went their own ways, mostly forming their own Baptist congregations, which completed the radical decoupling of spiritual and secular authorities. With his more moderate views, oriented toward a theology of order—not unlike Luther's views—Zwingli reached the "socially stable, economically agile, and politically predominant guild society"[17] and could henceforth count on its support. This development would reach an apex for once with the establishing of the *Prophezey* exegesis circle in Zurich, but especially with that of the court for marriage and morals (*Ehe- und Sittengericht*), a city authority made up of four secular and two clerical judges, with jurisdiction over practically all matters of social discipline.

Geneva

There are two things that cannot be separated from Geneva's Reformation:[18] first, like Luther in Wittenberg and Zwingli in Zürich, John Calvin was the outstanding personality in Geneva, who in his very own way ensured that the openness to Reformation ideas would be linked to political interests so that a sustainable and stable reform of the church and public life could go hand in hand. Second, the fate of Geneva was closely connected to that of Bern, as Geneva sought to close ranks with Bern in its wish to extract itself from the grasps of Savoy—thus entering into a new dependence, something that moved the council toward seeking independence again once and for all. The city, therefore, needed a reformer with a vision beyond the boundaries of the Swiss Confederation—and this was indeed Calvin, who looked toward Strasbourg and France, and not so much toward Zurich, Basel, or Bern. Geneva needed a cosmopolitan figure and therefore came to terms with Calvin despite all difficulties that it had with him for many years due to his severity and implacable nature when it came to doctrine and church life.

Calvin had a different understanding of the role of authority than did Zwingli and Luther. He was of the opinion that the clergy had the role of supervision of moral discipline and civic order, also with regard to those in power. It was not surprising, therefore, that this position would lead him to conflict with the city council, which was torn between its wish to extract itself from the grasp of Bern and its equally strong wish not to lose its sovereignty

17 Ibid., 408.

18 Cf. the brief but informative piece relevant to this context: Hans Rudolf Guggisberg, "Westschweiz und Genf," in *Die Territorien des Reichs*, 5:294–97.

to the church. Calvin established a consistory of 12 elders and the pastors, whose role it was to provide strict supervision, whereby the elders were also members of the city council (two were to belong to the small council, four to the middle council, and six to the grand council), so that measures of church discipline could soon be followed by secular punishment as well.

Hungary

During the Reformation Era, Hungary[19] found itself in the thankless role of serving, in general, as a buffer to the advances of the Ottoman Empire. Following the conquest of Mohács (1526) and Buda (1541), a large portion of Hungary had come under Ottoman control, with only a relatively small area in the North still belonging to the Habsburgs of Ferdinand I. There, however, magnate families—between 30 and 40 in number—with large landholdings, enjoyed considerable influence and power even in relation to the nobility, who were economically dependent on the magnates, and who not infrequently fled to the areas of Ottoman control. It was thanks to the magnates that the Reformation could spread rapidly and in the particular way it did. Without imposing a compulsory confession, they made Protestant preaching and practices possible, leading to a "slow but sure" process. It would, in fact, take quite a long time in some cases before the populace embraced the changes, but when it did happen, it had stability and durability. This was precipitated further by the fact that the confessionalization process was nearly always connected to the establishment of an educational and school system based on Melanchthon's ideas. As was also the case in Germany, but even more so, the Reformation and mother-tongue education supported the development of the language of the people and consequently the reshaping and establishment of Hungarian literature.

The magnates were able to expand their domain further when, following the Turkish victory at the Battle of Mohács, many prominent members of the clergy had perished, with only three bishops left in the country. As neither Hungarian king was interested in refilling those posts, a de facto process of secularization followed, which the magnates were able to put to their own use. Since for a long time after that the Catholic religious life had only a rudimentary influence, the stage was set for the adoption of Reformation thought. This was brought to Hungary by students, in particular, who had come to know the new doctrine in Wittenberg, and were met with particularly open ears in cities with German populations. In 1538, Mátyás Bíró Dévai prepared a catechism that supported him in his—and one may call it

19 Cf. Markus Hein and Éva Zs. Hein, "Ungarn," in *Theologische Realenzyklopädie* 34 (2002): 272–303.

as such—broad missionary activities, which he was able to carry out under the protection of the magnates even as he faced persecution from various quarters. Already in 1549, the former Wittenberg student Leonhard Stöckel completed the *Confessio Pentapolitana*, which was based on the CA *Variata*, and served as an example for other cities. Beginning in Debrecen, Reformed doctrine took root in the Ottoman part of Hungary, due to the efforts of István Szegedi Kis—a movement that found its apex in the adoption of the *Confessio Helvetica Posterior* in 1567.

Following the loss of its former splendour and the connected economic and social consequences, the Reformation represented hope for a new beginning within Hungary. Counter-Reformation efforts, which involved an attempt to regain influence through schooling, were therefore quite difficult. These measures were only met with some success once the archbishop of Esztergom, Péter Pázmány (1570–1637), succeeded in gaining some of the most important magnates for his cause, so that only the middle and lower nobility formed a Protestant majority in the Hungarian Diet. Only the Principality of Transylvania emerged as the protector of Protestants until it, too, lost its influence due to inept politics and ultimately the collapse of the Turkish occupation and the beginnings of the territory's re-Catholicization under Leopold I, who ascended to the imperial throne in 1658.

Netherlands

One can perhaps speak most readily of a people's Reformation, a Reformation "from below," when it comes to the Netherlands.[20] While the Reformation movement was used as a means of liberation from the Habsburgs, the beginnings of the movement did, in fact, trace back to the influences of humanism and the *devotio moderna* of the Brethren of the Common Life, who were very active in the Netherlands in particular, as well as of the strong Anabaptist movement. After Melchior Hoffmann conducted faith baptisms of numerous adults in 1530, these newly baptized Christians brought these new ideas back to their home parishes and fought there for the establishment of the practice. Despite persecution and reprisals—many Anabaptists became victims of the Inquisition—they were often quite successful finding many new supporters emerging from all social classes, who were able to get something out of the social concept and the apocalyptic notions that Hoffmann stood for. In this vein, new social structures were brought about, attaining monstrous dimensions in the Anabaptist Kingdom of Münster, which contributed to the Anabaptists being discredited everywhere. Meanwhile, new

20 Cf. Antoon E. M. Janssen and Peter J. A. Nissen, "Niederlande, Lüttich," in *Die Territorien des Reichs*, 3:200–35.

adherents would still join the more moderate Menno Simons. Later, it was French émigrés in particular who brought along their Calvinistic background, and the French-speaking southern provinces, which maintained close contact with Strasbourg. The 1561 *Confession de Foy* became the first Calvinistic creed in the Netherlands. Persecution by the authorities repeatedly forced Protestants to take flight, whether it was to Emden, where they joined John Laski, to London, or to Frankfurt. The resistance of the Netherlands to the rule of the Habsburg Philipp II, carried out in particular by the nobility and supported through the old traditions of the right to resistance, can only be viewed to a small degree as religiously motivated. Even the iconoclasm of 1566/67, which is commonly viewed as the "starting gun" for the uprising, did not emerge from religious interests: "It was not a great people's movement of economically and socially dispossessed. Several factors combined in this dissatisfaction: Calvinist idealism, blind religious zeal, anti-clericalism, economic-social dissatisfaction, and material goals all took turns in playing a dominant role."[21]

Calvinist-oriented parishes had, however, already been established, whose church orders were mostly prepared abroad for underground use in the Netherlands. Resistance to the imposed administrative system and the question of whether one needed to believe what the authorities decided was particularly virulent in these parishes, so that the new religious groups also provided a basis for political resistance. The 1568 Synod of Dordrecht focused on this relationship between church and state with a discussion of freedom of belief, and thereby exacerbated the contrast between the Spanish and Tridentine-minded southern and the Calvinistic-minded northern provinces even further. A planned religious peace was to provide that wherever at least 100 families belonged to a particular religion, people would be free to practice that religion. Both the insurgent Holland and Zeeland as well as the predominantly Catholic provinces of the South vehemently rejected this compromise. The formation of the Union of Utrecht by a number of insurgent provinces and cities in 1579 basically firmed up the confessional and political division of the Netherlands.

The Calvinization of the North—and the concurring (re-)Catholicization of the South—was supported by the authorities in that it always began with the prohibition of the practice of the Catholic faith. The actions of the authorities clearly aimed at the de-Catholicization of public life, which—even if the city rulers and provincial authorities declared themselves to be the protectors of the new faith—did not, conversely, constitute a "Calvinization" of public life; civic and church communities did not coincide, and the "secular" vote was considered decisive in elections for offices in schools, universities, and institutions for orphans, the poor, and

21 Ibid., 3:220.

the like. As a consequence, in these areas, a tolerant and pragmatic religious policy was established in line with the secular authorities.

Reformational Movements: A New Beginning in Europe?

This selected overview has made it clear that, in the mix of political and religious interests and motivations, a major role was played by the sovereigns' Reformation in the empire. Or perhaps it would be better—in order to include the variety of movements guided and mostly initiated "from above"—to speak of the authorities' Reformation. This would then include the Reformation in the cities and the concept of a reformation of parishes—one that researchers have critically received, and justly so—without ignoring the particular specifics.[22] This would, in any event, avoid the impression that there was a Reformation movement exclusively "from below," fully separate from any support of secular authorities and officials. Even the events in the Netherlands, which came closest to this idea, depended on support from the authorities. There is no question, however, that in fact the interests of the authorities coincided partly with what had been brewing among the people and in the parishes, and that, in return, the measures of the authorities also triggered something within the populace. As Manfred Rudersdorf puts it:

> As effective as the bourgeois Reformation in cities and the peasant parish Reformation were, with their albeit rather limited emanation, in the local and regional surroundings, it would entail an inappropriate relativization of the significance of the sovereigns' Reformation for the choice of faith in the Empire if this effectiveness were to be tantamount to reducing the German Reformation [. . .] much too one-sidedly to an "urban event." [. . .] The political interplay of forces that secured and guaranteed the survival of the new confession in the long run was undoubtedly to be located at the level of the early modern German territorial state.[23]

---

22 This remains valid, especially since Kaufmann established the following, building on his teacher Moeller and recent research: "The theological concepts of the reformers which were aimed at the religious integration of the municipality did more, generally speaking, to strengthen the authoritarian nature of the magistrates than to relativize it. [. . .] Congregational-communal or rather urban-republican traditions, which contributed to the Reformation movement enjoying particular support among the populace from which it often emerged, also became effective in the northwest German Hanseatic towns. During their phases of inauguration and establishment, the urban Reformations were Reformations of the magistrates and parishes; over time, however, the aspects of state rule would come to the fore." Kaufmann, *Geschichte der Reformation*, 420.

23 Rudersdorf, "Die Generation," 139f.

Our observations are not only due to an interest in history, but we also are bound to consider what these roots mean for us today as Protestants, in our churches, in interdenominational and interreligious dialogue; therefore, I will pinpoint my question and put forward only one thesis in response. The question is: In light of the Europe in which we live today, are there chances and openings for "the" Reformation, which, due to the divisions in the empire, gave way to many "Reformations" in the 16th century? Well, in this era in Europe, we live under fully different conditions, of which the separation of church and state certainly stands out. The discussions about whether "God" should appear in an European constitution underscores how thorough this separation is being conceived (thank God, nobody in Brussels or elsewhere has come up with the idea of questioning the Christian calendar . . .). A reform driven by the authorities would thus be unthinkable—in accordance with the principle of *ecclesia semper reformanda* that is valid for Protestant churches as well—as the church has to remain within its boundaries and the state must not get involved in the matter. Over all, this is a positive development that should be left undisturbed. On the other hand, it would be desirable for political actors and states to recollect and focus—with regard to their origins and formation, which occurred in close connection with religious moments—not so much on the historical aspects of church history as a whole and the Reformation movements in particular, but indeed on the content involved; on that which is "reformational," with the consistent self-understanding of reemphasizing that which is "Christian"—and which, at least in this regard, created a supportive and powerful common thread in the face of all its diversity.

CHAPTER 17

Walter Fleischmann-Bisten

Reformation, Radical Reformation, Anabaptists, and the Peasants' War

Reformation between Intolerance and Revolution

In the middle of the Reformation Decade leading up to the big 2017 anniversary, we are unavoidably faced with an immense obstacle: the darker sides of the 16th-century Reformation, which have left a legacy stretching into the most recent church and denominational history. The ecumenical, and even the interreligious, dialogues of the 21st century come to face this legacy time and time again. The Christian intolerance of earlier centuries did much to prevent the Reformation from unfolding its practically revolutionary potential for hundreds of years. However, it is precisely this that we now need as a type of Protestant elixir of life. I would thus like to cut a couple of paths here through some of this Reformation thicket of tolerance, intolerance, and revolution.

We first become aware of the Latin word *tolerantia* in Cicero's *Paradoxa stoicorum* of 46 BCE. The verb *tolerare* was used by the Stoics and in the New

Testament to mean "suffer, allow, and tolerate," including the meaning of voluntary endurance, and as an expression of superior patience and strength.[1] The church father Tertullian (c. 160–after 212) already used the term *tolerance* in connection with theological differences within the early church. This bitter truth is thus hard to explain: that just a few centuries, or even mere decades, after the end of the Roman persecution of Christians—because of the "Edict of Toleration" of Emperor Constantinc the Great in 313 CE—Christians, with the support of the state and church, would discriminate against supposed outsiders and theologically problematic groups as "heretics." Christianity "went from being a persecuted to a tolerated and then recognized and official church—and ultimately to a persecuting church."[2] Beginning in the 11th century, the church agenda not only included pogroms against the Jews, but also the persecution of Waldensians, Cathars, Hussites, and other minorities.

It is not a task for historians and denominational researchers to wag their fingers at developments such as these that appear questionable to us today. Sources always need to be interpreted in the context of prevailing political conditions and theological developments, that is, in their historical context.[3] I thus first attempt to understand why, even in the 16th-century centres of the Reformation (e.g., Wittenberg, Zurich, Strasbourg, Nuremberg, Geneva), the leading theologians lost—from our present point of view—their credibility and theological independence through their intolerant stance toward each other and toward the "left wing" of the Reformation. The Reformation stance on the peasants' demands and on the Peasants' War is of particular significance in this context. In the second section, I will look into the consequences of Protestant intolerance that continue to be a burden within ecumenical relations among Protestants, and will attempt to draw conclusions, especially with a view to the 2017 Reformation anniversary.

1 As discussed in Philipp David, "Was ist Toleranz?," in *Fundamentalismus und Toleranz*, ed. Tim Unger (Hannover, 2009), 9–27, at 12.

2 Ibid., 13. Cf. the edict of Emperor Theodosius the Great of 380: "According to the apostolic teaching and the doctrine of the Gospel, let us believe in the one Deity of the Father, Son and Holy Spirit, in equal majesty and in a unified Trinity. We authorize the followers of this law to assume the title Catholic Christians; but as for the others, since in our judgment they are foolish madmen, we decree that they shall be branded with the ignominious name of heretics, and shall not presume to give their conventicles the name of churches. They will suffer in the first place the chastisement of divine condemnation and in the second the punishment of out authority, in accordance with our will, shall decide to inflict. [. . .] The norm of a uniform religion is henceforth to be upheld in the Empire." Translation (of the bulk of the passage through the ellipsis) by Henry Bettenson, ed., *Documents of the Christian Church* (London: Oxford University Press, 1943), 31.

3 Cf. Ulrich H. J. Körtner, "Reformation und Toleranz," *Materialdienst des Konfessionskundlichen Instituts* (hereafter MdKI) 64 (2013): 3–8, at 3f.

The Darker Sides of the Reformation

The word *Toleranz* was coined in the German language by Martin Luther, of all people, as Albrecht Beutel explains. In his *Resolutions* of 1518, Luther declared that heresy could not be fought with "fire and sword" but only through religious persuasion.[4] Still, in his 1523 writing "On Secular Authority," Luther rejected all forms of force in matters of faith and conscience:

> How he believes is a matter for each individual's conscience, and this does not diminish [the authority of] secular governments. They ought therefore to content themselves with attending to their own business, and allow people to believe what they can, and what they want, and they must use no coercion in this matter against anyone. [. . .] so far from being something secular authority ought to create and enforce, faith is something that God works in the spirit.[5]

The death penalty was a last resort for Luther. Still, heresies had to be banned from the land due to their obscuration of the gospel. Luther's 1525 principle that "love endures all, faith tolerates nothing"[6] had its origins in his understanding of God's tolerance (*tolerantia Dei*) within the context of a theology of the cross. Luther was thus not able to accept any sort of indifference along the lines of "everybody should believe whatever they want." But he would soon plead for moderation for fear of violence and upheaval, and therefore soon reacted differently, following his original support, to the political changes deemed necessary (e.g., with regard to the demands of the peasants). He did this based on theological reasons and with consideration for the authorities that protected him and his followers.

We can observe, in any event, that Luther's tolerance for all other approaches to faith grew increasingly weak. The understanding of tolerance for the reformers as a whole—as Volker Leppin puts it—can be seen as a path between support, denial, and the granting of tolerance: being tolerated by those of the old Roman Catholic faith would have distorted Luther's own claim to the truth. "Being tolerated by the Antichrist would have meant leaving one's own acceptance to be decided by a power inimical to God." The lack of tolerance for the Anabaptists, for example, was, for Luther, due to "the classification of Anabaptism as blasphemy, while the decisive matter was the Anabaptists' rejection of an ordered ministry."[7]

---

4 Albrecht Beutel, "Der frühneuzeitliche Toleranzdiskurs. Umrisse und Konkretionen," in *Was ist Toleranz?*, 28–48, at 29 n. 1.

5 Translation from *Luther and Calvin on Secular Authority*, ed. and trans. Harro Höpfl (Cambridge: Cambridge University Press, 1991).

6 "Charitas . . . omnia tolerat, fides . . . nihil tolerat" in Martin Luther, WA 14:669, 14f.

7 Volker Leppin, "Toleranz im Horizont protestantischer Selbstverständigung," in *Schwierige Toleranz. Der Umgang mit Andersdenkenden und Andersgläubigen in der Christentumsgeschichte*, ed.

The Reformation stance on the demands of the peasantry and the Peasants' War of 1524/25 derived from a different conflict. The charge of intolerance is, in my opinion, unfitting if we take the historical situation into account. Unlike the numerous peasants' uprisings since the late 13th century, religious issues indeed played an important role in the German Peasants' War, as had been the case in the Hussite Revolution. Whether and how the influences of preachers who were reformation minded, however, affected the cause and course of the Peasants' War is difficult to determine since the effects of the Reformation could only be seen in southern Germany in 1524–1525. The Twelve Articles, the pivotal peasants' manifesto, however, was issued in Memmingen in March 1525, and reflects the influence of Luther with regard to authority and nonviolence. "There was, additionally, Zwinglian thought in the German southwest, Müntzerian ideas in the Black Forest and Thuringia, and much more. The important points are, in their essence, older than the Reformation like the talk of divine right and the spiritually founded rejection of serfdom."[8]

Without a doubt, Luther's polemics against the papacy and the entire church authority shook and eventually brought down one of the sustaining pillars of late medieval society. Among his numerous writings of 1520 and 1521, severe accusations of sovereigns and the nobility in general are to be found. Since his address "To the Christian Nobility of the German Nation," Luther repeatedly spoke out on questions concerning ownership, tithing, and usury. At this point, he expected an improvement of the Christian condition only from the authorities. Still, there were sections in "To the Christian Nobility" that call "the militia and the secular sword" to action should a council reject the reformation of the church.

"One must not doubt the mass effect of such statements," even if the Wittenberg upheavals of 1522 make Luther's turning toward nonviolence in matters of faith more than obvious.[9] Luther's twofold position in this set of issues becomes quite clear in his "Admonition to Peace Concerning the Twelve Articles of the Peasants" of April 1525. Luther speaks clearly to both parties, while rejecting the role of judge that was expected of him, but speaks instead most of all as pastor. While strongly criticizing the sovereigns as having caused the insurgence, Luther rejects the peasants' claim to be a "Christian association":

> They made use of the name of God unjustly, as they took up the sword, rebelled against the authorities, and wished to be their own judges. The

Marianne Delgado, et al. (Fribourg/Stuttgart, 2012), at 81–90, at 82 and 85.

8 Gottfried Maron, "Bauernkrieg," in Theologische Realenzyklopädie 5 (1980): 319–38, at 321 (hereafter TRE).

9 Ibid., 323f.

right of Christians is however not to fight back, not to take revenge, but to suffer! Luther is thus sensitive when it comes to the particular point in which social and political demands are made in the name of the Gospel. It is often overlooked that Luther indeed places both parties to the conflict on the same footing in the last part of his writing.[10]

One matter, however, has been decisive in the appraisal of Luther over the centuries: with the impressions fresh in mind of his travel into the centre of the peasants' revolts in northern Thuringia, where he felt closely confronted with what he saw as Thomas Müntzer's false prophethood, he added an annex to the second printing of his piece in May 1525, entitled "Against the Murderous, Thieving Hordes of Peasants." The text did not become known, however, until the peasants had already been bloodily defeated. We are not able to look into the different positions of other reformers within this paper; Melanchthon spoke out much more harshly than Luther, while Johannes Brenz took a very sensitive and conciliatory tone.

It is not surprising that the Catholic side placed the sole blame for the uprisings and their outcome with Luther and the Reformation. But even in the Marxist literature, which, for a long time, had one-sidedly lowered Luther to the status of a henchman of the court (*Fürstenknecht*), one could find other voices in the German Democratic Republic (GDR) era as well. Gerhard Zschäbitz, for instance, wrote as early as 1967 that Luther had not held the peasants in disdain, but that his stance was the product of his "class allegiance."[11] We can establish, generally speaking, in our context that the Peasants' War, in any event, did not "end the Reformation as a movement of the people" but "made it clear to the authorities in the affected areas that decisions would have to be made." Nor did the Peasants' War signify a victory for the "left wing of the Reformation," although there were links between the peasants in revolt and the Anabaptists both in Switzerland and elsewhere.[12]

The granting of tolerance can be seen in examples such as Sebastian Castellios's advocacy against Calvin's intolerance in Geneva and the role he played in the 1553 execution of the Unitarian-minded Michael Servetus,[13] and

10 Ibid., 327.

11 Cf. ibid., 329.

12 Gottfried Seebass, *Geschichte des Christentums* III, Theologische Wissenschaft 7 (Stuttgart, 2006), 136f.

13 Cf. Christian Link, *Johannes Calvin: Humanist, Reformator, Lehrer der Kirche* (Zürich, 2009), 70f., who recalls that Calvin added to his admonitions to paternal discipline as a trait of church discipline (*Institutes* IV, 12, 8) in the first edition of his *Institutes* in 1536 the following expansion that is unfortunately missing in later editions: "And not only are excommunicants to be so treated, but also Turks and Saracens, and other enemies of religion. Far be it from us to approve those methods by which many until now have tried to force them to our faith, when they forbid them the use of fire and water and the common elements, when they deny them

especially in the efforts of Philipp the Magnanimous, Landgrave of Hesse, who advocated for the tolerant treatment of the Anabaptists, and excluded the death penalty in any event.[14]

In 1529, the Second Imperial Diet in Speyer brought the entire political and theological dilemma into focus: fourteen imperial estates protested against the decision to impose finally the imperial ban against Luther and to get rid of him. They founded their stand in their understanding of the freedom of belief and conscience. These first "Protestants" demanded that "each individual has to stand and justify himself before God in matters that have a bearing on God's honour and our souls."[15] This Reformation view stood in opposition to the mandate that was renewed by the same diet to carry out the death penalty against all "Anabaptists." In most of the territories in which the Reformation had been introduced, Baptists had been persecuted as "Anabaptists" with the theological support of Luther and Melanchthon.[16]

Zwingli's sympathy for the much more radical consequences of a "Reformation from top to bottom" would soon also come to an end with the demands of "Anabaptists" and "Anabaptist-minded" groups, which emerged in the 1520s in Switzerland, Tirol, Franconia, and other regions. The Anabaptists, in the course of their intensive study of the Bible, came to the conclusion that the gospel only permitted baptism in faith and confession, and allowed for the strict separation of church and state. They thus refused to swear oaths or provide military service, and advocated for the freedom of belief—apart from the excesses in the Anabaptist Kingdom of Münster of 1534/35. This was expressed in a particularly impressive manner in the June 1534 petition of the imprisoned soapmaker, Leupold Scharnschlager, to the council of the Free Imperial City of Strasbourg:

> And if they seek to force you to adopt a faith that you—and each of you—cannot deem proper in your conscience, you could indeed never adopt it with a quiet conscience and forever wish to be free herein. I therefore ask you faithfully that you consider and take to heart that this is and must be the case for me and those like me, but that I and those like me also do not intend to maintain our faith through violence or resistance but instead, with the help of God's strength, for which we pray,

---

to all offices of humanity, when they pursue them with sword and arms." Trans. Ford Lewis Battles, *Institutes of the Christian Religion, 1536 Edition* (Grand Rapids, 1975).

14 Cf. Gury Schneider-Ludorff, *Der fürstliche Reformator* (Leipzig, 2006), 126–65.

15 Cf. the precise wording in Wolf-Dieter Hauschild, *Lehrbuch der Kirchen- und Dogmengeschichte*, Bd. 2 (Gütersloh, 1999), 113.

16 Cf. the overview in the report of the International Lutheran-Mennonite Study Commission, presented on 22 July 2010 as part of a celebration of reconciliation at the Lutheran World Federation (LWF) Assembly in Stuttgart, *Healing Memories: Reconciling in Christ* (Geneva/Strasbourg: Lutheran World Federation/Mennonite World Conference, 2010), 104–32.

with patience and suffering up until our bodily demise. [. . .] What would it mean to be in the right claiming something only for myself, and not to wish to grant the same to others? With this I refer to the freedom of belief.[17]

The stipulations of the 1555 Religious Peace of Augsburg[18] extended a certain legal equality with Roman Catholics only to the adherents of the *Confessio Augustana* and related groups. The Reformed (Calvinists) in the Electoral Palatinate, for example, were no longer persecuted as heretics because they accepted the revised 1540 version of the Augsburg Confession. The mutual intolerance among Protestants is evidenced in, for example, the words engraved in a Wittenberg building, which were rechiseled into its stone front in 1717: "*Gottes Wort und Lutheri Schrift, ist des Bapst und Calvini Gift*" ("God's Word and Luther's Scripture is poison to the Pope and Calvin").[19]

From Protestant (In)tolerance to Religious Freedom

The legal stipulations of the 1648 Peace of Westphalia was listing heavily toward intolerance, which would have considerable consequences. Even after the terrible experience of the Thirty Years' War, only Reformed Christians were granted equal status with the Roman Catholics and Lutherans. As we read in the *Instrumentum Pacis Osnaburgae* of 24 October 1648 in Article VII, paragraph 2: "In addition to the three aforementioned religious parties, none others should be tolerated [*nulla alia recipiatur vel toleretur*]." The degree to which this stance of intolerance with regard to other Reformation churches (Mennonites, Baptists, and later Methodists and others) continued to have an effect for centuries is reflected in the fact that even in a renowned theological lexicon only ten years ago, the decisions made in 1648 were described, without further explanation, as follows: "The sects were, however, excluded from the religious-legal guarantees of the Peace of Westphalia."[20]

The example of the Enlightenment development in England reveals the difficulties that the idea of tolerance met in the 17th century. The physician, philosopher, and politician John Locke and his works had great influence in the success of the Enlightenment. His writings and demands, as we can see in the following, made clear what he saw as a close connection between

17 Cited from Heinold Fast, ed., *Der linke Flügel der Reformation*, Klassiker des Protestantismus Bd. IV (Bremen, 1962), 119–30.

18 In the official language: *Ubi unus dominus, ibi una sit religio.* This would turn into *cuius regio eius religio* following the handbook by the jurist Johann Joachim Stephani *Institutiones iuris canonici* of 1599.

19 Cf. Volkmar Joestel and Jutta Strehle, *Luthers Bild und Lutherbilder. Ein Rundgang durch die Wirkungsgeschichte* (Wittenberg, 2003), 25.

20 Thomas Kaufmann, Art. "Westfälischer Friede," TRE 35 (2003): 679–86, at 683.

tolerance motivated by Christianity and human reason, also offering as a solution the possible separation of church and state:

> The toleration of those that differ from others in matters of religion is so agreeable to the Gospel of Jesus Christ, and to the genuine reason of mankind, that it seems monstrous for men to be so blind as not to perceive the necessity and advantage of it in so clear a light. [. . .] But, however, that some may not colour their spirit of persecution and unchristian cruelty with a pretence of care of the public weal and observation of the laws [. . .] I esteem it above all things necessary to distinguish exactly the business of civil government from that of religion and to settle the just bounds that lie between the one and the other.[21]

England's 1689 Act of Toleration provides the context for the concerns of Free-Church theologians over the discussion on the Constitution of Virginia since, even as concessions were made to nonconformists in England in matters involving the construction of chapels and the hiring of pastors, they continued to be denied important basic civil rights such as university and educational opportunities.[22]

The dissenters, nonconformists, and Congregationalists, all influenced by the theology of Martin Bucer and John Calvin, were not content with the outcome of the Reformation in 16th- and 17th-century England. Forced to emigrate to the New World despite the Act of Toleration, they were able to gain religious freedom as a constitutional right through an arduous process under the new political and denominational circumstances there. Roger Williams, a Baptist, and William Penn, who was a Quaker, are worthy of particular recognition in this regard.[23] In this context, Christian Link has called attention to the fact that, with regard to demanding religious freedom, particularly those churches influenced by Calvin "asserted particular influence on the development of modern democracy with the strong emphasis on the federal idea and lastly with their synodal-presbyterian system."[24] It was thus precisely those Free Protestant churches, which were put down as "sects" or "special communities" in Germany up to the Weimar Republic, that paved the way for the human right of religious freedom through their reception of the concept of tolerance and their adoption of the Reformation demand for freedom of faith and conscience.

Even the unions between Lutheran and Reformed Christians that emerged from the Enlightenment in the early 19th century in numerous

---

21 John Locke, "A Letter Concerning Toleration," trans. William Popple (unpub.).

22 Cf. Erich Geldbach, *Freikirchen—Erbe, Gestalt und Wirkung*, Bensheimer Hefte 70 (Göttingen, 2005), 78–85.

23 Cf. ibid., 70–78.

24 Link, *Johannes Calvin*, 72.

German territories showed unfortunate signs of intolerance due to the inequality of tolerance and religious freedom. Those Lutherans who rejected these unions for theological reasons, and who now belong to Germany's Free Lutheran churches, were forced to struggle with the great difficulties imposed on them by the official regional churches (*Landeskirchen*).[25] Within this context, Goethe's famous saying takes on a quality that was understandable and critical also within his time: "Tolerance should really only be a passing attitude: it should lead to appreciation. To tolerate is to offend."[26] As it was, forced baptisms continued to be carried out through the middle of the 19th century, even in Hesse, with parents facing severe punishment and being forced to emigrate to the United States—as in the case of Grimmel, a printer in Marburg.[27]

After the failure of the democratic Frankfurt Constitution of 1848/1849, and despite the growth of Free Protestant churches, which could no longer be slowed, it would take the Weimar Constitution of 1919 to end this inequality between official regional churches and Free Churches in the German Empire. This not only marked the end of the state church, but also constitutionally established the equality and autonomy of all religious communities (Art. 137). Additionally, the total freedom of belief and conscience was bestowed on every citizen of the German Empire (Art. 135).

It would, however, remain difficult to implement this equal footing, which would finally allow Adventists, Baptists, Free Protestant congregations, Methodists, and Mennonites to attain association rights. The founding of the Union of Evangelical Free Churches in 1926 and the creation of the Council of Christian Churches in Germany in 1948 with the help of numerous Free Churches both played a major role in overcoming old prejudices.

We can see how different the process was, outside of Germany, over the past hundred years—from the Reformation freedom of belief via a questionable idea of tolerance to a constitutionally recognized freedom of religion—if we look at the legal standing of all of the Free Churches that emerged from the Reformation in Austria and Switzerland. While, as far as I know, most cantons in Switzerland still do not uphold legal equality between the regional churches and many "Free Churches," the path was paved in summer 2013 for a new direction in this regard in Austria. With the ordinance of 26 August 2013,[28] the "Free Churches in Austria" association of the following

25 Cf. Hartmut Bartmuss, "Reformation und Toleranz—Anmerkungen zum Themenjahr," *SELK Info* 383 (January 2013): 2–3.

26 Johann Wolfgang von Goethe, *Maxims and Reflections*, trans. Elizabeth Stopp (New York: Penguin, 1998).

27 Cf. Geldbach, *Freikirchen*, 152–54.

28 Bundesgesetzblatt der Republik Österreich II 250/2013-Eintrag vom 27.08.2013; cf. the article by Karl Schwarz, MdKI 64 (2013): H. 5.

five Free Churches was finally legally recognized following a long and heated process:

- the Mennonite Free Church,
- the Union of Baptist Churches,
- the Association of Evangelical Churches,
- the Free Christian Pentecostal Church,
- and the Elaia Christian Churches.

These problems of recognition were connected to the particular foundation of the Austrian law of religion, which did not bring about complete equality for the Protestant churches of the Augsburg (Lutheran) and Helvetic (Reformed) Confessions until the Protestant Law of 1961. The legal recognition of a church or religious community was, for a long time, only extended to the Old Catholic Church (1877), the Moravian Church (1880), and Hanafi Islam (1912) alongside the historically existing churches and religious communities of Austria (such as the Roman Catholic Church, the Greek Catholic Church, the Greek Orthodox Church, Judaism, and the Lutheran and Reformed churches). The 1919 Treaty of Saint Germain, indeed, only recognized the free practice of religion in terms of an individual freedom of belief. Eventually, the Methodist Church (1951) and the Mormons (1955) would also be granted this status of the highest level of state recognition. Even the Law on the Status of Religious Confessional Communities (*Bekenntnisgemeinschaftengesetz*) of 1998 still distinguished between communities registered with the state and legally recognized institutions with a public legal status. To pass as the former, a community requires a membership of 0.2 percent of the entire population of Austria, or currently around 17,000 people. The above-mentioned Free Churches with some 160 congregations did not fulfill this requirement until they formed an association for state purposes, without, however, giving up their own independence. It was, however, for this reason that the Seventh-Day Adventists in Austria did not wish to join the group, as it does entail, among other things, common religious classes, something that raised identity-related concerns among the Adventists.[29]

Following this overview of intolerance among Protestants, it is practically a miracle that men (and one woman) representing Lutheran, Reformed, and United congregations and churches were able to agree on a common confessional text, for the first time in the history of Reformation churches in Germany, with the Theological Declaration of Barmen on 31 May 1934. Even if the confessional standing of the Barmen Declaration is not uncontroversial, Barmen served as a decisive impetus for the doctrinal discussions throughout Europe that led to the Leuenberg Agreement over 40 years ago,

29 Nachrichtenagentur APD Nr. 279/2013.

on 16 March 1973.[30] The Europe's Methodists joining in 1997 and at least a type of association agreement with the Baptists of Europe are hopeful signs of further bridges being built to firm up sustainable ecumenical relations among Protestants, after so many years of intolerance.

Conclusion

1. The Reformation divide between tolerance and intolerance remains a "topic of the history of the Reformation church's guilt and shame."[31] This view of EKD Vice President Thies Gundlach is, unfortunately, just as worthy of agreement as is the pointed appraisal of Helmut Kremers, editor-in-chief of *zeitzeichen* magazine: "If the reformers were in fact born with tolerance, much too often—and I would add much too long—it was left behind."[32]

2. The practically revolutionary potential of the Reformation with regard to the demands of the peasants, the excesses of capitalism, and for the path from the freedom of belief to the freedom of religion must be rediscovered and implemented today.

3. Even if the history of the Reformation and Counter-Reformation in the 16th and 17th centuries and through the Thirty Years' War was "practically emblematic in not tolerating the convictions of others" (according to Margot Kässmann, EKD ambassador for the 2017 Reformation Jubilee), contrary positions need to be recognized as well. This includes the fact that individual sovereigns (such as Philipp the Magnanimous of Hesse) and theologians (such as Martin Bucer and Johannes Brenz), as well as the vast majority in the Baptist movement, used biblical arguments in their support for the freedoms of conscience and faith.

4. The thesis of Baptist church historian and confessional researcher Erich Geldbach draws our focus to a problem area that is not new to the topic of this essay: "religious freedom is not the granting of toleration but an innate, inalienable human right."[33] The contribution of the Free-Church wing of the Reformation needs to be recognized more clearly than before in encyclopedias, handbooks, and even schoolbooks. Baptists, Quakers, and Methodists who emigrated and fled from England to North America in the 17th and 18th centuries fought hard for religious freedom as a human right. The basic ideas of the Bill of Rights of the U.S. Constitution (December

30 Cf. Walter Fleischmann-Bisten, "'Barmen' als Bekenntnis innerhalb der EKD. Konfessionskundliche Aspekte und Konsequenzen," *MdKI* 63 (2012): 8–11.

31 "Verdunkelter Christus," in *Schatten der Reformation: Der lange Weg zur Toleranz*, published by the EKD Church Office (Hannover: Kirchenamt der EKD, 2012), 4–6, at 4.

32 Cited from Walter Fleischmann-Bisten, "Die Stiefkinder der Reformation," in ibid., 15–17, at 16.

33 Erich Geldbach, "Religionsfreiheit," *MdKI* 55 (2004): 87–92, at 88.

1791) would find their way much later into the constitutions of Europe (Germany in 1919).

5. With a view forward to 2017, all of the churches and denominations, which have been meeting each other with intolerance and persecution for some 500 years, need to seek out new signs of reconciliation. Further steps are needed to build on the "healing of memories" that already occurred—entailing the statement of guilt and declaration of eucharistic communion between the regional churches of the EKD and the Mennonites (1996) and the declaration of full church communion between the Methodists in Germany and the EKD (1987).[34] The leaders of the EKD and its regional churches must move quickly to incorporate the churches of the Union of Evangelical Free Churches into the preparatory projects for 2017—something that needs to be done as well in Austria, Switzerland, and, indeed, all the churches of the Community of Protestant Churches in Europe (CPCE). Despite all the indignities, most Free Churches have not forgotten that they are also children of an incomplete Reformation.[35]

34 As the United Evangelical Lutheran Church of Germany (VELKD) has been an important trailblazer in this regard, it is not understandable why the ecumenical results already attained in Germany and other countries have not been carried forward into the process of reconciliation between Lutherans and Mennonites at the international level (cf. n. 16). Cf. Walter Fleischmann-Bisten, "Schuldbekenntnis ohne Tischgemeinschaft," *MdKI* 61 (2010): 81–82.

35 Cf. Walter Fleischmann-Bisten, "Kinder einer unvollendeten Reformation—Freikirchliche Rezeption von reformations-und Lutherjubiläen," *Freikirchenforschung* 20 (2011): 12–29.

CHAPTER 18

Erik A. de Boer

Reformation Jubilee and Confessionalization

The Christian church begins with Jesus Christ—no doubt about it. There is no church without Christ. As far as we humans are concerned, we can say that the church begins with the confession of the disciples: "You are the Messiah, the Son of the living God" (Matt. 16:16). Since then, humans have professed their faith in the Son of God, and we can find such confession in the New Testament.

The topic, as it was proposed to me, asks how the age of Reformation came to yield multiple confessions of faith—even to the extent of incurring fights of faith among reformers—and when such confessional development evolved into hyper-Reformation. In order to understand this evolutionary track, let me offer a bit more confessional history.

Confessing Phrases

A confession of faith that carries traits of a confessional formula is already provided by Paul in 1 Corinthians 15:3-5: "For what I received I passed on to you as of first importance: that Christ died for our sins according to the Scriptures, that he was buried, that he was raised on the third day according to the Scriptures, and that he appeared to Cephas, and then to the Twelve." The "received" and the "passed on" later become the notions of *traditio* and *redditio symboli*: confessing phrases of faith in God as Father, Son, and the Holy Spirit. Such formulas of faith are pronounced after the instruction of Christian doctrines, after the revelation of the mystery of faith and before the reception of baptism. They lead up to baptism. No credo, no access to the church. We may even say: there is no church without credo.

Confessional Narration

We encounter the term *kanôn pisteôs* or *regula fidei*, "the rule of faith," in the writings of the Apostolic Fathers and Apologists. It is a confession-like narrative of main biblical themes using a binary or trinitary structure. Such narratives or enumeration of the divine and historical facts of the Bible serve as a guide for the right faith.

It is on the basis of the trinitary structure of *regula fidei* that confessions like the Apostles' Creed were designed and persisted in this form in the West. At the Council of Nicaea, held in 325 CE, the ecclesiastical and secular authorities worked together for the first time on drafting a confessional text. The fourth century witnessed its extension into a credo called *Nicaeno-Constantinopolitanum.* The divinity of Christ and the Holy Spirit are confirmed. Since then, the church's confession is not only a positive rule of faith, but also a measure for uncovering heresy. In the fourth and fifth centuries, we find a large number of (handwritten) confessions of individual theologians or sacristans which (should) relate to the church confession and have been understood as such.

To summarize: personal and collective confessions of faith become public confessions of the church. The positive expression of true faith implies at the same time the denial of false doctrines. This state of affairs would remain in the West for centuries—as long as the Roman Catholic Church prevailed and could suppress any outsiders with the help of secular authorities. Only in the 16th century did the situation change radically. The movement that we call the "Reformation" led to new confessions.

The 16th Century: A Century of Confessions

The 16th century was a century of confessions, at least in terms of confessional texts. Such Reformation confessional texts differ from those of the early-church, ecumenical credos in many ways:

1. They describe, in any case in catechisms, church teachings on the basis of four main elements: Decalogue, Credo, Lord's Prayer, and the Words of Institution of the Sacraments.
2. They recognize the ecumenical credo and continue their theological evolution; in the *Confessio Belgica*, for example, in the doctrine of God and the doctrine of scripture, thereby taking the redemptive narrative as the basis for the whole confession of faith. In comparison with its model version, *La confession de foy* of 1599 from Paris, the primacy of the doctrine of God and the scope of the doctrine of scripture are striking in this Dutch confession of faith. These features can be understood as an approximation to the Roman Catholic Church and a clarification of their own position taken in the religious debates (e.g., the value of the canonical books).
3. The confessional writings of the Reformation often came into being through the interplay of secular and church leaderships. The *Confessio Augustana*—where the first part offers the dogmas that match with Rome and the second part offers controversial issues—cannot be understood if one disregards the political situations of 1530.

As already mentioned above, in the early phase of the Reformation, confessional writings did not involve such doctrinal formulations, neither on the Reformation nor on the Vatican side. The Roman Catholic Church developed her *Confessio Tridentinum* and *Catechismus Romanus* as late as 1563, at the end of the Council of Trent. Although dogmas were formulated earlier for the purpose of distinguishing between right and wrong teachings, they were only initiatives of theological faculties, without the support of papal or ecumenical authorities.

The development of the Protestant confessions of faith reflects the relationship between church and authorities. They were often initiated by disputation theses that would be discussed in a city so that a magisterial decision for the Reformation could be prepared. The climax of the confessionalization process happened between the years 1559 and 1565. The French churches adopted *La confession de foy*, consisting of 40 articles, at the first national Paris Synod. The Church of Scotland had the *Confessio Scotica* since 1560. In 1561, Guy de Bres also wrote a *confession de foy*, which was adjusted to the circumstances of the (French) Netherlands under the reign of King Philip II of Spain. It was adopted in 1562. The Second Helvetic Confession of Heinrich Bullinger was drafted in 1566 and was soon taken over by the Reformed Church in Hungary as well. This decade witnessed the shift of dimension of confessional evolution in the Reformed churches from the level of individual towns and regions to that of kingdoms and their kings. This marks the beginning of the era of confessional codification and delimitation.

The 17th Century: A Century of Dogmas

At the end of the 16th century, Reformed theology thrived in universities, making methodical progresses. This trend is referred to as Reformed Scholasticism and understood as a method of distinctions and instructions. In the Netherlands, disputations emerged concerning the authority of the *Confessio Belgica* and the Heidelberg Catechism, and also regarding the doctrine of original sin of children (baptism) and the doctrine of predestination. The Synod of Dordrecht of 1618–1619 adopted the *Canons* (dogmas or guidelines for instructions), a systematic response to the "Remonstrants" (a document of five articles which would lead to confessional and catechism changes). In my assessment, such evolution did not take place in Lutheranism after the conclusion of *The Book of Concord.*

It is controversial among researchers to what extent these *Canons* were influenced by the philosophical-theological method of Scholasticism. It is clear, however, that the *Canons* of Dordrecht aimed to serve first as a positive confirmation of the Heidelberg Catechism and the Dutch confession of faith, and second as a refutation of the positions judged as false doctrines.

Having mentioned the *Canons* of Dordrecht, it seems that we come to the point where ultra-Reformation is inevitably an issue.

Biographical Insight

I am, as we call it, a confessing member of a Reformed church that belongs to a church alliance of the Reformed churches in the Netherlands. Some distinctive features of this church group are as follows: (1) Not only all theology professors and pastors but also all elders and deacons have to sign the three ecumenical and three Reformation confessions of faith (to endow them with a certain canonical role). (2) We are not too familiar with confirmation classes, but, instead, with the catechesis for youth aged from 12 to about 18 years. Throughout the schooling years, children are also educated in the doctrines of the church. Then, a public confession of faith takes place and the youth are admitted to communion as confessing members. In my youth, the Heidelberg Catechism was taught in the catechesis; today, it stays more in the background. (3) Churches hold two worship services on Sunday; a teaching sermon is held in the afternoon service—almost always on the corresponding section of the Heidelberg Catechism.

All this is now, at the beginning of the 21st century, under great pressure. However, this biographical description may make it apparent how positively the confessional texts are understood in our tradition. Does the ultra-Reformation subsist—maybe in a pure culture—in a church reserve?

Celebrating Confessions?

By celebrating the "500 years of the Reformation," are we celebrating the birth of confessions, understood as confessional documents? Documents in the sense of Romans 10:9, in that they pass on in writing what is believed from the heart and professed with the mouth, and are adopted by us today?

The confessions of faith, which live divided in ecclesiastical organizations and their symbols, have come closer in ecumenical encounters and dialogues. There are consensus formulations, as, for example, the Leuenberg Agreement. The 20th century also saw the births of new confessions that were formulated as a reflection of certain contemporary issues, such as the Barmen Declaration in Germany and the Belhar Confession in South Africa.

Given these trends, is the 16th century overcome in terms of confessions? Can we leave the clashes among Catholicism, Lutheranism, Calvinism, Anabaptism, and so forth behind us? In my opinion, we should understand and celebrate the "500 years of the Reformation" with the help of the early-church terms *traditio* and *redditio*. *Traditio* in this sense means that the positive confession of the Reformation movement of the 16th century has been conveyed to us and that we, as its heirs, embrace it and return it. Returning as *redditio* means to express with our own words how we have understood the instructions of faith. Only if we relate to tradition, can we build tradition while working in our contemporary times: transference to the next generation through church teachings.

The elaborateness of the confessional texts of the 16th century is to be understood from their context. The systematic order of *capita* and the shape of the *articuli* are also determined by the era of its emergence. The verbatim biblical quotes, as found in confessional and catechism texts, are not always understood by us as occupying correct *loci probantia*, either. However, the confessional texts of the 16th century lead us back to the scriptures today. The credo of the church is born anew whenever we listen to the word of God, and will induce and entice us to confess. For there is no church unless there is credo.

CHAPTER 19

Martin Hirzel

Pietism

A Second Reformation?

The Reformation connections of Pietism and related earlier and later church-renewal movements are very complex. The development of this relationship between traditions was, on one hand, set into motion in early Reformation history and, on the other, formed by the situation in society and the church of the 17th and 18th centuries.[1]

Inherent to the churches of the Reformation is the wish to conceive and form the church in accordance with the early Christian ideal of the Acts of the Apostles and the *koinonia* ecclesiology of Paul's epistles. The reformers were not, however, moved by the call for *Reformatio in capite et in membris* ("reform of head and members") of the church, which had been heard time and again throughout the high and late Middle Ages ever since the Fourth Lateran Council,[2] that is, specific and comprehensive reform measures. The reformers expected the *reformatio ecclesiae* to result primarily from God's actions, through listening to the word of God. "Which is his church? The one

1 Martin Brecht, "Die Berufung von Pietismus und Erweckungsbewegung auf die Reformation," in *Freikirchenforschung 6* (1996): 1–9, here at 1.

2 Emidio Campi, "'Ecclesia semper reformanda.' Metamorphosen einer altehrwürdigen Formel," in *Zwingliana 37* (2010): 1–19, here at 4.

that hears his word," Zwingli once said.[3] "The *reformatio ecclesiae* was, for them, not indeed a reform of the institution of the church."[4] The church renewed itself from within through its occupation with the word of God in the context of the spiritual and social situation of one such as Luther, who personally struggled with the late-medieval practice of penitence, or Zwingli, who as a priest ministering to the people came to the view that the church no longer carried out its role in an urban society in accordance with the gospel. The actual reforms that took place during the Reformation era "went too far for some and not far enough for others."[5] Erasmus turned away from Luther because, in his opinion, Luther questioned the church and the pope too much. Thomas Müntzer and the Anabaptists broke away from the reformers, as they aimed for a renewal of life and the congregation in addition to the "renewal of faith." Luther and Zwingli were in general agreement in their rejection of too much compulsion and radicalism in bringing about the true church and the true Christian life. While Luther is known for his conviction that, in a practically automatic way, "from faith flow forth love and joy in the Lord, and from love a cheerful, willing, free spirit, disposed to serve our neighbour voluntarily,"[6] Zwingli saw the continual orientation of human righteousness with divine righteousness as important. The reformers rejected the paths of the Anabaptists and spiritualists inasmuch as they decided at an early stage to continue along the path of the Constantinian mainline church, and with the assistance of the secular authorities to remain the official people's church, which, from an ecclesiological perspective, would constitute a *corpus permixtum* as opposed to a "flock of the pure." There were, moreover, theological reservations with regard to justification by works when it came to placing too much emphasis on sanctification and Christian righteousness. Luther especially emphasized God's initiative in the formation of the renewed church. The introduction of church discipline to the Reformed churches could only slightly soften the tension between the early Christian ideal and the realities of the mainline churches. This tension would remain a characteristic of Protestantism.

How Pietism Came About

Pietism attempted a new response, different from that of the Reformation. How did this come about? Different reasons are cited for the development of Pietism, involving theology, the history of piety, and social

3 Ibid., 6.

4 Ibid., 7.

5 Here and henceforth, ibid., 8.

6 Martin Luther, "Concerning Christian Liberty," in *The Harvard Classics 36*, pt. 6 (New York, 1909), 14.

history. Traditionally cited are the "intellectualization" and "moralization" of the churches of the age of confessionalism, under the influence of orthodox theology, which neglected heartfelt faith for the sake of doctrine. One illustration of this is provided in what Goethe writes in *Dichtung und Wahrheit* (Truth and Fiction Relating to My Life) about his church lessons in mid-18th-century Frankfurt am Main:

> It will be taken for granted, that we children had among our other lessons a continued and progressive instruction in religion. But the Church-Protestantism imparted to us was, properly speaking, nothing but a kind of dry morality: ingenious exposition was not thought of, and the doctrine appealed neither to the soul nor to the heart. For that reason, there were various secessions from the established church. Separatists, Pietists, Herrnhuter (Moravians), Quiet-in-the-Land, and others differently named and characterized, sprang up, all of whom are animated by the same plain purpose of approaching the Deity, especially through Christ, more closely than seemed to them possible under the forms of the established religion.[7]

Recent research has, however, shown that orthodox theology has also been able to bring about vibrant forms of piety and church reforms. The attempt to approach God more closely than was possible in official religion, mentioned by Goethe in connection with devotional practice, can also be explained in terms of social history. Hartmut Lehmann presented several times how Pietism, as a religious movement, can be understood as a reaction to the numerous crises since the late 16th century, and during the 17th century in particular. While Luther and the two subsequent generations were still expecting and hoping for an imminent end to the world, later generations of believers lived through countless wars, famines, and epidemics, even both before and after the Thirty Years' War, instead of the promised coming of God's salvation. "How was it possible to be reconciled with the punitive God, in whose omnipotence one had entrusted oneself? How was one able to save one's soul and attain eternal life?"[8] Philipp Jakob Spener (1635–1705), with his church Pietism in the last third of the 17th century, was not the first to seek an answer to this question; long before him, English Puritanism, Jansenism, and the piety movement started by Johann Arndt (1555–1621) all sought answers to this external and internal crisis in the true Christian life.[9] As Lehmann's argumentation suggests, this "reform of life" involves the at-

---

7 J. W. von Goethe, "Truth and Fiction Relating to My Life," trans. John Oxenford (Philadelphia and Chicago), http://www.gutenberg.org/cache/epub/5733/pg5733.html.

8 Hartmut Lehmann, "Aufgaben der Pietismusforschung im 21. Jh.," in idem, *Transformationen der Religion in der Neuzeit. Beispiele aus der Geschichte des Protestantismus* (Göttingen, 2007), 103–19, here at 112.

9 Ibid., 112f.

tainment of a certainty of faith in face of the question of God within the context of continual catastrophes and wars. However, Pietism was surely also simply focused on coming to terms with the nonappearance of the end of the world, and on shaping the world in a positive manner; on the role of the church, which had been viewed negatively by many Pietists; and on the role of individual Christians in the world.

In terms of the history of theology and piety, the 17th century saw a change in eschatology, which brought about a new framework for the positive shaping of people's lives, the church, and the world. While Luther, as mentioned above, expected the end of the world to be imminent, and strongly emphasized God's activity in the lives of individuals, of the church, and the world, the Pietists were supporters of chiliasm, the doctrine of the millennial kingdom. Following Revelation 20, this involved the idea of a thousand-year kingdom on earth, in which the righteous would rule in the heavenly Jerusalem before the general resurrection. As Spener wrote in his *Pia Desideria*, "If we look at Holy Scripture, we cannot doubt that God has promised his churches a better condition here on earth."[10] The Pietists thus placed themselves in clear opposition to the Reformation. Chiliasm was clearly rejected in the *Confessio Augustana*, in Article 17.

Different Pietistic Ways of Connecting to the Reformation

Pietism connected with the Reformation in greatly differing ways, ranging from full identification with or mild criticism of the Reformation in ecclesiastical Pietism, to somewhat strong criticism in radical forms of Pietism. The radical Pietist Gottfried Arnold (1666–1714) followed this line in his 1729 "Impartial History of Churches and Heretics" (*Unpartheyschen Kirchen- und Ketzer-Historie*), in which he devoted an entire chapter to the "general deterioration following the Reformation."[11] In the various Pietistic varieties, the level of agreement with individual Reformation doctrines such as the doctrine of justification and ecclesiology stood in inverse proportion to the deficiencies of the Protestant churches that they listed. Accordingly, the self-image of Pietism as a Reformation or simply a church-reform movement was just as varied among its different expressions. While some Pietist groups, especially the ecclesiastical trends, saw themselves to be an addition, continuation, or completion of the Reformation, or as a second Reformation, others, especially the radical groups, distanced themselves strongly from the Reformation. I am not aware of the Pietists using term the "second Reformation"

10 Philipp Jakob Spener, *Pia Desideria*, ed. Kurt Aland, 3d ed. (Berlin, 1964), 43.

11 Brecht, "Berufung," 2.

as a self-designation. It was used instead as a slogan in church politics and a demand in response to perceived church deficiencies, also beyond Pietism. Werner Teschenmacher (1590–1638), the Reformed and humanistic-minded preacher at the court of Brandenburgian Kleve, called in 1633 for a "second Reformation" which should be "more complete and better."[12] Samuel Lutz (1674–1750), a Pietist from Bern, also spoke of expectations for a new second Reformation. "Lutz spoke of this expectation in his sermon held in 1728 to mark the 200th anniversary of the Reformation in Bern. At the time, he deemed it best not to look backward but ahead to a jubilee year of an entirely different kind, and reminded himself and his colleagues of their shared calling to be 'guardians of Jerusalem, roused by God to signs and harbingers of better times.'"[13]

We come closer to the classical Pietistic relationship to the Reformation with the Dutch Pastor Jodocus van Lodenstein (1620–1677), a representative of the *Nadere Reformatie* ("expanded, deepened Reformation"). Johannes van den Berg writes:

> In Beschouwinge van Zion, we see how much van Lodenstein was troubled in his last years by the state of the Reformed Church. He spoke extensively on the "deformity" of the church: Its doctrine he deemed pure but without the life of the church corresponding to it. What was important was not confessing the truth per se, as the truth had to become a living, personally experienced reality that would fill the whole heart—"Christ himself in our souls." In this context, his views on the Reformation were somewhat ambivalent. He saw the Reformation merely as an incomplete half-Reformation, even as a body without spirit. That was the Reformation in the form it had taken on in the course of history. This was, however, not to be the last word. His criticism of the form or "deformity" of the Reformation church did not, however, lead him to a devaluation of the Reformation as such: The Reformation did in fact intend and imply what was essential, the "killing of the flesh" and life from the spirit. However, one could not just stop at the wording, as it was the spirit that brings one to life. The contrast between word and spirit is the golden thread that runs through all of van Lodenstein's thought.[14]

---

12 Campi, "'Ecclesia semper reformanda,'" 12.

13 Rudolf Dellsperger, "Der Pietismus in der Schweiz," in *Geschichte des Pietismus, vol. 2: Der Pietismus im achtzehnten Jh.*, ed. Martin Brecht and Klaus Deppermann (Göttingen, 1995), 588–616, here at 603.

14 Johannes van den Berg, "Die Frömmigkeitsbestrebungen in den Niederlanden," in *Geschichte des Pietismus, vol. 1: Der Pietismus vom siebzehnten bis zum frühen achtzehnten Jh.*, ed. Martin Brecht (Göttingen, 1993), 57–112, here at 85.

This last aspect, the relationship between word and spirit, is also a major topic for Arndt, who also strove for a "reformation of life."[15] As suggested, van Lodenstein's views essentially corresponded with the later self-image of the Pietists, who sought to continue, deepen, and complete the Reformation. Incidentally, the motto *Ecclesia reformata semper reformanda* (the reformed church always reforming) demonstrably derives from van Lodenstein himself.[16]

The Case of Spener

In the following, I will use the case of Philipp Jakob Spener, the central figure of Lutheran church Pietism, to illustrate briefly a Pietistic view of the Reformation. This will be followed by a systematic theological look into the degree to which Pietism properly took on Reformation positions and in which ways it has passed it on to modern Protestantism in a modified form.[17]

The link to the Reformation provided Spener purely formal legitimacy for his reform aims, as phrased in classical terms in the *Pia Desideria*, a comprehensive program of church reform. This appeared in 1675 as the prologue to a new printing of a book by Johann Arndt. Spener made three major recommendations with regard to improving the state of the church: (1) increased reading of the Bible (individual reading, *Collegia Pietatis*); (2) reinforcement of the "universal priesthood"; and (3) strengthening of the awareness that Christianity consists of deeds and not of knowledge. On this third point, Spener writes in his *Pia Desideria*:

> . . . the Christian religion does not indeed consist in scholarship and the acerbity of probing questions as is being overly innovated in our times; but that we properly recognize the true God and our redeemer Jesus Christ from his word / profoundly fear / and love in true faith / call on him / be obedient to him in the cross and in our entire lives / love others with all our hearts as well / and gently help them.[18]

Spener saw himself affirmed by young Luther in all these points but particularly in the concern of a living internal faith that is also active in deeds. The favoured text on this point, also preferred by later Pietists such as August Hermann

---

15 J. F. G. Goeters uses this term in connection with dealing with the radical Pietists along the lower Rhine who were influenced by the Nadere Reformatie, cf. Johann Friedrich Gerhard Goeters, "Der reformierte Pietismus in Deutschland," in *Geschichte des Pietismus* 1:239–77, here at 268.

16 Campi, "'Ecclesia semper reformanda,'" 12.

17 This presupposes a "broad sense of the term Pietism" following Martin Brecht, with which an attempt is made to demonstrate traditional theological strands and connections in the history of piety; cf. Martin Brecht, "Einleitung," in *Geschichte des Pietismus* 1:1–10, here at 10.

18 Philipp Jakob Spener, *Die Werke Philipp Jakob Speners. Studienausgabe, vol. 1: Die Grundschriften Teil 2*, ed. Kurt Aland and Beate Köster (Giessen/Basel, 2000), 128.

Francke and John Wesley,[19] was written in Luther's 1522 "Preface to the Letter of St. Paul to the Romans": "Faith is a work of God in us, which changes us and brings us to birth anew from God. It kills the old Adam, makes us completely different people in heart, courage, senses, and all our powers, and brings the Holy Spirit with it. O what a living, creative, active, powerful thing is faith! So, it is impossible that faith ever stops doing good."[20] Spener agrees with Luther in the view that faith, as a work of God, does indeed bring forth good works. Despite this true Lutheran doctrine—which he also emphasized with regard to the meaning of the sacraments—he believed that many people were still incorrect in assuming that, by dint of justification through faith alone, works were not necessary or even dangerous. Such people no longer took morality so seriously, and had a false and imagined faith. With regard to the second suggestion to strengthen the universal priesthood, one can say that this, in its essence, corresponds with one of Luther's central Reformation insights, but which in its terminology was formed by Pietism and which can be viewed as an important heritage of the modern Protestantism. For Spener, taking the doctrine of universal priesthood seriously—that is, the activation of all baptized members of the church—entailed great potential for the church (greater vibrancy and radiance). The first suggestion of *Collegia Pietatis* was the most important characteristic of Spenerian Pietism, and is actually closely connected with the priesthood of all believers. He began to host this type of congregational assembly in his Frankfurt parsonage in 1670, a tradition with its origins in the Reformed church, as was practiced by Jean de Labadie (1610–1674).[21] The *Collegia Pietatis* were viewed as a sort of congregational assembly—which we would call a home church today—as an addition to services of the word in accordance with 1 Corinthians 14. Starting with this practical experience, Spener developed his concept of *Ecclesiola in Ecclesia.* A completely new strategy, different from what had previously been followed in the Lutheran church, was necessary to renew the church. One would have to work toward the gathering and fostering of the pious if one wished to improve and renew the church.[22] This model of a core congregation that enlivens the congregation as a whole was not meant to bring about separation. While the Protestant churches, following the Reformation and during the era of orthodoxy, used the instrument of church discipline as a means of correcting the fallible, in order to achieve a somewhat "pure" congregation, Spener, conversely, aimed at the improvement

19 Brecht, "Berufung," 4.

20 WA DB 7:11,6-10, trans. Bro. Andrew Thornton.

21 Johannes Wallmann, "Philipp Jakob Spener," in *Orthodoxie und Pietismus, Gestalten der Kirchengeschichte 7,* ed. Martin Greschat (Stuttgart, 1982), 205–23, here at 210.

22 Markus Matthias, "Collegium pietatis und ecclesiola. Philipp Jakob Speners Reformprogramm zwischen Wirklichkeit und Anspruch," in *Pietismus und Neuzeit* 19 (1993): 46–59, here at 67.

of the good. In this measure for reform, Spener also referred to a text by Luther, actually another Pietists' favourite Luther text, the "Prologue to the German Mass of 1526." In addition to the Latin and German Mass, Luther found a third form of worship service:

> But the third sort [of divine service], which the true type of Evangelical Order should embrace, must not be celebrated so publicly in the square amongst all and sundry. Those, however, who are desirous of being Christians in earnest, and are ready to profess the Gospel with hand and mouth, should register their names and assemble by themselves in some house to pray, to read, to baptize and to receive the sacrament and practice other Christian works. [. . .] In one word, if we only had people who longed to be Christians in earnest, Form and Order would soon shape itself. But I cannot and would not order or arrange such a community or congregation at present. I have not the requisite persons for it, nor do I see many who are urgent for it.[23]

This text may well reflect a discussion Luther had in 1525 with Kaspar von Schwenckfeld (1490–1561), who was very concerned with the moral realization of the Reformation, even before he joined the radical wing of the Reformation in later years.[24] We could provide further examples for Spener's reception of Luther. In general, however, Spener's high regard for Luther's Reformation becomes apparent when he spoke of the "dear Reformation."[25] It was clear to Spener[26] that there continued to be deficiencies in the Lutheran church. The departure from Babel was not yet complete. In his view, the Reformation had "to be completed. This is not possible without criticism of the existing deficiencies. It is warranted if it emerges from love and does not therefore signify the fouling of one's own nest that would please the Catholics, especially as they have enough to do to put their own house in order. He who belongs to the Lord must play a part in the task of reform."

While Spener's relationship to the Reformation was pragmatic and task oriented, Anton Wilhelm Böhme (1673–1722), following Spener, developed a historical view of the deterioration of the Reformation and its renewal in Pietism.[27] The revival movement of the early 19th century then had a

23 Martin Luther, "Prologue to The German Mass and Order of Divine Service, January 1526," in *Documents Illustrative of the Continental Reformation*, ed. B. J. Kidd (Oxford: Clarendon, 1911), 193–202.

24 Martin Brecht, "Das Aufkommen der neuen Frömmigkeitsbewegung in Deutschland," in *Geschichte des Pietismus*, 1:113–203, here 119.

25 Spener, *Pia Desideria*, 58.

26 Here and in the following Martin Brecht, "Philipp Jakob Spener, sein Programm und dessen Auswirkungen," in *Geschichte des Pietismus*, 1:279–383, here at 306.

27 Martin Brecht, August Hermann Francke und der Hallische Pietismus," in *Geschichte des Pietismus,* 1:439–539, here at 527.

more positive relationship to the Reformation, and strove toward a "return to the basic Reformation concerns."[28] Following upon the Enlightenment-era experiences in theology and the church, the Reformation appeared as a normative era which, in a way, was no longer surpassable.

Conclusion

Could Pietism be seen as a Second Reformation? Answers to this question differ in accordance with the theological position. It should have emerged rudimentarily here that Pietism took on different core concerns of the Reformation. This included, for example, the understanding of faith as a personal trust in God, that faith and a corresponding way of living belong together, the idea of the priesthood of all believers, the importance of the congregation, and the focus on the Bible. Moreover, speaking of the significance of the Reformation for the modern world, Pietism played an important role, even if it often appeared in opposition to the Enlightenment. The effect of Pietism on individuals (experience, the religious self, autobiography, journals) led to an upsurge in individuation, which would also serve to boost secularization and emancipation if a Pietistic way of thinking and living lost its connection to faith and the Bible. The relationship of Pietism to the Reformation becomes problematic for Reformation-oriented theology if the Reformation's basic understanding of God's word as the *verbum efficax*, which as a word of grace brings about forgiveness, righteousness of faith, and sanctification, is challenged through an overly strong differentiation of the word/ letter and the spirit. This occurs if the efficacy of the word, as it were, needs to be validated through an experience of rebirth or a describable conversion experience. The dimension of experience, which was rightfully emphasized following the Reformation, can then easily turn into an opposition to the primary concerns of the Reformation.

28 Gustav Adolf Benrath, "Die Erweckung innerhalb der deutschen Landeskirchen, in *Geschichte des Pietismus, vol. 3: Der Pietismus im neunzehnten und zwanzigsten Jh.*, ed. Ulrich Gäbler (Göttingen, 2000), 150–271, here at 155.

B. Social History

CHAPTER 20

Anne-Marie Heitz Muller

Impact of the Reformation on Women's Lives

Strasbourg in the 16th Century

Historians agree that the Reformation brought about profound changes in the lives of 16th-century women, but they remain divided in their interpretations: Do those changes attest to the improvement of their conditions or, conversely, to the reinforcement of the patriarchal system? In an attempt to rise above this dichotomous approach, I have focused this study on one of the major German cities of the 16th century, the Free Imperial City of Strasbourg, on its cultural and religious as well as demographic aspects. Analysis of various sources—be they theological treatises, biblical commentaries, catechisms, sermons, correspondences, or legal and medical sources—has made apparent the Strasbourg reformers' discourse on women, women's reactions to the Reformation, and the concrete impact of this new religious movement on their daily lives.

The reputation of the Strasbourg reformers as prominent biblical scholars and linguists is widely acknowledged. Although this would seem to have little to do with women's daily lives, it had a direct impact on their lives indeed.

Martin Bucer and his colleagues dreamed of making Strasbourg a holy city where all inhabitants could read the Bible daily, even at home. To realize this dream, they offered courses to adult men and women.[1] Bucer even encouraged Marguerite Blaurer, an educated woman, to pursue extensive studies and learn Greek to be able to read the New Testament in its original language.[2]

Not only did the Strasbourg reformers wish to make Strasbourg a holy city, but also—obviously in line with the strong imprint of the humanistic spirit in the region—a city of scholars. To achieve this goal, adult education was hardly sufficient. Therefore, they had to take charge of children's education. The first thing that comes to mind in this regard is the creation of the Johannes Sturm Gymnasium, whose quality of education attracted young boys from all over Europe. The Strasbourg reformers, following Luther's example, did not forget the girls in this matter, however. [3]

As early as 1524, they launched a resolute call demanding that girls' schools be created for all social classes in Strasbourg.[4] They repeated their call and proposed solutions for facilitating girls' access to schools. For example, they sought to divide the city into several districts, thereby assuring one girls' school per district to avoid a long journey for the children. In order to facilitate and favour girls' schooling, they also proposed that girls aged eight or younger be allowed to accompany their elder brothers to boys' schools.[5]

While still outweighed by boys' education in importance, girls' education attained an incontestable place in Strasbourg. By 1535, two community schools received 126 girls, while 304 boys attended primary schools, including 220 in Latin schools. Girls' schools kept evolving in the first half of the 16th century, and it was even envisaged, from 1545 onward, to provide education for the girls in the city-run orphanage. Under the influence of the reformers who insisted on the importance of education for all social classes, the city took over the remuneration of teachers who had thus far been hired by parents. Finally, a woman was

1 There are papers, such as *L'Apologie de Catherine Zell*, which document that Katharina Zell attended Bucer's courses.

2 *Briefwechsel der Brüder Ambrosius und Thomas Blaurer, 1509–1548*, t. 2, ed. Traugott Schiess (Fribourg: Fehsenfeld, 1910), esp. the letter dated 27 June 1534, 808.

3 In this regard, see especially two texts of Martin Luther: "An die Ratherren aller Städte deutscher Lands, dass sie christliche Schulen aufrichten und halten sollen," WA 15:27–53; and "Eine Predigt, dass man Kinder zur Schulen halten solle," WA 30/2:517–88.

4 BDS, 2, p. 397.

5 In dealing with the question of girls' schools in Strasbourg, I relied, besides on data resources, on three fundamental works: Charles Engel, *Les commencements de l'instruction primaire à Strasbourg au Moyen Âge et dans la première moitié du seizième siècle* (Strasbourg, 1889); Joseph Knepper, *Das Schul- und Unterrichtswesen im Elsass von den Anfängen bis gegen das Jahr 1530* (Strasbourg: Heitz, 1905); and Ernst-Wilhelm Kohls, *Die Schule bei Martin Bucer in ihrem Verhältnis zu Kirche und Obrigkeit* (Heidelberg: Quelle Meyer, 1963).

appointed the head of one of the municipal schools, starting in 1541. This was an exceptional event: it was not until over two decades later, in 1563, that Stuttgart, a widely recognized pioneering city in this field, created a girls' school, in which female teachers were paid by the city.

The primary goal of the reformers was not women's education itself but, rather, training good future housewives and Christian mothers. In practice, however, their ideas changed the lives of many girls, especially those from modest backgrounds who otherwise would never have had access to reading and writing. The same applies to many other areas: even if their stances were not feminist, as we understand the word nowadays, women profited from them. For example, they were revaluated not only in their roles as mothers and educators, but also in their work in the fields of social work and health care.

In the 16th century, female labour—although recognized in the Middle Ages—began to be discredited in society. Humanistic ideas, reviving the old misogynist texts, such as those of Aristotle, contributed to strengthen the separation between male and female spheres. Women were "reassigned" to take care of the private sphere, a trend that was further intensified through the emergence of capitalism and difficult economic situations at that time. This gave rise to the idea that women and foreigners "have stolen" men's work in the city.[6] With the growing concerns about the lack of employment, the depreciation of female labour gradually began to surface.

In the 16th century, while working was not a right for women, it was a duty for some of them: those who lived celibate, widows, and those whose husbands did not earn enough to support the family. Small auxiliary jobs started to develop. For example, women fabricated small objects while still taking care of their households that they then sold on the market. Others might cultivate a piece of land or supply their comestible products to farmers in the vicinity for resale, either raw or in transformed forms: they made sauerkraut, vinegar, and cheese, brewed beer, and made other items.

Some women, even housewives and mothers, were sometimes forced into prostitution, finding themselves in a situation with no other means to survive. They took advantage of the fact that Strasbourg was a city attracting many travelers, especially during the time of trade fairs that enjoyed a reputation throughout Europe.

In this context of progressive exclusion of women from the most secure and better-paying jobs (those within the corporations) on the one hand,

6 See Merry E. Wiesner, *Working Women in Renaissance Germany*, unpub. diss., Rutgers University, 1986. With respect to Strasbourg in particular, see Jean Rott, "Artisanat et mouvements sociaux à Strasbourg autour de 1525," in *Investigationes Historicae. Églises et Société au XVIe siècle. Articles rassemblés et réédités par Marijn de Kroon et Marc Lienhard* (Strasbourg: Oberlin, 1986).

and in the course of professionalization and masculinization of occupations on the other,[7] the reformers had an important role to play. Indeed, they contributed to the maintenance of women's low wages, as they were convinced that the best thing for a woman was to be married and, as such, her activities should be limited to supplementing her husband's salary. However, by revaluating and giving a theological significance to women-specific tasks, they also revaluated the professions of social work and health care, in which the majority of women already functioned.

As a matter of fact, many working women were engaged in hospitals, shelters for the poor, orphanages, and leper colonies. In these places, they did the same chores they were doing in their own homes: they were responsible for cooking, household spending, and care of the sick, children, and the elderly. They cleaned, did dishes and laundry, or sewed. Among the women who exercised such professions, widows were appreciated for their experiences and availability, given that they did not have children or, if any, only older ones. The second category of women who performed these works included married women whose husbands were sick or did not have enough income to meet the needs of the family. As a third category, young girls also worked in these health-care professions. Thus, they dedicated themselves to the service of their neighbours, which was the heart of the evangelical faith, and prepared themselves in some way for future family life by doing what would later be their domestic chores. Moreover, they could thus earn the necessary money for a dowry: after all, at the beginning of the modern age, the main goal of female labour was to prepare for the anticipated future embodied in marriage.[8]

Until then, however, women who were engaged in these types of activities were barely appreciated in society. The Strasbourg reformers gave a new dimension to their works by declaring that these women who worked in hospitals and leper colonies and received orphans were not just pursuing profitable tasks, but putting themselves in the service of their neighbours and, thus, to God. This may be seen in a municipal order, dating back to 1547 and inspired by the proposition of the reformers, specifying the duties of the servants of the hospital, which concludes: "In short, do not leave out

7 Merry E. Wiesner, *Women and Gender in Early Modern Europe*, 2d ed. (Cambridge: Cambridge University Press, 2000), 105–106, gives an example of knitting. The invention of the knitting machine at the beginning of the modern age prompted men to hijack this activity which, hitherto, had been female work. Thereafter, the works done by knitting women were depreciated and considered to be of inferior quality and sold at lower prices.

8 Olwen Hufton, *Frauenleben. Eine europäische Geschichte 1500–1800* (Frankfurt: Fischer, 1998).

anything that may be of service to the sick, always remembering that what is done to the needy is done to Christ himself."[9]

While the Strasbourg reformers' discourse proved to be useful for women, the actual craft and skill of these women should also be pointed out: they knew how to draw on the masculine discourse to conquer a new recognition and create new roles for themselves. Think, for example, of those women who had the courage to marry the first Strasbourg reformers and the importance they were able to give to this act and to the function they had created. Marrying a priest in the 16th century required a great deal of volition. The beginning of this century was marked by a movement of hatred toward the clergy. Laypeople, desiring a purer church, no longer tolerated seeing their clerics living in lust. Priests' concubines had become one of the most popular targets for pamphlets and critiques.[10] Notwithstanding these difficult circumstances, every first-generation Strasbourg reformer found a wife.

Martin Bucer himself was already married when he arrived in this Alsatian city, to Elisabeth Silbereisen.[11] She had been orphaned at the age of 16, and her relatives forced her to enter a convent. Shocked by the scandalous lifestyle of the clergy, and convinced that the marriage was consistent with the divine will, she was the first to take the plunge: she married Bucer, a defrocked priest, during the summer of 1522. In mid-May 1523, the couple settled in Strasbourg. At this time, the Alsatian city saw one priest's wedding after another. The motivations of these unions varied from one couple to another.

It seems that some of these marriages were motivated by love alone. Marguerite Drenss married the preacher Gaspard Hédion on 23 April 1524 with the consent of her mother, but against the will of her brother, who was vehemently opposed to the marriage: he asserted that if his sister married a priest, she would be deemed a sinner and, because of her illegitimate marriage, her future children would not be recognized. He sent several petitions regarding the matter to the Municipal Council.[12] He even presented other potential husbands to his sister, but Marguerite refused them all. Her

9 Otto Winckelmann, *Das Fürsorgewesen der Stadt Strassburg vor und nach der Reformation bis zum Ausgang des sechzehnten Jahrhunderts* (Leipzig: Verein für Reformationsgeschichte, 1922), 46.

10 Hans-Jürgen Goertz, *Pfaffenhass und gross Geschrei. Die reformatorischen Bewegungen in Deutschland 1517–1529* (München: Beck, 1987).

11 See Doris Ebert, *Bürgertochter—Klosterfrau—Ehefrau des Reformators Martin Bucer, Elisabeth Silbereisen: Familie und Lebensstationen* (Heimatverein Kraichgau, 2000).

12 See the study of these documents by Katherine G. and Thomas A. Brady, "Documents on Communalism and the Control of Women at Strasbourg in the Age of the Reformation," in *Anticlericalism in Late Medieval and Early Modern Europe*, ed. Peter A. Dykema and Heiko A. Oberman (Köln: Brill, 1993), 213–28.

brother, disappointed, had to admit that "she liked only this one," referring to Hédion.[13]

Some marriages took place in order to legitimize already existing unions. For example, in November 1523, Antoine Firn of the parish of St Thomas married his concubine of several years' standing.[14] At least five priests then followed his example during the month of January 1524.

Other marriages, although driven by love undoubtedly, were first and foremost motivated by personal theological convictions, as was the case with Katharina Schütz, the famous wife of the preacher Matthias Zell.[15] Katharina came from a wealthy and respected family. She received an extensive education, which was rather rare for a young girl of that time. She chose to lead a holy life and, therefore decided to live celibate. But after hearing Luther's message, she became a fervent adherent of the evangelical movement. She decided to underpin her commitment to the Reformation by marrying a preacher. She said, "I helped to institute clerical marriage,"[16] or even "By doing this, I wanted to give courage to all Christians and map out a road, which I hope has been established."[17] Zell himself entered this union out of conviction, not out of desire; Katharina Zell ascertained that the union had been "filled neither by beauty, nor by wealth nor by any other virtues that could be binding."[18]

It was also by theological convictions that the beautiful Wibrandis Rosenblatt became the successive wife of three reformers.[19] This young woman of 22 years, widow of the humanist Cellarius from Basel, wrote to Oecolampadius, preacher of the parish of Saint Martin of Basel, when he was looking for a spouse. They married in March 1528 upon Oecolampadius' decision. This union prompted many critiques focused not so much on Oecolampadius's clerical status as on the disparity of the couple: the 45-year-old reformer had married a beautiful young woman, 20 years his junior. Erasmus wrote about it with irony: "A few days ago, Oecolampadius married a young

13 Augustin Drenss, in ibid., 228.

14 Regarding this wedding, refer to *Supplication des pfarrhers/ unnd der pfarrkinder zu sant Thoman/ eim ersamen Rath zu Strassburg am rij December überantwurt* (Strasbourg, 1523), BNUS M.12.618, fol. Aiij.

15 A number of studies have been conducted on Katharina Schütz Zell. In particular, refer to Elsie Anne McKee, *Katharina Schütz Zell* (Leiden: Brill, 1999).

16 Catherine Zell, *Entschuldigung*, 1524, in ibid., 2:39.

17 Ibid., 39–40.

18 Ibid., 40.

19 These biographical elements were taken from two studies: a memorandum on Wibrandis Rosenblatt by Roland Herbert Bainton, *Frauen der Reformation, Von Katharina von Bora bis Anna Zwingli, 10 Porträts*, trans. Marion Obitz (Gütersloh: Gütersloher Verlagshaus, 1995), 84–102; and the article of Miriam Chrisman Usher, "Women and the Reformation in Strasbourg," *Archiv für Reformationsgeschichte* 63 (1972): 156–58.

woman not at all ugly, probably with the intention of whipping his flesh during the time of Lent."[20] Boniface Amerbach was even harsher in his expression: "The man is of advanced age, with trembling head; moreover, his body is so thin and exhausted that it is not unfitting to treat him as a living corpse! But he married a woman, more or less twenty years old, utterly distinguished . . . and full of life."[21] This union was a very happy one until Oecolampadius's death in November 1531. Following the advice of colleagues and friends of her deceased husband, Wibrandis married the Strasbourg preacher Capito, himself widowed by the plague that hit the city, in the summer of 1532.

Nine years later, the plague was still active. It took its toll on the lives of Capito and Elizabeth, Martin Bucer's wife. Following the last will of Elizabeth Bucer on her deathbed, her husband married Wibrandis.[22] The house then had six children, of whom only one was Bucer's and who also was physically and mentally ill, as well as Wibrandis's sick mother. Wibrandis managed this new household, gave birth to two children of their own, and adopted an orphaned niece. After Martin's rejection of the Augsburg *Interim*, when he had to take refuge in England, she agreed to follow him; after his death, she brought the whole family back to the continent. She died of the plague in 1564, which had already claimed the lives of so many members of her home.

The role of these reformers' wives was, in the first place, like that of all other women of this era, as a housewife and mother. By giving this role a proper status ("Stand"), the reformers called forth a revaluation of all wives and mothers and their domestic chores in the minds of men.[23]

Apart from this, reformers' wives had to play a broader role. These women were indeed given a real mission of demonstrating and promoting many spiritual values such as love and compassion. This was carried out through the care they gave to the weakest and the hospitality they lavished on many travelling guests. Katharina Zell, for example, said that "I receive everybody that knocks on my door, my house is always full of people."[24] Through this practice of living in a particularly open way and attentive to

---

20 It should be noted that Erasmus himself, a staunch opponent of the Reformation, founded his critique on the difference of age of the couple, not on the clerical status of Oecolampadius. *Erasmi Epistolae VII*, ed. P. S. Allen, no. 1977, 20 March 1528.

21 Amerbach, after 15 April 1528, ed. Alfred Hartmann, *Die Amerbachkorrespondenz* 3 (1947), no. 1253, 315.

22 See Bucer, *Briefwechsel der Brüder Blaurer* 2:92–93.

23 Heide Wunder-Kassel, "Frauen mischen sich ein—Protestantische und Katholische Frauenbewegungen im 16. Jh.," in *Frauen Mischen sich ein. Katharina Luther, Katharina Melanchton, Katharina Zell, Hille Feicken und andere.* Wittenberger Sonntagsvorlesungen (Wittenberg: Drei Kastanien, 1995), 105–106.

24 Catherine Zell, Letter to Conrad Pellican, 4 January 1549, in McKee, *Katharina Schütz Zell*, 2:109.

others, these women created homes representing true role models for their fellow citizens. Through their zeal for domestic works and their moral and intellectual qualities, these women strongly imprinted the *zeitgeist*. In addition, with the particularly warm welcome they reserved for many foreign guests, they ensured that the evangelical values were disseminated, both at regional and international levels.

These women essentially followed their vocation in, but not limited to, their homes. Katharina Zell, for example, felt that her status demanded of her to be committed to nondomestic activities as well.[25] She played an important role in various pastoral activities, so much so that her husband called her his "assistant"; she said,

> However, I also went to homes of the poor and rich. With love, fidelity and compassion, I supported the plague-infested and stretchered the dead, I visited people going through hardships and those suffering in cell towers and prisons[26] and those dying. I comforted them, always keeping in mind the words of the wise man: it is better to go to a house of mourning than to go to a house of feasting [*Eccl.* 7.2]. I have also learned a lot there, God be praised for that, and I can testify before God that I have done more work with my words and deeds than any workers or chaplains of the church, running and staying up day and night. Often I have neither eaten nor slept for two or three days. This is also why my pious husband, who liked it done that way, called me his only assistant.[27]

Finally, Katharina Zell could afford to play a political role, totally new at that time: for example, she stood up to defend her marriage, and she did not hesitate to take public stances to denounce before the municipal council the deplorable state of the hospitals in the city.

The conjunction between the tolerant atmosphere that reigned in Strasbourg in the first half of the 16th century, and the particular open-mindedness of Martin Bucer and his colleagues, allowed the Strasbourg citizens to experience real progresses at all stages of their lives. By giving new exegeses to the texts that had thus far been used to subjugate women, they could allow for real progress in their city, overcoming the prejudices of their time.

---

25 According to us, she was able to carry out these activites owing to a concurrence of facts and circumstances: her strong and independent character, having no children of her own, and her husband's extremely open attitude.

26 The *Annales de Sébastien Brant* describe these prison visits of Katharina Zell's; no. 4924, quoted by McKee, *Katharina Schütz Zell*, 2:231.

27 Catherine Zell, Letter to Ludwig Rabus, 30 December 1557, in ibid., 2:231–32.

CHAPTER 21

Marianne Carbonnier-Burkard

Reformation Jubilees

A Protestant Construction

In the book series *Cérémonies et coutumes religieuses de tous les peuples du monde* (*Religious Ceremonies and Customs of All the Peoples of the World*),[1] the volume devoted to Protestants contains a section on the Lutherans' "Reformation jubilees." The author and editor Jean-Frederic Bernard, the son of a Huguenot refugee pastor, depicts these customary centennial celebrations in the Lutheran states since the first Jubilee of 1617, which was celebrated on 31 October "in memory of the Reformation which began two hundred years ago by Luther."[2] From his vantage point, Bernard does not highlight how singular these commemorative celebrations were within Lutheran political circles, unrelated to the traditional church jubilees celebrated since the mid-Middle Ages and still less to the jubilees of the Old Testament. Indeed, he does not spend much time at all on this rare and local practice, limited to Lutheran states. It was not

1 Jean-Frederic Bernard and Bernard Picart, *Cérémonies et coutumes religieuses de tous les peuples du monde*, 10 vols. (Amsterdam, 1723–1737).

2 Jean-Frederic Bernard and Bernard Picart, *Cérémonies et coutumes religieuses de tous les peuples du monde*, vol. 3 (Amsterdam, 1733), 353–54.

until the second half of the 19th century, with the development of national memories, that Reformation jubilees surged in the Protestant states, now including the Reformed churches.

The revival of passion for commemorations at the end of the 20th century evoked, for about 20 years prior, historians' interest in various constructions of collective memory. Several recent works focusing on the Lutheran jubilees over the centuries, and on the jubilee practice based on it, have contributed to unveiling the denominational and political specificities of such commemorations.[3] Relying on them, I venture to address this question once more, including in the corpus of the Genevan and French Reformed jubilees, which were counterparts to the best-known Lutherans jubilees. I will distinguish two distinct epochs: the 17th and 18th centuries since the foundation year of 1617, and then the 19th century, the golden age of jubilees, carrying on to the early 20th century, in Lutheran Germany on the one hand and in the Swiss and French Reformed areas on the other.

The 17th/18th Centuries: The Jubilee Foundation Year of 1617 and Its Lutheran Confessionalization

The first jubilee in 1617

Prior to 1617, anniversaries of Luther's Reformation were already usually celebrated in towns or territories of the empire on the days fixed by respective local church orders or, after Luther's death, on the date of his birth or death. The idea of commemorating the date of the posting of Luther's 95 Theses in the fall of 1517 as the origin of the Reformation however emerged in 1617.[4]

It was launched by the theological faculty of the University of Wittenberg: Several young professors approached the High Consistory of Dresden to solicit Johann Georg I, the Saxon electoral prince, to authorize 31 October 1617 across his territory as a "*primus Jubilaeus Lutheranus*," as a "memorial day to be celebrated with solemnity and gratitude." The commemorative jubilees already had some predecessors in the academic Protestant world.

3 Winfried Müller, Wolfgang Flügel, and Iris Loosen, *Das historische Jubiläum: Genese, Ordnungsleistung und Inszenierungsgeschichte eines institutionellen Mechanismus* (Münster: LIT Verlag, 2004); Wolfgang Flügel, *Konfession und Jubiläum: zur Institutionalisierung der lutherischen Gedenkkultur in Sachsen 1617–1830* (Leipzig: Leipziger Universitätsverlag, 2005); Matthias Pohlig, *Zwischen Gelehrsamkeit und konfessioneller Identitätsstiftung* (Tübingen: Mohr Siebeck, 2007); Hartmut Lehmann, *Luthergedächtnis 1817 bis 2017* (Göttingen: Vandenhoeck & Ruprecht, 2012).

4 Hans-Jürgen Schönstedt, "Das Reformationsjubiläum 1617—Geschichtliche Herkunft und geistliche Prägung," in *Zeitschrift für Kirchengeschichte 93* (1982): 5–57; cf. Flügel, *Konfession und Jubiläum*, 54 s.

The University of Wittenberg for example celebrated its centennial year in 1602, calling it "*ein recht Evangelisch Jubelfest*" ("a proper Protestant jubilee"), with processions of professors and pastors as well as academic discourses and sermons.[5] Claiming their autonomy against the papacy, they evoked the tradition of the secular games of the antiquity with the "*carmen seculare*" of Horace.[6] By naming this form of commemoration a "jubilee," they also gave the traditional jubilees celebrated in the church since the year 1300 (and all the following centenaries) as proclaimed by the pope on the occasion of anniversaries and associated with the granting of indulgences a new meaning.[7]

The innovation of the professors of Wittenberg in 1617 consisted of the commemoration of one event in Luther's life at an assigned date: 31 October 1517. The posting of Luther's 95 Theses against indulgences, which were at the heart of Roman Catholic jubilees, was thus presented as an inaugural and emblematic moment of the Reformation. So the Wittenberg professor's project of a "Luther-Jubilee" in 1617 presented itself as a counterjubilee, polemic and ironic at the same time.

Two weeks later, another initiative of a Protestant jubilee ("Protestant" being used without Lutheran–Reformed distinction) was launched by Elector Frederick V of the Palatinate, who was Reformed and the head of the Protestant Union of the Empire, and his advisers. They pursued a double purpose: on the one hand, with armed conflict looming on the horizon, to strengthen the Protestant Union against the Holy Catholic League, and on the other to give full recognition to the Reformed, who were assimilated to "those of the Augsburg Confession," to benefit the religious peace of Augsburg (1555). On 23 April 1617, in an assembly held in Heilbronn, the representatives of the Protestant Union chose Sunday 2 November 1617 as the commemoration day to give thanks for the blessings that the Reformation had brought about, and at the same time to pray for the maintenance of the evangelical confession.

This initiative of the palatine prince must have aggravated the Saxon electoral prince, who insisted on the *Lutheran Concordia* and refused to join the Union. Taking this issue of a Reformation jubilee into his own hands, on 12 August 1617, he ordered that the Jubilee be celebrated in all of Saxon like a major church festivity, in the manner of a *triduum* on 31 October and 1 and 2

5 Andrea Lehmann, "Die Säkularfeiern der Alma Mater Viadrina (1606–1906)," unpub. diss., Viadrina European University, 2005, 12.

6 Pohlig, *Zwischen Gelehrsamkeit und konfessioneller Identitätsstiftung*, 118.

7 1300: Boniface VIII instituted a "holy year" every 100 years. Clement VI named it "Jubilee" in line with the Jewish concept of jubilee every 50 years, counting from 1350. Paul II, confirmed by Sixte IV, increased the frequency to 25 years: 1475, 1500, 1525, 1550, 1575, 1600, 1625.

November. Periscopes, models of sermons, and songs were prepared for the liturgical events of this holy day.

The magnificent Saxon programme was adopted by nearly all the Lutheran territories, and even by some of the Union (by the cities of Strasbourg, Nurnberg, and Ulm) and outside of the empire (in Denmark and Sweden). In the cities, the official ceremonies mobilized all the political, academic, and clerical authorities. The topics of the increasing number of speeches and sermons, which were subsequently published, included the principal concepts of the Protestant doctrine, with anti-Rome rhetoric as a counterpoint. Luther was presented as the hero who led the eschatological battle against the pope of Rome, an embodiment of the Antichrist.

A more topical theme was justification of the Reformation jubilee itself, and first and foremost the appropriation of the word *jubilee* because of its common use over three centuries. For Catholic controversialists, a jubilee without forgiveness of debt was only a "pseudo-jubilee," running counter to the Roman Catholic jubilees in which indulgences were distributed. Protestant preachers did not pay heed to this objection: according to them, the meaning of the jubilee (as laid out in Leviticus 25) was that of a memorial of thanksgiving for the liberation of formerly captive people (with Luther as the new Moses). Highlighting this function of a memorial, they presented the jubilee as an occasion for reawakening communal piety.[8]

As the Protestant jubilee aimed at reawakening the general public, its main target of mobilization was youth. J. F. Bernard describes one such event as follows:

> When the city of Ulm celebrated the Great Jubilee in 1617, a prayer was held specifically for this solemnity. All the students of the city were led to a church ceremony and catechized after the sermon before the whole congregation, which then prayed for the students' perseverance in the Lutheran faith and for that of their posterity. One week after the ceremony, each student was given a medal and a copy of the jubilee prayer book.

Multiplication of Reformation jubilees

While the Jubilee of 1617 gathered the entire Protestant side of the empire, only the Lutheran states carried on with this commemorative practice,

8 Jean Schillinger, "Jubilé ou Pseudojubilé? Polémiques entre protestants de Strasbourg et jésuites de Molsheim à l'occasion de la commémoration du centenaire de la Réforme (1617)," in *Glaubensformen zwischen Volk und Eliten. Frühneuzeitliche Praktiken und Diskurse zwischen Frankreich und dem Heiligen Römischen Reich/ Autorités, foi, perceptions. Croyances populaires et pratiques religieuses en France et dans le Saint Empire à l'époque moderne*, ed. Thomas Nicklas (Halle an der Saale: Universitätsverlag Halle-Wittenberg, 2012), 179–201.

thereby strictly confessionalizing it. It was along these lines that the centenary of the Augsburg Confession was celebrated in Saxony, and in several other territories in 1630, following the example of the Jubilee of 1617.

The jubilees during the Thirty Years' War were rather discreet, however, to avoid provoking the Catholic states. The Jubilee of 1667 (150th anniversary), which was ordered by Elector of Saxony Johan Georg II, was more distinguishable. He determined the date of 31 October to be the day for the celebration of the Reformation, without canonizing it, however (it often had to be moved to the Sunday before or after the set date). It was not until 1717 that the Reformation jubilee was celebrated in the majority of the Lutheran territories.

J. F. Bernard's description is based on the minutes of the celebrations held in Dresden from 31 October to 2 November 1717, and of those held from 25 to 27 June 1730:

> Nothing was arranged in advance for the solemnity of these jubilees. They are public rejoicing mixed with devotion: each state decides the extent of celebration according as it deems appropriate, analogous to the practice regarding the celebration of a victory in war. To mark their spiritual victory and the *overthrow of the papacy* in a considerable part of Germany and the North *through the victorious weapons of the antipapal Luther*, Lutherans sometimes launch a great jubilee day by a large assembly of representatives of the town or the state clad in black coats; they gather at the town hall at early dawn and go in procession to the main church, where there are also the clergy and academics coming also in procession from other parts of town. Then they enter the church to participate in the devotion of the celebration, in which they sing psalms and hymns to the sound of instruments and choir voices, pray and listen to the sermon especially addressing the given circumstances. Churches are adorned with flowers, etc. And often Communion is shared during the celebration of this jubilee.[9]

Clearly, in the Jubilee of 1717, the Lutheran pietists saw in Luther a "pious" man whose work they had to carry on, whereas the orthodox Lutherans celebrated the hero who slayed the medieval superstition and the papacy, and several German universities elevated all reformers and "witnesses of the truth" next to Luther.

9 Bernard and Picart, *Cérémonies et coutumes religieuses,* 3:353. The most detailed descriptions about the Jubilee of 1718 in different states can be found collected in *Hilaria evangelica* . . . (Gotha, 1719), by Lutheran theologian Ernst Salomon Cyprian (1673–1745).

The 19th Century to the 1930s: German Nationalization of Reformation Jubilees

The German nationalization of Reformation jubilees has its origin in the growth of German national sentiment during the 19th century.

1817: The political context is the "reaction" hostile to democratic ideas in the wake of the Congress of Vienna.

18–19 October, *Wartburgfest*: Some 500 students from 12 universities gathered together at the Wartburg to celebrate the victory over Napoleon and the anniversary of the Reformation at the same time, and also to demand national unification and democratic civil rights. In their speeches, Luther became a German patriot, because he founded the national culture and restored freedom to the Germans by defeating the pope of Rome.

31 October, Tübingen: Teachers, students, and representatives of the civil society and of corporations celebrated the Reformation jubilee and commemorated the victory of Leipzig with a great torchlight parade through the town.

The speeches and sermons of the Jubilee of 1817 varied in their views on Luther. For the *Aufklärer* (Enlightenment philosophers), Luther was the founder of the German language and its culture, and of the freedom of conscience. For the Prussian government under Frederick William III, he was the common father of the Reformation, a good opportunity to champion the ecclesiastical union of Lutherans and the Reformed. For orthodox Lutherans, Luther was first and foremost the theologian of fundamental truths of faith. For pietists, he was the advocate of the distribution of the Bible and mission to the Gentiles. All of them valorized themselves through Luther's achievements and the work of the Reformation, but no one was particularly interested in what Luther did on 31 October 1517.[10]

1867 (350th anniversary of 1517): This jubilee took place against the backdrop of the military victory of the Protestant Prussia over the Roman Catholic Austria in the battle for the symbolic heritage of the "Holy Roman Empire."

25 June 1868, Worms: The unveiling of the statue of Luther (*Das Wormser Lutherdenkmal*, sculptured by Ernst Rietschels from 1856 to 1868) was accompanied by festivities. This was the beginning of outdoor celebrations (i.e., not in a church) featuring open-air communal and folk festivals. Modern means of motorized transport (steamship and train) brought 100,000 visitors to Worms. It was a "festival of free thinking" and not a "religious festival,"

10 Only some rare pictures, which had appeared since 1806, referred to the posting of the theses on the door of the Castle Church of Wittenberg (Lehmann, *Luthergedächtnis 1817 bis 2017*, 25).

according to Abbot Marbach, who heard people shouting, "Long live the King of Prussia, German Emperor!"[11]

1883: Luther's jubilee (400th anniversary of his birth) in the German Empire. The political context was, since 1870–1871, one of triumph of the Protestant Germany over the Roman Catholic France (see Treitschke, 1834–1896), the creation of the German Empire, and the *Kulturkampf* (cultural struggles), precipitated by the proclamation of papal infallibility (1870) and the growing weight of the *Zentrum* (a Catholic party) in the *Reichstag* (German parliament). Luther was identified with the German nation, and the Reformation was regarded as the German revolution against the clerical power and Rome.

Wittenberg, Erfurt, Eisleben, and Eisenach witnessed festivals, the creation of museums and monuments, the planting of oak trees, and the inauguration of the *Archiv für Reformationsgeschichte* (Archives for Reformation History). In the United States, the Luther Jubilee exerted a certain level of impact, even outside the Lutheran churches. Luther was presented as one of the four founding fathers of the New World, along with Christopher Columbus, Johannes Gutenberg, and John Calvin.

1917: The fourth centenary of Luther's posting of his theses fell at the height of the First World War, in its fourth year. Since Luther was German, his trust in God and his unshakable determination to fight served as a model for the Germans.

In September 1917, when the Protestant churches in the United States were about to celebrate the jubilee of the Reformation of Luther, the president of the Society for the History of French Protestantism (SHPF), Frank Puaux, communicated to the president of the Jubilee Organization Committee the "fraternal feelings which unite the descendants of Huguenots of France to the descendants of the Puritans in America," without mentioning Luther. In December 1917, in his annual address as SHPF President, Puaux associated President Wilson's proclamation due to the American entry into WWI with Luther's declaration in Worms for the freedom of conscience and justice, saying that they were ridiculed by Germany, which had become "the plague and terror of Europe."[12]

1933: The 450th anniversary of Luther's birth was celebrated in Germany. The *Deutsche Christen* made the Reformer the messenger of the German *Führer*, using the slogan: "*Mit Luther und Hitler, für Glaube und Rasse*" ("with Luther and Hitler for faith and race"). In the meantime, the Confessing Church also claimed Luther, demanding the autonomy of Protestant churches.

11 *Revue catholique d'Alsace*, June 1868.

12 *Bulletin de la Société de l'histoire du protestantisme français* 66 (1917): 271–72, 276–77 (hereafter *BSHPF*).

1938: The 455th anniversary of Luther's birth, on 10 November 1938, falls on the day after the *Kristallnacht* ("Night of Broken Glass"). Nazis gave prominence to the "German Reformation" and Luther, honouring him as being "the greatest anti-Semite of his time, protector of the German people against the Jews." For their part, the Allied powers launched propaganda during the war associating Luther and Hitler with each other.

The 17th Century through Early 20th Century: Swiss and French Reformation Jubilees

Although the Jubilee of 1617 was held, in part, on the initiative of a Reformed prince, it did not find much echo outside the empire. In Geneva, Theodore Tronchin (1587–1657), rector of the Academy, called attention to the Reformation jubilee in his speech to promote the spirit of 1617: after outlining the history of jubilee since the secular games of the antiquity and denouncing the jubilee formula adopted by the popes of Rome to replenish the papal coffers, he praised two reformers, Luther and Zwingli. However, the idea of a Genevan jubilee was gaining ground. In August 1635, Geneva saw the commemoration—without public demonstration—of the day in 1535 on which the Council of Two Hundred abolished the Roman mass. Frederick Spanheim (1600–1649), rector of the Academy and theology professor, published on this occasion *Geneva restituta*, in which he justified the jubilee as the centenary of the birth of Geneva—republic, church, and academy—using the Reformation of 1535, calling it light after darkness (the parallel was drawn to the "secular games" that celebrated the birth of Rome).[13]

The Reformed churches of France seem to have overlooked the Jubilee of 1617.[14] Like the previous ones (1550, 1600), the Roman Catholic jubilee of 1625 stirred criticism on the regulation of such jubilees, unleashed by Charles Drelincourt, the preacher at Charenton: both Jewish and pagan ceremonies framed the practice of indulgences in ways that even the Council of Trent had difficulty justifying. The providential role of Luther in 1517 is mentioned in this connection, but no more.[15]

---

13 *Geneva restituta* (Geneva, 1636); see also another publication by Jacob Laurent, *Le Genevois jubilant* (1635).

14 It was not mentioned at the national synod held in Vitré in May 1617, still less at the next synod held in Alès in October 1620.

15 *Du Jubilé des Eglises réformées. Avec l'examen du jubilé de l'Eglise romaine*, (Charenton: Jean-Antoine Joallin, 1627), 154. A work partly inspired from *Traitté des indulgences, contre le decret du Concile de Trente* (trans. in French in a treatise by the Lutheran theologian Martin Chemnitz). *Briefve consideration sur l'an du Jubilé. Le vrai et grand pardon general de pleniere remission des pechés* (Geneva: Jaques Chouet, 1599).

Swiss and Genevan jubilees

It was the German jubilees in 1717, 1817, and 1883 that prompted the Swiss cities—foremost Zurich, Bern, and Geneva—to launch their own jubilees, each according to its own Reformation calendar, independent of the posting of Luther's theses in 1517.[16]

The second Lutheran jubilee of 1717 seems to have launched the Reformation jubilees in Switzerland. The first, in 1719, was the 200th anniversary of Zwingli's first preaching in Zurich Grossmunster, on 1 January. The Bernese, with their victory over the Roman Catholic cantons in 1712, saw to it that more limelight be shed on their own Reformation jubilee in 1728.

Geneva waited until 1735 to launch its jubilee, imitating the one of Bern.[17] It was celebrated on 21 August 1735 as a national holiday, scheduled in advance, with appropriate sermons, a prayer composed especially for the occasion by Jean-Alphonse Turrettini, a parade of pastors, teachers, and magistrates of the city, lights, and a banquet.[18]

The *Wartburgfest* in 1817 resonated with the students in Zurich and Bern: on 23 October 1818, they gathered to celebrate the tercentenary of Zwingli's arrival in Zurich as a preacher. They marched to the place where he was killed and founded a student union supporting a federal liberal state (Zofingen). However, the official Zwingli jubilee remained set on 1 January 1819. It was followed by those of Bern (1828), Basel (1829), and Neuchâtel (1830).

The Genevan jubilee in August 1835 followed the pattern of the Jubilee of 1735. Its motto, "Religion—Fatherland—Tolerance," however, expressed a certain anxiety about deconfessionalizing the jubilee. In fact, the Council of State had to keep confessional neutrality, because the new delineation of the cantonal territories included Catholic communes.[19]

---

16 These jubilees did not take place on an annual commemoration day in order to avoid overlapping with the day of "*jeûne genevois*" ("Genevan fast"), at the beginning of the 16th century and certainly in effect since the 17th century, not taking into account the day of "*jeûne fédéral*" ("federal fast") since the 19th century (1817, 1832).

17 The advocate of the jubilee within the *Compagnie* of Genevan pastors refers to the previous Reformation jubilees in Zurich, Bern, and Neuchâtel (5 November 1730).

18 Jean-Moïse Paris, *Le jubilé de la Réformation célébré à Genève le 21 août 1735* (Geneva: Cherbuliez, 1870), 37–59.

19 Mireille Lador, "Le Jubilé de la réformation de 1835 à Genève: 'Religion-Patrie-Tolérance,'" *Bulletin de la Société d'histoire et d'archéologie de Genève*, t. 25 (1995): 97–110. In Lausanne, jubilee-related projects to commemorate the Lausanne Disputation, in 1636 and in 1736, were met with indifference by the Bernese sovereign government; in 1836, the cantonal government refused to be involved.

The focus of Lutheran jubilees of the 19th century on the person of Luther also brought on the Reformed side a stronger focus on the other founding fathers of the Reformation.

Impressed by the memorial events around Luther since his student years in Germany, Jean-Henri Merle d'Aubigné (1794–1872), Reformation historian, Calvin admirer, and pastor of the Free Church of Geneva, launched a project of building a Genevan monument dedicated to Calvin in 1861: a building "destined to some useful institution," especially public conferences associated with the calling of evangelization. The proximity of the tercentenary of Calvin's death was expected to stimulate required energies. Only the ground could be dedicated in time, on 24 May 1864. However, it was out of the question to set up a "Calvin jubilee." At the most, one commemorated the "third centennial of John Calvin's death." Neither was a jubilee considered during the inauguration of the "Reformation Hall," in 1867.[20]

1884: Zwingli's date of birth provided an occasion for Zurich to hold a jubilee comparable (albeit more modest) to the Luther Jubilee in 1883 in Germany, prior to the solemn inauguration of the Zwingli monument in the following year (15 August 1885).

It was also the model of the Luther Jubilee of 1883 that the Protestant Church of Geneva envisaged when it considered commemorating the fourth centenary of Calvin's birth in 1909. Calvin himself was not so consensually admired in Geneva, however, compared to the adoption of the Reformation by the vote of the Genevan communes. In the early 20th century, he was still less remembered than ever before, because Michael Servetus's death at the stake obstructed the representation of Protestantism, and especially of Calvinism, as the forerunner of the ideals of freedom and human rights. In an attempt to escape a foreseeable malediction, Emile Doumergue, dean of the Faculty of Protestant Theology of Montauban and the "official" defender of Calvin's work, proposed to precede the Calvin Jubilee with an "expiatory monument" for Michael Servetus, on the occasion of the 350th anniversary of his execution, in 1903. Thus, it was accomplished: a clean sweep for a proposed "Reformation monument," in memory of the reformers—that is, not of Calvin alone—and the heroes of the history of human rights and the people.

Purged of its black memory with the expiatory monument dedicated to Servetus, Calvin has henceforth had the right to a bouquet of three jubilees in Geneva, at least in July 1909: one from the National Protestant Church on Geneva's becoming independent from the state (2–4 and 6–7 July), another

20 *Souvenir du troisième anniversaire séculaire de la mort de Jean Calvin ou inauguration du terrain de la Salle de la réformation, le 27 mai 1864* (Geneva: Ch. Gruaz, 1864). See Luc Weibel, *Croire à Genève: la Salle de la Réformation (XIXe-XXe siècle)* (Geneva: Labor et fides, 2006).

from the college (5 July) and still another from the university (7–10 July), which celebrated its 350th anniversary and at the same time laid the first stone of the Reformation monument (5–7 July).[21]

French Reformed jubilees

In France, it was not until the second half of the 19th century that projects of commemorative jubilees appeared among the Protestants.[22] The first that involved all the Reformed churches of France took place on 29 May 1859 for the third centennial of the Reformation in France, in memory of the first national synod of the Reformed churches of France (May 1559). The idea came into being at the Pastoral Conference held in Paris in April 1858, inspired, no doubt, by the Genevan Jubilee of 1836 and several other jubilees of French Reformed churches abroad since 1850.[23] Representing the theological "diversity" of Protestantism, and already tense on the subject of the confession of faith, the Jubilee Committee mobilized all the Reformed pastors of France, and also invited the Lutherans and Protestant churches abroad: "Reformed churches could dedicate Sunday, 29 May 1859 to a special sermon on the historical facts of the commemorated times . . . , accompanied by reflections and exhortations appropriate for the occasion."[24]

The minutes of the jubilee sent to the SHPF by 78 parishes testify to the success of the commemoration. The most important one took place in Nimes during three days, culminating in a giant open-air assembly at the place of the ancient assemblies of the desert.[25] Sermons and speeches, interspersed with the singing of hymns, including the chorale of Luther, recalled the French Reformation, the time of the martyrs of the 16th century, and the assembly of the desert. In the face of the general laxity of faith and the current context of confessional appeasement, everybody was urged to repentance and tolerance toward "our Catholic brothers."[26]

Nonetheless, this Jubilee of the "French Reformation" did not fix any annual memorial day of the Reformation in the French Reformed churches. When the SHPF committee launched the "Festival of the Reformation" in

21 Cf. Valentine Zuber, "La commémoration du quatrième centenaire de la naissance de Jean Calvin en 1909," in *Calvin. De la réforme à la modernité*, sous la dir. de François Clavairoly (Paris: PUF, 2010), 66–79.

22 The jubilee celebrated in 1817 by the Lutheran church in Paris and Strasbourg should be set aside as it is associated with the Luther Jubilee in Germany.

23 Jubilees of the French Protestant Church of London on 24 July 1850, of Frankfurt on 18 March 1854, of Emden on 5 November 1854.

24 *Troisième jubilé séculaire de la Réformation en France, 29 mai 1859* (Paris: Fischbacher, 1859), 11.

25 Ibid., 143–62.

26 Ibid., 230–32.

1866, it did not retain the date of the French Synod of 1559, on account of its being too scholastic. Albeit with hesitation, due to its "German" colorization, they chose the date of the anniversary of the public posting of Luther's 95 Theses as the signal of the "awakening of the Christian conscience"; so it fell on All Saints' Day (also a holiday in France), but this "cleared [it] of the memory relating too exclusively to the theses [of Luther]," to associate the day with "totally French memories."

The second great commemorative moment of the French Reformed took place in 1885 in the bicentennial of the Revocation of the Edict of Nantes. To tell the truth, the SHPF committee initiated this public commemoration with reservations. Since 1883, it had been exacted by the Societies of the Huguenot Descendants abroad.[27] However, in the context of a revival of anti-Protestantism since the French defeat in 1870, it was keen not to provoke any reproach of "reviving denominational hatred" by recalling a black day in the history of France and expressing solidarity with "foreign brethren." This is the reason for [the] SHPF's invitation to pastors to offer "memorial services" on Sunday, 18 October 1885, to precisely frame their theme: the commemoration should be "an act of humiliation and mourning on national level" and "fervent prayer to God for . . . the triumph of the ideas of tolerance and justice."[28] After the memorial services celebrated on Sunday in parishes, the SHPF ceremony itself took place on the evening of Thursday, 22 October, at the Oratory, in the presence of only one foreign delegate from the Walloon Church. The patriotic theme was retained in the speeches of the pastor Eugene Bersier (1831–1889) and the pastor and senator Edmond Pressensé (1824–1891), flanked by prayers and interspersed with hymns (including the Luther chorale).

Nationalism and growing anti-Protestantism imposed a blanket of silence on the tercentenary of the Edict of Nantes in the spring of 1898. This first "Edict of Toleration" was discreetly commemorated in Nantes, after the legislative elections in the great church, which was thus decorated with the national colours. Here again, the very few representatives of foreign societies and associations in connection with the SHPF and French Reformed churches were not invited to communicate their views.

The prospect of a jubilee on the occasion of Calvin's fourth centennial, in July 1909, did not escape the attention of the French Reformed churches, even though the anniversary of this born Frenchman was a priori irrefutable

---

27 In 1785, the old refugees' churches in Germany already celebrated the centennial of the edict of Potsdam (thus in Berlin: Jean A. Bocquet, *Sermon a l'occasion du jubilé séculaire de l'édit de Potsdam en faveur des réfugiés de France*: prononcé dans le temple du Werder le 29 octobre 1785 [Garde, 1785]); Erman, *Sermon prononcé dans le temple du Werder le 30 octobre* [1785] *à l'occasion du jubilé de la fondation des colonies francoises dans les Etats du roi* (Berlin, s.d.).
28 *BSHPF* (1885): 50.

for the (still) "National" Church of Geneva, supported by public institutions, and still vivid in a national memory. In 1909, in the context of the separation of church and state, and the "war of the two Frances," the jubilee of the reformer was a delicate matter for the French Protestants. The committee of the "Centennial Celebration of Calvin," chaired by historian Pastor Paul de Felice and composed of a majority of pastors and SHPF members, preferred to distinguish the French Jubilee from the Genevan Jubilee: it was "the illustrious French" that needed to be celebrated in France. While the date retained for the "national" public commemoration was the date of the Festival of the Reformation, the venue envisaged was in a secular place, the Trocadéro, not a church. In concluding his speech, Dean Doumergue did not hesitate to call Calvin a "powerful instrument of the French spirit and the spirit of God: *Gesta Dei per Francos*." More sober in expression, Pastor Jules-E. Roberty emphasized the role of the English Calvinist minority in the formation of the American Bill of Rights, the model of the French Declaration of 1789.[29]

Epilogue: The 1980s, or the "Era of Remembrance" (expression of Pierre Nora)

Since the late 1970s, the passion for commemoration, in Europe in general and in France in particular, has touched all kinds of "heritage" jeopardized by the rapid disappearance of social and institutional structures that safeguard stability in their transmission from generation to generation. This passion revived the Reformation jubilees, which had been in decline since the mid-20th century.

The success of *Lutherjahr* ("Luther Year") 1983 in Germany represented not only this general phenomenon, but also the political dimension of a Germany divided between the FRG and the GDR in the dusk of the Communist Eastern Europe. The reappraisal of Luther's role by GDR historians—Luther as the (Eastern) German precursor of modern revolutions—indirectly contributed to the reunification of Germany around their common hero.

In France, the commemoration of the Revocation in 1985 initially brought some distress to the SHPF and the Reformed Church of France: fears were expressed concerning the jeopardy of hagiography and the risk of collateral damages to the ecumenical climate. Therefore, the line of rigorously deconfessionalized history was claimed at all conferences and events in the French churches.

The commemoration of 1985 successfully set in motion the Protestant memorial cycle: 1987 (Edict of Tolerance), 1989 (French Revolution), 1998

29 Zuber, "La commémoration."

(Edict of Nantes). This cycle facilitated consensus around the flag of tolerance, a supreme value.

Against this background, the Jubilee of 2000 arrived. It was taken over by Rome, and only timidly celebrated by the Protestant churches. The Protestants could not help being astonished to see that the "Holy Year," so inaugurated in Rome by Pope John Paul II, served again as occasion for the promulgation of indulgences in the pure jubilee tradition of the Roman Catholic Church for seven centuries. The confessional disagreement on the definition of jubilee was (and is?) still there.

***

The promotion of Reformation jubilees in Germany from 1617 to 1917 was the result of the convergence of willpower between the political, academic, and ecclesiastical authorities of the Protestant states. These different entities jointly invented a form of festivity as an alternative to the jubilees of indulgences of the Roman Catholic Church. By periodically reactivating an identity conquered in precisely the place of indulgences, each of these entities has built, in pursuit of its own interests, a confessional Lutheran memory.

As for the Swiss and Genevan jubilees, from the 18th to the early 20th century, the Reformed commemorations, supported by the same institutions, emerged as weakened replicas of the Lutheran jubilees of Germany, lacking a consensual central figure.

In France, a Roman Catholic, and then secular, country, it is the concept of Protestant jubilee itself that has posed and is still posing a problem. While the "minority" memories, be they ethnic or generic, have had wind in their sails since the late 20th century, the Protestant churches are reluctant to claim a minority identity. This is why the Protestant jubilees in a minority situation, without their memory being supported at the national level or a model of identity, are intended to be kept confidential or become a euphemism for a separating identity.

CHAPTER 22

Frédéric Elsig

Caricature and Satire in the Age of Reformation and Confessions

From 16 October 2013 to 16 February 2014, the International Museum of the Reformation (IMR) in Geneva held an exhibition entitled *Hell or Paradise: The Origins of Caricature.*[1] This exhibition was inspired by the purchase in 2011 of two paintings by Egbert II van Heemskerck (London, circa 1700–1710) that depict Luther and Calvin each triumphantly arriving in hell (*Luther Entering Hell* and *Calvin Entering Hell*, Geneva, IMR, inv. 2010-71 and 2010-72, respectively). They set the thematic and temporal frames of the exhibition: highlighting the iconographic tradition leading to this pair of paintings and analyzing an entire epoch of satirical image that is characterized by an intense use of a new weapon of mass propaganda printing—right from the beginning of the Reformation up to the Enlightenment. In this essay, I will attempt to take stock of this phenomenon, with focus placed on the role the satirical image played during the era of Reformation and confessionalization.

1 This text replaces the lecture delivered at the congress by Isabelle Graesslé, director of the International Museum of the Reformation in Geneva.

Satire in the time of the Reformation and confessionalization:

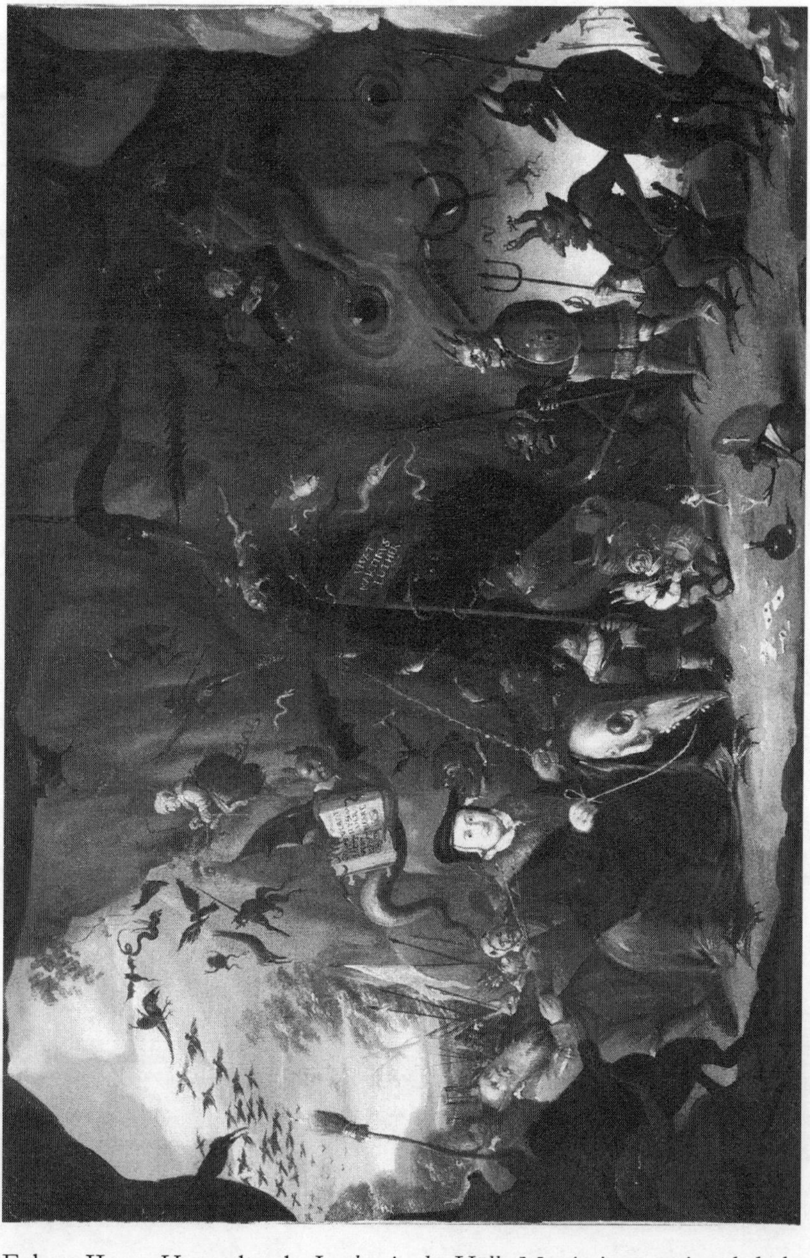

Egbert II van Heemskerck: *Luther in der Hölle.* Musée international de la Réforme (cat. 38), Genf. English: Luther in hell.

Egbert II van Heemskerck: *Calvin in der Hölle.* Musée international de la Réforme (cat. 38), Genf. English: Calvin in hell.

The Exhibition and Its Structure

The exhibition was divided into three parts and preceded by an introduction that made it clear that satirical themes used in the Reformation era already existed throughout the Middle Ages, dating back to the 12th century, using different media, from sculptures and drolleries adorning the margins of illustrated manuscripts to monumental paintings.[2] Among the works exhibited, a French book of hours created in the mid-15th century (Geneva Public Library, ms. lat. 33) contains one of the most common motifs of the period: a fox dressed as a monk preaching to a group of birds before devouring them. In order to emphasize the transition from single works to multiplied images, we juxtaposed the book with two prints that justified the Protestant propaganda by reinterpreting the polemical models of the Middle Ages at the very moment when the historian Matthias Flacius Illyricus was seeking to reproduce the origins of the Reformation: (1) a poster made in Geneva around 1536 inspired by an image of hell painted in 1401 by Giacomo Jaquerio, which was destroyed during the iconoclasm of 1535 (Geneva Centre of Iconography, inv. 44M02); and (2) a flyer created by Tobias Stimmer in 1576 that reproduces the 13th-century Strasbourg Cathedral with an animal parody of the procession and mass (Zurich, Central Library, inv. PAS II 14/10).[3]

The first part of the exhibition contained a necessary reflection on the status of such images. It showed the phenomenon of worship, on the one hand, and the phenomenon of destruction, on the other. To introduce this aspect, we used a copy of the *September Testament* of 1522 (Zurich, Central Library, inv. Zwingli 248) with illustrations by Lucas Cranach the Elder, based on the ideas of Luther himself. It contains the famous print in which the pope is associated with the whore of Babylon riding the seven-headed beast and wearing the papal tiara, an object of worship in the Catholic community. This strong image was reinterpreted several times during the 16th century, as illustrated by a remarkable enameled plate (Gandur Art Foundation, inv. FGA-OBJ-AD-53) created by Martial Courtois (Limoges, circa 1585) amidst the War of Religion.[4] We examined it as it was presented in a booklet written by Bernard of Luxembourg only a few months after the *September Testament*. In this booklet, Protestants were accused of being engaged in the personality cult of Luther, showing him as an idol inspired by the devil. It is called

2 Frédéric Elsig, "La ridiculisation du système religieux," in *Les marges à drôleries des manuscrits gothiques*, ed. J. Wirth (Geneva, 2008), 276–305.

3 C. Dupeux, P. Jezler, and J. Wirth, eds., *Iconoclasm: Life and Death in the Medieval Images*, exhibition catalogue, Historical Museum in Berne, 2 Nov. 2000—16 Apr. 2001; Strasbourg, Musée de l'œuvre Notre-Dame, 12 May–26 August 2001 (Paris, 2001), 386–87, cat. 214 (notes by C. Dupeux and R. Recht).

4 C. Grand-Dewyse, *Emaux de Limoges au temps des guerres de Religion* (Rennes, 2011), 402–404.

statua hereticalis (Zurich Central Library, 13430.5, fol. 7). On the opposite wall, the Protestant iconoclasm, which experienced two major waves in the 16th century, was depicted by two works that reflect the Catholic and Protestant points of view. On the one hand, the *De tristibus Galliae* (Lyon Municipal Library, ms. 156), an illustrated manuscript produced in Lyon around 1585 from the milieu of the Catholic League, depicts Protestants as monkeys, resorting to the wordplay of "Huguenot" and "*guenon*" (monkey).[5] It denounces their savagery and stupidity. Its frontispiece shows a preacher instigating Huguenots to loot the city of Lyon, symbolized by a lion (another wordplay), and to profane its sacred images, especially a crucifix. On the other hand, an engraving print of the Rijksmuseum in Amsterdam (Inv. RP-P.OB-76.780) justifies the Dutch iconoclasm of 1566 and shows Protestants equipped with brooms ridding the world of the onerous objects of the Catholic mass.[6]

The second part of the exhibition focused on the system, that is, primarily Protestant criticisms against Catholic dogmas and rituals. We introduced this category with the printed work that triggered a hostile atmosphere as early as 1521. Edited by Philip Melanchthon on the basis of Luther's ideas and illustrated once again by Cranach, the *Passional Christi und Antichristi* (Zurich Central Library, inv. 18.516.11) adopts the format of a traditional prayer book and uses each double page to juxtapose the exemplary life of Christ and the negative actions of the Antichrist depicted as a papal figure.[7] It provides two main phenomena: the first consists of a deformation of the iconographic themes and motifs of the Middle Ages, as demonstrated by an engraving inspired by the iconography of the Mystical Winepress, however, replacing Christ's blood with coins (Geneva, International Museum of the Reformation, inv. 2011-031). The second corresponds to the bipolarity between good and evil, heaven and hell, as demonstrated by a beautiful painting made most likely in Leiden in 1581 (Utrecht, Catharijneconvent Museum, inv. STCCs47). It portrays the parable of the Good Shepherd who leads Christians into the sheepfold and repulses the impostors seeking to enter the house of God by all means. Along the left-right axis, it shows a humble and young Protestant community listening calmly to Christ and opposing the outdated and greedy Roman Catholic Church. We could compare it to a print produced in Nuremberg 40 years earlier, which certainly served as its source of inspiration

5 S. Petrella, "Les Guerres de religion en images: le De tristibus Galliae et Jean Perrissin," in *Peindre à Lyon au XVIe siècle*, ed. Frédéric Elsig (Milan, 2014), 119–45.

6 W. Hofmann, ed., *Luther und die Folgen für die Kunst*, exhibition catalogue, Hamburg, Hamburger Kunsthalle, 11 Nov. 1983–8 Jan. 1984 (Munich, 1983), 144–45.

7 R. J. Dykema, *Lucas Cranach the Elder, Martin Luther, and the Passional Christi und Antichristi: Propaganda and Prayer in an Early Lutheran Flugschrift* (San Francisco, 2010).

(Nuremberg, Germanisches Nationalmuseum, inv. HB24).[8] Positioned a little apart to highlight museographically its unique character, a print (Geneva, International Museum of the Reformation, inv. 2005-198) serves as an example of the criticisms exercised within the Reformation, more precisely those of Lutherans targeting Calvinists.[9] It shows a dying man to whom Calvin personally recites the five hardest articles of his doctrine of predestination instead of reassuring him.

The third part was mainly concerned with the criticisms aimed at the emblems of a community (mostly Catholic) or individuals (mostly Protestant). A print made in Nuremberg in the 1520s (Berlin, Staatliche Museen zu Berlin—Stiftung Preussischer Kulturbesitz, Kupferstichkabinett, inv. 282-10) targets the sale of indulgences and the image of adoration associated with it: the *imago pietatis.*[10] It replaces the altar with a chest full of coins and the upper body of the risen Christ with that of the seven-headed beast alluding to the entire hierarchy of the Roman Catholic Church. In 1529, Johannes Cochlaeus replied to this caricature by showing Luther as the seven-headed beast and denouncing his multiple identities and evil character (Zurich Central Library, inv. 18.536).[11] And this counterattack process continues, for Lutherans took this caricature theme to engrave the *Seven-headed Calvinist Spirit* (Cobourg, Art Collections of the Veste Coburg, inv. XIII, 422, 59). This indicates an increasing aggravation of discourse since the opening of the Council of Trent in 1545, culminating in many prints that resorted to the register of scatology, as representatively demonstrated by the *Origin of Monks* (Berlin, Staatsbibliothek zu Berlin—Stiftung Preussischer Kulturbesitz, inv. YA 850). In parallel, it was also popular to play with the images that involve audience participation like these heads of a pope, cardinal, or bishop, which, when turned 180 degrees, become those of a demon, a satyr, or a madman. The same can also be observed in the medal exhibitions (Berne, Historisches Museum, inv. MA 914-916, 918) on a jug (Bonn, LVR-Landesmuseum, inv. 74.4219) and a small painting (Utrecht, Catharijneconvent Museum, inv. BMH s0056).[12]

---

8 R. W. Scribner, *For the Sake of Simple Folk: Popular Propaganda for the German Reformation* (Oxford, 1994), 27–28, 53–54.

9 A. Reiss and S. Witt, eds., *Calvinismus. Die Reformierten in Deutschland und Europa*, exposition catalogue, Berlin, Deutsches Historisches Museum, 1 April–19 July 2009 (Dresden, 2009), 60.

10 B. Latour and P. Weibel, eds., *Iconoclash: Beyond the Image Wars in Science, Religion and Art*, exhibition catalogue, Karlsruhe, Zentrum für Kunst und Medientechnologie, 4 May–4 August 2002 (Karlsruhe, 2002), 184–88.

11 F. Carey, ed., *The Apocalypse and the Shape of Things to Come*, exhibition catalogue, London, British Museum, December 1999–April 2000 (London, 1999), cat. 99.

12 P. Wachenheim, "A l'école d'Arcimboldo. Portraits politiques satiriques allemands et français (XVIe-XXe siècle)," *Francia. Forschungen zur westeuropäischen Geschichte* 37 (2010): 413–31.

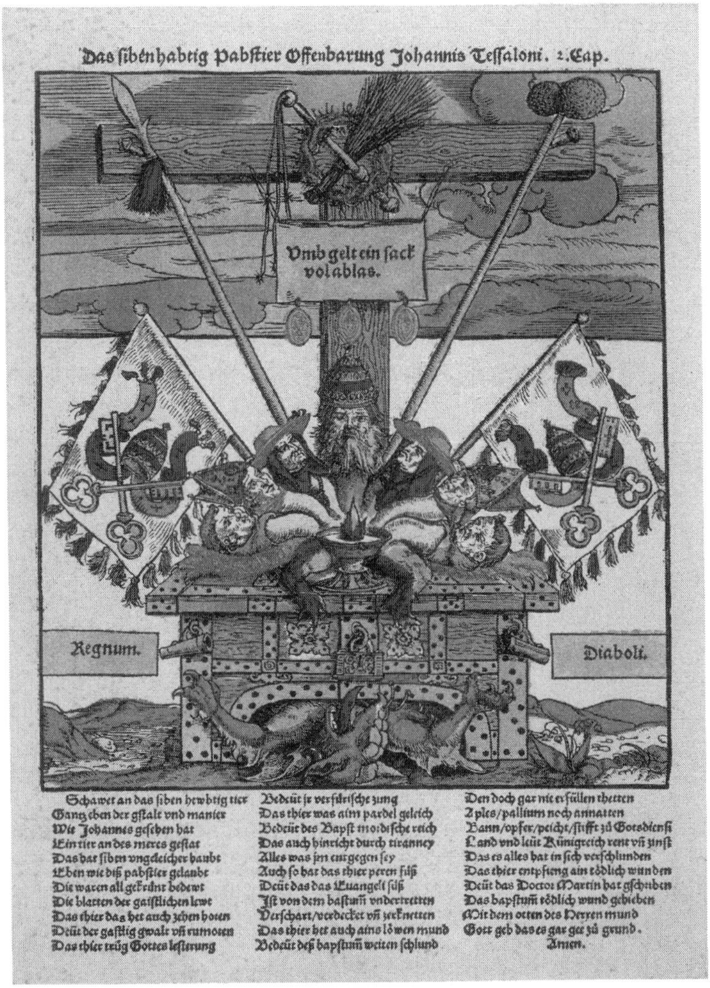

Bête papale à sept têtes (cat. 20). © bpk, Kupferstichkabinett/Staatliches Museen zu Berlin/ Jörg P. Anders.
English: The seven-headed papale animal (pope).

The Catholic response was to target the individuals concerned directly, in particular the founders of the Reformation. For example, a print (Cobourg, Art Collections of the Veste Coburg, inv. XIII 419,387) produced at the beginning of the Thirty Years' War hijacks the iconographic motif of travelling gypsies and features a perfectly recognizable Luther with a belly full of beer, fleeing with his wife and all his spiritual descendants to whom he literally gave birth.[13] Exhibited in its vicinity is a drawing (Munich, private collection), produced most likely in the late 17th century, which reflects the Catholic point of view regarding the inner-Reformation conflicts. Parodying the Battle of Carnival and Lent, it shows a ridiculous contest between Calvin and Luther, with the latter holding a feather duster to symbolize the vanity of such quarrel. A transition is made by the two paintings of Egbert II van Heemskerck that served as the occasion for reflection and the destination of this museographic stroll.

Finally, an epilogue addressed the images advocating religious tolerance; this is not to finish the tour of the exhibition with a happy ending, but to highlight the existence, albeit marginal, of an iconographic string that criticized the devastating effects of the confrontation and disseminated a pacifistic ideal. This is particularly the case with a print, produced from the milieu of Dutch Calvinists around 1600, that shows different denominations engaged in dialogue around a table under the guidance of *Ratio*.[14]

Post-Event Assessment of the Exhibition

One of the unique features of the exhibition was to contemplate the question of satirical images spanning over a long period of time, from the Middle Ages to the 18th century. It provided evidence that certain motifs and themes prevailed throughout the entire period. Above all, they were concerned with demonizing and ridiculing the opponents, most frequently pointing a finger at behaviours related to money or sex. It is also noteworthy that the use of apocalyptic and, more generally, infernal repertoire pervades these epochs. For example, associating the church with the seven-headed beast was the theme found in the ornament painting of the baptistery of the Padua Cathedral, created by Giusto De' Menabuoi in the mid-14th century, and two centuries later in the famous engraving of Cranach illustrating the September Testament, as well as in its successors.[15]

What is highlighted by such a finding is the decisive role played by the media used. Initially limited to the medium of paper, satiric images began to profit, as early as the 12th century, from more tangible media that assured their visibility. Thus, they appear in monumental paintings and sculpture as well as illustrated manuscripts and different types of private and unique objects. They experienced a major turning point with the adaption of printing, which allowed for reproductions and hence broad distribution in the forms

13 W. Harms, ed., *Illustrierte Flugblätter aus den Jahrhunderten der Reformation und der Glaubenskämpfe: Art Collections of the Veste Coburg* (Coburg, 1983), 62–63.

14 W. Hoffmann, ed., *Luther und die Folgen für die Kunst*, exposition catalogue, Hamburg, Hamburger Kunsthalle, 11 Nov. 1983–8 Jan. 1984 (Munich, 1983), 318–19.

15 S. Tammen, *Manifestationen von Antiklerikalismus in der Kunst des Mittelalters* (Frankfurt, 1993).

of books, flyers, and posters, that is, the predecessors of the ubiquitous modern posters. As such, it is the medium that determines different evolutionary phases of satirical images. As we have observed, the entire period addressed by the exhibition was characterized by the impact of printing. It has been followed by other satirical periods, defined in turn by the media of their dissemination: press, propaganda poster, television, and Internet. A religious caricature produced today hardly differs in its structure and content in that it always seeks to demonize the opposing parties and ridicule or soil what is sacred to them. It no longer has the force or virulence that its predecessors had in the Middle Ages and Renaissance era, but, owing to its instantaneous and global dissemination, its impact has become immediate and even more profound if the mocked religions do not share the same tradition and concept of images, still less of satirical images.

From this vantage point, we can better understand the dire efficacy of such images in the era of Reformation and confessions—an efficacy that had to compete amidst the growing tensions between confessions and the wars of religion. A rare print presented in the exhibition sheds light on this phenomenon (Paris, Bibliothèque nationale de France, reserve QB-201-7). The target of this print created by Wolfgang Meyerpeck in 1569 is Johannes Nas, bishop of Brixen and outspoken opponent of Luther. Resorting to the wordplay with "Nas" and "*Nase*" (the German word for nose), Meyerpeck transforms the head of Johannes Nas into a bagpipe, an instrument symbolizing lust, played by the devil to comfort the pope, depicted as Job in the worst state of his sufferings, mourning the fall of the Roman Catholic Church, which is likened to Babylon.[16] It is interesting to note that the pope leans against a tree on which hangs a famous image created in 1545 from Luther's milieu, which shows two farmers taking the papal tiara for a chamber pot. By using this as reference, Meyerpeck emphasizes the crucial role played by satirical image in the confessional conflicts. It is additionally noteworthy that it is his answer, in pictorial form using his iconographic expertise, to a pamphlet by Johannes Nas, directed in the preceding year against Luther: the *Anatomia lutheri*.

Another observation can be drawn from this investigation over long temporal and broad spatial dimensions. Whereas Protestants launched attacks as virulent as they were inventive, Catholics' counterattacks were rather discrete, both in their numbers and in their imagination. They seem to have preferred the literary medium such as pamphlets, while they reserved the use of image essentially for the dogma of religious painting. We can nevertheless verify that in the field of satirical images, they were most developed at the beginning of the confrontation. This is attested in the *Statua hereticalis* by Bernard of Luxembourg (1523), which responds directly to the September

16 Scribner, *For the Sake of Simple Folk*, 82, 134.

Testament of 1522, and the *Seven-headed Luther* in 1529, illustrating the pamphlet of Cochlaeus, an unequivocal answer to the *Papal Beast with Seven Heads* produced in Nuremberg shortly before. It should also be noted that the Catholic satirical images, for good reasons, never involved dogmatic questions, but only targeted individuals, mostly founders of the Reformation, especially Luther and Calvin. This happened with some delay, because it was necessary to wait until the iconographies of these founders were officially established. However, such iconographic images played a decisive role for the emergence of a new genre, namely caricature, defined as the ridiculous distortion of individual traits, a genre with a promising future.

Meyerpeck, Wolfgang (engraver), *Caricature contre la papauté,* 1569.
Bibliothèque natioanle de France, département Estampes et photographie.
English: Caricature against the pope.

Conclusion

The exhibition *Hell or Paradise: The Origins of Caricature* thus constituted an authentic laboratory where we delved into a thought-provoking investigation of the functions of satirical image. It was enriched through accompanying activities that played a mediating role for the general public to raise questions about the current reality of the phenomenon, thereby inviting illustrators and cartoonists to take a critical look at the exhibition. As a result, a catalogue was compiled within the framework of a master seminar of the University of Geneva. This catalogue was conceived to deepen the understanding of the functions of satirical image, following the structure of the exhibition.[17]

17 Frédéric Elsig and S. Sala, eds., *Enfer ou paradis. Aux sources de la caricature XVIe-XVIIIe siècles*, exhibition catalogue, Geneva, International Museum of the Reformation, 16 Oct. 2013–16 Feb. 2014 (Geneva, 2013).

CHAPTER 23

Martin Sallmann

Reformation and Democracy

Subsidiarity and the Priesthood of All Believers

The question of the relationship between the Reformation and democracy is a complex one. For one thing, the period between the Reformation of the early modern period and modern democracy spans over several centuries; for another, the terms are by no means unequivocal. Therefore, for a thorough examination of the links between the Reformation and democracy with a special reference to subsidiarity and the priesthood of all believers, it is necessary to differentiate both the historical timeframe and the terms accordingly.

Differentiation of the Terms

First of all, the Reformation encompasses the processes in the 16th century that, originating from the traditional Christian church of the Western world, brought forth the churches of the Lutheran, Reformed, and Roman Catholic confessions, as well as Anabaptism and the Anglican Church. This also denotes that there were different forms of Reformation: the Lutheran, Zurich, Upper German, Anabaptist, and, later, Genevan Reformations taking in different regions, lead by different central figures. While launched in the first half of the 16th century, churches were formed and strengthened in the second half, through theological teaching and ecclesiastical confessions, through devotional life in worship and daily routine, as well as church constitutions. These confessional churches also established particular relationships to their respective secular authorities. Over the succeeding centuries, they developed in different regions, each in its unique way, thus forming a diverse church landscape. It was not until the 19th century that the word "Reformation" became a term designating a historical epoch. In the context addressed here, a special significance is attributed to the diachronic aspect of the Reformation, specifically, the historical development of the early modern age into the contemporary times.

The term "democracy" is also to be differentiated historically. The ancient Greek democracy serves as the prototype of democracy: in those days, voting rights were possessed only by full citizens—that is, adult males of full status—there was no separation of powers, and democracy was pervasive in all aspects of social life. The notion of democracy as "self-governance of people" emerged in the 18th and 19th centuries. However, elements of such self-governance surfaced in medieval elective monarchies or European city-states. In the 16th century, Luther perceived the Confederation of Switzerland as a democracy. The terms and concepts of democracy were given their differentiated meanings in the 19th and 20th centuries, and can now hardly be overlooked. The embodiment of democracy is featured on different levels, namely, at the level of ideas, methods, institutions, and behaviour. Essential points at the level of ideas are the comprehension of freedom and equality. For the modern concept of democracy, freedom is to be delineated not only as freedom within the state, but also as freedom against the state. There is an area of human individuality in which the state may not intervene. Freedom no longer refers only to a particular social status of full citizenship, but principally to all people. Thus, freedom and equality are articulated at the level of human rights.[1]

Defining subsidiarity is more challenging because it appears in various areas such as politics, economics, and law. Subsidiarity denotes a particular relationship between individuals and institutions. Individual entities of self-determination and self-responsibility restrict the claim of regulations through institutions, to which they belong. Wherever self-determination and self-responsibility are not sufficient to fulfill certain tasks or solve problems, a higher organizational form intervenes to provide supports. State intervention

1 Immo Meenken, *Reformation und Demokratie.* Zum politischen Gehalt protestantischer Theologie in England 1570–1660. Quaestiones. Themen und Gestalten der Philosophie, Bd. 10 (Stuttgart-Bad Cannstatt, 1996), 31–33.

is curbed and claimed at the same time through the principle of subsidiarity. Martin Luther vehemently advocated the priesthood of all believers against the clergy of his time, arguing that priesthood is not necessary as a mediator between God and humans and that all Christians are equal and possess equal dignity before God. Although Luther treated this issue more cautiously in his later years and did not develop it further, it was singled out as a signum of Reformation theology, which lifted the privileged status of the clergy. The general priesthood represents the state of being Christian which is no longer classified into ranks or rungs.

The Historical Difference between the Reformation and Democracy

The question of the relationship between the Reformation and democracy gained in relevancy only with the decline of the feudal system under the *ancien regime* through the French Revolution; it made, therefore, a relatively late appearance. The Reformation as an era in the early modern times and the modern understanding of the post-Revolution democracy are not only far apart from each other by centuries, but also by intellectual-historical terms. Moreover, the Reformation developed in different places, in different political, economic, and social contexts, in different ways. The analysis of these relations with precisely differentiated notion of democracy is challenging, because it is difficult to pinpoint any direct historical-genetic lines from the 16th century down to our present day.

Thus, it is for this analysis necessary to make a distinction between primary, direct impacts and indirect, mediated impacts of the Reformation on the modern democracy.[2] Direct impacts can be identified by explicit or implicit references to theologians of the Reformation or to the doctrines and life of the confessional churches. Mediated impacts become manifest through intricate transmissions, through the life and work of groups, which convey, modify, and remodel ideas and insights. These mediated impacts are indeed more flexible, but also more difficult to be delineated. Direct influences of personalities or groupings on other individuals and groups are often difficult to prove in a historical-genetic approach. It requires explicit reference to works, notes in letters, or explicit comments in other sources. It is particularly difficult to demonstrate such links when they dissociate themselves from the individuals or groups and enter into a wider context of confessional, social, or political entities, developing and unfolding over several centuries in different historical contexts. Furthermore, if they are to be

2 Cf. Dietrich Ritsehl, "Der Beitrag des Calvinismus für die Entwicklung des Menschenrechts–gedankens in Europa und Nordamerika," in *Menschenrechte. 1. Historische Aspekte,* Forschung und Information, Bd. 30, ed. Ruprecht Kurzrock (Berlin, 1981), 58–70, here at 60f.

brought into context with other differentiated complexes such as democracy, human rights, and subsidiarity, which are also subject to their own historical evolutions, the task of discerning their impacts becomes extremely challenging, and the results should be carefully weighed. At any rate, there is much room for interpretations.

Various Reformation Themes of Modernity

Georg Jellinek, a German writer with Austrian origins, presented a positive association between the Reformation and human rights in the late 19th century, in which he assigned a prominent role to the freedom of conscience whose origin he saw in the Reformation. In their religious-sociological studies at the beginning of the 20th century, Max Weber and Ernst Troeltsch brought the Reformed and also the Puritan traditions into context with the emerging modernity. Weber interpreted the attitude of an intraworldly asceticism arising from the Puritan piety as the core driving source of the development of modern capitalism, as the Calvinist doctrine of double predestination could not assure the believers their salvation. Troeltsch argued that Protestantism relativized the ecclesiastical authority in the transitional period from the medieval to the modern ages, thus creating a room for the modern world. This earlier research ascribes the origin of modernity to Calvinist tradition, whereas the Lutheran tradition is labeled with a conservative reticence toward modernity. This stance, however, provoked protest already early on.

In the following, several themes, which are repeatedly referred to in regard to the relationship between the Reformation and democracy, will be depicted and the possible room for interpretation will be indicated.

Priesthood of All Believers—Equality of All People

At the peak of his clashes with the Roman Catholic Church, Martin Luther formulated the principle of a general priesthood. Depending on the argumentative context, he could base this on baptism, faith, or justification by Christ alone. The priesthood of all believers stands for the entirety of Christian existence. It abolished the distinction between clergy and laity as ecclesiastical classes. All Christians are in the same position before God and all have principally the task of ministry of word and sacrament. In the early years, Luther endorsed a congregation the right to assess all doctrines and to appoint and dismiss teachers. However, he did not institute the general priesthood as basis for a Protestant church order. Luther did not infer congregational implications from the priesthood of all believers. His statements about the priesthood of all people also became more reserved in later years.

Huldrych Zwingli advocated the congregational principle in the earlier stage of the Reformation: individual congregations were encouraged to assess the doctrines themselves and choose their pastors accordingly. This principle strengthened political communities that exercised a certain administrative and jurisdictional autonomy and voting rights. Farmers and Anabaptists adopted this principle, but could not implement it. Both in Zurich and Bern, individual congregations could at most retain the right to approve their pastors proposed by the secular and ecclesiastical authorities.

In John Calvin's theology, too, the principle of the priesthood of all people is uncontested. A believer is united with Christ through election. Christ's body is permeated with the Holy Spirit so that, without any distinction, all his members are guided by the Spirit. The diversity of members is reflected in the differentiation of the external order of the church.

The principle of the priesthood of all believers is of fundamental importance. All Reformers rejected the distinction between clergy and laity. This rejection was provoked by the abuse and privileges of the clergy within the traditional church; the general priesthood has thus its origin within the church itself. However, the consequent transfer of this principle onto a society of feudal order remained absent. Zwingli preferred aristocracy as governance, which he knew from his own experiences in Zurich. Calvin gave priority to an aristocratic form of government supplemented by democratic rights, and thus rejected both monarchy and democracy.

Synodal-Presbyterian Church Order

The *Ordonnances ecclésiastique* provided a fourfold ministry for the church leadership in Geneva. Pastors [*ministres*] and the teachers [*docteurs*] should exercise the ministry of the word. Pastors were co-opted from the collegium, confirmed and appointed by the town council, as well as accepted by the congregation through approval. Elders [*anciens*] and deacons [*diacres*] were elected by the town council after consulting with the pastors. The elders were chosen from among the Genevan citizens. Together with pastors, they formed a consistory that met weekly to exercise church discipline. In serious cases, the consistory could impose exclusion from communion. The secular authorities were thus involved in the composition of ministries. The consistory was a mixed committee that supervised the church discipline. At the same time, however, ecclesiastical and secular disciplines were clearly distinguished from each other.

In France, a congregation assumed a threefold ministry: pastors, elders, and deacons, who together formed a consistory. The consistory held the church leadership, represented the local church, elected pastors, and exercised church discipline. Congregations were integrated in provincial and general synods. This gave the Protestant church in France an independent structure that constituted a counterpart to secular authorities.

The Protestants who emigrated due to religious reasons and had sought refuge on the continent during the reign of Bloody Mary brought the presbyterian church model back to England. They demanded the abolition of the episcopal constitution of the Anglican Church and the introduction of a congregational order in biblical tradition. The presbyterian church order corresponded with the political participation of the lower nobility and the bourgeoisie in the parliament, but contradicted the privileges of nobility and bishops. Seeing that a church order reform was not possible, a part of the Puritan movement turned to separatism, rejected the Anglican Episcopalism and Calvinist Presbyterianism, and voted for the independence of individual congregations that were to enter into a covenant with Christ. These congregations adopted the Anabaptist ecclesiology and prepared congregationalism.

Persecution and Resistance in France and the Netherlands

In France, the Calvinist church grew into a strong minority that also gained political influence. In the course of the long civil war in the second half of the 16th century, independent regions were formed in the southwestern and southern regions with their own administration and excellent educational institutions in the wake of the bloody St. Bartholomew's Day Massacre. It has often been pointed out that in this process the Huguenots transferred the Calvinist model of church leadership to the political realm.

The civil war in the Netherlands led to the separation of the Seven United Provinces, the Dutch States-General, under the sceptre of Holland. Before that, Calvinists had come to the country from the South as emigrants for religious reasons. At the Synod in Emden in 1571, a synodal-presbyterian church order was adopted for the congregations. These church orders were implemented in the northern provinces, and consistories were established in towns.

Under the pressure of persecution, Monarchomachs developed the right of resistance against the unjust and tyrannical authorities, considering the established positive law, the Roman law, and biblical passages on covenant. They argued that feudal law provided for the reciprocity of rulers' rights and duties, so that the monarch was himself bound by it. Biblically, the double covenant was established between God and the monarch with his people, on the one hand, and between the monarch and his people, on the other. The right to resistance, however, was not developed by the Huguenots alone; it was claimed by the Catholic party as well.

Covenant and the Social Contract

The covenant theology inspired by Heinrich Bullinger and John Calvin was adopted and further developed by Puritanism, wherein a distinction was made between a covenant of works and a covenant of grace. The covenant of works was obliged to the compliance with the Decalogue that leads to eternal life. The Decalogue, however, brought the sinner to despair, remorse, repentance, and finally to Christ. The covenant of grace promised to the sinner the justice of Christ, which is received by faith. Faith, which is a gift of God, joyfully seeks the sanctification of life in alignment with the Decalogue. Although the federal theology was combined with a doctrine of predestination, according to which God had irrevocably elected people for salvation or damnation, the idea of reciprocal commitment soon arose. As God had shown God's grace, for example, by rescuing them from the Spaniards or, later, through the land appropriation in the New World, the people were in debt to abide by the divine law. If this obligation was neglected, the entire people was threatened by misery.

In early congregationalism, this mutual commitment of the covenantal idea received an active reinforcement from the people. The assembly of believers, which is placed under God's rule, entered into a covenant with God in which they declared their will to be obedient to the divine law, and God for God's part declared this assembly as God's own people. Robert Browne regarded this mutual voluntary agreement as constitutive of a congregation, but also of any form of exercising sovereignty, thus also in the political sphere.

The distinction of a twofold covenant was adopted from the French Protestantism: a covenant is made between God and the king with his people, on the one hand, and between the king and his people, on the other. While the king is God's vice-regent, failure to fulfill his tasks endows the people with the right to resistance.

Assessment and Appraisal

It is hardly controversial that the Reformation tradition in general—and the Reformed theology in particular in its diverse forms of Puritanism—exerted an impact on the course of modern society. However, the magnitude of this impact is controversial. Especially, the transition from theology to politics and from worship to society is difficult to appraise. One thing should certainly be considered, though: neither Presbyterianism nor Congregationalism was motivated by modernizing politics, but by the pursuit of true faith and church order reflecting it. Nevertheless, the priesthood of all people, presbyterian church order, and federal theological thought processes likely formed the mindsets that fostered democratic attitudes. Such effects are to be probed in their respective historical contexts. It is also important to note that the Lutheran tradition did not simply take a conservative stance as against the Reformed tradition. Rather, the historical and politico-social circumstances are of greater importance for the reception and development of the different theological traditions.

C. Dogmatics

CHAPTER 24

Christophe Chalamet

The "Unintended" Reformation?

Reflections on the Reformation, Individualism, and the Secular Age

As the Western world, including the United States, is becoming more and more secularized, people feel the need to reflect on this long and massive evolution, and they look for historical factors which have led to our current situation. At times, they do it with some nostalgia: they regret the times when most church services were well attended, when churches were, as the French saying goes, "at the centre of the village," not just geographically but in all regards. The cleric was a person of authority, with much influence in the area.

How did we go from there to here, from masses being involved in Christian devotions, to relatively empty churches, massive indifference, and an attitude that religion is a "personal," "intimate," "private" affair? Could it be that the Protestant Reformation, initiated by Martin Luther in the second decade of the 16th century, had something to do with this?

The thesis that the Reformation spurred secularization and individualism is far from new. Already in the 16th century, many Roman Catholic observers were concerned that the reformers, by placing scripture above the church tradition, were opening the doors wide to all kinds of arbitrary, and widely diverging, interpretations of scripture. Modern theologians concur in saying that there are individualistic tendencies in Reformation theology and that ecclesiology is the "weak link" in Protestant theology.[1]

This critique was repeated by another Genevan thinker a few centuries later. In the second of his "Letters Written from the Mountain," Jean-Jacques Rousseau writes: with the reformers, "the individual mind is established as

1 Albrecht Ritschl's interpretation of justification within the frame of the kingdom of God can be interpreted as an attempt to overcome individualism within Protestantism by recovering a sound teaching about the "kingdom" and the "church." Here was his overall goal, against all the Pietist reductions to the individual (cf., for instance, J. Chr. von Hofmann): ". . . unter dem leitenden Gedanken des Reiches Gottes die Versöhnung durch Christus und die Rechtfertigung im Glauben . . . als die Hauptsache oder als das Eins und Alles der christlichen Lehre gelten können." *Die christliche Lehre von der Rechtfertigung und Versöhnung*, vol. 1: *Die Geschichte der Lehre* (Göttingen: Marcus, 1870), 561. He commends Calvin for considering the believer only insofar as the believer is a member of the community (194–96, 203); still, Calvin could have gone further along this line (245). *L'orthodoxie luthérienne, puis le piétisme, ont poussé dans la direction de l'individualisme* (301, 347, 349, 364). As is well known, Karl Barth took over the "battle" against individualist reductions in his debate with Rudolf Bultmann. For Barth, the *pro nobis* precedes the *pro me.* For Brunner, the fact that Calvin treats the theme of the church only in the final volume of his Institutes is an expression and a cause of "the oft-lamented protestant individualism." Emil Brunner, *Das Missverständnis der Kirche* (Zurich: TVZ, 1988), 11. For chez Calvin, ". . . la foi est considérée essentiellement comme une réalité individuelle à laquelle la communauté de la foi s'ajoute, mais comme ne faisant pas partie de sa nature. Ce qui signifie que Calvin, bien qu'il soit dans la pratique et éminemment homme d'Église et fondateur d'Église, sépare de l'Église la foi comprise dans un sens individualiste. À supposer que les croyants aient besoin de l'Église, ils sont croyants même indépendamment de l'Église. C'est aussi la conception actuellement en cours chez les protestants réformés. À cette conception s'oppose diamétralement la conception catholique, non seulement la catholique romaine, mais également la conception de l'orthodoxie grecque, des anglicans et des vieux-catholiques qui, marquant au fer rouge cet individualisme, le considèrent comme une hérésie essentielle, parce que pour eux. . . . Église et foi constituent une unité de même nature et que l'on ne peut absoluement pas s'imaginer la foi sans l'Église." Emil Brunner, *Dogmatique*, vol. 3: *La doctrine chrétienne de l'Égise*, de la foi et de l'achèvement, trans. Frédéric Jaccard (Geneva: Labor et Fides, 1967), 33–34. Paul Tillich writes: "The interest of early Protestantism was . . . so much centred around individual justification that the idea of a 'Gestalt of grace' in our historical existence could not develop." Paul Tillich, *The Protestant Era*, trans. James Luther Adams (Chicago: University of Chicago Press, 1948), xx. ". . . le protestantisme à ses débuts s'est tellement centré sur la justification personnelle que l'idée d'une '*Gestalt* de grâce' dans notre existence historique n'a pas pu s'y développer." Idem, *Substance catholique et principe protestant*, ed. A. Gounelle (Paris-Geneva-Québec: Cerf-Labor et Fides-Laval, 1996), 236. "Das Interesse des frühen Protestantismus war indessen so stark um die individuelle Rechtfertigung zentriert, dass der Gedanke einer 'Gestalt der Gnade' in unserer geschichtlichen Existenz sich nicht entwickeln konnte." Idem, *Der Protestantismus als Kritik und Gestaltung. Schriften zur Theologie I*, Gesammelte Werke, Bd. 7 (Stuttgart: Evangelisches Verlagwerk, 1962), 21.
For further information on the critique of individualism by Adolf von Harnack, see also Alfred Loisy, *L'Évangile et l'Église* (Paris, 1902), 165, 167–68.

the sole interpreter of scripture; thus the authority of the church is rejected; thus each is put under his own jurisdiction for doctrine. Such are the two fundamental points of the Reform: to acknowledge the Bible as rule of one's belief, and not to admit any other interpreter of the meaning of the Bible than oneself."[2]

Rousseau then raises the following possible objection: if arbitrary, individualist readings of scripture were one of the two key ingredients of the Protestant Reformation, then how did ecclesial communities emerge? How did "bodies"—indeed, ecclesial "bodies"—see the light of day ("*comment ont-ils fait corps*")? Rousseau's answer is clear: "they united in this, that all acknowledged each of them as competent judge for himself."[3] The "glue" for the Protestant churches was therefore precisely their individualistic dogma, according to Rousseau. "The very diversity of their manners of thinking about all the rest was the common bond that united them."[4] "As a Reformed church, the Church of Geneva, then, does not and should not have any profession of faith that is precise, articulated, and common to all its members."[5]

This "freedom" is what Rousseau cherished in Protestantism. "Let someone prove to me today that in matters of faith I am obliged to submit to someone else's decisions, beginning tomorrow I will become Catholic, and every consistent and true man will act as I do."[6]

The big question is, indeed: How did we get from there (the reformers and their theologies) to there (Rousseau, modern liberal theology which prolongs Rousseau, and us)?

Answering that question is not easy. It can be addressed on several levels: on the level of theology, especially on the supposed presence of

2 Jean-Jacques Rousseau, *Letter to Beaumont, Letters Written from the Mountain, and Related Writings*, ed. C. Kelly and E. Grace, trans. C. Kelly and J. R. Bush, *Collected Writings of Rousseau* 9 (Hanover, NH: University Press of New England, 2001), 154. "Voilà donc l'esprit particulier établi pour unique interprète de l'Écriture; voilà l'autorité de l'Église rejetée; voilà chacun mis pour la doctrine sous sa propre jurisdiction. Tels sont les deux points fondamentaux de la Réforme: reconnaître la Bible pour règle de sa croyance, et n'admettre d'autre interprète du sens de la Bible que soi." "Lettres écritres de la montagne" (deuxième lettre), in Jean-Jacques Rousseau, *Œuvres complètes*, ed. Raymond Trousson and Frédéric S. Eigeldinger t. 6 (Geneva-Paris: Slatkine-Champion, 2012), 255.

3 Rousseau, *Œuvres complètes*, ". . . ils se réunissaient en ceci, que tous reconnaissaient chacun d'eux comme juge compétent pour lui-même," 255.

4 Ibid., "La diversité même de leurs façons de penser sur tout le reste était le lien commun qui les unissait," 256.

5 Ibid., 157. "L'Église de Genève n'a donc et ne doit avoir comme réformée aucune profession de foi précise, articulée et commune à tous ses membres," ibid., 260.

6 Ibid., 155. "Qu'on me prouve aujourd'hui qu'en matière de foi je suis obligé de me soumettre aux décisions de quelqu'un, dès demain je me fais catholique, et tout homme conséquent et vrai fera comme moi," ibid., 256.

individualistic tendencies in such-and-such theology. Here, ecclesiological considerations are of particular importance. But there is theology and then there is the reception of theology. Calvin is not the same as Calvinism. Calvin may have wished to ground the believer's certitude of salvation, but clearly participants in the broad tradition he formed, which we call Calvinism, may still have had deep existential concerns regarding their own eternal status. These concerns, in turn, may have triggered particular ways of living. That is, of course, the starting point of Max Weber's well-known thesis on the affinity between Calvinism and capitalism.

Clearly, Rousseau projected his own (and his fellow Deists') views of freedom and conscience into the reformers' world. It is Kant, not Luther or Calvin, who thought it could not have been God who addressed Abraham and ordered him to sacrifice his son Isaac (Genesis 22). The reformers were indeed "bound" by scripture and had absolutely no interest in arbitrary readings of scripture. All they wanted was to rediscover the gospel, not fashion a new one according to their own whims. They viewed themselves as listeners of scripture, not as critics of it. This is where they "stood" (as Luther put it in Worms in 1521); they could not do otherwise. The idea that the reformers promoted freedom of conscience is an aberration. Most people nowadays are (unlike in the 18th, the 19th, and early 20th centuries) aware of that.

But that does not resolve in any way the lingering question: What about the "unintended" consequences of the Protestant Reformation? Sure, the reformers were bound by God's word in scripture. But did they not, by opposing "the" church, open the door to individual stances that are attitudes of confrontation, rather than obedience, to the "community" which the church is? By focusing so much on "justification," did they not orient theology and the Christian faith toward an individualistic understanding of Christianity? After all, who is the object of justification: a community or an individual who trusts in God's promise and gift?

Brad S. Gregory's recent book *The Unintended Reformation* seeks to show one thing, which the subtitle of the book clearly indicates: *How a Religious Revolution Secularized Society*. According to Gregory, nowadays "anything goes so far as truth claims and religious practices are concerned," and that deplorable situation is "an extension and latter-day manifestation of the full range of views produced by the Reformation unfettered."[7] John Milton, Roger Williams, and other "radical Protestants" of the 17th century, who "claimed that an individual Christian was no more bound to institutions, traditions,

7 Brad S. Gregory, *The Unintended Reformation: How a Religious Revolution Secularized Society* (Cambridge, MA: Harvard University Press, 2012), 112. On that same page, Gregory acknowledges Luther's concern with regard to arbitrary interpretation of the Christian faith. All further page references are cited within the text.

authorities . . . than was an individual philosopher as construed by Descartes, Spinoza, or Hobbes," these "radicals" "simply spelled out what was implicit in Luther, Calvin, and every other sixteenth-century Protestant reformer" (215). What the Reformation "produced absent the power of political authorities standing behind hermeneutic authorities" is the following: "the aggregate of whatever individuals happened to prefer" (355). The *sola scriptura* "generated" an "open-ended arbitrariness" (374). Protestant pluralism "derives" from the *sola scriptura.* That is a "fact," according to Gregory (353). "By rejecting the authority of the Roman Catholic Church, the Reformation eliminated any shared framework for the integration of knowledge" (326). The Reformation's "failure derived directly from the patent infeasibility of successfully applying the reformers' own foundational principle" (368), namely the *sola scriptura*, which opened the door already in the 1520s to "radical doctrinal skepticism and relativism" (369). "By rejecting the Roman Catholic Church's authority and much of medieval Christianity, the Reformation pushed the Republic of Letters in a secularizing direction: instead of being a network focused *on* the renewal of Christendom, it became a refuge *from* divisive, disruptive, and embattled religious affairs" (335). Gregory states his thesis in the clearest way in the conclusion: "the Reformation is the most important distant historical source for contemporary Western hyperpluralism with respect to truth claims about meaning, morality, values, priorities, and purpose. . . . Against the intentions of anti-Roman Catholic reformers but as a result of their actions, the church became the churches" (369).

Gregory is obviously correct to think that the Protestant Reformation triggered a diversity of ecclesial communities (and yet weren't there several Christian "churches" long before the 16th century?), and he is well aware that the reformers would have been shocked to see how Rousseau interpreted Protestantism (364). But does he adequately take into account the *many* lively debates which preceded 1517 and the failures of medieval Christianity?[8] In a way, his stance is akin to Alasdair MacIntyre's overly dramatic vision of the modern collapse of ethics in the opening pages of his book *After Virtue.*[9]

---

8 Gregory does not share Rousseau's naïve "nostalgia": "Quand les premiers Réformateurs commencèrent à se faire entendre, l'Église universelle était en paix; tous les sentiments étaient unanimes . . ." Rousseau, *Œuvres complètes*, 267. In a presentation on Gregory's book on 8 May 2012, Mark Noll points out that the "damage done by Protestants to the medieval ideal depended in virtually all instances on failures of medieval Christendom." Noll's response can be viewed at http://vimeo.com/41909963.

9 Gregory acknowledges his debt to MacIntyre on p. 5, and MacIntyre gives high praises to the book on the back cover. Of course, inside the book (359) one finds a harsh—but unfounded—critique of MacIntyre's most important opponent, Jeffrey Stout. Gregory, like MacIntyre and Stanley Hauerwas, is interested in "habituation in Christian virtues within a shared way of life" (350). He deplores this: "There is no shared, substantive common good" (377). Gregory

Despite the last chapter's title, "Against Nostalgia," the reader receives the impression that Gregory "regrets" the 16th-century schism. But is it the job of historians to "regret" the past? Doesn't this "regret" invite suspicion that nostalgia is indeed present, despite the last chapter's title, in such a narrative? The grain of truth in Gregory's bold but simplistic thesis (the subtitle of the book, for which Gregory himself must take responsibility, seems to posit a sort of mono-causality: our secularized world is the result of one single religious revolution: Luther's) has to do with the danger of arbitrariness within Protestantism, sometimes in the name of the Spirit's "illumination." But Gregory's book overlooks the *much-greater* source of secularization in our world: the *modern* revolution and in particular the deistic ideas, rather than the Protestant Reformation. The turning point, as Charles Taylor suggests, cannot be found in the 16th century, but rather towards the end of the 17th century, with the ideas evolving even further in the 18th century. The reason for our "secular age" is multifaceted and cannot be reduced to one historical event. Additionally, one has to carefully analyze the evolvements of Protestantism in the late 16th and the 17th century, while being on the search for the movement which eventually led to our Western, secular world.

My goal in this analysis was neither to grant absolution to the reformers nor to clear Protestantism of any responsibility within the great historical movements which shaped our contemporary world. It is obvious that the Latin (Western) Schism has led to a fragmentation of Christianity and to intent discussions on philosophical and theological questions (not to even mention the bloody conflicts). One-sided explanations, however, are no help, and provocative and catchy subtitles like Gregory's may be successful in a bookstore, but are actually truly inadequate and regrettable.

seems to be convinced, unlike "some Protestants," that theology without metaphysics is intellectually unsustainable (332).

CHAPTER 25

François Dermange

Calvin's Economic Ethics

Capitalist, Socialist, or Something Else Entirely?

Associating Calvin with capitalism or socialism is an anachronism. Not only did these terms come into being much later, but the underlying ideas themselves were incomprehensible in the 16th century. We can bring these terms closer to his time only by seeking their elective affinity as done by Max Weber (1864–1920) over a century ago in *The Protestant Ethic and the Spirit of Capitalism*[1] and, more recently, by André Bieler (1914–2006) for socialism.

The Protestant ethic as discussed by Weber is not "ethics" per se, a theologically grounded normative theory, but an ethos, a body of norms culturally internalized in customs whose transgression is sanctioned by social reprobation, without having to be explained. In this sense, the Protestant ethic is not the one of Luther or Calvin, but the psychological and practical impact of their ideas on social action within the groups coined by their influence. From this standpoint, Weber was well aware that he would not

1 Max Weber, *L'éthique protestante et l'esprit du capitalisme: suivi d'autres essais [1904–1905]*, ed., trans., presented, and annotated by Isabelle Kalinowski (Paris: Flammarion, 2000).

find in Calvin, in any form whatsoever, traits encouraging capitalism.[2] Rather, it was through Calvin's *Wirkungsgeschichte* ("historical influence"), Calvinism, Puritanism, and, finally, the secularized ethos driven by industry bosses that Weber could detect this sense of capitalism.

As for capitalism, it is neither the economic and social system of the liberals, nor the system denounced by Marx, but a "mindset" which is presented, for example, in Benjamin Franklin's advice to a young man[3]—a mentality seeking a legitimate gain in a systematic and rational manner in pursuit of a calling: "An economic action is called *capitalistic* if it rests on the expectation of profit by the utilization of opportunities for exchange, however on formally peaceful chances for profit."[4] As such, the "spirit of capitalism" refers to an internalized view of the world, whose primary features are individual initiatives; instrumental rationality (reason centred on pursuing the means and not the ends); the intention of material acquisition, trade and competition; and an appetite for risk-taking.

So, Weber supports the idea that the development of modern capitalism cannot be explained by the "natural" game of "pure" economic laws, as claimed by the economic liberalism, nor by the ultimate way of economy determining the relationship between social strata, as argued by the Marxists. It cannot be reduced either to the sole intention of individuals to improve their living conditions (Adam Smith), to maximize one's interests (Werner Sombart), or to make a profit. The emergence of new economic behaviours and concepts is linked to a new ethos nurtured especially, among a variety of complex factors, by the new spirit of the Reformation. Thus, the Reformation would have served capitalism initially until the moment that, now crowned by success, it could do without this support, having already established its own power base of operation.

Today, however, "capitalism" is no longer just a mindset ("spirit of capitalism") but a socially coercive force: the Puritan wanted to be a man of trade—we *must* be one.[5] In this regard, Weber speaks of the "iron cage" or "iron box" ("*ein stahlhartes Gehäuse*") in which we would gradually allow ourselves to be locked. Henceforth, no one has the liberty any longer to give his or her life a meaning different from that imposed by the outside society: individualism, competitiveness, success, utility conceived in definite terms, and so forth. Economic science itself presupposes that individuals act rationally, that is, they pursue their own selfish interests, solitarily acting, to maximize their

2 Ibid., 150, 160.

3 Ibid., 89.

4 Max Weber, "Avant-propos au 'Recueil d'études de sociologie des religions,'" in *Sociologie des religions* [1922] (Gallimard, 1996), 493–94. (English title: *Collected Essays on the Sociology of Religion.*)

5 Ibid., 300.

enjoyment. However, not only is such a definition of rationality by no means a self-evident matter, but all serious economists know that this is fiction. Nevertheless, we act as if it were true, to the point of making it one of the principal keys to the social life. Consequently, "capitalism" follows a nihilistic logic where everyone finds themselves taken up in a spur gear:

> Imagine the consequences of that comprehensive bureaucratization and rationalization which we see as premise today. In private enterprises of big industry, as well as in all economic enterprises equipped with modern organization, "calculability," rational calculation, is manifest at every stage. It reduces each individual worker to a cog in the machine and, seeing oneself in this light, one's own preoccupation becomes more and more only whether one can become a bigger cog. . . . The problem which besets us now is not *how* this evolution can be changed, for that is impossible, but what will come of it.[6]

So, I will beat around the bush and tackle this issue sideways, not on its sociological field but by probing its relationship to theology. Although Calvin is not at the centre of Weber's analysis, Weber retains at least two essential elements which he associates with Calvin's rationalization of the Reformation: the new implication given to asceticism and self-demonstration of the election by professional success.

The rationalization process inaugurated by Israeli prophets would find in Calvin, in fact, its culminant point.[7] Not only did the Reformation disenchant the world by removing the magical means of salvation and confession, but Calvin further advanced the movement of rationalization with his notion of sacraments and salvation.[8] In denying the merit of works, the Reformation necessarily left its followers to wonder if they were saved. Luther reassured them with a spiritual and mystical response; Christians could experience that they were God's "chosen vessels" and could be united with Christ. However, Calvin rejected these emotional and mystical elements. For him, it was enough to hold to the decree of the sovereign God who predestined from all eternity those elected to salvation and to persevere in unshakable trust in Christ resulting from true faith.[9] Such a response was sufficient for Calvin, but not for his followers.

Moreover, in line with the same process of rationalization, asceticism was given a shift in meaning. For a long time, asceticism had consisted in renouncing worldly riches in order to turn to the true riches that Christians

6 Cited by Isabelle Kalinowski, "Leçons wébériennes sur la science et la propagande," in Max Weber, *La science, profession et vocation* (Agone, 2005), 255. (The English translation here is an existing translation that was adapted to the French translation.)

7 Weber, *L'éthique protestante*, 166–67.

8 Ibid., 166–67, 190.

9 Ibid., 164.

found in God. It involved a voluntary deprivation of one's goods. Calvin turned the direction of asceticism from renunciation to action.[10] According to him, the world exists to serve God's glory and Christians are there to increase, as far as their resources allow it, God's glory on earth by accomplishing the divine commandments.[11] They should therefore enjoy the world as if they were not enjoying it, but without renouncing its riches, because they could be useful to others and serve the glory of God.

Calvin's disciples linked these two elements. Since predestination left them in solitude and anxiety,[12] they found the means to ensure their election in occupational activities carried out with the greatest possible efficiency. While claiming to be saved by grace through their faith, the Reformed and the Puritans used the results of their occupational pursuits as the objective basis for their *certitudo salutis*.[13] If they succeeded, they did what God expected of them as God's agents and instruments; thus they could be sure to be on the right side. Faith was proven (*bewähren*) by tangible signs.[14]

Did Weber read Calvin correctly? Yes and no. No, because he radicalized Calvin's position and gave importance to certain elements—to predestination in particular—that obviously did not belong to the ethics of the Reformer. In particular, how can we forget that the central theme of the *Traicté très excellent de la vie chrestienne* (*Of the Life or Conversation of a Christian Man*), written in 1539 and published in part in 1551, and taken up again throughout the successive editions of the *Institutes*,[15] was precisely the union with God? At the end of the progressive regeneration of human faculties, which is the object of sanctification, the opposition between freedom and obedience, passivity and activity, divine justice and human will is overcome: "The goal of our regeneration is to realize in our life a harmony and agreement [*symmetria et consensus*] between God's righteousness and our obedience, and thus to confirm the adoption through which God accepted us as God's children."[16] This state where God and a human being are thought in terms of *symmetry* and

10 Julien Freund, *Etudes sur Max Weber* (Geneva: Droz, 1990), 157–58. (English title: *Sociology of Max Weber*)

11 Weber, *L'éthique protestante*, 185.

12 Ibid., 165.

13 Ibid., 178–80.

14 Ibid., 184.

15 John Calvin, *The Life of a Christian Man*: for a long time in the concluding part of the *Institutes* (ch. 17 of the 1541 edition and ch. 21 of the 1545 edition and the successive ones), finally included by Calvin in Book III, chs. VI-X of the last edition (1559).

16 *Institutes of the Christian Religion (Inst.)* III, VI, 1. (Translation note: an existing translation was adapted to match the French version)

consensus is precisely the state of a "sacred union" (*unio mystica*) by which the believer enjoys Christ and all riches that are in him.[17]

Admittedly, however, Weber is right when he argues that Calvin redefines asceticism. If Calvin begins indeed to put the attachment to the riches in heaven as antithetical to worldly riches,[18] he gives a good reason not simply to denounce the riches of this world: "This does not suit Christian meekness for anyone, as if in hatred of the human race, to flee to the wilderness for solitude, and to desert the duties which the Lord has especially commanded to all of us: i.e., to help each other."[19] The gospel, then, discovers a new "antithesis." Dangerous as they are per se, riches are not less useful to others, and in serving others they are allowed to serve God.[20]

Because they love God, Christians try to "use the gifts of God purely with a pure conscience," without greed, immoderate profusion, or arrogance.[21] So they omit "all shows of superfluous and vain abundance,"[22] and by the example of the early Christians simply live soberly and happily.[23] However, because they also love their neighbours, Christians will not part from riches which can be used for good causes.[24] God did not want God's children to be useless here in this world, but they come through for one another,[25] "are helpful to one another, and are joined in a mutual bond of charity."[26]

As such, the ethics of the reformer favoured a sober pursuit of social efficacy in the use of riches, particularly by providing workplaces which allowed everyone to find his or her calling. However, even if we are to agree with Weber in this regard, the motivation for this ethics was by no means connected to predestination. If "Christian love of neighbours" took the form of occupational activities in service of the earthly life of the community that was neither to compensate for the solitude of the believer, as claimed by

17 *Inst.* III, XI, 10.

18 John Calvin, *Commentaires du Nouveau Testament* (Paris: Meyrueis, 1853), t. 1, p. 187, on Matt. 6:19. (English: *Calvin's Commentaries on the New Testament*, Matt. 6:19. ". . . particularly, when God allows us a place in heaven for laying up a treasure, and kindly invites us to enjoy riches which never perish.")

19 *Inst.* IV, XIII, 16. (Translator's note: an existing translation was adapted to match the French version.)

20 Calvin, *Commentaires du Nouveau Testament*, t. 1, 189, on Matt. 6:24; t. 1, 371 on Luke 16:1-15.

21 *Inst.* III, XIX, 9.

22 *Inst.* III, X, 4.

23 Calvin, *Commentaires du Nouveau Testament*, t. 2, 483, on Acts 2:46.

24 Ibid., t. 1, 372, on Luke 16:1-15.

25 John Calvin, *Sermons on the Epistle to the Ephesians, in Opera quae supersunt omnia*, ed. G. Baum, E. Cunitz, and E. Reuss (Braunschweig and Berlin: Schwetschke, 1863–1890), v. 51, col. 736, on Eph. 5.

26 Ibid., col. 732, on Eph. 5.

Weber,[27] nor to reintroduce a theology of works, as was sometimes suspected by Lutherans, but because "helping each other"[28] was the means to give a concrete sense of love.

Calvin has nothing in common with the ideal type of Puritan merchant hardening steel during the "heroic age of capitalism," as described by Weber,[29] and if utilitarianism of selfish and hedonistic individuals has Christian roots, as Nietzsche thought,[30] it is nothing more than an appalling caricature.

Is Calvin then a socialist well ahead of his time? I doubt it. One reason is convincing enough. Socialism, in its various forms, aims at abolishing social classes and defending equality for all,[31] whereas Calvin is not hostile to the ruling class. His vision is, rather, that of a body which lives from the interdependence and differences of everybody. This model applies to political, economic, and even male/female relationships. In each case, God requires those in superior position to ensure justice for the others as they deserve it. In this sense, the ethics of the reformer is one of responsibility and equity rather than equality and freedom. It does not want to abolish class distinctions, wealth, or intelligence, but in keeping with the gospels, much will be asked of those to whom much was given. As in the parable of the talents, each is the steward of what he or she has received. He or she is not the owner of his or her riches. One's riches are there to serve others.

We are all commanded to serve one another following the Golden Rule of not doing unto others what we would not like them to do unto us. Bound to the gospel, Christians go even further: for more justice still, loving them in doing to others what they would like done unto themselves, starting with the poorest and most vulnerable.

27 Weber, *L'éthique protestante*, 172.

28 *Inst.* IV, XIII, 16.

29 Weber, *L'éthique protestante*, 180.

30 Friedrich Nietzsche, *Par-delà le bien et le mal*, trans. Patick Wotling (Paris: Flammarion, 2000), §228. (English title: *Beyond Good and Evil.*)

31 See in particular, André Bieler, *La pensée économique et sociale de Calvin* (Geneva: Georg, 1959), and idem, *L'humanisme social de Calvin* (Geneva: Labor et Fides, 1961), wherein, as noted by W.-A Visser't Hooft, Bieler depicts Calvin as a "socialiste personnaliste," 5. In Calvin, *Prophète de l'ère industrielle* (Geneva: Labor et Fides, 1964), Bieler presents a more nuanced viewpoint, favouring a "humanisme réaliste," distinct from liberal and socialist ideologies (55).

CHAPTER 26

Douwe Visser

Reformation and Politics

Between Prophetic Voice and Blind Obedience

During the Second World War, there was some hesitation in Germany in the Confessing Church (*Bekennende Kirche*) to pray for Dietrich Bonhoeffer. Some within the church could not accept the fact that he was part of a resistance movement that wanted to bring the Hitler regime to an end, even by means of violence. For the same reason, some objected after the war to naming a street in Berlin after Bonhoeffer. Although the church and its leaders did not want to give up its right of freely confessing its faith—that was the very reason for the existence of the Confessing Church—some felt that right should not go so far as to overthrow the (still-perceived) legal German government. Bonhoeffer himself struggled immensely with this. His justification of armed resistance by comparing the situation with the example of a drunken driver on the Kurfürstendamm wounding and even killing people is well known. Bonhoeffer said that in such a case one would not help much by giving pastoral care to the victims. It would be best, he said, to stop the drunken driver by *all* means. On the other hand, however, he always felt that the final justification of his actions was in the hands of God. He would stand as a sinner before God depending on God's final forgiveness.

When in South Africa after 1948 the apartheid system became part of every aspect of society, opposition from churches within and outside the country became stronger and stronger. For quite a few Christians, armed resistance against this destructive system was regarded as a necessary final option. The World Alliance of Reformed Churches adopted at its General Council in Ottawa in 1982 the motion to condemn the theological justification of apartheid as a heresy. The word *heresy* is very strong, and can only be seen as something that has to be opposed by *all* means. Little consideration was given, in the end, to the opinion that this meant resistance to a lawful government of a sovereign state. In fact, the apartheid regime was seen as an unlawful government and by no means as God given. The Belhar Confession, speaking out against an ideology of apartheid, clearly states in article 5: "We believe that, in obedience to Jesus Christ, its only head, the church is called to confess and to do all these things, even though the authorities and human laws might forbid them and punishment and suffering be the consequence."

To speak out against power, to go as far as disobeying a ruling government, is justified by many biblical examples. The words of Acts 5:29 are very clear: "We must obey God rather than any human authority." These words were spoken by the apostle Peter, who, together with the apostle John, was standing before the Sanhedrin, arrested because of their preaching in the name of Jesus. Answering the question of the high priest as to why they continued with their unlawful preaching, Peter said—with the words quoted above—that they could not do otherwise. They had to obey God more than they had to obey human authorities.

Peter's words are quite similar to words spoken at a different time and place in history. When Socrates stood before the court of justice in Athens in 399 BCE, he was accused of tempting the young men of the city to give up the traditional faith. He then said: "Men of Athens, I am happy with you and I love you but I will obey God more than you." Therefore, Socrates refused to give up his challenging way of questioning the young men of Athens. The words of Socrates were generally known among the educated people in the ancient world. It may even have been that Luke, the author of Acts, knew these words.

The difference, however, between Socrates and Peter is that the God to whom Socrates made reference is a different one than the God or, better, the *gods* his judges believed in. That difference of faith did not exist between Peter and his judges. For Peter, as for those he opposed, God was the God of Israel. And to obey God more than any human authority was part of the tradition of Israel's religion. In Daniel 1, we read that Daniel and his friends refused to eat the food the king had ordered them to eat. The food was not "kosher," and eating it would go against their obedience to God. More horrible is the story in 2 Maccabees 7 of seven brothers and their mother who refused to eat pork and died as martyrs. The Jews have more than shown that they obey God more than any human authority.

So, Peter and his judges did not differ about the principle that they had to obey God more than any human authority. They differed about Jesus and whether obeying him was obedience to God or, instead, disobedience. For now, the debate about Jesus is not relevant. What is relevant is the deeply rooted principle in Israel's tradition, confirmed by the followers of Jesus, that God has to be obeyed more than any human authority. This can lead to deep conflicts with human authorities, as shown by examples in both the history of Israel and the history of the church.

In the Bible, however, is a passage that seems to contradict Peter's words that God has to be obeyed more than any human authority. In Romans 13, Paul writes: ". . . whoever resists authority resists what God has appointed, and those who resist will incur judgment." These words not only seem to contradict other passages in the Bible, but it also seems that Paul himself did not follow his own words. Paul had been imprisoned and finally went to Rome, because he had come into conflict with the authorities. So he seems to have applied Acts 5:29 more than Romans 13.

Romans 13:1-7 follows chapter 12, wherein Paul has a long exposition about "doing good." That passage concludes in verse 21 with the words: "Do not be overcome by evil, but overcome evil with good." Then, after 13:1-7, comes verse 8 with the words: "Owe no one anything, except to love one another." The obedience to the authorities can therefore not be in conflict with the surrounding principles cited in 12:21 and 13:8. Even in 13:1-7, Paul makes reference to doing good, as in verse 3: ". . . rulers are not a terror to good conduct, but to bad." The underlying assumption can therefore only be that obedience to the authorities is in line with "doing good." If not, then God has to be obeyed more than any human authority.

The Reformation started from this principle that God has to be obeyed more than any human authority. Luther's words in 1521, standing before the Diet of Worms, "Here I stand. I can do no other," are a direct application of Acts 5:29. It does not make much difference whether he said these words or not, as they are now "*communis opinio*." Either way, real or legendary, they are a confirmation of his conduct. Disobedience to the authorities lies at the origin of the Reformation, whatever the contradictory developments thereafter may have been. It is even part of the word used when referring in general to the followers of the Reformation: "Protestant." The root of the word does not simply mean "to protest" in the sense of being opposed to, but it is the

Latin word *protestari*, which means "to declare publicly." As such, it means not being silent whatever the consequences may be. So, in the name *Protestant*, Acts 5:29 becomes reality.

Not always, of course, have Christians acted in the way that Peter did, not least in those times when rulers were an absolute terror to good conduct. It is now more than a century since the First World War began. Protestant preachers on both sides of the belligerent parties totally condoned the aggression. "The Holy Spirit now is the War Spirit," a German preacher said. An English preacher gave thanks for the God-given glorious hour. By the next World War, the *Deutsche Christen* (German Christians) were fully behind Hitler. Luther, who stood firm before the Diet in Worms, later aligned with the powers slaughtering the rebellious farmers. Churches both have spoken truth to evil powers and have aligned with evil powers. It would not be a problem to give many examples of the latter.

Even in the most flagrant situations of churches aligning with evil powers, however, they would not contradict the principle that, in the end, God has to be obeyed more than any human authority. They would have said: by obeying the authority we support, we obey, God. So, as with Peter and his judges, the question is not about the principle, but what it concretely means to obey God. This, however, makes the principle of obeying God more than human authorities a risky matter. One could list the following obstacles to the principle itself:

- How can you be sure to know what God wants you to do? Do I not refer to what is, in fact, what I want and what brings me advantage as being the will of God, like the South African apartheid that made the white race privileged over anyone else?
- When others are told to do something because they have to obey God, they have little room for doubt or debate. The crusades were organized from the principle of obeying God—*Deus le vult!*—and there are more examples where people felt morally forced to do things because they believed it was God ordering them.
- Already in the past, but certainly now in modern times, economic, social-ethical, and political matters are so complex that it is very difficult to point to the right way to go by saying, "This is what God wants us to do."
- In an age of postmodernism, the "great truths" are less prominent. Theology has become very complex and biblical exegesis is a process of endless nuancing. We live more with questions than with answers.

- Certainly, in large parts of the world, churches have lost power and authority. Christians have a marginalized position and live in multi-religious societies.
- Religion, also Christianity, has in many cases become above all therapeutic and self-confirming. It has lost much of its confronting nature.

Against the background of these obstacles, we can now come to the main question of whether the church, and especially the churches of the Reformation, can still have a prophetic voice in the sense of being a witness of the way we should go even when the consequence is confronting individuals and societies. What authority for such a prophetic voice could there still be, if any? Here, as a conclusion, are some principles to consider:

1. John Calvin saw the ideal state as having a religious role in preventing religious crimes (sacrilege) and ensuring a public form of religion. Calvin also maintained that the state has a duty to protect personal property, keep public peace, and enable business to operate unfettered by fraud or other crime. In Calvin's theology, human life is set in relation to the life of God. Life for the honour of God is based on faith in God, who put God's own life at stake for the benefit of humankind. Our common journey forward as a people of faith is accompanied by our life-giving God. For a modern, secularized state, however, Calvin's principle of the ideal state has applicable elements, but cannot be taken over as a whole. As the British political thinker Quentin Skinner rightly says:

   > The religious upheavals of the reformation made a paradoxical yet vital contribution to the crystallizing of the modern, secularized concept of the State. For as soon as the protagonists of the rival religious creeds showed that they were willing to fight each other to the death, it began to seem obvious to a number of politique theorists that, if there were to be any prospect of achieving civic peace, the powers of the State would have to be divorced from the duty to uphold any particular faith.

2. It should also be clear right from the beginning that a modern, secularized state cannot follow an argument based on the principle that it is God's will to go in a certain direction. We cannot be as the Old Testament prophets who were speaking in the context of a theocratic society. We should not even long for such a society.

3. Prophetic witness has to be convincing witness. It is good to nuance and to have thorough preparation before coming out with the message. However, we should not think that a clear message is not possible. The exegesis and application of biblical texts may be a complicated process, but firm standpoints can be taken. Take, for instance, this passage from

Psalm 146:7-9: "The LORD sets the prisoners free; the LORD opens the eyes of the blind. The LORD lifts up those who are bowed down; the LORD loves the righteous. The LORD watches over the strangers; he upholds the orphan and the widow, but the way of the wicked he brings to ruin." This is not just an ornament of clarity in an ocean of floating words that go into all directions. This is the guiding theme of the Old Testament. As for the New Testament, Jesus is a person full of surprises and has a multilayered personality. However, the person who struggles for honesty and integrity, who works for peace and justice, is not far from Jesus, notwithstanding the ages that separate us.

4. Modern societies may be very complex, making it difficult to point out what is evil; however, it is not impossible. There may have been a lot of discussion about the document adopted by the World Alliance of Reformed Churches in 2004, known as the Accra Confession (or "Accra Statement," as some prefer), and it may be true that things could have been said in a better way, but who would deny that there is something rotten in the state of the modern world economy? It is not a church that keeps silent that will get respect. Better a church that is confronted than a church that is ignored. But the prophetic voice is not just shouting out loud. It requires building up thorough expertise. Emotions may be a good start, but they should not be in conflict with critical rational thinking. A church should also be self-critical and not just opting for the right, politically correct ideology. It should also be firmly grounded in its own tradition. We are not the first to speak out.

5. It is true that in most societies the church has a marginalized position. That is a blessing in disguise, because a church that is powerful can easily be corrupted to align itself with other powers in order not to lose influence. The Reformation stands, after all, in principle, for a certain degree of anticlerical thinking.

6. Throughout history, churches may have moved back and forth between speaking with a prophetic voice and showing blind obedience to authority, but, in fact, these are not alternatives. This is because obeying God *still* means not to be silent as regards the story of the gospel, even though this may transpire with modesty, or almost in complete silence, or, especially, incidentally; this could still be sufficient for a particular moment in a particular situation. When, however, the passion to obey God by not being silent about what you have seen and heard is lacking, the Spirit is quenched. This is self-evident, because a church that is silent dies.

D. Ecumenism

CHAPTER 27

Wolfgang Thönissen

Luther's Dispute with His Catholic Opponents

The Example of Purgatory

Late Medieval Criticism of Indulgences

Beginning in the 11th century, the distribution of indulgences became one of the central religious practices in the Middle Ages.[1] This inevitably involved serious abuses right from the beginning. In his work, Nikolaus Paulus elaborates on this abuse and proposes to distinguish between the theology and the practice of indulgences, because he is able to demonstrate that many indulgences had been granted improperly and even falsified.[2] Despite the downright ambiguous formula of indulgence, *a poena et a culpa* ("from punishment and from guilt"), it was always evident in theology and devotional literature that it was not about a remission of guilt, but an abatement

1 *Th. Lentes*, Nikolaus Paulus (1853–1930) und die "Geschichte des Ablasses im Mittelalter," Einleitung zur 2. Auflage, in idem, *Geschichte des Ablasses im Mittelalter*, vol. 1 (Darmstadt, 2000), XXXVIII.

2 *Th. Lentes*, ibid., XXII.

of the temporal punishment for sins. From this standpoint, Paulus is in line with Protestant historiography, although his main thesis, that indulgences had always been correctly granted to the believers,[3] must undergo a more rigorous scrutiny today.[4] Joseph Lortz, in his 20th-century Catholic Reformation historiography, regards the selling of indulgences as reflecting the decline of the late medieval church, which provides him a stronger basis from which to describe Luther's opposition to the corrupt Catholicism.[5] The argument of Bernd Moeller, a Protestant church historian, however, is far more differentiated when he asserts that there was no sign of disintegration of the medieval world as regards late-15th-century religious life in Germany.[6] The 15th century can actually be called one of the "church's most pious times in the Middle Ages."[7] Against this assessment, the deplorable states regarding the practice of piety around 1500 turn out to be "a complex state of affairs."[8] Despite the ubiquity of indulgences and the multiple criticisms of its abuses, Moeller goes on to judge that, given the rigorous penance regulations, a "trace of the gospel" took effect and came forth in the invention of indulgences.[9] While holding this view, Moeller does not deny that, in the concentration of the sheer amount of indulgences in the hands of the pope, the selling of indulgence itself became a "universal fundraising source."[10] Considering that the indulgences are said to have been ubiquitous in the second half of the 15th century,[11] albeit only in some regions, there is no longer any doubt about the extent and intensity of the anti-indulgence mood in Germany. Evidences of increasing contempt for indulgences are found in many sources, not only in Luther.[12] As Wilhelm Ernst Winterhager writes, "The great chagrin over the indulgences which pervades among the populace and all sectors of society was . . . the decisive breeding ground for Luther's success."[13] Anti-indulgence

3 Nikolaus Paulus, *Geschichte des Ablasses am Ausgang des Mittelalters* (Darmstadt, 2000), 121.

4 Cf. G. A. Benrath, Art. "Ablass," in *Theologische Realenzyklopädie* (*TRE*) 1 (1977): 351.

5 Cf. J. Lortz, *Die Reformation in Deutschland* (Freiburg-Basel-Wien, 1982), 193–210; E. Iserloh held the same view.

6 B. Moeller, "Frömmigkeit in Deutschland um 1500," in idem, *Die Reformation und das Mittelalter. Kirchenhistorische Aufsätze*, ed. J. Schilling (Göttingen), 73–85.

7 Ibid., 81.

8 Ibid., 84.

9 B. Moeller, "Die letzten Ablasskampagnen. Der Widerspruch Luthers gegen den Ablass in seinem geschichtlichen Zusammenhang," in ibid., 54f.

10 Ibid., 55.

11 C. Neuhausen, *Das Ablaßwesen in der Stadt Köln vom 13. bis zum 16. Jahrhundert* (Köln, 1994), 274.

12 W. E. Winterhager, "Ablaßkritik als Indikator historischen Wandels vor 1517. Ein Beitrag zu den Voraussetzungen und Einordnung der Reformation," in *Archiv für Reformationsgeschichte* (*ARG*) 90 (1999): 16f.

13 Ibid., 20.

discourse was practiced even before Luther's appearance. Caution is also advisable in reading Winterhager's theses, however. The criticism of indulgences between 1500 and 1517 arose from various motives, events, and objectives. As Christoph Volkmar shows, the indulgence itself was not questionable for Duke Georg of Saxony, but the practice of proclaiming individual sermons regarding indulgences—in this case, those of John Tetzel—was. Duke Georg, who allowed the circulation of Luther's 95 Theses in Saxony, did not advocate a general criticism of indulgence, but he used Luther's criticism of them for his own purposes. What Duke Georg ultimately criticized was the unbridled spread of indulgence campaigns across the nation that financially threatened his own campaigns of indulgence and carried the urgently needed revenue out of the country. Luther's attack on indulgences served Duke Georg's purposes insofar as he used it only as a pretext for fending off foreign indulgences. Volkmar writes, "This does not offer any reason for inferring that the Duke Georg basically distanced himself from the practice of indulgences."[14] Although the formula "no indulgence, no Reformation" holds its validity despite its terseness, the concerns for reform were by no means only the reformers' exclusive principal motif. From this perspective, general ecclesiastical reform efforts and the Wittenberg reform movement take their courses concurrently, and to some extent confluently.

The Context of the Late-Medieval Penitential System

Whoever wishes to understand Martin Luther's theses on indulgences should properly reconstruct the controversy regarding their institution in the early modern church against the background of the late medieval practice and teachings of the church on penance. The penitential system which sprang from the monastic roots in the form of the monastic penance is characterized by the absence of reconciliation, that is, the unrepeatable rehabilitation of the penitent into the church. This was replaced with the practice of satisfaction as an orderly means of pastoral care and penance strongly legitimized by the Western penitential system. Penance prescription was calculated by the penitential tariffs recorded in so-called penitentials by virtue of the stance that penitents are only responsible for sinful actions (as opposed to sinful intentions) "according to which guilt can only be assessed on the basis of objective facts and remedied by a calculable compensatory performance."[15] The practice of completion of penance by means of redemptions and commutations or even by proxy constitutes the breeding ground for the emergence of

14 C. Volkmar, *Reform statt Reformation. Die Kirchenpolitik Herzog Georg von Sachsen 1488–1525* (Tübingen, 2008), 379, cf. 373–84.

15 R. Messner, *Feiern der Umkehr und Versöhnung*. Gottesdienst der Kirche. Handbuch der Liturgiewissenschaft 7/2 (Regensburg, 1992), 165.

indulgences.[16] While the prescription, abatement, and absolution of penance had always been associated with the church's penitential system administered by church officials, the indulgence, according to the research of Nikolaus Paulus, constituted something new in Western medieval church history. General indulgences granted irrespective of an act of penance can be tracked back only to the 11th century.[17] The *indulgentia* is not aimed at mitigating the imposed penance, that is, removing guilt, but at granting pardons for the temporal punishment of sins remaining even after the forgiveness of sins. For this punishment, the priest and the congregation can intervene and support the penitent through prayers and intercessions. In indulgence, therefore, we should see remission with an unequivocally clear aim of obtaining satisfaction, which is the third integral part of sacramental penance after contrition (*contritio*) and confession (*confessio*). In the course of the interiorization of penance after the turn of the first millennium, the emphasis of penitential process shifts to the confession and its underlying contrition through which guilt is forgiven before God, whereas satisfaction is devaluated.[18] The decisive weight of repentance to be redeemed from punishment and guilt is the true contrition of love; this leads to the distinction between *contritio* and *attritio*.[19] The intercessory individual abatement of punishment for the penitent (*absolutio*) is replaced by the "grace granted generally, rightfully and as evenly as possible (*dispensatio*) to each individual willing to perform penance, nourished by the inexhaustible store of spiritual merits administered by the church."[20] This view draws on the principal of a distinction of the punishment of sins, namely, between the eternal and temporal punishments. This raises a difficult problem of determining the effectiveness of the performance of the penance that the priest imposes.[21] The shift from satisfaction to contrition leads to a change in the practice of penance. Within the scope of this change in the church's practice of piety, indulgence comes to play a virtually ubiquitous function for the late medieval piety.[22]

---

16 Benrath, "Ablass," 459.

17 Nikolaus Paulus, *Geschichte des Ablasses im Mittelalter. Vom Ursprunge bis zur Mitte des 14. Jahrhunderts*, 2 vols. (Darmstadt, 2000); idem, *Geschichte des Ablasses am Ausgang des Mittelalters.*

18 Messner, *Feiern der Umkehr und Versöhnung*, 173f.

19 H. Vorgrimler, *Buße und Krankensalbung*, Haus der Geschichte (HDG) IV(3) (Freiburg i. Br., 1978), 144f.

20 Benrath, "Ablass," 349.

21 B. Hamm, "Von der Gottesliebe des Mittelalters zum Glauben Luthers. Ein Beitrag zur Bußgeschichte," *Lutherjahrbuch* 65 (1998): 25.

22 B. Moeller, "Die letzten Ablasskampagnen. Der Widerspruch Luthers gegen den Ablass in seinem geschichtlichen Zusammenhang," in Schilling, ed., *Die Reformation und das Mittelalter*, 53–72.

Luther's Motives in the Indulgence Controversy

The launch of the indulgence controversy in the fall of 1517 is one of the major milestones of church history.[23] Even contemporaries such as Melanchthon saw these events, in retrospect, as the decisive turning point for the historical development that would eventually be called the Reformation.[24] With hindsight, Superintendent of Gotha Friedrich Myconius characterized the indulgence controversy as originating from a pastorally motivated opposition to the existing practice of indulgence.[25] The picture of the pastor worried about his penitents, as Lothar Vogel has recently described, is a prevailing image of the Reformer still today both in scientific and in popular depictions. Although the relationships between the indulgence controversy and other social and political factors have been expounded in numerous studies now, the pastoral motive still occupies the prominent position in explaining the causes of the indulgence controversy and the direct motivation for Luther's actions. However, can this characterization be verified by Luther's own statements?

Reading Luther's statements, it soon becomes clear that his 95 Theses were meant to be an academic text that was not initially intended for the general public.[26] These theses were written to launch a disputation as a preparation for a doctrinal definition. From this, it can be inferred that not the confessional, but the "pulpit and lectern were the decisive elements in Luther's life for his entrance into the indulgences controversy."[27] It was not from his role as a confessor, which Luther was without doubt, but from his own practice of penance that he gained his decisive soteriological awareness that "the true repentance can only come from the love for God and for God's righteousness."[28] When Luther began to combine this insight gained in Staupitz with the holy scriptures, he developed the meaning of penance—drawing on the Greek word *metanoia* as a change of mind—as recognition of one's sinfulness. The first thesis on indulgence contains a decisive theological insight which, while not putting him actually in opposition to Scholastic theology and the medieval theology of penance, allows him to follow in the footsteps of late medieval theologies to rediscover a New Testament insight which had been almost lost in the course of developing a medieval institute

23 L. Vogel, "Zwischen Universität und Seelsorge. Martin Luthers Beweggründe im Ablassstreit," *Zeitschrift für Kirchengeschichte* (ZKG) 118 (2007): 187–212, here 187.

24 Cf. the preface to the second volume of Luther's works from 1546 (CR 6:155–70, No. 3478).

25 *Geschichte der Reformationsgeschichte*, ed. O. Clemen (Leipzig, 1914), 20–23.

26 Vogel, "Zwischen Universität und Seelsorge," 197.

27 Ibid., 203.

28 Cf. in his letter to Staupitz of 30 May 1518 (WA 1:525–27). Cf. R. Wetzel, "Staupitz und Luther," in *Martin Luther. Probleme seiner Zeit*, ed. V. Press and D. Stievermann (Stuttgart, 1986), 75–87.

of penance as sacramental confession, that is, the practice of lifelong daily repentance in keeping with the word of God as an independent way of realizing repentance and reconciliation in the life of the church and of individual Christians. This seems to confirm the problematic relationship between the theology of penance and the criticism of indulgence. It can only be a secondary aspect whether it is possible to merge the considerations of modern theological rationality and the salvation sought by Christians under the scriptural principle, in returning to the biblical core message.[29]

Luther's Intentions in the Beginning of the Indulgences Controversy

Luther himself repeatedly and elaborately took a stand in the indulgences controversy. His letters to various people written within a period of half a year provide an insight into his motives. Luther's opposition to the selling of indulgences surfaced after the jubilee of 1500 with increasing intensity. However, he criticized not only the abuse associated with it, but also the documents accompanying the sale of indulgences, primarily the *Instructio Summaria* of Albrecht of Mainz, the sermons spread by Johannes Tetzel, and the antitheses of Wimpina-Tetzel. To resolve the chagrin caused for believers, Luther understood his theses as a warning to several clerical aristocrats whose theological positions he doubted and proposed a disputation among scholars. To this end, he posted—as he himself called it—a disputation note (*Disputationszettel*) with which he challenged the scholars to dispute about this controversial issue. Luther saw himself entitled to dispute publicly on controversial matters, following the academic tradition, by virtue of the fact that he was a professor at a university approved by the pope.[30]

For Luther, indulgences were a "self-deception of souls." To eliminate this delusion and out of love for the truth, he ventured into this "perilous labyrinth of disputation."[31] Indulgences are good for "nobody whosoever . . . except for the sleepy and the idle on the way of the Cross of Christ." However, Luther not only wanted to dispute about the problem of indulgences, "but also about the God-given power of attorney to absolve punishment and forgive sins, so also about incomparably more important issues," as Luther himself asserted.[32] As such, he puts penance in the very centre of his disputation. Luther directs his attention to the three parts of penance: *contritio*, *confessio*, and *satisfactio*, with a particular focus on the third one. He condemns the view of those "who put so much importance to repentance that almost

29 Cf. Winterhager, "Ablaßkritik als Indikator historischen Wandels vor 1517," 67.

30 Luther to Pope Leo X, end of May 1518, in WA 1:528.

31 Luther to Spalatin, 15 February 1518: WA.B 1:146.

32 WA 1:528.

nothing remains from the whole act of penance except some purely external performances of satisfaction and the most cumbersome confessions."[33] By taking offense at the slightest part of penance, although not at the satisfaction itself, but at the "remission of this inferior performance," he intends to break through to the doctrine of true penance.

Luther does not want to set norms, but to dispute—this is his explicit aim. He does so by referring to the views and teachings of the entire church, giving priority to scholasticans, Scholastic philosophers, mystics, and the Bible.[34] He does not see his duty as establishing a binding doctrine in this matter, but as putting forward his objections to contradict those "of which I earnestly wished that they would have announced nothing but the truth in their sermons."[35] With this, he seeks to "prove scientific perverseness and instability of those doctrines."[36] He does not want to agree with one side or the other, but wants to expound important issues in the disputation, "until the holy church will determine how to think about it in the future."[37] Luther refers to the Bible, church fathers, and ecclesiastical law, as he sees them as not in contradiction with the topics he raises. Much more, it seems absurd to him that things are preached in God's church which "we cannot justify."[38] Thus, he sees himself obliged to bring this controversial issue to disputation in fulfillment of his duty as professor.

The Dispute over Purgatory

The 95 Theses, Luther's Resolutions, the objections of Johann Eck and Sylvester Prierias, as well as Luther's respective answers together constitute an inherently logical, causal, and temporal context, though this is not always clearly discernible. A particular problem is the chronological order of various documents, so that it is yet to be clarified which responses correspond to which challenges raised by the theses. Luther's Resolutions on the theses are his answers to Tetzel's unprinted theses. However, the Resolutions, written in May 1518, also contain passages referring to or citing Eck's Obelisks (*Obelisci*) and Luther's Asterisks (*Asterisci*) of March 1518. But the dialogues on certain issues go beyond the second half of 1518, as does the dispute with Prierias, which began in June 1518. Finally, the question has to be raised as to what extent post–1518 replies by Luther's opponents—for example, those by Prierias up to 1520—should also be included.

33 Luther to Johannes von Staupitz, 30 May 1518: WA 1:526.

34 Luther to Johannes von Staupitz, 31 March 1518: WA.B 1:160.

35 Luther to Hieronymus Schulz von Brandenburg, 22 October 1518: WA.B 1:138.

36 Luther to Johannes von Staupitz, 31 March 1518: WA.B 1:160

37 Luther to Hieronymus Schulz von Brandenburg, 22 October 1518: WA.B 1:138.

38 Ibid.

Thesis 14: *Imperfect piety or love on the part of the dying person necessarily brings with it great fear; and the smaller the love, the greater the fear.*[39]

All fear and horror come from mistrust; mistrust is the cause of horror, despair, and damnation[40]—this is how Luther brings thesis 14 to the point in his Resolutions. This thesis seems ludicrous to Eck. What is this about? It concerns the justification of purgatory, as Eck points out in his antitheses: purgatory does not have to do with the perfect or the imperfect love, nor with the perfect or imperfect grace, but with the punishment owed due to sins.[41] Therefore, Eck adduces the argument that the imperfect love of a child does not scare it. Luther's thesis, however, seems to take a different direction: in his reply to Eck, he makes it clear that even the most perfect love of an adult cannot provide protection from fear and horror; it actually leaves him or her in an even greater temptation. In the end, it is probably insignificant whether a child has an imperfect love, and an adult a perfect love that protects him or her from fear or horror. This argument does not seem to unfold further, because Luther agrees with Eck that the crucial question is what the perfection or imperfection of love or unatoned punishment has to do with purgatory. Here Luther comes to the point: referring to the Dist. 35 (correctly, it should be called 25 of Gratiani Decr.[42]), Luther makes clear that it is not a question of unatoned punishment, but of guilt and sins (*culpa et peccata*); purgatory exists for the sake of sins, not punishment. Luther calls such a sin the imperfect love—the one love through which humans love themselves and their life more than God. Luther pursues this train of thought further in the Resolutions.

Thesis 15: *This fear or horror is sufficient in itself, to say nothing of other things, to constitute the penalty of purgatory, since they come very close to the horror of despair.*[43]

Prierias ferociously accuses Luther of heresy in theses 14 and 15. Luther gives an equally clear answer: "The existence of purgatory is absolutely certain to me."[44] There are three of Luther's sentences which Prierias rebukes in particular: (1) Those who are in purgatory do not know if they will

39 "Imperfecta sanitas seu charitas morituri necessario secum fert magnum timorem, tantoque maiorum, quanto minor fuerit ipsa."

40 "Venit ergo omnis turbatio ex diffidentia, omnis securitas ex fiducia in deum, fiducia autem ex caritate, quia necesse est, ut is tibi placeat, in quem confidas" (Köhler, 48).

41 The dispute in the background here is whether the imperfect repentance is sufficient for the forgiveness of sins, so a repentance without love for God.

42 *Decr. Gratiani Pars* I, dist. XXV. can IV "Qualis."

43 "Hic timor et horror satis est se solo (ut alia taceam) facere penam purgatorii, cum sit proximus desperationis horrori."

44 Resol (MüAusg., 182)

be saved.[45] (2) Those who are being cleansed fear great evil like children.[46] (3) Fear itself is enough to constitute purgatory.[47] Luther defends himself sturdily against these accusations and therefore undertakes to give elaborate answers. First, much space is taken up by the dispute over authorities. However, Luther responds precisely to the accusations raised: (1) The inferences Prierias draws do not withstand the evidence: Can it be honestly claimed that those who are in purgatory know they will be saved? Could not the opposite also be true? Does not the prayer of the church—that hell may not devour it—suggest that some are heading toward hell? So who can deny that there are uncertainties in regards to purgatory? (2) How can anyone feel the pains from a punishment if he or she is not afraid of it? If it were as Prierias asserts, then there must be two kinds of pain, the one on earth, the other in purgatory. In addition: What sense does it make, as Prierias pretends, to just talk about fear in relation to a future evil, given that the souls are in fact in present evil? Therefore, we had better to assume this: the punishment of purgatory is the horror of damnation and thus a fear of future evils that a dying man undergoes.[48] (3) On the third accusation: Luther does not want to say that fear alone is sufficient as punishment or as an understanding for the punishment from which souls suffer. This is certainly not the whole punishment, but the horror of damnation is—it may be said—a catchy image or, even better, a symbol to illustrate the punishment in purgatory. It is brought to the attention by the "*sit proximus*" of thesis 15. In the Resolutions regarding thesis 15, a clarifying hint finally points to the core of the dispute: with Augustine and against Thomas Aquinas, Luther pleads for the nonillustrative nature of purgatory, that hidden sanctuary of the souls of which we cannot know anything.[49] Almost like a modern theologian, Luther seems to warn his opponents to profess knowledge about something that is absolutely hidden to human beings. His clear testimony to purgatory is also to be understood from this perspective. Whereas Luther does not deny it, he wants to dispute the ways and means of his perception.

45 "Quod hi, qui in purgatorio continentur, nescient se salvandos" (Köhler, 53).

46 "Quod qui purgantur timeant, praeterquam filialiter" (Ibid.).

47 "Quod hic timor se solo satis sit facere poenam purgatorium" (Ibid.).

48 "Poena purgatorii est timor future mali i.e., horror damnationis" (Ibid., 54).

49 "Nihil de igne et loco purgatorii loquor, non quod ea negem. . . . Ego vero interim cum b. Augustino remaneo, scilicet quod receptacula animarum abdita sint et remota a nostra cognition. . . . Mihi certissimum est purgatorium esse" (Ibid., 49f.) Quotation by Augustine, "Enchiridion ad Laurentium sive de fide, spe et caritate . . ."

Thesis 16: *Hell, purgatory, and heaven seem to differ as do despair, almost-despair, and assurance of salvation.*[50]

The dispute over the understanding of purgatory continues. Thesis 16 is closely related to thesis 15. Luther compares purgatory with despair; it is to some extent (*prope*) despair, between hell (despair) and heaven (*securitas*). Wimpina-Tetzel had already labeled "*prope desparatio*" as fallacy. Eck considers it an impudent thesis. Souls know that they will be saved, but through fire. Luther replies by asking from where his knowledge originates, given that there are just so many theological opinions in circulation among Scotists and Thomists. Luther reiterates his argument: the horror of the soul makes people instinctively uncertain.[51] If all teachers were of the opinion that the punishment of purgatory is the same as that of hell with the exception of despair, then the assumption cannot be wrong that purgatory is close to despair. Therein, Luther does not claim that purgatory is despair like hell, but he avoids saying that purgatory is salvation, only through fire. The disputation here seems to heat up on the question of the certainty of salvation. Prierias, too, holds on to the conviction that those who are purified can have a certain assurance of their salvation, and therefore are not desperate, because they have the hope of release. Behind this, however, there is the crucial question of how punishments are taken away.

Thesis 17: *It seems necessary for the souls in purgatory that fear and horror decrease and that love ought to proportionately grow and increase.*[52]

Two questions are at the centre of Luther's disputation with Eck and Prierias. Eck impales Luther's thesis on growing and increasing love on the question of merits. Wherever the tree falls, there it will remain lying, Eck argues with Ecclesiastes 11:3, according to merit or demerit. Luther apparently is not willing to answer this question, but he inquires once more very precisely: Does Eck want to contend that the cleansed do not get better through the redemption of their sins in purgatory? Is there no increase in good or evil in purgatory? Can the cleansed really not get better? Again, Luther's skepticism surfaces: Who will ultimately know how the souls are doing in purgatory? From another side, Prierias examines the present problem, which Luther addresses with the growth and increasing of love, from a different point of view. He accuses Luther of inconsistencies in this reasoning, because he takes fear, horror, and damnation as his starting point. If Luther then wants to find a way that fear could be expelled, then it can probably only be the way of

50 "Videntur infernus, purgatorium, celum differre, sicut desperatio, prope desperatio, securitas differunt."

51 "Addo, quod horror animae natura sua facit incertum hominem" (Köhler, 56).

52 "Necessarium videtur animabus in purgatorio sicut minui horrorem ita augeri charitatem."

love. Fear against love seems to be the alternative in the eyes of Prierias. In response, Prierias now claims that those who suffer in purgatory are pilgrims, insofar as they are retained from salvation, with the restriction, however, of not taking it for granted (*autem non simpliciter*). Prierias concludes: they do not grow in love. If they were to grow, it would be a charity for them to stay longer in purgatory in order to come out of it in more perfect states. Luther counters Prierias's antithesis with the objection that it must then also be a charity if no saint were to die or martyrs were to suffer until the last day, because if love could become more and more perfect, then all would persevere in the state they are in now to become even more perfect. As this argumentation does not take effect here, however, then it would be of no use in regards to purgatory either.

> Thesis 18: *Furthermore, it does not seem proven, either by reason or by scripture, that souls in purgatory are outside the state of merit, or of the growth of love.*[53]

In contrast to his opponents, Luther insists on his argument of thesis 17 that the souls in purgatory are either in a state of merit or of growing in love. Wimpina-Tetzel considers this thesis simply false. Eck regards it as presumptuous, as does Prierias. The reason is clear: souls do not deserve, but pay (*solvendi non merendi*). Love must be gained in life, not in purgatory, Eck argues. As such, two assertions are frontally opposed: souls are in a state of merit or not (*in statu merendi*). Luther resorts to a polemical discourse, calling on Eck for disputation, with the limitation that he himself is not ultimately sure of each aspect. Prierias admits that for one or another argument there are neither scriptural nor ecclesiastical proofs. Consequently, they cannot reach any agreement on this question. Luther confirms this by admitting that they may only proceed to probable evidence. Whether Thomas interferes positively or negatively, it does not change the probability of the thesis unless it is a matter of faith. Luther confesses that he denies what Prierias positively claims. Therefore, he considers the disputation to have reached its end. Luther must admit that this issue cannot be further elucidated.

> Thesis 19: *Nor does it seem proven that souls in purgatory, at least not all of them, are certain and assured of their own salvation, even if we ourselves may be entirely certain of it.*[54]

Wimpina-Tetzel and Eck consider Luther's thesis as false. Eck is convinced that departed souls know more than the living. They know that they are dead and do not despair. Luther takes up again what he wanted to say:

53 "Nec probatum videtur ullis aut rationibus aut scripturis, quod sint extra statum meriti seu augende charitatis."

54 "Nec hoc probatum esse videtur, quod sint de sua beatitudine certe et secure, saltem omnes, licet nos certissimi simus."

not all who are in purgatory are sure of their salvation.[55] Luther holds the certainty (*certitudo*) or even the assurance (*securitas*) of this knowledge as presumptuous. Therefore, he does not deny that some are certain, but not all. In the background of this is, for Luther, the experience of refutation of faith. However, what does certainty in faith mean? Those who are dead in faith are not sensitive to pain; only those who perceive their disbelief and feel pain because of it know that faith is living within them. Luther invokes against Eck by inversing the argument: if only the souls know that they move toward salvation, so we do not know about it. All this shows Luther how easy it is to steer any dispute to sophistry. Knowledge, certainty, faith, and unfaith are obviously difficult issues to assess. Thus, a dispute fails to materialize.

> Thesis 25: *That power which the pope has in general over purgatory corresponds to the power which any bishop or curate has in particular in his own diocese and parish.*[56]

With thesis 25, Luther concludes the dispute with both Eck and Prierias on the question of the jurisdiction of the key office. His conclusion, consistent with the whole church, is: the jurisdiction of the pope and the key office do not extend to purgatory.[57] In contrast, Luther proclaims the power to pray and the intercessions (*potestas orandi et intercedendi*). Does this view pervert the whole system of church governance, as Eck accused Luther? Luther does not claim that all ecclesiastical authorities have the same authority. The pope may call upon the entire church for general intercessions and prayers for the souls, as bishops may call upon their respective dioceses and priests on the All Souls' Day, on general penance days, and during mass for the dead. But Luther considers a jurisdiction of the key office over purgatory as false.

The Outcome of a Reconstruction of the Dispute between Luther and His Opponents

What are the topics addressed by Eck and Prierias? Can we recognize lines of a consistent theology? With his theses, Eck defends the dignity of the sacrament of penance. The dispute relates, in his view, to the third part of sacramental penance, *satisfactio*. The sacramental-instrumental understanding of the sacrament makes it necessary for Eck to extend the office of the keys to the punishments imposed by God and by the office itself. This entails the conclusion that even the deceased who are in purgatory can have the punishments incurred while living absolved by virtue of the office of the keys. This means in turn that the theology represented by Eck knows more about

55 "Non omnes sint certae in purgatorio de sua beatitudine" (Köhler, 70).
56 "Qualem potestatem habet papa in purgatorium generaliter, talem habet quilibet Episcopus et curatus in sua diocesi et parochia specialiter."
57 "Ego cum universa ecclesia nego esse clavibus potestatem in purgatorium" (Köhler, 85).

purgatory and its operative mode than is generally asserted. Sylvester Prierias's statements are even more comprehensive. The sacrament of penance, in particular the understanding of repentance, is at the centre of his theological understanding. Prierias represents the conviction that the imperfect repentance (attrition) could be cured by the office of the keys. Thus, he represents unambiguously a Scotist position. If Luther takes up the significance of repentance for a sinner's redemption and represents this, then he is obviously closer to the theology of Thomas Aquinas. This places also in this context the focal point of theological reasoning for the expansion of the power and impact of the office of the keys and of absolution, one of the most serious issues in the late Middle Ages.

Luther's opponents repeatedly accuse him of denying the teachings of the church in this or that question whenever he represents this thesis. A detailed analysis shows, however, that Luther by no means denies the church's teachings; he only represents particular views on some issues and provides interpretations over which he wants to dispute. The phrase "I want to dispute" is repeatedly used. His opponents, however, do not want to dispute to clarify the question at hand; they want to establish him as a heretic. Luther admits to his opponents that he is not certain in all questions.

Luther turns several times against the philosophy and theology of Johannes Duns Scotus. So, the dispute over the theses appears to be a dispute over the sophistry of late Scholastic theology. Vis-à-vis Prierias, the scope of the dispute is mainly restricted to the theology of Thomas Aquinas, which is understandable, since Prierias relies on his monastic brother. However, Thomas does not appear as absolute enemy of Luther, but implicitly as a warrantor. To prove his thesis, Luther first refers to scriptures, second to the church fathers, above all Augustine, then finally to the ecclesiastical law. The question of authorities plays a prominent role in the dispute.

What is new about Luther's theology? Faith makes one not only completely remorseful, but it also justifies the sinner. With his theses, Luther seeks to defend the true theology. This seems to be in accordance with the most important authority for Luther, that is, the theology of Augustine. As Luther incorporates faith into the question of repentance, the first outline of the later exclusive dichotomy of repentance and faith is already manifest. However, it cannot be understood as an alternative to the tripartite division of penance here, because Luther unequivocally represents the traditional tripartite division. Here, however, a top-notch theological thesis attunes itself: in dealing with the traditional doctrine of penance of the late Middle Ages, Luther develops the final form of his doctrine of justification.[58] It is a product of his

58 "From his experience with the doctrine of penance sprang the final form of his doctrine of justification, according to which the sinner is justified through the assertion of the Gospel

engagement with the late medieval theology and not its prerequisite. Viewed from this vantage point, the question of the Reformation discovery is not to be narrowed down to the question of a rupture and hence an abrupt transition to a different theology—not just another form of theology—but to embody the idea of a highly complex interaction of historical circumstances, actual process, and historical impact. Therefore, I disagree with the thesis of Reinhold Seeberg, who approvingly quotes G. A. Benrath:

> Not only has the Reformation taken its beginning in a criticism of the medieval doctrine of penance, but its central and essential ideas can also be described as a replacement of the sacrament of penance. . . . Thus, with the burst of the sacrament of penance by Protestantism, the whole medieval notion of religious life was repealed, and it was necessary to establish an appropriate replacement for it, which can be found in the Protestant doctrine of justification and sanctification.[59]

At least at this point of time, we cannot speak of a replacement of the sacrament of penance by the new theology of justification.

Luther rightly rejects his opponents' accusation that he is a heretic. Luther does not deny what his opponents accuse him of; he repeatedly confirms the church's teachings on central issues of faith. However, he makes use of a clear distinction of the office of the keys from God's action within the wide range of various theological views in the complex context of the sacrament of penance. This includes first and foremost a clear distinction between *culpa* and *poena*, then adherence with the high medieval doctrine of repentance and a renewal of the doctrine of declaratory absolution that prevailed up until the early Scholasticism. Luther vehemently rebuffs any attempts to extend the power of the office of the keys to the realm of purgatory. Thus, Luther is a staunch advocate of the sacrament of penance and its integrity. He sees in the indulgence and its practice dilution and deception of the church's doctrine of penance. Therefore, the depiction of a fundamental attack on the sacrament of penance by Luther, as claimed by the older dogmatic historiography, cannot be lent credence.

(*promissio*) in the form of the external word (here absolution) in which the word becomes a certain, truly engaging faith (*fides*) (and so creates assurance of salvation), as in this process the sinner is guided to and joint with Christ through the Holy Spirit" (Messner, *Feiern der Umkehr und Versöhnung*, 192).

59 R. Seeberg, *Die Theologie des Johannes Duns Scotus* (Leipzig, 1900), 397f.

CHAPTER 28

Viorel Mehedinţu

A Dialogue That Turned into a Monologue

Correspondence between Tübingen Theologians and Patriarch Jeremias II of Constantinople, 1573–1581

While reading the letters between Tübingen theologians and Patriarch Jeremias II of Constantinople,[1] two themes of central importance caught my attention. They are pervasive throughout the whole exchange of letters: "scripture and tradition" and "justification." This essay focuses on these two themes, which will be examined from the perspectives of both Protestant and Orthodox theologies.

It was in this correspondence that the understanding of scripture and tradition as well as of the doctrine of justification became serious topics for the first time in their respective church histories. Over the centuries since then, almost down to the present time, the opinion has been more or less formed that the Protestant churches are churches of scripture, while the

1 In *Wort und Mysterium* (Witten, 1958).

Orthodox Church is a church of tradition. This concept of scripture here and tradition there is indeed a reduction of the actual standpoints of the two churches.

The Relationship between Scripture and Tradition

In the letters of the Tübingen theologians

In their correspondence with Patriarch Jeremias II with which they hoped to achieve an agreement to the Protestant doctrines, the Tübingen theologians emphatically put a high value on clarifying the significance of scripture and tradition in their mutual relationship. I have deliberately refrained from speaking of this relationship "within the church," because in the passages of the two letters in which this topic was addressed (15 pages total), the word *church* was mentioned only once (in a negligible context). For them, the scripture is the "criterion for assessing all doctrines and statutes, religious practices, human traditions and works with respect to the Word of God, the Almighty of all things" (second letter, 133).

Their appraisal of tradition varies widely, ranging between its veneration and its deprivation. The Tübingen theologians' ambivalent attitude toward the church fathers is demonstrated in the following assessment: "While we most sincerely appreciate the efforts that the fathers put into interpretation of scripture and often make use of it ourselves, those interpretations should not be considered indispensable to such an extent as to deny that the true and genuine meaning and significance of scripture can also be found without the interpretations and comments of the fathers, only with the help of the Holy Spirit" (141).

The special significance of the dogma of the ecumenical synods lies solely and exclusively in its conformity with the holy scriptures. This conformity with scripture resembles a quality seal of each tradition. The truth of the dogma springs from its "accord with the divine words" (136). This does not necessarily mean, however, that only what comes clearly and directly from scripture can be accepted. "So we readily endorse the designation of the Son of God as 'coessential' although it not to be found in the Holy Scriptures" (142). The adoption of this dogma is explained by the same principle: "because there are allusions to this word in several places in the Holy Scriptures" (142). As regards this, other designations may also be mentioned, such as "person, substance and nature, as used in the early church confessions and taken up anew in the Lutheran confessions, although they are not directly mentioned in scripture."[2]

2 Edmund Schlink, *Theologie der lutherischen Bekenntnisschrifte*, 3d ed. (Munich, 1948), 37.

This outlines the gist of the view that the Protestant theologians of Tübingen held regarding scripture and tradition. Their interest in this topic was peculiarly manifest in their two letters. The scripture, which they reiterate as rule and norm and describe as the "infallible and irrevocable criterion," becomes a raster, a formal principle against which everything should be measured.[3] It conveys the impression that the scripture, once placed on a high pedestal, was assigned first and foremost a juristic and supervising function for tradition, to prevent it from transcending its borders. Indeed, the relationship of the scripture to tradition appears to consist only in this function. We are left with the impression that they, with the scripture held high in their hands, wanted to put all existing traditions to strict scrutiny. In their letters, they use the term *tradition* primarily in the sense of the tradition of interpretation.

They do not go into the aspect that tradition served an important function in the church. Their very open view on scripture narrowed their view of tradition and it escaped their attention that in the church, tradition was an inherent and lively association with the scripture. This possibly happened because the church played virtually no role in their proceedings. Apart from the early church's dogmatic decisions, which passed the test of the scripture, they had a very critical attitude toward tradition. They argued in their letters as if they had no church and no living tradition in it. Essentially, they do justice neither to the church nor to its tradition because their view of scripture was one-sidedly boiled down to its meaning without any real-life references to church or tradition. Where else should scripture prove itself as a yardstick criterion, if not in the church in its living relationship to tradition?

The Tübingen theologians were not aware at that time that the Reformation sprang from the Western tradition, although they separated themselves to a great extent from the Roman Catholic Church. Filioque, for example, one of the topics broached in the correspondence, is a chapter of Western tradition which dates back to Augustine. The *Confessio Augustana Graeca*, which they sent to Patriarch Jeremias, is nothing other than their own tradition. This confession has been much appreciated up until today and constitutes a basis for the Protestant doctrine as well as the confession of faith of the church. Edmund Schlink's writings on tradition have been generally endorsed: "The stance of the Reformation towards tradition is not yet discernible by considering only its concept of tradition. It should rather be examined how they *de facto* used tradition."[4]

3 Edmund Schlink, in *Ökumenische Rundschau* 1 (1960): 48.

4 Edmund Schlink, "Zum Problem der Tradition," in *Schriften zu Ökumene und Bekenntnis*, ed. Klaus Engelhardt and Günther Gassmann (Göttingen: Vandenhoeck & Ruprecht, 2004), 199.

Even the Lutheran and Reformed churches have a tradition. The great book of the confessions of the Lutheran church, *The Book of Concord*, presents an extensive tradition which, in its specific and programmatic manner, relies not only on scripture, but deliberately on the early church's doctrinal decisions as well, by referring to the church fathers, as proven by the *Catalogus testimoniarum* that was appended to it. With respect to the concept of tradition, Martin Luther's fundamental work is also representative, as is John Calvin's for the Reformed Church, to mention only two figures here. Have they not been quoted more often than any other church fathers, both in Eastern and Western Christianity?

The most important and intrinsic part of the apostolic tradition, vital for salvation, was taken up in the New Testament, not only in order to safeguard this tradition better against distortion as scripture or to occasionally use as a reference work, but also in order that it would continue to play its role as a living reality in the church. Tradition needs scripture, and vice versa. "The scripture needs tradition so that the apostolic witness of Christ event becomes a present-life event through transmission instead of remaining a closed-up event."[5] Not only scripture, but also tradition unalterably belongs to being church. There is no church without tradition.

The reconsideration of the phenomenon of tradition and its reappraisal has led to fundamental studies for quite a while already in Protestant theology.[6] The traditional *sola scriptura* has been considered, in light of the importance of tradition, to be "in need of interpretation" in order to revise misinterpretations in the understanding of tradition.[7]

To conclude this section, I would like to expound another aspect of tradition that is referred to by Protestant studies, particularly since this understanding of tradition is also shared by the Orthodox theology. The New Testament scriptures incorporate some of the oral apostolic tradition. The Tübingen theologians came to broach this question briefly, without elaborating it further (first letter, 138). The original tradition has not been taken up in scripture in its entirety. This does not mean, however, that something essential for salvation is missing from scripture, but merely that the apostolic oral tradition was more extensive than the portion incorporated into it. Long before these theologians, Luther also shared this opinion: "*Alterum mysterium est in Ecclesia non satis esse et libros scribi legitimate, sed necessarium eat Medici et audiri. Ideo nihil enim scripsit Christ, sed omnis dixit, Apostoli pauca scripserunt, sed Plurima*

5 Viorel Mehedinţu, *Offenbarung und Überlieferung: neue Möglichkeiten eines Dialogs zwischen der orthodoxen und der evangelisch-lutherischen Kirche* (Göttingen: Vandenhoeck & Ruprecht, 1980), 188.
6 Ibid., 165–211.
7 Gerhard Ebeling, "'Sola Scriptura' und das Problem der Tradition," in *Wort Gottes und Tradition*, 2d ed. (Göttingen, 1966), 91.

dixerunt."[8] We even find this confirmed in the scripture at the end of the gospel of John (21:25). Referring to this biblical passage, another Protestant theologian writes: "The Gospel of John . . . emphatically points out, even in great detail, not the finality of his presentation, but rather the inexhaustibility of tradition and hence, intentionally or unintentionally, opens the way for reshaping and restructuring of traditional heritage—as it also occurred."[9]

Scripture, tradition, and church in the letters of Patriarch Jeremias II

Although the Tübingen theologians wrote in their first and second letters about the significance of scripture as the criterion for dogmas and all other traditions, the Patriarch did not answer them directly, as they might have expected of him. An explicit, theologically founded hierarchy between scripture and tradition cannot be found in his writing. However, a close perusal of the biblical passages quoted in his letters reveals that, compared with his references to church fathers, the Patriarch underpins the majority of his statements by referring to scriptural passages. His letters are replete with such passages.

Patriarch Jeremias identifies the norm of truth as follows:

> The community of Christ is, to speak in accordance with the divine Paul, the pillar and foundation of the truth. No gates of hell will overpower them, according to the divine promise of the Lord, . . . because it is built firmly on the rock and on those in which the truth is anchored. Whoever belongs to the congregation of Christ alone belongs well and truly to the truth, and whoever does not completely belong to the truth does not belong to the congregation of Christ. (first letter, 53)

This time we witness a different understanding. Does this imply that scripture has been dethroned? I strongly doubt it. With these key sentences, the Patriarch expresses an idea of unity among scripture, tradition, and church. He only justifies formally, not contents-wise, what the norm of the truth is, which he sees in the church with everything it includes: scripture and tradition. While his presentation is not considered to be a theological treatise, it is nevertheless very interesting. He portrays the church as the "foundation of the truth." The church is for him not an entity which determines this norm from within itself. A careful reading of his statement makes it clear that he justifies this authority of the church with a biblical quote from 1 Timothy 3:16. His last and most persuasive reasoning is anchored in scripture. The church is the one that gives a voice to scripture during worship. Its words are

---

8 WA 5, 537.

9 Hans Frhr.v. Campenhausen, "Die Entstehung des Neuen Testaments," in *Das Neue Testament als Kanon*, ed. Ernst Käsemann (Göttingen: Vandenhoeck & Ruprecht, 1970), 113f.

received as the words of Christ. What other meanings are conveyed through his statement that the "congregation of Christ [is] . . . the pillar and foundation of the truth"? By *congregation*, he means the community of believers. He brings truth and community together. The community has been assembled not to determine the truth, but to find out what truth is. Jeremias calls it the "congregation of Christ," that is, the community around Christ, with him in its midst. The church is not simply the community of those who believe in Christ. Within this community, the believers are not among themselves, but this community is a special one, a community of believers assembled together along with the divine persons. In the church "the Trinitarian Persons meet with humans."[10] The truth dwells in this kind of community. The truth of the church is one person, Jesus Christ.

According to his letters, tradition plays a major role for Patriarch Jeremias alongside the holy scripture.[11]

The liturgical-sacramental character of tradition as a work of the Holy Spirit

The church is closely associated with tradition in its essence. Tradition not only means the transmission of the truth of salvation, but also the permanent re-presentation of the salvific history in Christ, materialized ever anew and present *hic et nunc* by the Holy Spirit. Here, it becomes clear what inherent connection exists between scripture, tradition, and the church. All three are seen by Patriarch Jeremias as one living unity. They constitute a unified ensemble for him, which he so experienced in the life of worship in his Orthodox Church. This unitary view may have prompted him to overlook the necessity to reciprocate the persistency with which the Tübingen theologians distinguish and separate tradition from scripture.

Maybe he did not respond to it because he actually intended to present the teachings of his church. This was the issue at heart for him. The Tübingen theologians did not make things easy for him, and vice versa. This understanding of tradition was not familiar to the Tübingen theologians, judging from their letters. As little as one would have expected it of them, certainly one might have expected it of the Patriarch. He could have drawn their attention to the pneumatic character of tradition, if he himself had penetrated into the inner layer of this worship in his description of liturgy, that is, the impact of the Holy Spirit through whom the history of salvation becomes a

10 Viorel Mehedințu, "Die Einheit der Kirche aus orthodoxer Sicht nach Johannes 17, 21," in *Einheit als Gabe und Verpflichtung. Eine Studie des Deutschen Ökumenischen Studienausschusses*, ed. W. Bienert (Frankfurt am Main, 2002), 79.

11 Mehedințu, *Offenbarung und Überlieferung*, 255ff.

present event. He does not succeed to put precisely this in a nutshell. Without the impact of the Holy Spirit, tradition degenerates into a lifeless transmission of traditional good. Without the impact of the Holy Spirit, absolutely nothing happens within the church.

Patriarch Jeremias refers to liturgy as a formal presentation of the history of salvation according to its external course. "The pneumatic character of tradition in the Orthodox Church is closely linked to its liturgical-sacramental aspect. . . . Christ's redemptive work, which constitutes the central theme of the liturgical-sacramental tradition, would remain an external, inaccessible act to humans without the Holy Spirit in whom and through whom Christ is present in the church."[12]

Through this understanding of tradition, both sides of the correspondence would have come closer together. They would have had the opportunity to verify that despite the different forms of worship, something similar happens in the inner layer of their services. Both sides missed this opportunity. Actually, they are not the only ones who missed it. In the worldwide ecumenical dialogue as well, this aspect of Christian worship has been neglected and not considered an important issue for far too long. Perhaps the time was not ripe then and the status of theologies did not allow it. Yet, this is not enough reason to exonerate the participants of the correspondence because they did not sensitively listen to each other; instead, their sole interest was to present their own teachings.

Justification by Faith and Good Works

From the perspective of the Tübingen theologians

"Justification" denotes "making just" or "being made just." This concerns human beings. They were made just by God. The reason is explained in *Confessio Augustana* (CA 4). Humans were not justified for nothing, for no reason; "for Christ's sake, through faith, so we believe that Christ suffered for us and that for His sake we are forgiven our sins and given righteousness and eternal life." Humans are justified freely, but this was not for free. Jesus personally took our place and paid a very high price for us. Those who have fallen as deep as humans have cannot rise again on their own. Only Jesus is righteous before God. Christ's righteousness has God attributed to us. What is expected of us is that we believe in it.

This "so we believe" is the main concern of the Tübingen theologians. They compare faith with the hand "through which we receive what our Saviour Christ accomplished for us" (first letter, 148). *Sola fide* and *sola gratia*

12 Ibid., 258.

are two core concepts of the Protestant doctrine of justification, which are rediscovered repeatedly in their two letters. These two *solas* are tirelessly and relentlessly defended against good works. Only in this way, completely without works, justification remains God's sovereign and absolute redemptive act. Justification deals with the sole efficiency of God. Humans are only receivers; otherwise they would, in some way, contribute to their own salvation. This notion would diminish the justifying act of God in Jesus Christ, as it would be "an unworthy endeavour to divide our salvation between us and Christ" (second letter, 201). Because the Tübingen theologians thought that Patriarch Jeremias brought faith and works together, not clearly separating them from each other, they put much effort into this issue. Whoever believes him- or herself justified along the path of fulfilling the law shall know this: "so this is how our salvation will have gone." God's law cannot be fulfilled. "It commands us to live in outwardly visible obedience and pious customs. . . . God looks exclusively into the heart" (second letter, 200). Humans cannot restore the original righteousness and relationship with God. Only Jesus Christ could reconcile us with God: *reconciliatio propter Christum* (Apol. IV, 37, 191).

If works are completely excluded from justification, this does not mean in the least that they are not urgently necessary all the same. "Nevertheless, we sincerely urge our listeners—not only casually—to do good works commanded by God" (first letter, 153). We are not doing good works by ourselves, but with Jesus Christ who "caused them within us" (ibid.). Good works are not to be separated from faith. In this sense, they are signs of good faith. Only a good tree can bear good fruit. So, it is valid, we are justified by faith alone, which is, however, not without works. "*Sola fide nusquam sola*."

The consequences of justification consist not only in the forgiveness of sins or the favour of Christ's justice due to faith, in making or declaring righteousness. Not only do humans receive another status before God, but the justifying work of God cannot linger without affecting us, our being and our life. God's justifying act encompasses much more. After the first creation of the human being, God creates the same again. God creates a new human out of the old: "*ex iniustis iusti efficiamur seu regeneremur*" (Apol. IV, 184, 117). In this realm of the consequences of justification, the Tübingen theologians share the same view as Patriarch Jeremias in quite a few respects: "Now you have enumerated many points in this article on justification which are also entirely unchallenged in our midst" (second letter, 196).

Faith and works in the letters of Patriarch Jeremias II

Although he was repeatedly confronted with justification-related terminology in both letters, Jeremias's terminology comes nowhere near to the doctrine of justification. Accordingly, he does not quote any New Testament passages to which the Tübingen theologians referred. He pays no attention to the doctrine of justification, nor does he pose any comprehension questions to his correspondence partners. Instead, he brings up his understanding of Christ's redemptive work, without referring to any specific chapter of the dogmatic, which did not exist at that time. The doctrine of salvation was not treated separately, but within Christology and pneumatology, where it actually happens. The Patriarch uses the word *judgment* to refer to God's final judgment. In his letters, the Patriarch writes about "the great and unspeakable love of God and his Christ for us" as the ground of our salvation. The term of God's "philanthropy" is repeatedly mentioned, as is the term of grace.

The issue of faith and works occupies a more prominent proportion in his letters, as is the case with the Tübingen theologians. One may suspect a mutual conditionality here. Patriarch Jeremias speaks much of Christian life. His letters are, above all, paraenetic writings in which he makes recommendations for a virtuous life. He calls the path of virtue the royal path. By way of example: "The grace . . . will not be granted to those who do not strive" (first letter, 59). ". . . so let us not bear malice"; ". . . so let us prevail over passion and badger them with repentance and confession. This is the time of labours, fights and struggles. . . . So let us fight as long as we are still in the stadium" (second letter, 184–85). "We have to run, strenuously indeed" (first letter, 63). This kind of running is, however, only possible with support: "If we walk along this path, we need the driving force of God. Guidance is in God's hand, but we have to strive for the worthiness to be taken by his hand" (first letter, 62).

The significance that the Patriarch ascribes to such sentences is either the preparation for the participation in the event of salvation or the consequence of faith. "Humans cannot receive the forgiveness of their sins unless they turn to God through repentance, and have living faith in good works, as we have said before and will never cease to say" (first letter, 60). What he recommends in the works preceding the reception of salvation is meaningful only as preparation. This is still being practiced in the Orthodox Church.

This is the point that I think the Tübingen theologians misunderstood in thinking that the Patriarch gave works a prominent role very close to faith and did not distinguish their functions enough by not separating them from each other. To see to what extent Patriarch Jeremias considered good works to be fitting for salvation, I have excerpted some examples from numerous statements: "But we should not rely on works . . . even after we have done everything, according to the word of the Lord, we are still unworthy servants" (first letter, 65). "For there is nobody, indeed nobody, who would find mercy and philanthropy for his deeds under precise scrutiny" (ibid.). "Moreover, our works, if they are being judged—even if they are almost perfect—are nothing" (first letter, 68). Nevertheless, what such works achieve has still some meaning: ". . . our attitudes show that we are grateful and obedient to the Commandments and do what is good and virtuous" (ibid.). Humans can only respond to Christ's work of salvation with a "sacrifice of praise," as it is termed in the Orthodox liturgy.

The Doctrine of Justification as Understood by the Tübingen Theologians

First, on *sola fide* and *sola gratia*, which belong to the core concepts of the doctrine of justification. As true and undisputed as it is that humans receive the justice of Christ by faith alone, this fact should not give rise to the impression that *sola gratia* is absolute and independent. Faith has no effect whatsoever without Christ, however deep the trust in him is. He is the one who induced not only the so-called objective justification through his death, but also the subjective act of faith that grants us a personal share in his redemptive sacrifice. It is not the faith itself that justifies, but what is believed in and to which faith is directed. *Sola fide* shall point to *solus Christus.*[13] *Sola gratia* is also to be understood in such a manner, so that we, in receiving divine grace, do not receive it as an entity isolated from God. Grace is not something that God sends us. God is gracious.[14] Grace is not something dispatched from God to us. "Receiving grace is receiving the Triune God in his uncreated energies emitted from his nature as divine act, occurring for and in us. The inseparability of grace from God's nature and the perichoretic state of existence of the divine hypostases is the reason that the presence of each of the Persons of the Trinity includes that of the others."[15] Faith and grace are relational concepts. They connect us to Christ or, more precisely, he comes to us in faith. In the Orthodox theology, there is the personal concept of "participation" in this context. The attainment of salvation happens in the personal encounter with Christ. The name of Jesus was mentioned increasingly rarely in the correspondence in comparison to *sola fide* and *sola gratia.*

From the two letters, we also learn little of the impact of the Holy Spirit within faith. This is not a human achievement. Faith is "a very powerful work of the Holy Spirit that changes hearts" (Apol. IV, 99, 181). "Everything that

13 Ernst Kinder, "Christus und der Rechtfertigungsglaube," in *Evangelisch-lutherischen Kirchenzeitung* 2 (1952): 1.

14 Cf. Viorel Mehedinţu, "Art. Gnade, 2," *Orthodoxe Gnadenlehre*, Evangelisches Kirchenlexikon (EKL), 3d ed., 2 (1989): 225–29.

15 Viorel Mehedinţu, "Die orthodoxe Erlösungslehre," in *Von Gott angenommen-in Christus verwandelt. Rechtfertigungslehre im multilateralen ökumenischen Dialog*, Beiheft zur ökumenischen Rundschau 78 (Frankfurt am Main, 2006), 245.

happens in the church in connection with the salvation in Christ is the work of the Holy Spirit. Nothing happens without his intervention."[16]

Sola fide seems to have exerted its effects in the direction that the resurrection of Christ does not come forth within the doctrine of justification, as if our salvation was not achieved by the risen Christ. It was through his resurrection that he completed his work of salvation. The same Christ who was subjected to innocent suffering and death for us is the Risen One who gives us a share of his victory over death and sin. The justification without his resurrection would remain incomplete. We were redeemed not only through his sufferings and death on the cross, but no less by his resurrection. These two belong together.

Another question that I pose to the authors at both sides of the correspondence is where and how the participation in the Christ event occurs. In the description of justification, word and sacrament are hardly mentioned. The church, if I am not mistaken, is not referred to with a single word. Is it possible that the participation in the redemptive work of Christ takes place even outside the church, in *sola fide*? Neither of the letters offers any information on the fact that the church is the place where the word is proclaimed and the sacraments are celebrated in worship and where salvation in Christ becomes present through the power and the impact of the Holy Spirit and where justification is personally granted. The entire description of the Reformation doctrine of justification focuses on *sola fide* without any reference to Christ, means of salvation, and the church. In this description, there is no room for the church, unlike in the seventh article of the Augsburg Confession, where the church is described as the "the *assembly* of all *believers* among whom the *Gospel is preached* in its purity and the *holy sacraments are administered according* to the *Gospels.*"

None of those involved in the exchange of letters provides an ecclesiology. At that time, the doctrine of the church was not under discussion.[17]

Here are some further reflections on the understanding of justification. Justification is presented in Protestant theology as categories of legal thought—justify, do justice, declare justice, attribute and impute, just to name some. Justification places us before the tribunal of God where justice is administered, where one is accused, convicted, and acquitted. Justification is a judiciary act. It involves an indictment and a fearsome punishment. The punishment is horrible. The boundaries of this legal process are smashed and the juridical system is abolished when the good and absolutely innocent one is punished and the guilty party is set free. At this point of the procedure, God's intervenes and freedom is granted to humans, but not to his son, Jesus

16 Ibid., 242.

17 Bernhard Lohse, *Luthers Theologie* (Göttingen, 1995), 295.

Christ. His duty was: "to remove sin by the sacrifice of himself" (Heb. 9:26). He is "the Lamb of God who takes away the sin of the world" (John 1:29).

Why has God chosen this path of sacrificing his son? Solely out of love for us humans: "For God so loved the world that he gave his only Son, so that whoever believes in him may not perish but have eternal life" (John 3:16). God's grace and love break through right in the middle of the tribunal.

The Protestant doctrine of justification is largely based on Romans and Galatians, in which the apostle Paul copes with the Pharisees' understanding of righteousness. Justification is oriented mainly in compliance with these New Testament writings, whereas convincing verses are also found in Paul's other letters and other parts of the New Testament which may be useful for a comprehensive understanding of the sacrificial death of Jesus.

In Orthodox theology, it is held that the concept of justification as a central concept of the understanding of salvation does not reflect the entire spectrum of the New Testament. Additionally, it still holds the conviction that the legal terminology alone is not the most suitable form to present the deep original meaning of the sacrifice of Jesus.[18] This is not only an Orthodox view. The well-known theologian Jürgen Moltmann, also from Tübingen, writes in this regard: "The terminology of justification was turned into a thoroughly legal terminology of indictment and acquittal in *foro Dei by* Melanchthon."[19] These Orthodox objections should not overlook that within the doctrine of justification, essential aspects of the Christian faith were worked out that also served as inspiration for other Christian theologies.

"The love of God the Father toward humans who, for humanity, send his Son to the world and to let him endure the death on the cross, and the love of the for humans self-sacrificing Christ"[20]—in the face of this immeasurable divine love, the notion of righteousness steps back. Along this line, I would like to refer to another great Protestant church theologian, Edmund Schlink, who, in his seminal work Ökumenische *Dogmatik*, points out that it is not possible to speak of God's righteousness without mentioning his love at the same time.[21]

For the theology of the Orthodox Church, the cross of Jesus is first and foremost the revelation of God's love for the fallen human being. "But God proves his love for us in that while we still were *sinners Christ* died for us" (Rom. 5:8). In the theological writings of the church fathers, Jesus Christ was often called *philanthropos*, as he is still called in worship services today. God's love is at the heart of the Orthodox understanding of salvation: "God is

18 Mehedinţu, "Die orthodoxe Erlösungslehre," 224.

19 Jürgen Moltmann, *Geist und Leben der Kirche* (München, 1991), 169.

20 Mehedinţu, "Die orthodoxe Erlösungslehre," 227.

21 Edmund Schlink, *Ökumenische Dogmatik* (Göttingen, 1983), 428.

love" (1 John 4:8). God's love, which operates *ad extra* in the history of salvation, has its roots, its source, in the intertrinitarian relations *ad intra*. The doctrine of the Trinity occupies a central position in Orthodox theology because, in the words of Nissiotis, it is the "foundation on which the Orthodoxy stands and from which the life and theology of the church have unfolded."[22] By God's love, the love of the three divine persons is meant, wherein the Son the God is on Golgotha, so intensely experiencing this love while suffering in the torment of death. "No one has greater love than this, to lay down one's life for one's friends" (John 15:13). The destination of Jesus' sacrifice is also to be understood in the context of this understanding of love as the heart of salvation. Jesus did not suffer an innocent death to satisfy God for the sin of humankind or to measure up to God's righteousness, but for humans' sake, in order to free them from sin and death and to empower them to a new life in community with him. So what actually happened is not *satisfactio Dei*, but *sanatio hominis*. Anastasios Kallis writes in this regard: "This is not juridical, but a therapeutic process."[23] The term *Heiland* ("healer"), a German designation of Jesus, is also to be understood in this sense.

Due to the close relationship between liturgy and theology in the Orthodox Church, it goes without saying that God's love is experienced and praised in songs and chants in worship time and time again. The Holy Spirit is praised in the doxologies as "the philanthropic and life-giving Spirit."

The understanding of the history of salvation in Christ as a sacrifice of love in the more recent Orthodox theology is not opposed to the understanding of justification in the Protestant churches, especially because the notion of God's justice is also an important concept in Orthodox soteriology. Jesus himself calls God "righteous Father . . ." (John 17:25). The Romanian theologian Dumitru Staniloae writes in this regard: "God's justice and mercy cannot become separated from each other within his relationship to us."[24] The mystery of the redemption of humankind through Jesus Christ is so inexhaustible that it cannot be completely explained by a particular theology alone.

The question is, How does the Holy Spirit work in us? Basically, this can be answered with the following dictum: the Spirit works in us, but not without us. How is it then associated with the human participation in the reception of the saving grace? Each person participates in his or her redemption with absolutely no contribution, but takes part in it "through personal acceptance of salvation, and is personally redeemed and thus personally involved

22 N. A. Nissiotis, *Die Theologie der Ostkirche im ökumenischen Dialog. Kirche und Welt in orthodoxer Sicht* (Stuttgart, 1968), 19.

23 Anastasios Kallis, *Brennender, nicht verbrennender Dornbusch. Reflexionen orthodoxer Theologie* (Münster, 1999), 293.

24 Dumitru Staniloae, *Orthodoxe Dogmatik*, vol. 2 (Zürich-Gütersloh, 1990), 226.

in the work of his/her salvation throughout his/her life."[25] In other words, individuals take part in the bestowal of their salvation by virtue of faith. Their role is limited to receiving consciously and accepting gratefully God's saving action for them and drawing consequences from it throughout their lives. "Therefore, my beloved, be steadfast, immovable, always excelling in the work of the Lord, because you know that in the Lord your labour is not in vain" (1 Cor. 15:58). The notion of the earned merits, the "arithmetic of merits," is foreign to the Orthodox Church.[26] "In the works as necessary consequences of faith extends the operation of the Holy Spirit working in our faith. His impact does not stop when out of faith works are following."[27]

In light of the understanding of the relationship between grace and works, the relationship between divine grace and free will becomes manifest. According to the Orthodox understanding, free will is part of the essential nature of human beings. It belongs to God's image in human beings. Although it is strongly mitigated through sin, it is not lost. Deprived thereof, humans would no longer be wholly human. The will is also under the influence of the Holy Spirit. "Now the Lord is the Spirit, and where the Spirit of the Lord is, there is freedom" (2 Cor. 3:17). To what extent is the free will of an individual involved at the moment of receiving the saving grace? Does God overlook human freedom if God alone redeems human beings? Does God take their freedom into account? A person devoid of will cannot be of God's plan. God "needs their approval; he wants that humans are willing to be redeemed on their part."[28] God does not grant grace to humans against their will. God turns to other means: God strengthens their will and supports them. Preservation of human free will and its involvement in salvation are to be understood in this sense. "Therefore, beloved . . . work out your own salvation with fear and trembling; for it is God who is at work in you, enabling you both to will and to work for his good pleasure" (Phil. 2:12-13). God's will and work do not happen without the human willingness in the sense of the statement made by Augustine: "The One who created you without you will not save you without you."[29]

25 Sergei Bulgakov, *Die Orthodoxie. Die Lehre der orthodoxen Kirche* (Trier, 1996), 167.

26 Ibid., 168.

27 Mehedințu, "Die orthodoxe Erlösungslehre," 252.

28 Ibid., 251.

29 Lohse, *Luthers Theologie*, 281.

CHAPTER 29

Johanna Rahner

Reform or Reformation?

The Councils of Trent, Vatican I, and Vatican II

Thesis 1: Reform is intrinsic to the church—this is a claim that deserves our proverbial "Amen." Not every reform, however, merits our "Yes and Amen"—we must demand certain criteria.

Thesis 2: "Reform" is a distinct theme for each epoch of church history. Initially, it had rather a structural nature, that is, *ad intra*, and thus was mostly aimed at removing concrete grievances (*re-formatio* was made necessary due to *de-formatio*; with "*reformatio in capite et in membris*" ["reformation in its head and its members"] and "*Gravamina*" ["complaint" or "grievance"] as slogans of the 13th to 15th centuries, especially the 16th century). With the Reformation, however, the question of reform developed a fundamentally new format regarding both its valid basis for theology and its contents, especially those visible elements having to do with credibility, fulfillment, and real-life aspects of faith and realization of faith (i.e., criterion of "salvation"; *ad extra*). From this perspective, however, *reformatio* becomes a notion that must be comprehended from multiple perspectives and, hence, has to be interpreted in a confessionally open way. Therefore, *reformatio* rewrites not only the Reformation as a renewal movement, but it can also determine more closely the self-reflection of the Roman Catholic Church, launched by the Council of Trent, in the sense of a "Catholic Reform."

Thesis 3: The significance of the Council of Trent for the Roman Catholic Church was first and foremost an apologetic one. But this was also understood as the church's dogmatic response, positioned deliberately opposite to the Reformation, to the challenges posed by the reformers' theology (be they the arguments about scripture and tradition, biblical canon, original sin, doctrines of eucharist and sacraments, indulgence, icons, or veneration of saints), and thus a self-ascertainment and demarcation (cf. the canons!). Within the Catholic realm, the council brought other, also important, impulses, even though not unique and not always decisive, for reform toward the Catholic renewal, which was a central pastoral concern of the time. This renewal itself was broader and older in its origin than the council and the Catholic reform movement that the reformers triggered. Viewed in this light, the impulses for reform of the late medieval church, which began even before the Reformation, were taken up and implemented as a response to the Reformation. These impulses continued with or without interruptions throughout the Reformation, even as they were obviously influenced by the Reformation and hence positively (!) absorbed it. Admittedly, the decisions of this council made in relation to its reform decrees constituted, for the most part, half-hearted compromises (whose implementations were sometimes even repealed) and its doctrinal texts have outright "minimalistic" dimensions (Hubert Jedin), that is, limiting their scope to the condemnation of certain doctrines. At the same time, in the course of their reception—occasionally against the intrinsic intention of the council—they sometimes served the purpose of cementing denominational differences and thus did justice to the confessional catchword of the Counter-Reformation, because henceforth the Catholic reform orchestrated itself in the explicitly antireformation direction. "The Tridentinum has become a shell into which to withdraw" (Hubert Jedin), and this led to that increasingly petrified corset of "Tridentinism" (Yves Congar), wherein its mythology—centrally forced and reinforcing the Roman Catholic centralism—became the label of a whole epoch and at the same time represented the burdensome legacy of the council.

Thesis 4: A brief look at the impact history (*Wirkungsgeschichte*) of the Reformation is enough to discover what proved decisive: The inherent plurality, which, for example, was a good tradition in the medieval church, became reduced to a uniform identity and ideology in the confessional age—on both sides of the confessional border. The interdenominational competition in the same geographic region forced each denomination to determine an exclusive identity, make it a norm, and impose uniformity. Denominational identity became group identity, and the church's self-understanding was defined as "tribal ecclesiology" (Roger Haight), which no longer dared to permit internal differentiation. Consequently, the Roman Catholic Church and its positional diversity experienced "spiritual impoverishment" in the wake of the Reformation (Bishop Wanke).

Thesis 5: In hindsight, this actual church-dividing character of the Reformation will have to be ascribed to the ecclesiological consequences of the reformers' theology. However, the historical exploration has certainly led to a partial relativization of many an evaluation. In the 15th century, the centrally forced papalism took a narrow and only provisional victory over the conciliarism that sprang from the misery of the occidental schism. The fronts, however, were not as consolidated as they seem, and the dynamics arising from the ecclesiological reminiscences of Reformation theology were an eloquent testimony to the fact that the 16th century was sitting on an ecclesiological volcano, precisely because the dispute between centralist forces and their regional antagonists still persists. The same remains true for Trent. It was only after the Tridentinum that papal-centralism was purported to be the unique characteristic of the Roman Catholic Church. For this reason, much of what was taken for granted by the medieval theologians, be it the plurality of church structures or diversity of liturgical forms, disappeared from the Catholic world stage through the post-Tridentine uniformity constraint. This "Tridentinism" reached its heyday and doomsday in the Catholic canon law with the First Vatican Council (Vatican I) and its reception history. The one-sided ecclesiological positioning, along with the fragmentary character of this council, displayed its insufficiency. The Second Vatican Council (Vatican II) intercepted this one-sidedness again and resumed an open-minded tradition which had been lost in the aftermath of the Catholic profile formed by the Counter-Reformation; this tradition interpreted the Tridentinum and Vatican I, and not the other way round. As such, however, it coped better with the ecclesiological questions of the Reformation than the post-Tridentine confessionalization.

Thesis 6: While well anchored within the permissible range of medieval theology, the Reformation-driven contouring of the theology of grace became more dynamic through its declaration of the exclusiveness of grace as the basis of salvation, *sola gratia*, and the exclusiveness of faith in the attainment of salvation, *sola fide*—stances that went beyond the theological foundations of the Middle Ages, where the soteriological was located in the ecclesiological—because, in the end, it dared to think ahead in a different way and in a modified form. This insight was particularly attributable to the systematic work of Otto Hermann Pesch on the Catholic side, who unveiled the forms of thought (*Denkformen*) of the Reformation and medieval (then again, also extending to the post-Reformation Catholic) theologies, which were different from each other and therefore *not* conveyable eventually. Nonetheless, Pesch urged all successors to take to heart that these different forms of thought were to be interpreted as complementary models of understanding, thus making it possible for this denominationally opened perspective to implement a changed appraisal of rupture, novelty, and originality, on the one hand, and of continuity and progress, on the other hand, which led to a changed perception of the Reformation and its concerns.

Thesis 7: With Vatican II, the Roman Catholic Church adopted an open approach to the insight that their own identity should no longer be delimiting, excluding all others, but should be steadily determined from the double perspective of *ad intra* and *ad extra*. While Trent aimed at drawing boundaries, the aim henceforth was to become aware of similarities, with a changed basic stance in the core content ("Truth in Dialogue"). Against this background, the Roman Catholic Church was compelled to view herself as a church in the process of constant reform. "She is at once holy and always in need of purification, and always follows the way of penance and renewal," "she never ceases to renew herself."[1] The church needs a "constant Reformation."[2]

Ad intra, this dynamization led to a perception and appreciation of the diversity and plurality of the one truth, handed down and to be passed on, as well as the knowledge of its personal-existential, and thus communicative, basic dimension.[3] This involved factors such as situational, historical, and linguistic differences, as well as differences of mentality. Each different form of thought was to be interpreted as a complementary model of understanding. This ran counter to the temptation of henceforth making the question of truth simply a question of "either/or."

Ad extra, this led to a changed attitude toward other confessions, including an eschatological dynamization of self-understanding and self-determination as the church of Jesus Christ.[4] Ecumenism and dialogue are permanent basic obligations of the church's own, in a certain sense now "open," identity.

---

1 Dogmatic Constitution on the Church of the Second Vatican Council, "*Lumen Gentium*," nn. 8, 9; hereafer LG.

2 Decree on Ecumenism of the Second Vatican Council, "Unitatis Redintegratio," n. 6, cf. also nn. 4, 5; hereafter UR.

3 Dogmatic Constitution on Divine Revelation, "Dei Verbum," nn. 2-6, 8; Decree on the Mission Activity, "Ad Gentes," n. 22.

4 Cf. subsistit [LG 8.2]; the "non plena communio" of non-Catholic Christians [LG 14f.], up to the axiom of the universal will of salvation of God who embraces all peoples [LG 16]).

Thesis 8: The Vatican II texts used the term *reformatio* only once (UR 6) and preferred, instead, the notion of renewal—*renovatio*. However, the ideas of change, adequate adaptation, and above all being affected and challenged by the "signs of the times" were perceivable in every council paper as a pervasive, overarching idea. The very first words of the first document of the council brought this decisively and concisely to the point: ". . . to adapt more suitably to the needs of our own times those institutions which are subject to change."[5] Such dynamics of change did not arise from the misery of abuse, but were in conformity with the council's fundamental shift of perspective. The "pastoral basic intention" of the council was not just a question of (linguistic) style (i.e., refusal of judgments), but had basic hermeneutical consequences. Vatican II did not just bring something new; it was a new way of "council." This involved especially the perspective of going forward—beyond and above the simple "progress in the understanding of the doctrine of faith"!

Thesis 9: The council texts themselves thereby reflect the fact that the council understood itself as a council of transition, at the beginning of a process which did not come to an end, even with the council's conclusion. This is self-evident even within its texts. Methodologically, the texts used the juxtaposition technique. Sources were cited from tradition and recontextualized at the same time. In particular, in subject areas in which the council ventured to think afresh or, rather, to consider the course of things from other angles than the temporarily (but obviously not mentally) close 19th century, the old and the new appeared together face to face. Meanwhile, this new contextualization changed the interpretation and implication of the old and provided a new way of understanding differently, or a different way of understanding anew. For the council, tradition was therefore not the mere conveyance of old formulas, but the lively restoration of their contents in new, modified horizons.

Thesis 10: Recently, attempts have been made, in the wake of Pope Benedict XVI's Christmas greetings to the Roman Curia dated 22nd December 2005, to apprehend this dynamic more concretely by attributing a "hermeneutic of continuity" or "discontinuity" to it, that is, by more closely determining the council's relationship to its prehistory, specifically by guarding it against misunderstandings. Pope Benedict himself spoke of the "hermeneutic of reform" in conjunction with the "hermeneutic of rupture." Two points must be considered here.

---

5 Constitution on the Sacred Liturgy, "*Sacrosanctum Concilium*" (hereafter SC), 1.

First, we must note that Vatican II—and this applies to every council of church history—was of course not launched with the idea of overthrowing its own doctrinal tradition (and thus its identity). Nevertheless, it has changed things from the ground up. From historical standpoints, it is obvious that the council consciously broke from the "monotony of the Catholic," as developed throughout the confessional age (with even more reinforcing dynamics in the 19th and early 20th centuries), in the form of a standardized and uniformed unity model. Of course, the council understood this formal "rupture" as a rediscovery of the original "Catholic" in the sense of *ressourcement* ("return to the source") and *aggiornamento* ("opening").

Second, Pope Benedict XVI clearly established the idea of "reform" as a leitmotiv of the council. Having fallen into disrepute before the council (respectively as the aftermath of the Counter-Reformation constellations of the Roman Catholic Church since the mid-16th century, reinforced through the 19th-century developments with their antihistorical "sentiment," which led directly to the interpretation of "inalterability" as a distinctive feature of "truth"), the idea of (necessary) change established itself as a leitmotiv of the council. The closely related idea of *ressourcement* had already gained a foothold, not only in various pre-council movements, but also in a wide variety of doctrinal decisions[6] and alongside with it the idea of change through renewal. This idea experienced a breakthrough along with the program of *aggiornamento* inspired by Pope John XXIII.

Thesis 11: Without an understanding of the council's prehistory—above all from the Tridentinum up until the end of the "long 19th century," that is, Vatican I and its long reception history—as inherent to its character, there can be neither an adequate understanding of Vatican II nor an appropriate answer to the question of the right of domicile of the theological concerns of the Reformation in today's Roman Catholic Church. This insight takes the council seriously as a consequence of its (pre-)history, because experiences have taught the church that things cannot be simply left "as they are," but fruitful, proactive thinking is necessary. The conciliary reform impulses win their dynamics from the orientation toward their origin itself. This, finally, leads to the question: How much continuity may be upheld and how much rupture is needed to be able to stay faithful to one's mission and hence to oneself in a changing world?

6 Cf. the encyclical of Pope Pius XII, "*Divino Afflante Spiritu*" [1943], and the liturgical reforms in "*Mediator Dei*" (1947).

Part Five

The Churches and the Reformation Jubilee

CHAPTER 30

Thies Gundlach

In the Beginning There Was Freedom

Since 2008, Protestant churches in Germany have been preparing for the Reformation Jubilee 2017, jointly with federal and state governments, under the banner of a "Luther Decade." The thematic years of the Decade explore the core aspects of the religious and social transformations of Europe, and later the whole world, which unfolded in close association with the Reformation. Thereby, for the first time, the Reformation churches are jointly preparing this jubilee; that is, not the German (VELKD) or international (LWF) Lutheranism alone, but the whole community of the Reformed, United, and Lutheran churches in the EKD (Evangelical Church in Germany) are preparing for this big event together. This is possible due to the Leuenberg Agreement of 1973, 40 years old as of 2013, which overcame the mutual condemnations of Reformation churches. Furthermore, the EKD has been trying, by means of diversified participatory board structures and international conferences, to get smaller (free) churches, pre-Reformation movements, and other denominations marginalized by the Reformation to join in. The participation of the Roman Catholic Church, however, is coined by the view that the Reformation caused the schism of Western Christendom and that this loss of unity should serve as the all-defining measure for evaluating the Reformation. Therefore, for the Catholics, it can be called a "commemoration" of the Reformation at best and acts of penance are more appropriate than festivities. In this context, the question of what to celebrate in 2017, as already raised on multiple occasions, is an absolutely justified question to which the current Protestantism can only respond that there is and will not be *the* answer, but, rather, constantly renewed and different answers, even self-contradictory ones, until 2017. A part of this plurality will be explored in the following reflections. There are, in my view, three dimensions from which the answers to the question about the meaning and goal of the Reformation Jubilee 2017 can and should be sought; namely (1) a theological-existential dimension, (2) a historical dimension, and (3) a commemorative-cultural dimension.

Theological-Existential Dimension: What Shall We Celebrate 500 Years Later?

In 2012, the Berlin Theological Journal published a special issue entitled "Perplexed before the Reformation Jubilee 2017?" This title is aptly articulated and peculiarly alarming at the same time, and only a Reformation Jubilee rich and strong in content will uphold the churches against such tugging and pulling toward tourism and trivialization. Or, put as a mission statement: we can only reach beyond Luther pretzels and Luther figurines by finding theologically, spiritually, and culturally relevant formulations that can express the quintessence of the Reformation event 500 years ago and are, at the same time, accessible for modern people who are unpracticed in spiritual things. In this regard, it is significant, seen from a higher vantage point, that the preparations for the jubilee are intensely taking place in the new *Bundesländer* (federal states) of the Federal Republic of Germany, that is, in areas with one of the highest secularization rates in Europe, where it is a particular challenge to impart those "spiritual things" to the "unpracticed." The Reformation churches must make it clear to the supposedly "religiously unmusical" people (Max Weber) why the Reformation Jubilee marks a key turning point in the history of the Western world, including their own history, and why this history has constantly exerted its impact until today and shall never cease doing so.

Reflections on the current context of the jubilee

In this section we will look at the spiritual core of Reformation awakening and see how it radiates its light into the present and the future. The starting point of my reflections here is the basic thesis formulated by Volker

Leppin: "Reflecting on the Reformation means from a Protestant view to reflect on the gospel of Jesus Christ—hence on the common foundation of Christian proclamation." This is the starting point of everything that revolves around 2017 as Christ-centred or ecumenically oriented festivity; the Reformation churches want to celebrate the gospel, not themselves. Additionally, it is to be kept in mind that 2017 will be the first jubilee that is marred neither by the self-assertion of a threatened denomination (1617) nor the demarcation from Catholicism (1717), neither a national awakening (1817) nor a national just-war fatalism (1917), and still less by delineation from the East German interpretations of Luther (1983). It is a free, unbiased portrait of Reformation insights in the current context. After 100 years of ecumenical movement and 70 years after the Holocaust, we should and must also shed light on the shadows of the Reformation, in addition to its driving forces toward freedom, education for all, broadened worldviews and professionalism, love of neighbour, and the modernization of gender relations. Since the German idealism, the Reformation has been associated with the beginning of modernity; discussions about this association have become an unbroken, ever-recurring tradition, also depending on researchers' own interests. With the necessary historical distance, we may characterize the Reformation Jubilee 2017 with the following insights, which in my opinion meet general approval:

1. The jubilee places the rediscovery of the gospel in the centre, not the establishment of a new church.
2. The date 31 October 2017 is a symbolic one, on which the beginning of a fundamental spiritual and social differentiation will be commemorated. Divisions and separations were neither intended by Luther in their dimensions nor recognized by his contemporaries as such.
3. No one "brought about" the Reformation and its subsequent separations, no one steered them; they happened and they are, as such, part of God's history with God's world.
4. The Reformation message of justification as the key discovery of the Reformation theology is the core of the breakthrough of freedom. The four converging points of *soli* (*sola fide*, *sola scriptura*, *sola gratia*, and *solus Christus*) are still fundamental points of reference for the formulation of these insights.
5. Besides our gratitude for the rediscovery of the gospel and the breakthrough of freedom, we also feel shame over the reformers' spiteful and intolerant statements and the phases and developments in confessional history that led to great suffering.

6. The classic portrait of "Martin Luther the Hero," who guided humanity from the Middle Ages to modern times with his spiritual orientation, does not reflect the state of historical research on the person of Luther and his work.
7. For the future shaping of Protestantism, the jubilee in 2017 is multiply auspicious: it is internationally celebrated within the scope and framework of the Leuenberg Agreement and free of an anti-Catholic flavour.
8. All churches and denominations coined by the Reformation are invited to celebrate 31 October 2017 together in order to present the contemporary churches and denominations in remembrance of the commencement of their common belief.

There are undoubtedly many other important aspects that are associated with the Reformation Jubilee, but its principal challenge is already clear: if the churches wish to come out of their cocoons in view of all these points, they must find current and understandable content, compatible language, and a generally comprehensible message for their substantial concern. This can only be achieved through clarity and reduction of complexity. What, then, should constitute the core of the Reformation Jubilee 2017?

The historical starting point

Martin Luther grew up in an insecure world and (therefore?) in a spiritually and theologically "hyped-up" church: godly affairs were meticulously defined and administered to every last detail and there was an indulgence, a saint, a side altar, or a prayer sequence for every existential contingency of everyday life. Fears, doubts, hollowness, and grievances were often "assigned" instead of "assuaged," and piety was extremely ritualized. The world was something scary for people of that time, as was God. After the death of Jan Hus in 1415, the ensuing 100 years witnessed widespread queries, doubts, and skepticism, but these still were only met with defensive resistance. By 1500, there surged—to a large part harnessed by the emerging humanism—a deep discomfort with the state of affairs in the scientific community and the (Scholastic) theology. While there was a very serious and profound tradition of piety around 1500, as exemplified by the "observant monasteries," this period saw the rampant banalization, commercialization, and trivialization of piety, driven to extremes by the competition among places of pilgrimage with their inflationary marketing of miracles, grotesque shows, and collections of bizarre relics ("Jesus' diapers") in addition to increasingly eccentric forms of indulgences. "The inflation of salvation-offers around 1500 harboured the seed of self-questioning and prompted the individualization of forms of appropriation."[1] Not *everything* was dark in the late Middle Ages, but *much* was indeed in need of reform.

Is there something here which reminds us of the present situation? Is our generation, 500 years after the Reformation, in a "pre-Reformation" kind of situation? Is our generation as buzzing and banal and as mercantile and trivial as people back then? Martin Luther sought the key to his reform concerns in the answer to the question about *the merciful God*: his main concern was the salvation of souls in the last judgment, because he was afraid of the punishments that shall befall sinners after death. How can we transcribe this question Luther raised about the merciful God in modern terms? How can his question be conveyed in a world which hardly knows God, has little concern about the last judgment, and is convinced that "hell is other people" (Jean-Paul Sartre)? What words are to be used today to pose Luther's question of the merciful God if one cannot assume a religious, Christian premise?

Legitimate updates?

How can I keep myself fit? Being healthy is all that matters! Sometimes we get the impression that physical health has now taken over the role that the salvation of souls used to play. Health is a predominant issue everywhere; people spend astonishingly large amounts of money on health, and are dreadfully afraid of its absence.

How can I prove myself right? Being in the right is all that matters! Martin Walser wrote a small book on the subject of justification and postulated that a society that knows no justification can produce only self-opinionated dogmatists. Nowadays, looking at the rampant public tribunalization and scandalization, we cannot but admit that without final judgment in the spirit of divine grace, we deal with each other most ungraciously.

The main point is that I am profiting from it! The totality of relevance—proving efficacy at all costs—is another component of the new redemptive faith. Faith and God must be useful for me so that I can justify faith with its intrinsic values (in modern terms, with the social capital). Faith is so wonderfully useful and so convenient, God is doing me a service (I will succeed; or it is okay to belong to the so-called weak and feeble, etc.). Again, I am afraid that God has no desire to be useful.

Luther's question is, in any case, "useful" in one sense: it asks you and me about God, about something that is our ultimate concern (Paul Tillich), neither about my knowledge nor my actions, but about the certainty of feeling (Friedrich Schleiermacher) or the inner attitude. Luther's question creates and strengthens the question about the inner person, the soul, the space

1 Thomas Kaufmann, *Geschichte der Reformation* (Frankfurt am Main, 2009), 84.

within myself meaning not only reflection, but also support and a home while traversing the vicissitudes of life. If this question about God—even amidst doubt, seeking, accusation, absence, and so forth—can no longer be asked within myself and in the world, it becomes lonesome and silent, empty and banal, inside of me and around me. A soul not asking about God is like a fish on dry land and a house with no windows; it is darker than it should be and narrower than necessary.

"Justification of sinners by faith alone"—this basic formula of the Reformation insight must be interpreted in close association with the soul: remembrance of the Reformation deals with *easing the soul* of the fears of our time. The central Reformation insight can be unfurled in three steps of conquering fear: *exodus from fear—retreat in God—re-entry into the world.* This is the grammar in the background of the Reformation breakthrough, so to speak, the basic architecture that attempts to hold the overwhelming diversity of insights and aspects together.

And it's plainly clear: because we live in a highly individualized age (of which most of the Reformation insights are not insignificant), only individual approaches to Reformation insights are available. In principle, every person, every milieu, every class, and every existential situation should be able to place its respective history of liberation from fear in the memory of the Reformation. The paths to the Reformation breakthrough 500 years ago have become, as it were, existential archetypes of all liberation paths today. An old insight serves here as a basic recipe: show me your fear, and I will tell you what redemption you are seeking. Each individual can recognize him- or herself in this triad of "exodus from fear—retreat in God—re-entry into the world," because his or her way out of today's fears and constraints, imprisonments and bondages, contain these three dimensions, if they want and can be understood spiritually.

Exodus from fear—retreat in God—re-entry into the world: but is this *three-step fear conquering* apt for our time? Is the catchphrase "exodus from fear" a comprehensible point of reference for the many "unpracticed" people of today? Does our world, our generation, including the future generation, have the same fears that are curable by the retreat in God? This question cannot be difficult enough, because it belongs to the sobriety of self-perception that our discourse about God often has the effects of medicine which claims to cure a disease that no one has, and of the solution of a problem that would not exist without theology. Or, theologically speaking: because we have an extremely weak hamartiology (doctrine of sin), hardly anyone understands our soteriology (doctrine of salvation). However, this is a basic form of all Christian reflection right from the first days of Christendom: Jesus Christ is the salvation of the whole world, because the whole world is in disaster. Jesus

Christ died for our sins, because all human beings are sinners. The proclamation of faith has a point of reference as healing and medicine only insofar as there is awareness in us—as vague as it may be—in what a desolate and hopeless world we are living. However, in the absence of such awareness of living in dark and hopeless situations, inwardly and outwardly, the promise of liberation is vain and empty. Consequently, the question to be raised is as follows.

What sorts of existential dead-end situations are there today that may serve as starting points for the Christian discourse of sin and salvation? The central slogan from which to proceed is, in my opinion, formulated by the French sociologist and psychologist Alain Ehrenberg, in 2008: "The Weariness of the *Self*: Diagnosing the History of *Depression* in the Contemporary Age."[2] With this *phenomenon of an "overstrained self"* manifesting itself in a never-ending series of new aspects, the radicalized globalization and countless alternative offers to each and every thing releases a stress about decision making, which not only prompts the escape into depression, but also creates a mass of overstrained citizens who constantly display stop and brake signals. Their selves, stressed by various invading options, develop signals calling for redemption. We come across such signals incredibly often today, even in the church. Behind these signals is often a deep fear that goes beyond one's capacity to cope, and thus one can only be freed from it. This fear of being overstrained only worsens if we try to overcome it with more performance and commitment. Even the opposite alternative, that is, plain proclamation of a time-out, is not equal to overcoming that stress, but merely a transposition of overstraining on a purported alternative lifestyle. What I am convinced of is that it is at this juncture that we can and must raise our voices in order to present the doctrine of justification, the Reformation-specific spirituality, just this "retreat in God," more plausibly.

Why We Remember the Past

Not only the churches in Germany, Europe, and worldwide that stem from the Reformation, but also the whole modern society are preparing for the Reformation Jubilee 2017; in 2011, the German Bundestag deemed it to be a "world-class event." It is not a church party; rather, the whole society commemorates its "mythical-legendary emergence" with its sense of a constructional aspect. Commemorative jubilees have an aspect of self-contouring: Who are we? Where do we come from? What do we want to be? Basic existential questions are processed in commemorative festivities. They interpret and provide reassurance; they clarify and bestow confidence. In the

2 Alain Ehrenberg, *The Weariness of the Self: Diagnosing the History of Depression in the Contemporary Age*, trans. Enrico Caouette, et al. (Montreal: McGill-Queen's University Press, 2009).

multireligious, pluralistic, and highly individualized society of today, however, there is hardly any legend of origin that defines and affects all people. Neither the quincentenary of the discovery of America (1492–1992) nor the bicentenary of the French Revolution (1789–1989) could constitute such a unified undertaking of interpreting our common origin. Of course, the 500-year celebration of the beginning of the Reformation in 1517 will not affect all social groups in the same way and to the same extent, but it will certainly touch a very large portion of today's society. For example, 24.5 million people in Germany are members of Protestant churches, of whom about 660,000 persons are full-time employees of the Evangelical Church in Germany (EKD), along with its member churches and their social-welfare agencies. Additionally, churches have 1.1 million volunteers in Germany. Worldwide, the year 2017 will mobilize millions of people around the globe. The World Communion of Reformed Churches (WCRC) and the Lutheran World Federation (LWF) have around 150 million members, and there are nearly half a billion Christians belonging to Protestant denominations worldwide. And since the Reformation has influenced all Christian churches, a broad interest of all Christians in this event may be assumed.

With the upcoming jubilee, and seizing the opportunity to make it a central turning point in its history, German society is undertaking efforts to clarify its fundamental spiritual roots that go beyond a purely commercial, rational, and pragmatic common ground. This attempt can be explained by the principle that the culture of commemoration satisfies the need for "consolidating our fleeting existence."[3] Not only churches must strengthen the certainty of faith, but society also faces the challenge of promoting identity and integration. This draws on the principle that the stronger the dynamics of change are developed in the present, the more culture of memory becomes necessary. The "shrinkage of the present" (Hermann Lübbe) leads to the intensification of commemorative festivities, and the increasing insecurity of identity boosts the number of commemorative locations and dates. Therefore, the plausibility of the Reformation Jubilee for the present society consists in a sort of "blessing of memory."

It will benefit the whole society to memorize and update the basic insights of the Reformation because it can clarify our origins, make the present comprehensible, and mitigate the fear of the future. Given that it deals with core issues such as the question of human dignity, the concept of freedom, the social responsibility of all, and the cultural identity of the present, a society strengthened by Reformation stories is a society free of fear, more self-aware, and confident: to put it in a nutshell, it is *a society capable of conquering fear.*

3 Friedrich Schiller, "Was heißt und zu welchem Ende studiert man Universalgeschichte?" (Inaugural lecture in Jena, 26 May 1789), *Akademische Buchhandlung* (Jena, 1789).

However, this target image is only achievable if we remember the historical facts in a sober and informed manner; therefore, accurate historical research is an indispensable, integral part of every memory, and key to each reasonable retrospection. Thereby, we should not underestimate the fact, however, that historical research is never neutral in reporting things "as they happened," but always adopts interest-based approaches and lets one-sided standpoints creep in. Therefore, we certainly welcome the attempt to describe the history of the Reformation(s) in as historically accurate a way as possible, as recently undertaken by the LWF and the Secretariat for Christian Unity in Rome. At the same time, this Vatican–Lutheran joint historiography gives us an opportunity to see that such attempts are still in their infancy, as the common narration has taken up only a few, very Lutheran-specific memories of the Reformation history. With this in mind, the Evangelical Church in Germany is observing with keen interest every historical study that will come about on the road to the Reformation Jubilee (such as the Luther biography by Heinz Schilling) and is looking forward to historical specification.

This is the place to clarify our invitation to the Roman Catholic brothers and sisters; I assume that there is no ecumenical disagreement in view of the existential-theological interpretation of the Reformation insights as expounded above, so that the Roman Catholic Church can also accept it as a missionary task to free souls and societies of fear. Yet, it takes getting used to the idea of the Reformation Jubilee 2017 as an event for the entire society, not only due to the justified concern that the throne–altar alliance is here happily celebrating its resurrection, but also due to the vague link to the basic idea of associating the contemporary, modern world in a particular way with the Reformation awakening. As much as an air of throne–altar alliance must be avoided at all costs, it is incomprehensible that the Roman Catholic brothers and sisters are so concentrated (if not to say "fixed") on the division of the church. There are quite a few indications that, for example, in the Second Vatican Council some of the central insights of the Reformation have been incorporated—so can we not celebrate just these achievements together? Furthermore, it is well known among the insiders of ecumenical matters that the churches stemming from the Reformation and the Roman Catholic Church have different ecumenical goals, with the former striving for the reconciled diversity of and the latter for the visible unity of the many churches. Therefore, there is hardly any substantial progress in the current ecumenical landscape. But why are these differences repeatedly on the agenda as a crucial point when it comes to the Reformation Jubilee? There are—thank God—many good and important ecumenical agreements regarding 2017, but as far as these fundamental questions of evaluating the 500-year-old Reformation are concerned, the two churches are estranged and find themselves confronted with an either-or kind of dilemma between either jubilee or commemoration. I would be happy to see the rapprochement take still-further steps.

How We Want to Celebrate 2017

One problem in organizing the jubilee festivities is, admittedly, the tension between accurate historiography and the current culture of memory; it is a question of principle, given that narrating history is, in contrast to a historical reconstruction of the given historical event, staging the event in a present settings. "Updating" of history requires creative, poetic talents to make "my" or "our" history out of "the" history. Of course, this principle can be abused; one can thus dispose a historical event, charging it with pathos, or superimpose one's own interests upon it. Historicizing is the only remedy against this. However, one cannot stop at historicizing; otherwise, history is fossilized within history. We have to recognize and reflect on the risk of abuse instead of anxiously seeking to avoid it.

If we want to establish a present relevance and future-oriented significance for a historical date, we should not leave it in the hands of historical research alone, because we otherwise run the risk of losing the current relevance of memory. We can draw some important lessons from these reflections on commemoration as we interpret and plan the Reformation Jubilee 2017: it is historically irrefutable that Martin Luther, the Augustinian monk and theology professor, wrote 95 Theses on the penitential practice. What is contested, however, is the existential but irrelevant fact about the nailing of those theses to the door of the Wittenberg Castle Church: Did Luther himself, or somebody else, or even *anybody* actually do it? Already during Luther's lifetime, this event of theses-nailing became the symbol of the Reformation movement that spread across Europe within a few years and led to profound changes throughout the intellectual, cultural, and political world. As such, it is not the historical veracity of the theses-nailing that is celebrated in its 500th anniversary 2017, but the symbolic beginning of comprehensive dynamics. Celebrating the Reformation Jubilee also involves compressed commemorating and storytelling in such a manner that the temporal relevance is embedded in the history. This reference to the *zeitgeist*, in whatever definition it may be presented, makes the historical memory an existentially relevant narrative. Only those capable of demonstrating such narrative relevance will be victorious in the commemorational competition. Today, a generation of the 21st century asks what significance the Reformation in 1517 might have. Any interpretation and corresponding organization of the jubilee depends therefore on the *zeitgeist*; whoever wants to avoid this *zeitgeist* in organizing jubilee events will celebrate alone.

What kind of "back to the future" is interesting today, not only to the churches forged by the Reformation or Christians, but to all people? The Reformation placed the conscience of each individual in the centre and initiated a mental shift, which undoubtedly did not prevail immediately and everywhere, but left its traces in deep layers of life. Through the Reformation discovery, a new inner freedom of humankind emerged in the world that has subsisted ever since. Reformation is the (re)discovery of a primary inner freedom, which is why so many impact-filled stories are arrayed around this new freedom: Luther's posting of his theses, Luther's courageous response to the emperor and the empire, Luther's marriage with Katharina, not to forget Zwingli's sausage meal during Lent, Calvin's zeal for social reform, Melanchthon's educational initiatives, Bugenhagen's consolidated practice of loving one's neighbour, and many others. Reformation narratives that have fascinated people throughout the centuries are stories of freedom and courage, new beginnings, and self-awareness. Even the new, albeit not-yet modern, images of women of the Reformation breathe this upright course. From an existential viewpoint, the Reformation lives in people's memories of a mixture of fearless freedom and bold self-awareness that not only resisted the then-authorities of church and state, but also proved worthy in the existential dimensions of closeness and love, friendship and trust. Along these lines, the Reformation narrative in the 21st century can have a form of a fear-conquering movement founded on the retreat in God and leading to the responsible reintegration into the world. This new self-awareness of those who are liberated from the fear of their time can embody the topicality and relevance of the memories of the Reformation. Of course, those who place such freedom in the middle of the occurrence should not be surprised by the diversity that can arise from it. Moreover, had this torch of freedom not been betrayed and obscured, denied and abused even, in the Reformation, we would now have only saints to remember. Neither Martin Luther nor the other reformers were free of guilt. Their extremely polemical confrontation with the believers of the old religion and the pope, Luther's brutal statements on Jews in his later years, the cruel persecution of Anabaptists and peasants, and many other wrongdoings cast appallingly dark shadows on this unique departure. But these shadows should not let us forget the discovery of the Reformation, namely, that even today the story of the small monk Martin Luther, who showed freedom and courage at Worms before the great emperor and the whole empire, can still be told. And this is remembered very fittingly with the words supposedly pronounced by him: "Here I stand, I can do no other, so help me God. Amen."

CHAPTER 31

Anne Burghardt

Challenges and Opportunities of the Jubilee

A Lutheran Perspective

In this essay I will follow the guidelines that have been set up by the "Special Committee: 500 Years of Reformation" and approved by the Lutheran World Federation (LWF) Council in June 2013, as they are helpful for addressing both aspects: the challenges and the opportunities presented by this jubilee. The special committee was truly a global body, bringing together representatives of the Lutheran churches from all seven LWF regions—Africa, Asia, Central and Western Europe, Central and Eastern Europe, Northern Europe, Latin America, North America—in order to guarantee that the whole global community of LWF with its diverse regional expressions was heard.

Goals

Based on the recommendations of this committee, the LWF aims with the commemoration of the 500th anniversary of the Reformation to:

- Strengthen the communion among the member churches;
- Explore the meaning of Lutheran identity;

- Strengthen its ecumenical commitment.

Principles

In preparing ourselves for the Reformation anniversary we are working along three principles:

- Reformation today is a "global citizen"—that is, it is worldwide, not just West-centric;
- In the preparations we are committed to ecumenical accountability;
- Churches of the Reformation are churches in ongoing reformation;

Opportunities and Challenges Related to These Goals and Principles

Reformation as a global citizen and strengthening communion among member churches

The heritage of the Reformation today is a global one. The Reformation and Lutheranism do not "belong" only to the "classical" Lutheran countries anymore, but they have for quite some time now been global citizens. Around 40 percent of Lutherans are presently living in the global South, and the number is growing. How does this affect our Lutheran identity, or identities? Hence:

> *The Reformation anniversary in 2017 offers a chance to bring the global aspect of the Reformation more into consciousness.* This aspect will also be emphasized by the fact that the LWF Assembly 2017 is going to take place in the global South, that is, in Namibia.
>
> *The minority-situation perspective of many LWF member churches may not be overlooked while preparing for the Reformation anniversary. This includes a special task for the LWF: to become the voice of those whose voice is not heard.* Therefore, it is, on the one hand, important to listen carefully to the needs of the member churches and support them, especially the ones with minor resources, in preparing for the anniversary in terms of communication and sharing of information. On the other hand, it is LWF's task to bring these issues to the joint table so that they are relevant for all our member churches and, at the same time, to guarantee that the experiences and expressions of being Lutheran in different contexts become relevant to the whole, worldwide communion—also for our big northern member churches. LWF sees its function as being a "catalyst" for its member churches in preparing for the anniversary.

> *It is relevant to explore the meaning of* communio *within the LWF*, as one of the goals of the anniversary is to strengthen the communion among the member churches of the LWF. Founded in 1947 as the federation of Lutheran churches, the LWF has become a communion of churches. There have been quite a few studies on the understanding of this *communio* at the LWF in the 1990s already; however, this is a reflection that needs to continue, both in regard to the relations inside the *communio* as well as to the external relations of the *communio* as a whole.
>
> *Unity in diversity in the Lutheran world* has been formulated by the LWF as a value that needs to be kept in mind by commemorating the Reformation anniversary. The principle "unity in diversity," on the one hand, requires theological reflection about common theological ground and, on the other hand, asks how to approach the sisters and brothers in Christ who belong to the same *communio* but represent different interpretations of Lutheran theology.

Exploring the meaning of Lutheran identity and of ongoing reformation

Many member churches of the LWF have expressed their wish to explore the meaning of the Lutheran identity in their context while approaching the anniversary of the Reformation. This includes the attempt of several member churches, especially in the global South, to emancipate themselves from the heritage of their "mother churches" and express their Lutheran identity in ways which would be more rooted in their local context. There are, however, also member churches, especially in the Nordic countries, who have been living in a majority-church situation for centuries and have sometimes found themselves in a position where being a Lutheran has been something "self-evident." Hence, we need to challenge ourselves in deeper discernment of our Lutheran identity and its implementations in the changing contexts:

> *Addressing the question about the Lutheran identity is not about celebrating our particularity as Lutherans, but about exploring the central theological convictions that have enriched this branch of the Reformation, its impact on society, and its relevance for today.* According to the LWF's self-understanding, to be Lutheran is to be evangelical, sacramental, diaconal, confessional, and ecumenical. While these central convictions of the Lutheran tradition do not belong uniquely to Lutherans, its distinctive patterns and emphases shape the way in which the LWF responds to the challenges and questions of today. However, the distinctiveness of these patterns and emphases needs to be explored again and again—from the role and hermeneutical

understanding of scripture and Lutheran confessional writings that unite all member churches of the LWF, to the diaconal approach of the church in its holistic mission.

The church must be open to constant renewal. The church should always examine its theology, practices, and structure in the light of the principle *Was Christum treibet*—"what 'promotes' Christ." Seen as a central principle, this helps to prevent situations where secondary questions would take precedence over the gospel. While continuing to ask for contextualization of the gospel today, it should also not be forgotten that the questions human beings ask today are not always necessarily completely new in their essence. The question of justification, for instance, is as relevant today as it used to be in Luther's time. What has changed is the understanding of which institution human beings need to justify themselves before.

Ecumenical accountability and strengthening of ecumenical commitment

The LWF has declared that the approach to the Reformation anniversary needs to be ecumenically sensitive and accountable. The aim is to remember with gratefulness the theological heritage of the Reformation while working for greater joint understanding and joint witness with Christians from other traditions to fulfill the prayer of Christ "that they all will be one."

The LWF is looking for ways for shared journey toward the 500th anniversary of the Reformation together with its ecumenical partners. The Reformation Jubilee offers a unique possibility to reflect together on the meaning of reformation and renewal in the life of our churches, to consider what has been the special contribution of the Reformation for the wider Christian community, and to ask how we relate ourselves to the renewal in our respective churches. The meaning and possibility of joint witness, including joint liturgical and study materials as well as diaconal projects, must be explored.

The ecumenical encounter includes also an invitation to Lutherans for critical self-reflection. While not neglecting the central convictions and achievements brought about by the Reformation, we should also challenge ourselves to ask what could be learned from other Christian church families—including aspects of pastoral care and spirituality, for instance. However, critical self-reflection also includes addressing the difficult and painful parts of the Reformation heritage, such as the persecution of the

Anabaptists or the fact that, while seeking for the renewal within the church, the Reformation led to a greater disunity of the body of Christ.

The commemoration of the anniversary of the Reformation shall also provide discussions about the understanding of reform and renewal in different religions. This discussion is especially important in modern pluralistic societies where use of common public space needs to be addressed.

A Thematic Approach

Main theme

Liberated by God's grace

(Related readings: Rom. 3:24; Eph. 2:8-10; Gal. 5:1; Luke 4:16-21)

This theme was inspired by the very central Lutheran understanding of the human being who is justified by God's grace. The challenge is to explore this statement through the questions "From what?"and "What for?"—enabling the exploration of the Lutheran understanding of the doctrine of justification and being free to serve the neighbour.

Subthemes

The subthemes are phrased in a way that enables the addressing of contextual challenges that the Christian community faces in today's world. The challenge is to explore these themes in a way that enables the identification of certain concepts, attitudes, and global policies that people "liberated by God's grace" reject because they are incompatible with the gospel:

Salvation—not for sale: This conveys the central message of the doctrine of justification—a message that salvation is God's free gift—and expresses a clear critique of contemporary practices and concepts that treat salvation as a commodity on the "religious market." Another important aspect to be addressed by this subtheme is the need for self-justification that many human beings today feel.

Human beings—not for sale: This underscores that every individual is a unique person created in God's own image and must therefore be fully respected in her or his dignity and integrity. On this basis, issues of particular social relevance such as human trafficking and economic policies that create or increase poverty can be unpacked and receive due attention.

Creation—not for sale: This underlines theologically that nature has to be fully respected and protected as God's good creation, entrusted to human care. Therefore, it cannot be subject to exploitative human domination nor can its resources be concentrated and exploited as commodities.

A Sustainable Approach

While planning and preparing for 2017, however, it is important to keep in mind "What happens on 'October 32.'" Materials, plans, and events should be planned in such a way that the 500th anniversary of the Reformation does not become a "dead end" in itself, but will hopefully serve as a possibility to find and create new ideas, new hope, and new insights.

CHAPTER 32

Aiming Wang

The Reformation Jubilee and Christianity in China

A Brief Overview of Chinese Protestantism

To begin, we must recognize that the study of the Reformation in China has long remained confined to the areas of culture, literature, and sociopolitical studies from a Marxist-Leninist point of view. Since the publication in the early 1980s of Max Weber's works in China, including *The Protestant Ethic and the Spirit of Capitalism*, we have seen an increase in university research dedicated to the relationship between universal values and Protestantism. This tendency seems to remain strong in regards to a better understanding of the Reformation among Christian intellectuals, and especially as concerns Calvin, John Knox, and Puritanism in particular.

Nevertheless, theological and church research on the Reformation in the Chinese language has been very scarce and limited, despite the publication of translations even under difficult conditions. The current policies of the national church, that is, the China Christian Council (CCC) and the

Three-Self Patriotic Movement (TSPM), create limitations to the careers of Christian academics. These restrictions have an effect both within the organization of this church at the national level as well as outside of this framework. It is, however, this church that is currently recognized by the authorities, in political and financial terms, following a model based on that of the Soviet Union some 60 years ago.

Second, we can still assess how the situation is currently evolving in a more encouraging manner. Throughout the country, at the parish level, we can find more pastors with a better educational background, while a large number of believers from all social classes, but predominantly from the middle classes and the elite, have been joining the churches. This state of affairs has had an influence on the programs of foreign-mission societies, which have carried out a large part of the evangelization. A large number of Chinese academics have studied in the West, in particular in the United States. They have made friendships with other Christians and come to know the fellowship with the church communities there.

According to the Pew Research Center report of 10 February 2013, approximately 640 million people in China of all ages were affiliated with a religion. Thirty years ago, few researchers, even in mainland China, were willing to take a stance on whether or not religion had survived Mao Zedong's Cultural Revolution (1966–1976). It has, however, become clear today that religion has not only survived but that hundreds of millions of Chinese people now have a certain religious faith, according to the Pew study. It is remarkable to discover that, with 68 million believers, China now has the seventh largest number of Christians in the world.

I would like to steer our attention here toward the fact that the Chinese authorities have openly declared that the number of Protestants within CCC-TSPM has risen to slightly over 23 million. This signifies that the majority of Protestants are mainly involved in the house-church system. Some international missionary societies have even estimated that there are at least 80 million Protestants in China outside of the governmental national-church organization.

I do not intend to discuss the state of the churches in China here. I would simply like to note that Christianity is expanding in every social class. This reality needs to be taken into consideration if we wish to understand the problem of religious freedom and human rights from a Christian point of view, and to interpret the significance of the 2017 Reformation Jubilee for the church in China.

Finally, we need to take into account that traditional Chinese ideology had been constituted by Confucianism from the time of the Han Dynasty (206 BCE–220 CE) and during all the subsequent dynasties until 1905. Today, however, the state ideology is based on the theories of two European thinkers, Karl Marx and Friedrich Engels, mixed with the ideas of Lenin and Stalin. Current China is thus ruled by a purely Western ideology!

Generally speaking, our objective is to identify the historical forces that have driven Chinese intellectuals and elites who hold positions of responsibility. What is now possible in today's Chinese society? How is it that Calvinism can now be seen as the great force that constitutes the basis for the thought—if not, indeed, for the religion—of the Chinese Christian elite?

Luther, Melanchthon, Zwingli, Calvin, and Knox in China

The first Protestant missionary, Robert Morrison (1782–1834), arrived in China in 1807. Western missionaries worked very hard throughout China, covering nearly all segments of society and the poorest classes in particular. Intellectually speaking, they did not, however, put together sufficient resources when it came to university research and the necessary theological education required to educate Chinese Christian leaders as well as the people of the church.

When the People's Republic was founded, missionaries were given three years to leave the country. Before the revolution, however, their contributions primarily involved *diakonia* and less frequently theology, leading to ecclesiological, theological, and structural deficiencies.

This is why there has yet to be a Chinese translation of Luther's important works. Only two volumes have been published by the official publishing house, but they were translated by non-Christians with inadequate vocabulary. This means that the influence of Martin Luther, with these two volumes, is very limited within the church. The theological students of the officially recognized church only have use of this old version of the two Luther volumes as a reference for the study of Luther's thought. This version was in fact translated during the Second World War by the board of the Nanking Theological Seminary with the support of missionaries from the United States.

It is therefore worrying that research on Martin Luther in today's China remains very weak, from a sociopolitical or cultural perspective, not only at the university level but also within the framework of the aforementioned national-church organizations, CCC-TSPM. Among Luther's ideas, only the doctrine of justification by faith is known and the subject of interpretation. Justification would seem to be understood as the isolation or separation of faith from moral responsibility. The subject of justification is the interpreters themselves, and not the Lord, in the common and literal sense, Chinese. This means that all research on the theological legacy of

Philipp Melanchthon is ignored and does not correspond to anything in the Chinese world. However, it is precisely Melanchthon's interpretation of this extremely important doctrine of Luther as well as his works that provided, both theologically and politically, the solid foundation of the Reformation.

The same can be said for Zwingli and the other reformers. From a Chinese point of view, there is only one text that speaks of the theological significance of Zwingli with regard to covenant theology and tradition, which served as a model for the great tradition of Puritanism and the evangelical movements in the United States in the subsequent centuries. In numerous rural Chinese parishes, we can find traces of Zwinglian liturgical and architectural influence, even if hardly anyone is able to remember that there had been a tradition in China extending back to this reformer.

Finally, we are faced with a surprising phenomenon in China with regard to the great Reformation figure, John Calvin. Around 30 years ago, the image that Chinese intellectuals had of Calvin was badly misunderstood and terribly damaged due to Stefan Zweig's (1881–1942) famous novel, *The Right to Heresy: Castellio against Calvin*, published in 1936. The book was generally viewed as a historical work, and many people in China, due to their personal experience and the suffering that they continue to endure today, conflate severity and totalitarianism. This has led to Calvin being a symbol of dictatorship and tyranny for a long time.

Nevertheless, as mentioned before, since the publication of Max Weber in Chinese, an increasing number of Chinese intellectuals, and students in particular, have been fascinated by the spiritual and theological writings of Calvin and his followers. Their deep concern for ultimate truth, universal values, and authentic piety, anchored in a strong sense of responsibility and duty in the secular world, and the like, which form the basis of the thought of Calvinist and Puritan missionaries, have encouraged and sustained them in the end. I would like to add that, while most of Calvin's writings, just like those of Luther, have yet to be translated into Chinese, numerous introductions to and interpretations of Calvinism and Puritanism have exercised a deep influence over the past ten years.

John Knox, John Wesley, and Jonathan Edwards, whose thought came to China via experts and Christian associations, kindled great interest in and enthusiasm for Calvinism-Puritanism. This is reflected today in the form of evangelical movements all throughout the country.

The Crisis: Dangers and Opportunities

I would now like to discuss briefly the crises involving the character and orientation of the church in China.

Historical identity: Ignoring the fact that Martin Luther is the foundation of the entire Reformation weakens the continuation and progress of evangelization in China. An understanding of the legacy of Calvin and the Reformed tradition could be mixed in with Confucian moralism, thus adding to the texture of Chinese national identity.

The political context: What are the concerns of the Chinese authorities with regard to the growth of the church and the evangelical movements throughout the country? One could objectively define at least five kinds of concerns that absolutely need to be taken into account in the development of a Chinese Protestant theology: (1) the question of ideology; (2) the nationalistic thought; (3) the concisive effect of Confucianism on society; (4) syncretism; and (5) sociopolitical issues in general. I cannot of course develop all of this here, but simply confirm that the official concerns require a hermeneutical approach that has yet to emerge.

The theological crises of the church: These have taken on an ever-greater urgency for a number of reasons:

- The evangelical and Pentecostal movements represent an important segment of rural Christians; the historical church, Luther and Calvin, as well as the Western Protestant tradition do not have a place there.
- The following of gurus, according to a phenomenon inspired by the Congregationalist model, constitutes the strongest tendency among the local churches of China. In these areas, the historical church has no significance, especially with regard to the rule of faith and church doctrine. The leader plays the dominant role.
- Issues involving syncretism and relativism, as raised by the future Pope Benedict XVI in the 1960s, can serve to describe the range of unregistered church organizations spread throughout China's cities.

These crises are troubling and obvious. We are faced with difficulties if we view ourselves to be the heirs to the Reformation tradition in China.

The phenomenon of elites preferring Calvinism has been identified by numerous Western researchers studying house churches in Beijing. This constitutes, in my opinion, an opportunity for the future growth of the church in China.

Suggestions for an Effective Solution

First of all, we need to organize university research on the Reformation through more intensive, systematic studies on the works of the reformers, including Luther, Zwingli, Melanchthon, Calvin, and others. This type of research would need to be done from the perspective not only of church history, but also of church doctrine and theological ethics. In my opinion, it is urgently necessary to form a society or NGO to realize these historical endeavours in Chinese, perhaps using the United Bible Society as a model. There are numerous Christian academics outside the CCC-TSPM system who have great talents and gifts to this end. Most of them were formally educated in various universities in the United States, Germany, and other countries. Setting up such a special organization dedicated to research on the Reformation in Chinese, involving an academic and objective university program, would constitute an important historical step within the context of today's China. There exists a universal truth, but how and where can we prove this, and how can we discover this based on the Bible and Christian tradition, and on the church in particular?

Second, this research on the Reformation needs to be ecumenical, as there is a serious lack of understanding within China's Protestant churches when it comes to the great tradition of Christianity within the Roman Catholic Church. They continue to place themselves above the Catholic tradition and are essentially unaware of the importance of the order of faith, the creeds, confessions, doctrinal disciplines, and the like. There are a great many Catholic priests and nuns who demonstrate the spiritual power of the Christian faith by bearing witness through their behaviour in today's China, all while a great many Protestant churches have developed separately around charismatic leaders, who, like gurus, act arbitrarily in the name of God! I am currently conducting a systematic study on theological historicity of Cardinal Ratzinger, later Pope Benedict XVI, as an important point of reference for the future of the church in China.

Third, the research on the Reformation needs to be hermeneutical. We need to be very attentive in entering into dialogue with other spiritual systems. Even as human languages are quite rich, they are also very limited when it comes to discussing and examining questions of values, virtues, and truth. The Chinese vocabulary concerning the Christian faith is indeed very superficial and limited in comparison with the vocabulary available for Confucianism, Taoism, Buddhism, or Marxism-Leninism.

Finally, I would like to propose that research on the Reformation needs to be missionary, and encourage evangelical people from all the corners of Chinese society to get a clear idea about the riches that the reformers have to offer for the future of China. The Christian elites of China have been fascinated by a large number of principles, including the doctrine of law and gospel, the forensic understanding of justification by faith, the three *soli*, the third use of the law, freedom of conscience and the right of resistance, and so forth, which need to be interpreted and systematically linked to the modern history of humanity. The dream of democratic government, primacy of law, democracy, fundamental human rights, and the like should one day be theological concerns in the research of the Reformation legacy in China!

The Reformation Jubilee can become a historical opportunity for Chinese Christians to draw up a road map for a promising future; the legacy of the great reformers and their spirit could increasingly become a tradition of relevance to Chinese Christianity. We are now faced with the difficult task of ecclesiastical development within the church, a serious challenge indeed! And it is a whole topic unto itself. Yet I am able to remain optimistic, even if the prospects may seem rather gloomy in the short term. In the longer term, an optimistic perspective could be derived from the great influence of thinkers such as Karl Barth, Dietrich Bonhoeffer, and others. There are positive signals along the way toward the fulfillment of hope in China!

CHAPTER 33

Kurt Cardinal Koch

Commemorating the Reformation from an Ecumenical Perspective

I thank you sincerely for your invitation to this closing ceremony of the International Congress on the Commemoration of the Reformation in 2017.[1] This invitation is at the same time an expression of your wish to commemorate the Reformation not in a closed circle of Reformed and Lutheran churches, but also to include us Catholics and to take an ecumenical perspective in general. This reflects your recognition of the fact that the Reformation concerns not only the churches and church communities emerging from the Reformation, but also other churches, especially the Roman Catholic Church, as it also led to the division of Western Christianity and, as such, has left wounds on both sides, just as a divorce does.

1 A short speech delivered at the closing ceremony of the International Congress "500 Years of the Reformation: Challenge and Implications for Today" held in the St. Peter Church in Zurich on 9 October 2013. In this translation, in order to respect the position and the meaning of the author, we strictly use the wording "Reformation" and "commemoration of the Reformation," instead of "Reform" and "the Reformation Jubilee" as announced though the organizers of the congress. This difference is the mark of the whole input.

Ecumenical Questions to the Commemoration of the Reformation

With your invitation, you give expression to the fact that a commemoration of the Reformation, after more than 50 years of ecumenical dialogue, can no longer be done in the same manner as in previous jubilees. We Catholics gratefully welcome this ecumenical sensitivity and are happy to accept the invitation to a common commemoration. This involves, of course, attentive listening to each other, how the inviting and invited parties understand this common commemoration, and how they may play their respective roles. In this sense, I understand my essay as an attempt to formulate the questions to be raised to the commemoration of the Reformation from the Catholic—and thus an ecumenical—perspective.

Reformation and reform

First and foremost, it should be borne in mind that "reform," a word of far more fundamental meaning, is the word underlying "reformation," and that the interaction of these two realities is to be examined. On the one hand, the Reformation is understood as a process of reform within the church through the rediscovery of the gospel and the concentration of the life of Christians and the church on the person of Jesus Christ. The Reformation is clear proof that a true reform of the church can only come from a deep encounter with the Word of God, in which the church finds its true identity.

On the other hand, however, the Reformation cannot lay an exclusive claim on the reform of the church. Only a brief look at the history of Christianity already shows that whenever critical situations arise, the church has always been reminded of the primacy of the word of God in its life and mission. Let's just think of St Francis and St Dominic, the two founders of their respective mendicant orders, who did not wish to create new orders in the first place, but to reform the church from within, especially by choosing a *sine glossa* evangelical form of life faithful to the gospel in its literal entirety. We may also think of St Charles Borromeo who, after his formal entry into the bishopric in Lombard, diagnosed the lack of preaching as one of the most common shortfalls of the clergy and saw his primary mission as bishop in "being witness, proclaiming the mystery of Christ and preaching the Gospel to every creature."[2] Additionally, in the more recent past, in the same line of thought, the Second Vatican Council initiated a similar reform of the church[3]

2 Quoted from G. Alberigo and Karl Borromäus, *Geschichtliche Sensibilität und pastorales Engagement* (Münster, 1995), 39–40.

3 Cf. Klaus Koch, "Was bedeutet heute 'Reform' der katholischen Kirche in der Schweiz? Zur Lage der Konzilsrezeption," in *Karl Borromäus und die katholische Reform. Akten des Freiburger*

by re-endowing the word of God with the centrality that it is entitled to have in the life and mission of the church. If we remember these and many other reform processes, it is inappropriate to identify reform and Reformation with one another. History demonstrates that Reformation cannot be, and is not, the only answer to the church's need for reform. Thus, given that reform has a larger radius than the Reformation, the right question to be raised is how the continuous need for reform of the church and the historical process of the Reformation relate precisely to each other.

Reformation and schism

To answer this question, I invite you again to take a brief look at the incontestably most radical reformer of the church, namely St Francis of Assisi. His memory brings to light that it was not the powerful Pope Innocent III who preserved the church from collapsing and renewed it, but a small and insignificant monk, whereby it should be borne in mind that Francis did not reform the church without or against the pope, but only in communion with him. While Francis is a successful example of a radical reform of the church in agreement with the church hierarchy, all of the church reforms undertaken by the reformers led to schism. This is the main reason that it is with pain that the Roman Catholic Church shares the joy of the necessary church reform achieved, because it finally led to the division of the church, along with its many negative effects. Consequently, the commemoration of the Reformation cannot be an occasion for joyous celebrations for us Catholics, but also an occasion for reflection, confession of sin, and repentance.

This attitude corresponds well to the real concerns of the Reformation, especially the one of Martin Luther. His main concern was a thorough reform of the whole church, and by no means a reformation in the sense of a rupture of unity, thus resulting in the emergence of new forms of churches, to which it ultimately led. If we take Luther's intention seriously, we should see in the historical facts that his intention could not be realized at that time, not only due to the failure of the Roman Church of that time, but also by the nonsuccess of the Reformation itself, as the Protestant ecumenicist Wolfhart Pannenberg rightly judges: "The emergence of a particular Protestant ecclesiasticism was a makeshift compromise, considering that the initial goal of the Reformation was the reform of the whole church."[4] This historical insight can only mean, to put it the other way round, that only with the ecumenical

Symposiums zur 400. Wiederkehr der Heiligsprechung des Schutzpatrons der katholischen Schweiz, ed. M. Delgado and M. Ries (Freiburg/CH–Stuttgart, 2010), 365–94.

4 Wolfhart Pannenberg, "Reformation und Einheit der Kirche," in idem, *Ethik und Ekklesiologie. Gesammelte Aufsätze* (Göttingen, 1977), 254–67, at 255.

efforts for the restoration of unity is a full realization of the Reformation itself also addressed. It may thus be expected that the common commemoration of the Reformation will be an occasion to attain new and courageous impetuses for the process of ecumenical rapprochement.

Reformation and tradition

The historical fact that all of the Reformation movements in the 16th century led to schisms and the emergence of new church communities makes it necessary to establish a fundamental distinction between reform and Reformation. By its very nature, a reform can never have the result that the reformed is no longer identical with its preceding form that had to be reformed. As a reform affects the concrete form of manifestation and its implementation, but never the essence of that which is to be reformed. Otherwise, it would be a change of nature which would make the thing to be reformed into something wholly new. This standpoint entails the question, from an ecumenical perspective, as to whether the Reformation movements in the 16th century saw themselves in this sense as reforms of the church or, rather, if they led in a far more radical sense to a changing of nature. This question arises above all from the fact that while the reformers understandably had big problems with the medieval paradigm of the papal church, instead of returning to the early church paradigm, they increasingly parted—to a greater extent the Reformed than the Lutherans—from the ecclesiological fundament that had been formed since the second century and is shared by the Catholic Church along with all Orthodox and Oriental-Orthodox Churches, namely the sacramental-eucharistic and episcopal basic structure of the church.[5] Because the church is there, according to the early church understanding, where the episcopate is in the sacramental succession of the apostles, and hence the eucharist is given as a sacrament over which priests and bishops preside, it is quite natural to come to the conclusion that the Reformation gave rise to another type of church or, given the fact that these churches soon parted from each other and still other types emerged, the churches emerging from the Reformation also consciously want to be church in a different way.

This leads us to raise an even more fundamental ecumenical question, namely the one about the relationship between the Reformation and tradition—more specifically, the question as to how the Reformation relates to the entire tradition of the church of which we have, after all, 1500 years in common. And on this wider horizon, answers may be found to the question of how we, the ecumenical partners respectively and collectively, view

5 Cf. Klaus Koch, "Die apostolische Dimension der Kirche im ökumenischen Gespräch," *Communio. Internationale katholische Zeitschrift* 40 (2011): 234–52.

the Reformation: whether we continue as was common in the past to consider it as a rupture with the previous tradition of Christendom, through which something new emerged, or if we see it in a lasting continuity with the whole tradition of the universal church. This question was posed years ago by the then-Cardinal Walter Kasper, my predecessor as the president of the Pontifical Council for Promoting Christian Unity, to the churches and church communities emerging from the Reformation in view of the commemoration of the Reformation, whether they perceive the Reformation as "a new paradigm which sets themselves apart 'protestantly' from the Catholic through a continuing fundamental difference," or whether they understand it in an ecumenical sense as "reform and renewal of a universal church."[6] The answer to this question is determinant not only for the ways in which we Catholics can participate in the commemoration of the Reformation, but also and especially for the direction and continuation of the ecumenical dialogue of the Roman Catholic Church with the churches and church communities emerging from the Reformation.

Reformation and ecumenical unity

Looking back on the past directly directs our gaze toward the future, with the question arising, in view of the commemoration of the Reformation, as to the destination of our ongoing ecumenical journey. In this regard, we have to recognize that the goal of the ecumenical dialogue has become increasingly ambiguous over the recent years. This is a crucial problem because, devoid of a common goal, the ecumenical partners are at the risk of proceeding in different directions and hence drifting further apart than before.

The main problem here is that there are currently two understandings of ecumenical unity, with substantial differences in profiles and denominational marks, which defy each other. While the Roman Catholic Church, together with Orthodoxy, adheres to the ecumenical vision of visible unity in the common belief, sacraments, and church ministries, quite a few churches and church communities emerging from the Reformation have come to advocate a different ecumenical vision, namely the postulate of mutual recognition of all existing ecclesial realities as churches and thus as part of the one church of Jesus Christ. This view is very close to the position of the Protestant New Testament scholar Ernst Käsemann, according to which the New Testament canon does not constitute the unity of the church, but justifies the

---

6 Cardinal Walter Kasper, "Ökumenisch von Gott sprechen?," in *Denkwürdiges Geheimnis. Beiträge zur Gotteslehre. Festschrift für Eberhard Jüngel zum 70. Geburtstag,* ed. I. U. Dalferth, J. Fischer, and H.-P. Grosshans (Tübingen, 2004), 291–302, at 302.

variety of denominations.[7] With this theory, he also attempted to justify the large schisms biblically, thereby paying the high price of relativizing the biblical canon in favour of one canon, which carries a one-sidedly Pauline mark, within the whole body of canon, and thus diluting the visibility and legal constitution of the church in favour of an invisible church.[8] Even though the Protestant postulate of a mutual recognition of all ecclesial realities as part of a church, which has a prominent standing in current ecumenical discussions, does not advocate a basic indivisibility of the unity of the church, this church would merely be the sum of all existing ecclesiastical forms. The upcoming commemoration of the Reformation, therefore, has to consult on whether it will serve to legitimize further an ecclesiological pluralism advocated by the Protestant side, or if it will be regarded as a vital opportunity to seek afresh a common goal of ecumenical dialogue, allowing it to be guided by Jesus' call for unity expressed in his high priestly prayer (John 17).

From Historical Conflict to Ecumenical Communion

These are the four decisive questions to be raised from an ecumenical standpoint in relation to a common commemoration of the Reformation which I have formulated with deliberate poignancy not only to stimulate the subsequent panel discussion, but also because I have to respond to the topic of this closing session: "2017 is a chance." This opportunity can be specifically an ecumenical one, if we have the courage to understand the commemoration of the Reformation as a welcome opportunity to reconsider our current ecumenical situation and to venture into new directions in the future. This commemoration of the Reformation will especially become an ecumenical opportunity if we implement the three focus areas that are at the heart of the document prepared by the Lutheran-Roman Catholic Commission on Unity in view of the commemoration of the Reformation, which is also applicable to the conversation with the Reformed churches. This document bears the significant title: "From Conflict to Communion." Let me present these three pillars in the following.

First and foremost, the title impels us not to come too hastily to "communion," but to bear the "conflict" as well. We have every reason for this if we consider that the Reformation led to schism and bloody religious wars in the 16th and 17th centuries, above all the Thirty Years' War that changed then-Europe into a red sea. Additionally, it has to be assessed as a heavy burden remaining from the Reformation time that this gloomy conflict had a

7 Ernst Käsemann, "Begründet der neutestamentliche Kanon die Einheit der Kirche?," in idem, *Exegetische Versuche und Besinnungen.* Vols. 1 and 2 (Göttingen, 1970), 214–23.
8 Cf. Gerhard Lohfink, "Der Kanon und die Vielzahl der Konfessionen," in idem, *Gegen die Verharmlosung Jesu. Reden über Jesus und die Kirche* (Freiburg, 2013), 178–91.

long-range effect of precipitating the emergence of secular nation-states with strong denominational boundaries. And if we further consider that while it is true that the Reformation of Martin Luther freed itself from the domination of the papacy entangled in political turmoil, it soon fell under a similar dependence on the princes, and Lutheran authorities, among others, delivered a theological justification for the persecution of Anabaptists. In addition, the Reformation in Switzerland was also not introduced without violence. In the face of such historical memories, it may not then be so easily asserted that the Reformation gave birth to the "freedom of the church." Rather, both sides have good reasons to bring complaint and to repent for the misunderstandings, malignancies, and injuries that we have inflicted on each other over the past 500 years. By all means, such a public act of *repentance* will have to be the first step toward a common commemoration of the Reformation.

Second, an essential way of overcoming such a painful history of separation is to write it down together, which has been done in the document "From Conflict to Communion." This document should be regarded as a result of the struggle undertaken by the Catholic side to present a historically and theologically more adequate picture of the Reformers and the intensified efforts on the Protestant side to deliver a fairer picture of the Middle Ages and the Roman Catholic Church in that time. This historically nuanced view should also be appreciated as a ripe fruit of the ecumenical dialogues over the past decades. This leads us to the second pillar of the common commemoration of the Reformation, namely *gratitude and joy* for the mutual rapprochement in faith and life, as has happened over the past five decades, also in retrospect of the long and shared history before the Reformation and the schism.

Finally, from the repentance in the face of the historical suffering and from the joy over the ecumenical communion achieved thus far, hope arises as the third pillar: a *hope* that the common commemoration of the Reformation will give us the opportunity to take further steps toward the long-cherished and hoped-for unity and not to rest on the laurels of our achievements. This ecumenical document "From Conflict to Communion" makes an important contribution because it reminds us of the visible unity of the church as the goal of our ecumenical efforts. Therefore, 2017 will be an opportunity if it will not mark the end but a new beginning of the ecumenical struggle for full communion between the churches and church communities emerging from the Reformation and the Roman Catholic Church, whereby the triad of repentance, gratitude, and hope will manifest in harmony, with none of them lagging behind if it wishes to be perceptible as a symphonic triad.

Part Six

Evaluating the Jubilee Conference

CHAPTER 34

Michael Bünker

A Polyphony of Protestant Voices

The traditional polyphonic *Zäuerli* song without lyrics, typical of the Protestant part of Canton Appenzell, could already be heard during the opening worship service. Did the local organizers perhaps mean to allude to the polyphony within Protestantism, which cannot be overlooked in our common orientation to 2017 and the occasion of the 500th anniversary of the Reformation? Congress participants arrived from all over the world with their respective churches' particular history, current context, and views on the anniversary year. The situation in Europe changed fundamentally 40 years ago with the signing of the Leuenberg Agreement. This vibrant church community of Lutheran, Reformed, United, and Methodist churches, along with others such as the Waldensian and Bohemian Brethren, whose Reformation dates back long before the 1517, has made it possible, and indeed even directly calls for, the churches to celebrate the Reformation anniversary together. The Reformation was a European event that changed both church and society fundamentally. Now, the Protestant churches have joined each other on the way to the year 2017 within the Community of Protestant Churches in Europe (CPCE), which dates back to the Leuenberg Agreement. In Austria, for example, the Methodist, Reformed, and Lutheran churches are preparing for the occasion together. The Evangelical Church in Germany (EKD) and Federation of Swiss Protestant Churches (FSPC) joining together to organize this congress is another clear sign of this growing community and the conviction that organizing the Reformation Jubilee as a German occasion fixated on Luther would diminish it.

Through a series of important talks and numerous workshops, discussions, presentations, exhibitions, and side events, the congress has served to bring to light the different degrees of preparation, the central topics to be taken into account, and the perspectives for the anniversary year. Thereby, it has become apparent that any common orientation with regard to 2017 comes thanks to a common agreement and does not merely depict the historical facts of the Reformation for everyone. This is indeed a good thing, as it makes it impossible to tarry in nostalgic ways of commemoration, only facing the past. Focused acutely on the year marking Luther's 95 Theses, it is, in fact, all about the primary concern that characterized the Reformation in its variety of developments: the rediscovery of the gospel of God's free grace and its changing power for the church and society. This is indeed a reason to rejoice and to celebrate! In its call for a European celebration of the Reformation, the CPCE stated in the final report of its 2012 General Assembly that the "Gospel brings a breath of fresh air, banishes fear, gives new life, grants freedom, opens our eyes to the needs of others and banishes mournful spirits. Whenever we experience this amongst ourselves, we feel the stirrings of the Reformation among us. It is when the Christian churches allow themselves to be guided by the Gospel that the Reformation is properly honoured." So, is this celebration all about the potential of Reformation theology for the 21st century, as Ulrich Körtner put forth in his Zurich presentation on the four *solae*?

This Reformation Jubilee differs from those of previous centuries in that it is the first in the era of ecumenism. The opening address by Rowan Williams and the closing presentation by Cardinal Kurt Koch, as well as the participation of Orthodox dialogue partners at the congress, brought this to light. Does this mean that there will be a common celebration? Following the cardinal's presentation, which spoke not only of terminology ("commemoration" instead of "jubilee") but also of clear conditions ("By all means, . . . a public act of repentance will have to be the first step toward a common commemoration of the Reformation"), it would appear advisable not to set expectations too high for now. But who knows? The shadows of the Reformation, and confessionalization in particular, were indeed openly discussed by the Protestant churches themselves at the congress. The representatives of smaller churches that consider themselves to be diaspora churches are, however, particularly looking forward to the anniversary. They found an opportunity in Zurich to exchange ideas and to be enriched with new concepts and approaches. All of this is demonstrating how the "major" churches, in this case the FSPC and EKD, have taken on responsibility at the European and even global level. A follow-up—preferably at the halfway mark in 2015—is greatly desired!

CHAPTER 35

Ibrahim Wushishi

Why We Celebrate the Jubilee

I would first like to attempt to define the term *Reformation*. The *Collins English Dictionary* defines the Reformation as a religious renewal movement of the 16th century, with protests against abuses leading to the development of the Protestant churches. The reformers rejected certain developments within the church, feeling the need to act toward restoring the church's purity and spirituality.

The Protestant Reformation movement in Europe started with Martin Luther's 95 Theses in 1517 and concluded with the Peace of Westphalia in 1648. While the movement began as efforts to reform the Roman Catholic Church, it led to the division of the church, as many concerned Christians in the West rejected the doctrines and practices of the church, such as the selling of indulgences. The largest groups to emerge from the Reformation were the Lutherans, Reformed, Calvinists, Presbyterians, and Anabaptists, while other Protestant confessions can also be generally traced back to the Reformation tradition. The International Congress on the Reformation Jubilee sought to bring together people from a wide variety of countries with different cultural backgrounds and diverse experiences to discuss and exchange ideas on the 500th anniversary of the Reformation in 2017.

Some circles cast doubt on the idea of the Reformation Jubilee and that our reflections on the Reformation era could contribute to the search for answers to today's problems and challenges in society and the church. However, if we forget our roots and origins, it would make it difficult for us to see the way before us. The idea for the congress therefore surfaced just in time—as a contribution toward considerations on the legacy of the Reformation, on what the reformers lived and suffered for, what they died for, and how we can connect this to the struggle for justice and peace in our modern world, whether in the West or in Africa. This presentation would not be complete without referring to the legacy of the Reformation founders.

The reformers, in their struggle for change in the church, called for people to be liberated from "fear, superstition, and uncertainty to provide hope for the future and a framework for lives of stability." Yes, indeed! They worked for human freedom and dignity in prayer, and continued their struggle in the face of all opposition out of a high regard for personal freedom: the reformers saw it as unworthy of the godhead to be confined behind walls or to be represented in images. They therefore preferred inner spiritual prayer and direct communion with the godhead to an external form of worship that would use ceremony and form to speak to the senses and to create a direct connection between the finite and infinite. The Reformation should be viewed as a movement of liberation from papism and as the beginning of an era of freedom and independence. Most reformers came from modest backgrounds; their accomplishments are proof that God's Spirit, who works through chosen instruments, is stronger that any armies or navies. These modest servants of God brought about great achievements and became the voice of the voiceless in society and the church.

The reformers in no way intended to split from the Roman Catholic Church. The movement was supposed to serve particularly to reform and to do away with traditions that the reformers viewed as standing in opposition to holy scripture. This included, for example, plans for the construction of vast cathedrals, rampant corruption in the church, and the fact that only clergy were permitted to study and read scripture.

One positive contribution of reform was clearly the invention and use of the printing press for translations of the Bible into numerous vernaculars, including my own native language, Jju (spoken by a small ethnic group in southern Kaduna State in northern Nigeria). The Bible thus becomes accessible to all and people are encouraged to read and study it whether in church, at home, or whenever they have the time. The question, however, remains: How many of the churches and people for whom this unlimited opportunity exists today are actually willing and prepared to do so? It is indeed mostly older people in Europe who read the Bible and live in accordance to it. Many young people have no interest in the church or in reading the Bible. In Africa, on the other hand, most people, and young ones in particular, are active in the church. They concentrate in their Bible study on passages involving miracles or wealth, as the focus shifts from the good news of salvation to the good news of healing or prosperity, with churchgoers asked at times to cultivate and maintain their relationship with God.

I had a number of questions when I received the invitation to the conference since at first I did not think either the 500th Reformation anniversary or this congress itself to be necessary. I struggled a great deal with it, even once I had already accepted the invitation. But now I thank God that the congress has quenched my thirst for knowledge, and that I have been able, upon returning to Nigeria, to explain the significance of the jubilee to others with similar questions. I also came face to face with another aspect of the Reformation: Africa was not a centre but, instead, a product of the Reformation. That is why we have had much to learn with regard to the church in Africa from the Reformation legacy and the reformers' struggles—efforts in the struggles against corruption, in the fight for peace, justice, and dignity in Africa, and in our role of prophetic responsibility as the church. After the congress, it became clear to me that the jubilee is not a triumphant celebration of the Protestant church, but, instead, a celebration of the growth of God's kingdom, of the fact that the Bible is available and accessible in different languages, and of the freedom of believers to worship, pray, and read the Bible and thus to seek a connection to our creator without limitation.

The conference also brought us face to face with the challenge of learning from the efforts, the dedication, and the personal commitment and sacrifice of the reformers 500 years ago, in that they held fast to their truth despite all opposition and rejection. We need to demonstrate similar commitment if the church is to be able to fight successfully against the ills of our society today. We may doubt at times whether progress is even possible, but in the words of Nelson Mandela, of blessed memory: "It always seems impossible until it's done." Yes, indeed! There were surely those, 500 years ago, who doubted that Martin Luther, John Calvin, and others could bring about any real change—and yet we are now able to attest to the success of their struggles, and not only in the Protestant but also in the Roman Catholic Church. The church must not allow itself to be impeded in its efforts to fight against the ills of society and to provide a voice to the voiceless, even in the face of vehement opposition and rejection.

The Reformation legacy has also had its grim sides, for example, the fragmentation of the church into thousands of denominations, years of religious violence and wars such as the German Peasants' War, the Thirty Years' War (1618–1648), which brought about the death of countless people in the

Holy Roman Empire, and the persecution of smaller sects on the part of both Protestants and Catholics. The positives have, however, outweighed the negatives by far, and the congress focused on the question of how we can best put the positive legacy of the Reformation to use in order to strengthen the unity of the church, with regard to the ecumenical movement, to the Roman Catholic Church, as well as with people of other beliefs within our modern society. The jubilee celebration will need to place an emphasis on the freedom of belief, on justice, peace, and human dignity—just like Luther during his own struggles, when he posted his 95 Theses, or when he famously said in front of the court, "Here I stand; I can do no other, so help me God!"

I would like to thank the organizers for the outstanding choice of speakers, who explored their topics very effectively. It was an excellent idea to invite Cardinal Kurt Koch from Rome as well, who participated in a panel during the conference. I was personally fascinated by his answers to the questions and by his openness. It is important that members of the Roman Catholic Church and adherents to other faiths continue to participate in conferences involving the discussion of the Reformation. It did, however, come to my notice that there was a lack of young people and that only a few representatives of Africa were on hand. I would therefore like to call for participation and involvement of the youth and the churches in Africa in the planning and celebration of the jubilee. These groups can then contribute to the preparations and celebrations from their own perspectives.

In conclusion, I would like to underscore that the church in Africa and elsewhere should take the 500 years that have passed since the Reformation as an occasion for thorough reflection on prophetic responsibility when it comes to decrying the ills of our society, to critically questioning bad practices, to promoting tolerance, to doing away with corruption in church and society, to protecting the weak, and to being the voice of those who have no voice in society. The church of Jesus Christ needs to return its focus to scripture: no human invention must be permitted to take the place of the Bible or to determine how the word of God is applied in the life and ministry of the church. The Protestant church needs to hold fast to this truth just as it did 500 years ago.

CHAPTER 36

Frank Fornaçon

Free Evangelical Churches and the Jubilee

Christians of Free Churches from Germany, Switzerland, and other countries attended the International Congress on the Reformation Jubilee 2017 held in Zurich from 6 to 10 October 2013. For them, the congress was an inspiring experience that may provide an important impetus for the coexistence of Lutheran and Reformed churches on the one hand and various Free Churches on the other.

Who Came Together?

The Reformation Jubilee 2017 ought not to become a denominational jubilation. This was the common tenor of many of the speeches given at the International Congress, which was attended by over 200 specialists from church, theology, and politics, representing churches from 35 different countries. Some of them were representatives of Free Churches: Mennonite, Free Evangelical, Methodist, Moravian, and Baptist churches coming from as near as Germany and as far as Cuba and Cameroon. The Association of Evangelical Free Churches in Germany (VEF) was represented by Prof. Dr Markus

Iff, Dr Oliver Pilnei, and Peter Jörgensen from Ewersbach, Elstal, and Berlin, respectively. Additionally, Bishop Rosemarie Wenner and Bishop Theodor Clemens from Bad Boll and Frank Fornaçon from Kassel came as representatives of other German Free Churches. The Federation of Swiss Protestant Churches (FSPC) invited the Swiss Free Churches (VFG) and especially the Mennonite Church. Their representative was Mister Spiess (representing both the VFG and the Swiss Evangelical Alliance).

What Was It About?

The goal of the congress was to prepare for the Reformation Jubilee 2017 in a European, ecumenical, and international context. The jubilee in Wittenberg (the posting of the 95 Theses) should not compete with Zurich or the Upper German Reformation, and anti-Catholic rhetoric should be avoided. Many speakers referred to the persecution of Anabaptists during the Reformation era. The implications of the Reformation discoveries (through Christ alone, by grace alone, by faith alone, by scripture alone) should be made salient in their contemporary meaning and bear fruit beyond the confines of central Europe. The gospel, as has been repeatedly emphasized, shall be at the heart of the jubilee.

What Role Will Be Played by Ecumenism in 2017?

The majority of participants did not have great expectations with regard to the contribution of Cardinal Kurt Koch, who is responsible for ecumenical relations in Rome. He emphasized in his speech that the celebration of the Reformation as a jubilee needs to include a repentance for the schism that occurred back then. Otherwise, we can only speak of a Reformation commemoration.

Efforts were clearly made to include the Reformation churches outside of the Lutheran World Federation and the World Communion of Reformed Churches in the celebration. In this regard, care should be taken on the part of Free Churches to ensure that this opportunity will not be wasted. In view of the jubilee, as was clearly pointed out in an informal meeting of the representatives of Free Churches, not only should the historical events (persecution of Anabaptists) be taken seriously, but the current tensions between mainstream denominations and Free Churches should also be broached. Free Churches should take part in jubilee festivities at local, regional, and national levels in all forms of commitment.

Voices of Participants

Peter Jörgensen, delegate of the Association of Evangelical Free Churches, in the seat of the federal government in Berlin, experienced the symbolic power of the places he visited during the tour through the Old Town:

> Jews, Muslims, Catholics, and Anabaptists—their goose was cooked in Zurich and elsewhere during and long after the Reformation period. We commemorated their lives and deaths at historical sites. "The excluded" has retained its meaning even today as a term describing many Protestant groupings that are and will remain minorities wherever they are vis-à-vis the mainstream society which has a different religious convictions. The status of a national church is not granted to the Protestant tradition everywhere. Everybody knows what it is like to be a part of "the excluded." So, a common platform that fosters the development of mutual sensitivity for each other can easily be found. Pentecostals, Methodists, Baptists, and other Protestant churches are regarded as "big ones" around the world. With many relations constantly in motion, what is "large" today can become "small" tomorrow. The questions of how to interact with minorities and what religious freedom means are answered differently depending upon whether they are answered from the experiences of those without power or from those in power. It still is a great challenge to deal with power in such a way that those without power are recognized, their dignity is respected, and their freedom is safeguarded. It remains to be seen whether the Reformation Jubilee 2017 will succeed in meeting this challenge by expanding the horizon and gauging the power and absence thereof solely on the basis of the measure of confessing to Jesus and following his footsteps.

Rosemarie Wenner, bishop of the United Methodist Church in Germany, summed up the congress events with the following statement:

> The Reformation Jubilee will be more colourful and authentic, once the contributions of the International Congress held in Zurich from 6 to 10 October 2013 are received. Not only the churches stemming from the "Swiss Reformation," and thus more related to Zwingli and Calvin than Luther, but also many small Lutheran churches across the world have expressed that it will not be enough for them to come to Wittenberg in 2017 as guests. It was declared in many speeches that the Protestant churches will not celebrate themselves but, rather, the "uncovering of the gospel" (e.g., Gottfried Wilhelm Locher, FSPC, in the closing press conference).
>
> Now it's up to us, small churches in Europe that stem from the Anabaptist movement born and persecuted during the Reformation period or from more recent Protestant revivalism, to make our histories and our

special concerns heard during the festivities. Thereby we should not limit our voices to the "healing of memories," important as that is. We also have things to contribute when it comes to dealing with the question as to how the renewal stimulated by the rediscovery of the primary concerns of the Reformation may occur today.

Prof. Dr Markus Iff, Ewersbach, stresses the theological aspects of the congress in his summary notes:

All speeches, panel discussions, and workshops revolved around three questions that are also essential for all Free Evangelical Churches in Europe:

1. History and theology: common theological roots and themes. Where do we come from and who are we?
2. Theological foundation: being Protestant today. What are the topics to be attended to until 2017?
3. Significance and responsibility: Protestant witness today. How can we witness the Gospel as "a joyful *deliverance* from the godless biddings of this world for a *free, grateful service to God's creatures*?"

From the perspective of a scholar, it was remarkable that both theological keynote speeches were delivered by university professors with Reformed theology background.

Prof. Dr Peter Opitz, director of the Institute of Swiss Reformation Studies at the University of Zurich and a highly regarded Reformation theologian, expounded the contributions of the Swiss Reformation to the Reformation history. He pointed out that the church, according to Zwingli's understanding, is a community of learning and communication in which all humans are principally equal before God and hence can learn from each other. A church as an heir of the Reformation, therefore, is a grateful and confessing community before God and humanity today. In this community, reconciliation is exemplarily realized and it stands up for justice and reconciliation in the world.

Prof. Dr Ulrich Körtner, professor of systematic theology at the University of Vienna, gave a systematic-theological introductory speech on the understanding of faith and of consequential reality in the Reformation theology under the title "An Exclusive Faith: The Fourfold 'Alone' of Reformation Theology." In this introductory speech, he aptly referred to comparable passages in Luther's Large Catechism and the Reformed Heidelberg Catechism in order to illustrate the doctrine of justification as the theological core and common heritage of Reformation theology for today and to shed light on the consequences thereof also for Protestant ethics.

The sociohistorical, political, church-historical, fundamental-theological, and ecumenical backgrounds of the Reformation phenomena were elucidated and discussed in workshops by delving into the questions "Where do we come from?" and "Who are we?" The director of the *Institute* for Confessional Studies in Bensheim, Dr Walter Fleischmann-Bisten, led the working group that shed light on the "dark side" of the Reformation, including the intolerance toward and persecution of Anabaptists. He pointed out that the Reformation history is also a history of shame and guilt that must also be remembered. Therefore, we have to conclude that Reformation Jubilee 2017 cannot be held at the confessional or national levels, but solely at the ecumenical level. Unfortunately, the project "Healing of Memories" launched in view of the Reformation Jubilee has so far only been applied bilaterally between the EKD (Evangelical Church in Germany) and the DBK (German Bishops' Conference). However, the Evangelical Church in the Rhineland has launched a subproject in the meantime with the involvement of Free Churches.

The congress was impressive with respect to its international dimension, which was especially conspicuous in the multifaceted panel discussions on the hermeneutical challenges of the Reformation today and the opportunities and challenges for the life and witness of churches in various contexts. This was an eloquent expression of Protestantism as a global and pluralistic movement. It was peculiarly interesting from the perspective of Evangelical Free Churches to hear the reflections and statements on the possibilities of the Reformation Jubilee from the Lutheran and Reformed churches that are minorities in their countries (e.g., Poland, France, and Argentina).

In his opening speech on the heritage of the Reformation, Rowan Williams, former archbishop of Canterbury, referred to the rediscovery of scripture as a source of true teaching of the gospel. The question about the Bible in the life of the church (how to understand the *sola scriptura* today) and the hermeneutical approach to scripture were repeatedly discussed during the congress. This is also of importance for Evangelical Free Churches specifically, when they look for their roots within the Reformation events. How can we advance the words of comfort or command of scripture to guide individual believers and the churches alike to the gospel of Jesus Christ as professed in scripture?

In view of the Reformation Jubilee, the main concerns of the VEF will be to make its voice heard in different contexts (academia, church and social policies, adult education, etc.) and to document its understanding of "being Protestant" as a heritage of the Reformation process (e.g., through materials for congregations, trainings for pastors, conception of sermon series and home group magazines, conferences and seminars, and publications of academic literature, for example, V. Spangenberg, ed., *Luther and the Reformation from the Perspective of Free Church. Kirche—Konfession—Religion* 59 [Göttingen, 2013]).

Theodor Clemens, bishop of the Moravian Church in Germany (*Herrnhuter Brüdergemeine*, Bad Boll), asks who owns the Reformation in his final contemplation:

> It belongs not only to the Lutheran and Reformed churches, but to the whole of the ecumenical movement. All churches have been influenced and forged by the spirit that led to the Reformation, which indeed transformed them.
>
> The Reformation Decade makes it apparent that what is celebrated is not an event that happened in a certain year, but actually a renewal process that has changed the world. Thus, the Reformation does not even belong to churches alone.
>
> The Reformation neither began with Martin Luther, nor ended with him. Therefore, in many European countries, 2017 will not be the only year of commemoration of the movement that renewed the church. For the churches in the Czech Republic and the German Moravian Church, 2015 will be a very important year in which the death of Jan Hus in Constance will be commemorated.
>
> Throughout the congress, emphasis was placed on the *solus Christus* as the central concern of the Reformation. We need to go on a journey together to find out its meaning and implications for us in the ecumenical movement and for people of our time.
>
> It was striking to see male and female participants arriving from all four corners of the world forming a community during the communion service as the opening ceremony of the congress. Especially moving was the moment of the confession, as all through the congress the dark sides of the Reformation were again and again remembered. During the tour in the city, we remembered the Anabaptist movement and other marginalized groups.
>
> It was with great pleasure to receive the hearty invitation of the Evangelical Church in Germany to cooperate in the preparation for the Reformation World Expo to be held in the summer of 2017 in Wittenberg under the motto, "Let us celebrate, pray, rejoice." It would certainly be good if we, as Free Churches, accepted this invitation together.
>
> Despite the contentment we perceived on seeing the emphasis placed on the diversity of Christian witness in the churches during the final session as well as in many other sessions of the congress, we recognize that the question of achieving a more palpable community and of advancing on the way to unity still remains a great challenge for us as churches. Differences, open questions, and tasks were discussed in this regard as well. Free Churches stemming from the Reformation and forged by Pietism have certainly been bestowed with an important take of bringing forth the *solus Christus* and the desired necessity for unity in discussions with the Pentecostal and the evangelical and charismatic movements.

We, as Free Churches, should also ask ourselves critically and be ready to be asked what contributions we can make towards the unity of Christians.

Zurich and the memory of the works of the Swiss Reformers provided the congress with a particular appeal and width and brought the topic into a broader context.

Oliver Pilnei, director of the Institute for Staff and Community Development in Elstal, has focused his interest on the ecumenical dimension of the congress:

The initiators used the congress to search for "the reforming" of the Reformation in an ecumenical setting. Obviously, this does not lend itself to a straightforward conceptual frame and needs further elaboration. The lecture given by Professor Opitz (Zurich) makes it clear that the typical Lutheran reading that highlights Luther's Reformation discovery covers only one aspect of this wide-ranging movement. There, as well as in other places, the gospel of Jesus Christ was rediscovered. This fact serves as an invitation to Free Churches to answer the question as to how they may contribute theologically and historically to the bouquet of the Reformation in view of 2017. With regard to the Baptist tradition, we may name, inter alia, a consistent and thorough understanding of freedom of religion and conscience as well as the priesthood of all believers. The speech by Cardinal Kurt Koch and the ensuing panel discussion with Margot Kässmann were both intense and sobering. It became apparent that Rome is unwilling to join the celebration. It was emphasized anew that the churches stemming from the Reformation are a "different type" of church. These statements were primarily directed toward the Lutheran and Reformed churches while all other Reformation churches were not considered. This experience teaches us to happily live in ecumenical coexistence with Roman Catholic brothers and sisters at a local level, to maintian the courage to continue such efforts, and not to expect too much from the official church.

The congress made intensive networking with the representatives of other churches possible. A total of 250 participants came from five continents, 35 countries, and a large number of denominations. Discussions were held with ambassadors for the jubilee, members of high consistories, and bishops. We could also talk with Petra Bosse-Huber, the successor to the EKD bishop Martin Schindehütte, head of the Department for *Ecumenical* Relations and Ministries Abroad.

VEF and BEFG (Union of Evangelical Free Churches [Baptists] in Germany) will have to encourage their respective member churches and local congregations to understand themselves as part of the Reformation movement, to communicate the extent to which this is so, and to be actively involved in the ecumenical events of the jubilee year—at the local, regional, and federal levels.

Frank Fornaçon, member of the BEFG Presidium and one of the VEF representatives in the Steering Committee of the Protestant Churches for the Reformation Jubilee, emphasized in his evaluation of the congress the unfinished tasks with respect to the relationship between established and Free Churches:

> By all the joy about the retrospect and confession of the injustices committed upon the Anabaptists during the Reformation period, the formation of the current landscape of interchurch relationships is important to me. There are still outstanding tasks, such as the appointment of Free-Church religion teachers, the difficulties experienced by kindergarten teachers in finding posts in Protestant schools, and discrimination against Free-Church colleges (necessitating cooperation with other Protestant colleges on an equal footing). All this is indicative of the fact that the established churches are strongly focused on maintaining their power and that they have not yet understood the necessary solidarity of all churches in this secularized society. By the same token, Free Churches have a debt of obligation as well: they must make their contribution regarding the role that churches should play in society from their perspective. Moreover, they must be open to discussion to determine what mutual theological recognition as churches means.

Claudia Haslebacher, United Methodist Church, Bern, commented on the congress from the perspective of the Swiss Free Churches. She regards it as a challenge to strengthen the common ground between the Reformed and Free Churches:

> The congress on the Reformation Jubilee made the extent of the diversity of the effects of the Reformation era down to the contemporary era clear as well as the scope of difference in the self-presentation and lifestyle of the churches born during the Reformation period, in different countries and cultures.
>
> In Switzerland, we could hear different voices ranging from "We do not celebrate ourselves, we celebrate the gospel" (Gottfried Wilhelm Locher) to a voice from the canton of Aargau in the regional group that goes in the direction of making the Reformation Jubilee an occasion for strengthening the cantonal Reformed churches. From the Mennonite side, representing the radical wing of the Reformation, it was emphatically voiced in the regional group work that we not forget this part of the Reformation. Swiss churches have a long way to go before they can organize the Reformation Jubilee in harmonious unity.

The Swiss Free Churches and communities have an even longer way to go to get involved and find their place in the whole process. I consider it important that Evangelical Free Churches, whether they came into being during or after the Reformation period, do not exclude themselves from this process. A Swiss participant frankly stated, "The German Express will also roll over us in Switzerland in 2017. We must decide how we will actively participate as Swiss churches. In my opinion, this also applies to Free Churches: the Reformation Jubilee will come and be celebrated in the cantonal churches, be it in 2017 or later. The Free Churches and communities need to consider carefully whether they really want to exclude themselves from the events or rather contribute to them. This is especially true if this is actually not a celebration of a particular church, but of the gospel, since this is indeed what we proclaim as well!"

CHAPTER 37

Hanspeter Jecker

Anabaptist and Mennonite Churches and the Reformation Jubilee

The Reformation is a key event in modern church history. It is the direct origin of the two mainstream Protestant churches in the Lutheran and the Reformed traditions. Both churches are steering toward their quincentenary celebrations in the coming years. The big year for Lutherans is 2017, when they will remember the posting of Luther's 95 Theses in Wittenberg in 1517, and for the Reformed it is 2019, when they will remember the beginning of Ulrich Zwingli's preaching activities in Zurich.

Compared to these two mainline churches, the number of Anabaptist-Mennonites belonging to the Mennonite World Conference is respectively small. Nonetheless, they share the same origin with their birth dating back to the Reformation period. The first believers' baptisms took place in Zurich in 1525. This event manifested, for the first time in Europe, the independent path they had taken with increasing deviation from the mainstream Reformation movement. If the jubilee is to be celebrated also from an Anabaptist-Mennonite aspect, the year 2025 comes into view.

Due to ecumenical networking over the past few decades, it is only natural that, already during the ongoing preparations for various jubilees, the intensified interdenominational relationships come to yield their fruit, so that the denominations no longer march completely separated. Nonetheless, it can be described as a historical novelty that the International Congress on the Reformation Jubilee was jointly organized by the Evangelical Church in Germany (EKD) and the Federation of Swiss Protestant Churches (FSPC).

The congress organizers declared that the central concern of the Reformation Jubilee should not be a self-celebration, but the "uncovering of the gospel." What is at stake are not denominational boundaries, but the foundation of faith, namely, Christ. The jubilee shall be celebrated with people of all denominations who are willing to share the joy thereof. The message of the Reformation should be brought beyond the boundaries of Protestant churches and increasingly give answers which meet the challenges of the 21st century. Thereby, however, the dark sides of the Reformation should also be brought to the surface during the celebrations.

At the congress, most participants represented EKD and FSPC member churches. A few individuals came from Evangelical Free Churches. Within this group, the two representatives of the Swiss Mennonite Conference were the only two who, strictly speaking, represented churches that date back to the so-called radical wing of the Reformation.

In the following, I will neither write a comprehensive report nor a detailed evaluation of the congress. It is, rather, an attempt to formulate important impressions and concerns from an Anabaptist-Mennonite standpoint. The first part is addressed to the mainland Protestant churches,[1] and the second part, to our own Anabaptist-Mennonite churches.

Impressions and Concerns Relating to the Protestant Churches

It creates an appreciative and optimistic atmosphere that the Anabaptist-Mennonite churches as heirs of the "radical wing" of the Reformation were invited to this preparation congress after centuries of persecution, repression, and discrimination.

We are pleased to witness that both in plenary lectures and in quite a few workshops, not only the repression of Anabaptism has been named as a serious and dark aspect of the Reformation, but numerous steps toward rapprochement and reconciliation have also been mentioned. They have taken place in the last few decades between Anabaptist-Mennonite churches and

1 Within this document, the term Protestant church is used to describe all the churches which are members of the Community of Protestant Churches in Europe (CPCE), http://www.leuenberg.eu.

Lutheran or Reformed churches and are expected to serve as a foundation for further development.

Yet, this frequently repeated openness to involve the heirs of the radical Reformation in the preparations for the Reformation Jubilee has hardly been reflected concretely in the organization and procedure of the meeting. This reinforces the impression that the following question has not yet been clearly answered: In the preparation of the Jubilee, what is the role to be played by this part of the Reformation which does not ascribe to the sphere of Luther, Melanchthon, Bucer, Zwingli, Bullinger, and Calvin, but is usually referred to as the "radical wing," now substantially represented by the Anabaptist-Mennonite churches as its historical and theological heirs?

If this part of the Reformation were to play its role in the jubilee preparation, it is important to keep in mind that the churches concerned are not members of the Community of Protestant Churches in Europe and hence contacts must be established beyond these boundaries.

The inclusion of the "radical wing" of the Reformation might prove helpful on three levels. As a preliminary remark, however, it is important to say that the following points should by no means overemphasize the witness and contribution of Anabaptist-Mennonite churches. We are well aware of our own deficits, which have been demonstrated in our own history as well as during the course of ecumenical encounters. Additionally, these events and encounters made us gratefully recognize how we can learn from the traditions of other churches. Out of such encounters with other churches, we have been encouraged to submit our own positions for discussion.[2]

1. The point repeatedly highlighted during the congress as a main purpose of the Reformation Jubilee is the "rediscovery of the gospel" for and through the contemporary world. We are all aware, however, that the common men and women in the streets are usually least interested in the gospel and Christian faith. The main argument they advance against it usually is the following: such horrible crimes have been committed in the name of the Bible, the church, and God that these are the last things they want to be bothered with.

Confronting the dark side of one's own tradition, including the centuries-old repression of Anabaptism and other religious nonconformists by

2 Cf. Fernando Enns, ed., *Heilung der Erinnerungen—befreit zur gemeinsamen Zukunft. Mennoniten im Dialog. Berichte und Texte ökumenischer Gespräche auf nationaler und internationaler Ebene* (Frankfurt/M. and Paderborn, 2008), ferner Gesprächskommission Schweizerischer Evangelischer Kirchenbund SEK und Konferenz der Mennoniten der Schweiz KMS (eg.), Christus ist unser Friede. Schweizer Dialog zwischen Mennoniten und Reformierten 2006–2009 (Bern, 2010). http://www.kirchenbund.ch/sites/default/files/publikationen/pdf/Christus-unser-Friede.pdf. Cf. also the article "Konfessionsgespräche, bilaterale," http://www.mennlex.de/doku.php?id=top:konfessionsgespraeche-bilaterale.

the mainline churches, opens up the opportunity to name and confess to the injustice committed. This will remove stumbling blocks that contemporary believers often refer to as the main obstacles toward faith. In other words, it would open up new perspectives for the proclamation of the gospel today.

2. The inclusion of the "radical wing" of the Reformation in the jubilee preparations enhances the chance that several issues that might otherwise remain in the shadows will be in the public spotlight. This may be beneficial in multiple ways.

- It highlights the question of faith and church membership as a voluntary act, and thus being Christian as a not-self-evident matter.
- Thanks to the Christological anchoring in a theology of devotion and willingness to suffer, Anabaptist-Mennonites represent more radical and sustainable forms of peacemaking, conflict transformation, and nonviolence, not only at home and in the church, but also in local, national, and international contexts. This will remain on the agenda even if the ecumenical public appeal shall fade.
- The aspect of critical distance to state and government is also of importance. The scope of the shameful and frightening consequences of this deficit area of the church are exemplarily illustrated by the two world wars (the year 2014 marks the centennial of the outbreak of the First World War and there will be opportunities to address this issue also from the ecclesiastic standpoint!).
- Further, a concrete transformation of lifestyle is at the centre of our tradition. This arises from authentic encounters with God and also embraces areas such as poverty and wealth or sickness and healing.
- Thereby, the Holy Spirit plays an accompanying role both in comfort and claim of faith, in all becoming and growing, in all endings and new beginnings.

As a marginal note, I would like to add that in the account of the growing number Christians in the southern hemisphere, the above-outlined set of issues may even be of greater importance than the well-known classical Reformation questions (doctrine of justification, free will, sacraments, etc.).

3. Finally, a third chance presents itself to the Protestant churches through the inclusion of the radical wing of the Reformation in the jubilee preparations: many Evangelical Free Churches, down to parts of the more recent evangelicalism and Pentecostalism, see their own theological or ecclesiastical predecessors in the radical wing of the Reformation. Notwithstanding that direct continuities and associations are lacking among these groups, the integration of the Anabaptist-Mennonite tradition in the jubilee preparations would augment the probability for a relationship between official and Free

Churches, often fraught with tension, to be broached during the process. The same is true for the large traditional churches and the often equally sensitive relationships with their own internal "pious wings." Here and there alike, mutually discriminating general revilements leave their marks and catchphrases such as "liberal impious Bible critics" or "pietistic evangelical fundamentalists" are quickly picked up.

The fragmentation and disunity among Christians is considered another serious stumbling block for quite a number of contemporaries when attempts are made to give them an understanding of the gospel. The more such stumbling blocks are disregarded in the planning of the Reformation Jubilee, the less likely it becomes to reach the declared goal of "rediscovering the gospel."

Impressions and Concerns Relating to the Anabaptist-Mennonite Communities

The organizations of Anabaptist-Mennonite communities are encouraged to reflect as soon as possible on their possible thematic contributions to the Reformation Jubilee.

In a first and broader sense, we need to be concerned with the contents of our contributions as Anabaptist-Mennonite communities. In the preceding section, I have enumerated several possible issues to which Anabaptist-Mennonite points of view might be contributed. This list is certainly not exhaustive, but should be critically reviewed and supplemented. It will be necessary to coordinate the procedures of the national Mennonite conferences at European (AMG, KMS, ADS, AEEMF, etc.) and global levels (MWC).[3] This does not require a big organization, but the willingness to be involved.

In a second and narrower sense, it concerns the question of envisioning our own Anabaptist-Mennonite Jubilee of 2025. In doing so, it should be kept in mind that the objectives of our reflection should go beyond how and where and with what goal we want to celebrate this occasion as a worldwide community of Anabaptist churches. We will also have to deal with the dark sides of our movement besides its strengths. Thus, we will be confronted, for example, with the question of the innumerable fragmentations within the movement and the persistent unwillingness to be reconciled among the different groups.

It is unlikely that we will celebrate our jubilee alone. Given the frequent and positive interpersonal and interdenominational encounters at local and regional levels following bilateral dialogues with the Roman Catholics,

3 AMG: Arbeitsgemeinschaft Mennonitischer Gemeinden in Deutschland; KMS: Konferenz der Mennoniten der Schweiz; ADS: Algemene Doopsgezinde Sociëteit; AEEMF: Assocition des Eglises Evangéliques Mennonites de France; MWC: Mennonite World Conference.

Lutherans, Reformed, Adventists, and others, we are called to find appropriate and honest as well as appreciative and sustainable ways to validate this growing fellowship on the occasion of our jubilee. The year 1525 was, from an Anabaptist perspective, a year of hopeful departure and at the same time a year of painful rupture of church communion. Jubilees should embrace the memories of both.

Martin Schindehütte

Afterword

An afterword, really? Such a title can be misleading, causing some to assume that the congress is a closed chapter in itself. However, the contributions documented in this volume show that this congress cannot be seen as anything else but a single prologue—a foreword. From multifaceted perspectives, it points out that which will have to be elaborated and accessed further, in greater breadth and depth.

An ecumenical dialogue has been launched about what the Reformation means, not only for Protestant churches, but also for all churches, and what the Reformation has in store for their future.

The Reformation is dialogue-centred by nature. This insight had to be gained at a high and painful price in history. The reconciling potential of a "unity in diversity" is now openly at hand. Yet, it is still more of a potential than of a reality. This applies first to the ecumenical dialogues among churches, and then for dialogue among religions as well.

The Reformation shed light afresh on "God's powerful claim upon our whole life." This liberates us for "free, . . . grateful service for God's creatures." This responsibility for the world has to be introduced in culture, society, and politics. The different contexts of the contributions of the congress have shown what kind of efficacy can be embodied in the commitment of churches.

Reformation is not an event that should be remembered, but a common path. The congress has shown how this fellowship can be shaped. Now we are called to take further steps together.

The general assembly of the World Council of Churches showed a broad ecumenical framework within which the Reformation Jubilee can also be prepared and modeled: as a station along the common pilgrimage to justice, peace, and conservation of creation; as a cultural, social, and spiritual milestone for the wandering people of God.

A vibrant contribution on the road to 2017 was made by the presentation of national, regional, and local projects during the International Ecumenical Congress in Zurich, which are only hinted at in this documentation. Church federations and communities as well as some national churches are already paving the way for the Reformation Jubilee 2017 with many ideas and suggestions: from the Community of Protestant Churches in Europe (CPCE) and the Lutheran World Federation (LWF), to the Evangelical Church in Germany (EKD), the Evangelical Lutheran Church in Italy, the Evangelical Church AB (Lutheran) and HB (Reformed) in Austria, and the United Protestant Church of France, up to the Dutch Foundation Refo 500.

The congress has also kindled lively discussions about the issues that the Reformation left unsolved or the homework that should inevitably be addressed by the Reformation churches by 2017:

1. Reformation and violence
2. Reformation and subjectivism
3. Church, religion, and society
4. Unsolved theological tasks of the Reformation in relation to the Reformation Jubilee
5. To what extent can the CPCE model of "reconciled diversity" be applied in reality?
6. Freedom and responsibility for the world
7. Communication of the gospel today
8. Bible and religious pluralism within and beyond the church
9. Ethical challenges: Why have bioethical issues become a church-dividing factor?
10. The dark sides of the Reformation and the reformers

11. How can we speak about the gospel in a convincing and authentic manner today?
12. Reformation and education
13. Return of "the holy" and "the religious"

Foreword instead of afterword, foresight instead of hindsight, marching on instead of stepping back! This shall be documented in this publication. May the congress achieve this.

Many cordial thanks to all who have contributed to this!